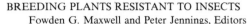
ATMOSPHERIC MOTION AND AIR POLLUTION
  Richard A. Dobbins
INDUSTRIAL POLLUTION CONTROL—Volume I: Agro-Ind
  E. Joe Middlebrooks
BREEDING PLANTS RESISTANT TO INSECTS
  Fowden G. Maxwell and Peter Jennings, Editors
NEW TECHNOLOGY OF PEST CONTROL
  Carl B. Huffaker, Editor
INDUSTRIAL LOCATION AND AIR QUALITY CONTROL: A Planning Approach
  Jean-Michel Guldmann and Daniel Shefer
PLANT DISEASE CONTROL: Resistance and Susceptibility
  Richard C. Staples and Gary H. Toenniessen, Editors
AQUATIC POLLUTION
  Edward A. Laws
MODELING WASTEWATER RENOVATION: Land Treatment
  I. K. Iskandar, Editor
AIR AND WATER POLLUTION CONTROL: A Benefit Cost Assessment
  A. Myrick Freeman, III
SYSTEMS ECOLOGY: An Introduction
  Howard T. Odum
INDOOR AIR POLLUTION: Characterization, Prediction, and Control
  Richard A. Wadden and Peter A. Scheff
INTRODUCTION TO INSECT PEST MANAGEMENT, Second Edition
  Robert L. Metcalf and William H. Luckman, Editors
WASTES IN THE OCEAN—Volume 1: Industrial and Sewage Wastes in the Ocean
  Iver W. Duedall, Bostwick H. Ketchum, P. Kilho Park, and Dana R. Kester, Editors
WASTES IN THE OCEAN—Volume 2: Dredged Material Disposal In the Ocean
  Dana R. Kester, Bostwick H. Ketchum, Iver W. Duedall and P. Kilho Park, Editors
WASTES IN THE OCEAN—Volume 3: Radioactive Wastes and the Ocean
  P. Kilho Park, Dana R. Kester, Iver W. Duedall, and Bostwick H. Ketchum, Editors
LEAD AND LEAD POISONING IN ANTIQUITY
  Jerome O. Nriagu
INTEGRATED MANAGEMENT OF INSECT PESTS OF POME AND STONE FRUITS
  B. A. Croft and S. C. Hoyt, Editors
PRINCIPLES OF ANIMAL EXTRAPOLATION
  Edward J. Calabrese
NONCONVENTIONAL ENERGY RESOURCES
  Philip R. Pryde
VIBRIOS IN THE ENVIRONMENT
  Rita R. Colwell, Editor
WATER RESOURCES: Distribution, Use and Management
  John R. Mather
ECOGENETICS: Genetic Variation Susceptibility to Environmental Agents
  Edward J. Calabrese
GROUNDWATER POLLUTION MICROBIOLOGY
  Gabriel Bitton and Charles P. Gerba, Editors
SALINITY TOLERANCE IN PLANTS: Strategies for Crop Improvement
  Richard C. Staples and Gary H. Toenniessen, Editors
CHEMISTRY AND ECOTOXICOLOGY OF POLLUTION
  Des W. Connell and Gregory J. Miller
ECOLOGY, IMPACT ASSESSMENT, AND ENVIRONMENTAL PLANNING
  Walter E. Westman

(*continued on back*)

WASTES IN THE OCEAN

ENVIRONMENTAL SCIENCE AND TECHNOLOGY

A Wiley-Interscience Series of Texts and Monographs

WASTES IN THE OCEAN

Editors: Iver W. Duedall
Dana R. Kester
Bostwick H. Ketchum
P. Kilho Park

Volume 1: INDUSTRIAL AND SEWAGE WASTES IN THE OCEAN
Editors: Iver W. Duedall, Bostwick H. Ketchum, P. Kilho Park, and Dana R. Kester

Volume 2: DREDGED-MATERIAL DISPOSAL IN THE OCEAN
Editors: Dana R. Kester, Bostwick H. Ketchum, Iver W. Duedall, and P. Kilho Park

Volume 3: RADIOACTIVE WASTES AND THE OCEAN
Editors: P. Kilho Park, Dana R. Kester, Iver W. Duedall, and Bostwick H. Ketchum

Volume 4: ENERGY WASTES IN THE OCEAN
Editors: Iver W. Duedall, Dana R. Kester, P. Kilho Park, and Bostwick H. Ketchum

Volume 5: DEEP-SEA WASTE DISPOSAL
Editors: Dana R. Kester, Wayne V. Burt, Judith M. Capuzzo, P. Kilho Park, Bostwick H. Ketchum, and Iver W. Duedall

Volume 6: NEARSHORE WASTE DISPOSAL
Editors: Bostwick H. Ketchum, Judith M. Capuzzo, Wayne V. Burt, Iver W. Duedall, P. Kilho Park, and Dana R. Kester

WASTES IN THE OCEAN
Volume 5

DEEP-SEA WASTE DISPOSAL

Edited by

DANA R. KESTER
GRADUATE SCHOOL OF OCEANOGRAPHY
UNIVERSITY OF RHODE ISLAND
KINGSTON, RHODE ISLAND

WAYNE V. BURT
COLLEGE OF OCEANOGRAPHY
OREGON STATE UNIVERSITY
CORVALLIS, OREGON

JUDITH M. CAPUZZO
DEPARTMENT OF BIOLOGY
WOODS HOLE OCEANOGRAPHIC INSTITUTION
WOODS HOLE, MASSACHUSETTS

P. KILHO PARK
OFFICE OF OCEANIC AND ATMOSPHERIC RESEARCH
NATIONAL OCEANIC AND ATMOSPHERIC ADMINISTRATION
ROCKVILLE, MARYLAND

BOSTWICK H. KETCHUM
WOODS HOLE OCEANOGRAPHIC INSTITUTION
WOODS HOLE, MASSACHUSETTS

IVER W. DUEDALL
DEPARTMENT OF OCEANOGRAPHY AND OCEAN ENGINEERING
FLORIDA INSTITUTE OF TECHNOLOGY
MELBOURNE, FLORIDA

A WILEY-INTERSCIENCE PUBLICATION
JOHN WILEY & SONS
New York   Chichester   Brisbane   Toronto   Singapore

Library of Congress Cataloging in Publication Data:

Deep-sea waste disposal.

(Wastes in the ocean; v. 5) (Environmental science
and technology, ISSN 0194-0287)

"A Wiley-Interscience publication."
Includes indexes.

1. Waste disposal in the ocean.   2. Factory and trade
waste.   I. Kester, Dana R.   II. Series.   III. Series:
Environmental science and technology.

TD763.D44   1985   628.4′459   84-27147
ISBN 0-471-89331-5

CONTRIBUTORS

ACKERMAN, DONALD G., Radian Corporation, 3200 East Chapel Hill Road, Research Triangle Park, North Carolina 27709

BIRD, JERRY L., University of Texas at Austin, Marine Science Institute, Port Aransas Marine Laboratory, Port Aransas, Texas 78373

BROADUS, JAMES M., Marine Policy and Ocean Management Program, Woods Hole Oceanographic Institution, Woods Hole, Massachusetts 02543

BROWN, FRANCIS C., Department of Chemical Engineering, Northeastern University, Boston, Massachusetts 02115

BURT, WAYNE V., College of Oceanography, Oregon State University, Corvallis, Oregon 97331

CAPUZZO, JUDITH M., Department of Biology, Woods Hole Oceanographic Institution, Woods Hole, Massachusetts 02543

COLWELL, RITA R., Department of Microbiology, University of Maryland, College Park, Maryland 20742

DEWAR, WILLIAM K., Curriculum in Marine Sciences, 12-5 Venable Hall, University of North Carolina, Chapel Hill, North Carolina 27514

DUEDALL, IVER W., Department of Oceanography and Ocean Engineering, Florida Institute of Technology, Melbourne, Florida 32901

FAY, ROGER R., Department of Oceanography, Texas A&M University, College Station, Texas 77843

FLIERL, GLENN R., Department of Earth, Atmospheric and Planetary Sciences, Massachusetts Institute of Technology, Cambridge, Massachusetts 02139

FOX, MARY F., Graduate School of Oceanography, University of Rhode Island, Kingston, Rhode Island 02881

FRAZER, JANE Z., Chevron Research Company, 576 Standard Avenue, Richmond, California 94802

GRIMES, D. JAY, Department of Microbiology, University of Maryland, College Park, Maryland 20472

HAYES, BENJAMIN W., Bureau of Mines, U.S. Department of the Interior, Avondale, Maryland 20782

KESTER, DANA R., Graduate School of Oceanography, University of Rhode Island, Kingston, Rhode Island 02881

LANCASTER, BRUCE A., Biology Department, Woods Hole Oceanographic Institution, Woods Hole, Massachusetts 02543

LANKES, WILFRIED, Lehnkering Aktiengesellschaft, Schifferstrasse 26, 4100 Duisburg 1, Federal Republic of Germany

LEE, WEN Y., University of Texas at Austin, Marine Science Institute, Port Aransas Marine Laboratory, Port Aransas, Texas 78373

LESCHINE, THOMAS M., Institute for Marine Science, University of Washington, Seattle, Washington 98105

LOVORN, THOMAS F., Lockheed Advanced Marine Systems, 3929 Calle Fortunada, San Diego, California 92123

MORGAN, CHARLES L., Lockheed Advanced Marine Systems, 3929 Calle Fortunada, San Diego, California 92123

NAUKE, MANFRED K., Marine Environmental Division, International Maritime Organization, 4 Albert Embankment, London SE1 S7R, England

NEMSER, NELSON L., Department of Chemical Engineering, Northeastern University, Boston, Massachusetts 02115

O'CONNOR, THOMAS P., National Oceanic and Atmospheric Administration, National Ocean Service, Rockville, Maryland 20852

PARK, P. KILHO, National Oceanic and Atmospheric Administration, Office of Oceanic and Atmospheric Research, Rockville, Maryland 20852

ROBERTSON, ROBIN, Science Applications, Inc., 379 Thames Street, Newport, Rhode Island 02840

SIMS, ROBERT, R., JR., Science Applications, Inc., La Jolla, California 92038

SINGLETON, FRED L., School of Science and Health Professions, Department of Biology, Old Dominion University, Norfolk, Virginia 20742

SPAULDING, MALCOLM L., Department of Ocean Engineering, University of Rhode Island, Kingston, Rhode Island 02881

WASTLER, T. A., Marine Protection Branch, U.S. Environmental Protection Agency, Washington, D.C. 20460

WEITKAMP, CLAUS, Institut für Physik, GKSS-Forschungszentrum Gmbh, 2054 Geesthact, Federal Republic of Germany

XU, HAUI-SHU, Department of Microbiology, University of Maryland, College Park, Maryland 20742

SERIES PREFACE

Environmental Science and Technology

The Environmental Science and Technology Series of Monographs, Textbooks, and Advances is devoted to the study of the quality of the environment and to the technology of its conservation. Environmental science therefore relates to the chemical, physical, and biological changes in the environment through contamination or modification, to the physical nature and biological behavior of air, water, soil, food, and waste as they are affected by man's agricultural, industrial, and social activities, and to the application of science and technology to the control and improvement of environmental quality.

The deterioration of environmental quality, which began when man first collected into villages and utilized fire, has existed as a serious problem under the ever-increasing impacts of exponentially increasing population and of industrializing society. Environmental contamination of air, water, soil, and food has become a threat to the continued existence of many plant and animal communities of the ecosystem and may ultimately threaten the very survival of the human race.

It seems clear that if we are to preserve for future generations some semblance of the biological order of the world of the past and hope to improve on the deteriorating standards of urban public health, environmental science and techology must quickly come to play a dominant role in designing our social and industrial structure for tomorrow. Scientifically rigorous criteria of environmental quality must be developed. Based in part on these criteria, realistic standards must be established and our technological progress must be tailored to meet them. It is obvious that civilization will continue to require increasing amounts of fuel, transportation, industrial chemicals, fertilizers, pesticides, and countless other products; and that it will continue to produce waste products of all descriptions. What is urgently needed is a total systems approach to modern civilization through which the pooled talents of scientists and engineers, in cooperation with social scientists and the medical profession, can be focused on the development of order and equilibrium in the presently disparate segments of the human environment. Most of the skills and tools that are needed are already in existence. We surely have a right to hope a technology that has created such manifold environmental problems is also capable of solving them. It is our hope that this Series in Environmental Sciences and Technology will not only serve to make this challenge more explicit to the established professionals, but that it also will help to stimulate the student toward the career opportunities in this vital area.

Robert L. Metcalf
Werner Stumm

PREFACE TO
WASTES IN THE OCEAN

This is the fifth of six volumes considering the problems of *Wastes in the Ocean* in which we consider the following subjects:

Volume 1: "Industrial and Sewage Wastes in the Ocean,"
Volume 2: "Dredged-Material Disposal in the Ocean,"
Volume 3: "Radioactive Wastes and the Ocean,"
Volume 4: "Energy Wastes in the Ocean,"
Volume 5: "Deep-Sea Waste Disposal," and
Volume 6: "Nearshore Waste Disposal."

The objectives are to present a comprehensive overview of the state of our knowledge concerning the disposal of waste in the ocean and to present new and original contributions to the evaluation of the impact of the disposal of waste materials on human life and well-being, on the marine biota, on amenities, and on legitimate uses of the ocean. The chapters included in all volumes of this series have been subjected to both external and editorial reviews. We are especially grateful to the reviewers of these chapters for the time and effort they devoted to the development of the final manuscript.

The burgeoning human population on earth and the continuing development of complex industrial technology have inevitably led to enormous increases in both the quantity and the kind of waste material that must be disposed of in ways that do not cause an intolerable degradation of our environment. The optimum solution to the problem is to recycle the waste material in ways that produce a beneficial effect. This is not always possible and various types of treatment can be employed to minimize the quantity of wastes and to make the product of the treatment less damaging to our environment. Even after treatment, there will be some residue that must be contained or discharged to the environment.

The options for environmental discharge are limited: on land, into the atmosphere, or into the hydrosphere. Before any one of these particular environments is selected for any specific waste material there should be a careful scientific analysis of the possible impacts of such a disposal operation. It is hoped that this series will provide the framework for the evaluation of the impact of specific types of wastes in the ocean.

From time immemorial people have been disposing of waste materials into the marine environment or into the rivers and streams which ultimately lead to the sea. For millennia it was assumed that the ocean was so vast that our puny efforts would have no measurable or damaging impact. Within the last century it has become clear that some semiconfined bodies of water were being seriously degraded and that the disposal of wastes into the hydrosphere must be managed and controlled in order to preserve the integrity of the ocean. We now know that some pollutants are distributed worldwide and can be identified and measured in the waters of the open sea far from the source. The problems associated with ocean disposal of waste material require careful and critical evaluation so that we may assume that the valuable resources of the sea are preserved and protected for future generations. This will require the most careful evaluation of the impact of waste disposal at sea so that we may use the oceans wisely.

We are very thankful to Mr. Treville Leger, Editor, John Wiley & Sons, for his constant encouragement and for being very helpful in the preparation of these volumes.

The Editors

PREFACE

Historically, the deep ocean has been used only to a limited extent for the disposal of wastes. The direct input of wastes to the open ocean has included the disposal of contained material, the sinking of obsolete ships, discarded munitions, at-sea incineration, and discharges from barges and other vessels. As problems with waste disposal on land become more acute, it is inevitable that the marine environment will receive increased attention as an alternative disposal medium. International agreements and national policies have placed a high value on minimizing oceanic pollution through waste disposal management. Considerable research has been devoted to identifying actual and potential impacts of waste disposal in the marine environment.

Most of the research conducted thus far on the effects of open ocean waste disposal has not identified direct evidence for environmental degradation, although such effects are difficult to monitor. It seems likely that the ocean can safely disperse and assimilate limited amounts of some types of wastes. But what are the limitations? It is evident that some regions of the open ocean are more favorable than others for waste disposal because of differences in circulation, chemical conditions, biological productivity, and fisheries.

The chapters in this volume are concerned mainly with discharges that occur near the sea surface. We have not included the dumping of contained wastes on the seafloor. Radioactive wastes, a principal example of contained wastes, are considered in Volume 3 of this series. However, there have been other types of contained wastes such as nerve gas and obsolete explosive munitions disposed on the deep ocean floor. Upon decomposition of these containers, this mode of waste disposal can release wastes to the deep sea.

This volume begins with an overview of the use of the open ocean for waste disposal and compares the characteristics of the deep ocean with those of nearshore marine environments. Part II presents investigations related to incineration of combustible wastes at sea, a mode of waste disposal that appears to have a number of advantages over other alternatives. Part III examines studies of liquid industrial wastes that have been dumped at open ocean disposal sites.

The development of new marine resources may increase the waste burden to the ocean. It is likely that marine ferromanganese nodules will one day be an important source of certain metals such as copper, nickel, and cobalt. Recovery of these metals from nodules will produce considerable amounts of wastes which may be discharged to the marine environment. Although such operations have not yet occurred, Part IV presents three considerations that will help to define the waste disposal problems associated with deep-sea mining of ferromanganese nodules.

The material in this volume emphasizes investigations pertaining to the natural and physical sciences, but economic factors are of primary importance in determining policy and a course of action. The economics of a deep ocean transport system are examined by one chapter in Part V. This volume is concluded by a general consideration of the feasibility of deep ocean waste disposal that is based on sound scientific and technical factors. Knowledge of the marine environment is increasing at a rapid rate. Timely application of this information to waste management is essential to maximize our use of the ocean for fisheries, transportation, and energy and material resources.

Many people have contributed to the preparation of this book. We would like to thank the reviewers of each chapter, who made many helpful suggestions. We greatly appreciate the work of Theresa D. Bewig for editorial assistance and co-ordination of manuscript preparation, and Ellen E. Main for reference research and manuscript preparation. Many of the illustrations were done by Barbara J. Struttmann. Preparation of this book was supported in part by the National Ocean Service, U.S. Oceanic and Atmospheric Administration.

DANA R. KESTER
WAYNE V. BURT
JUDITH M. CAPUZZO
P. KILHO PARK
BOSTWICK H. KETCHUM (1912–1982)
IVER W. DUEDALL

Narragansett, Rhode Island
May 1985

CONTENTS

GLOSSARY OF ACRONYMS   xvii

PART I. INTRODUCTION

1. Waste Disposal in the Deep Ocean: An Overview   3

   T. P. O'Connor, D. R. Kester, W. V. Burt, J. M. Capuzzo, P. K. Park, and I. W. Duedall

PART II. INCINERATION AT SEA

2. Development of International Controls for Incineration at Sea   33

   M. K. Nauke

3. Research on At-Sea Incineration in the United States   53

   D. G. Ackerman, Jr., and R. A. Venezia

4. Ocean Incineration: Contaminant Loading and Monitoring   73

   R. R. Fay and T. A. Wastler

5. Methods to Determine Hydrogen Chloride in Incineration Ship Plumes   91

   C. Weitkamp

6. Incineration at Sea: Experience Gained with the *M/T Vesta*   115

   W. Lankes

PART III. INDUSTRIAL WASTES: MODELLING, MICROCOSMS, AND BIOLOGICAL EFFECTS

7. A Three-Dimensional Numerical Dispersion Model for Acid-Iron Waste Disposal   125

   R. Robertson and M. L. Spaulding

8. Motion and Dispersion of Dumped Wastes by Large-Amplitude
    Eddies   147

    G. R. Flierl and W. K. Dewar

9. Fate of Ocean-Dumped Acid-Iron Waste in a Stratified Microcosm   171

    M. F. Fox and D. R. Kester

10. Microbial Studies of Ocean Dumping   187

    F. L. Singleton, D. J. Grimes, H.-S. Xu, and R. R. Colwell

11. Zooplankton Population Responses to Industrial Wastes Discharged
    at Deepwater Dumpsite-106   209

    J. M. Capuzzo and B. A. Lancaster

12. Pharmaceutical Wastes at the Puerto Rico Dumpsite: Sublethal
    Effects on a Marine Planktonic Copepod, *Temora turbinata*   227

    W. Y. Lee and J. L. Bird

PART IV. DEEP-SEA MINING WASTES

13. Modelling the Coagulation of a Solid Waste Discharge from a
    Manganese Nodule Processing Plant   243

    C. L. Morgan and F. T. Lovorn

14. Distribution of Cr, As, Se, Ag, Cd, Ba, Hg, and Pb in Pacific
    Ocean Ferromanganese Nodules   259

    J. Z. Frazer, B. W. Haynes, and R. R. Sims, Jr.

15. Disposal of Rejects from Ferromanganese Nodule Processing   271

    F. C. Brown and N. L. Nemser

PART V. ECONOMIC ASPECTS OF DEEP-SEA DISPOSAL

16. Economic and Operational Considerations of Offshore Disposal of
    Sewage Sludge   287

    T. M. Leschine and J. M. Broadus

PART VI. CONCLUDING REMARKS

17. Disposal of Wastes in the Deep Sea: Oceanographic Considerations   319

*D. R. Kester, W. V. Burt, J. M. Capuzzo, P. K. Park, and
I. W. Duedall*

Author Index   335
Subject Index   341

GLOSSARY OF ACRONYMS

AAS	Atomic absorption spectrophotometer
ACOE	U.S. Army Corps of Engineers
ASTM	American Society for Testing and Materials
BOD	Biological oxygen demand
DWD-106	Deepwater Dumpsite-106
EIS	Environmental impact statement
EPA	Environmental Protection Agency
GC-MS	Gas chromatograph–mass spectrophotometer
GEOSECS	Geochemical Oceans Sections Study
IMCO	Inter-Governmental Maritime Consultative Organization
IMO	International Maritime Organization
LDC	London Dumping Convention
NEA	Nuclear Energy Agency
RCRA	Resource Conservation and Recovery Act
TTO	Transient Tracers in the Ocean

PART I: INTRODUCTION

1

WASTE DISPOSAL IN THE DEEP OCEAN: AN OVERVIEW

Thomas P. O'Connor

Ocean Assessments Division
National Oceanic and Atmospheric Administration
Rockville, Maryland

Dana R. Kester

Graduate School of Oceanography
University of Rhode Island
Kingston, Rhode Island

Wayne V. Burt

College of Oceanography
Oregon State University
Corvallis, Oregon

Judith M. Capuzzo

Department of Biology
Woods Hole Oceanographic Institution
Woods Hole, Massachusetts

P. Kilho Park

Office of Oceanic and Atmospheric Research
National Oceanic and Atmospheric Administration
Rockville, Maryland

Iver W. Duedall

Department of Oceanography and Ocean Engineering
Florida Institute of Technology
Melbourne, Florida

Abstract	**4**
1.1. Introduction	**5**
1.2. Past and Present Practices	**7**
1.3. Dumping into Surface Waters in the Deep Sea	**12**
1.4. Characteristics Distinguishing the Deep Sea from the Coastal Ocean	**12**
1.4.1. Physical Characteristics	12
1.4.2. Chemical Characteristics	16
1.4.3. Biological Characteristics	18
1.4.4. Geological Characteristics	20
1.5. Closing Remarks	**23**
Acknowledgments	**24**
References	**24**

ABSTRACT

Incineration at sea, industrial and sewage waste disposal in the surface mixing zone, and disposal of low-level nuclear wastes, obsolete munitions, and nerve gas onto the seafloor have been the main uses of the deep sea for waste management. In 1981 the wastes disposed of in the deep sea consisted of 48×10^4 t of liquid industrial wastes and 2×10^4 t of sewage sludge by the United States; 1.5×10^4 t (solids) of sewage sludge by the Federal Republic of Germany; 5300 t of liquid industrial wastes by Denmark; 99 t of solid industrial wastes by the United Kingdom; and 9400 t of low-level radioactive wastes [α 7.8×10^{13} Bq; β and γ 5.7×10^{15} Bq (^{3}H 2.8×10^{15} Bq)] by several European countries. Also in 1981 at-sea incineration of slightly more than 10^5 t of organic wastes from Belgium, France, the Federal Republic of Germany, the Netherlands, Norway, Sweden, and the United Kingdom was carried out in the North Sea. Unique oceanographic features of the deep sea include its large dilution capacity; the long residence time of deep-sea water (on the order of 10^2 y); low biological productivity in the surface water of the open ocean (~ 50 g m^{-2} of carbon per year); the existence of an oxygen minimum zone at several hundred meters deep in the mid-latitudes; and the abyssal-clay regions showing sedimentary records of tens of millions of years of slow, uninterrupted deposition of fine-grained clay. Any deep-sea waste disposal strategy must take into account oceanic processes and current scientific knowledge in order to attain a safe solution that will last for centuries.

1.1. INTRODUCTION

Most wastes disposed of in the ocean initially enter the nearshore waters of estuaries, bays, and continental shelves. These regions, and unique upwelling zones,
comprise about 10% of all oceanic areas and support more than 99% of the commercially exploited fisheries (Ryther, 1969). Except for transoceanic shipping,
commercial and recreational uses of the sea occur in the same nearshore regions
that are most often used for waste disposal. However, there are potential dangers
to human health, food supplies, and ecosystems when the nearshore regions are
used extensively for waste disposal. It is therefore prudent to consider alternative
disposal methods. The deep ocean as a waste disposal environment is one such
approach.

Chapters in this volume are mainly concerned with discharges that occur near
the sea surface. We have not included the dumping of contained wastes on the
seafloor. Radioactive wastes, a principal example of contained wastes, are considered in Volume 3 of this series (Park et al., 1983). However, there have been other
types of contained wastes such as nerve gas and obsolete explosive munitions disposed on the deep ocean floor (Inter-Governmental Maritime Consultative Organization, 1981). Upon decomposition of these containers, this mode of waste disposal can release wastes to the deep sea.

The input of wastes to nearshore waters occurs through pipeline discharges (Fig.
1.1a), nonpoint sources such as atmospheric input (Table 1.1), and runoff and from
ship and barge dumping (Fig. 1.1b). Disposal into surface waters or the deep ocean
has occurred only from disposal vessels and from at-sea incineration (Fig. 1.1c),
where stack emissions eventually settle into the sea. In California, where the continental shelf is quite narrow, a pipeline discharge below the permanent pycnocline
of the ocean at a depth of 400 m has been proposed (Brooks et al., 1982; Jackson,
1982).

In this chapter we define deep ocean disposal as that which occurs in waters
deeper than 200 m. This criterion is somewhat arbitrary, but it excludes most continental shelves and includes waters that have a permanent pycnocline, with the
exception of the polar regions, where deep and bottom waters are formed at the
sea surface.

There have been three basic approaches to disposing of wastes: containment,
decomposition, and dilution. Disposal on land or in containers on the seafloor represents the containment approach. Incineration, pyrolysis, and secondary or ter-
tiary sewage treatment are examples of decomposition. This second type of disposal approach generally produces additional wastes such as acidic gases, ash, and
sludge that must be considered in an overall waste management plan. Because of
the dispersive nature of the oceanic environment, the disposal of wastes in the
ocean is often an example of the dilution strategy. Deep ocean disposal of liquid
industrial wastes, as practiced by the United States of America and other countries,
has been designed to enhance initial and subsequent dilution of the waste by discharging the material into the turbulent wake of a moving vessel (Ketchum et al.,
1981; Duedall et al., 1983). The oceanic disposal of solid wastes such as dredged

Figure 1.1. Input of wastes to the ocean from different sources: (a) sewage outfall discharge in deep water covered by boulders; (b) vessel disposal at sea (photograph courtesy of M. H. Orr); and (c) *M/T Matthias II*, incineration of organic wastes at sea (photograph courtesy of H. Compaan).

Table 1.1.   Annual Emission of Five Metals in the Atmosphere by Industrial and Natural Activities (10^3 t y^{-1})[a]

Metal	Industrial Sources	Natural Sources					
		Windblown Dust	Forest Fires	Volcanic Activity	Vegetation	Seasalt Spray	Total Natural Sources
Cd	7.3	0.1	0.012	0.52	0.2	0.4	1.2
Cu	56	12	0.3	3.6	2.5	0.08	18
Ni	47	20	0.6	3.8	1.6	0.04	26
Pb	450	16	0.5	6.4	1.6	5	20
Zn	310	25	2.1	7.0	9.4	10	54

[a]Adapted from Salomons and Forstner (1984).

material and fly ash may result in the formation of areas of localized contamination on the seafloor, which may appear to be a containment approach (Duedall et al., 1985). It is possible, however, for wastes on the seafloor to be remobilized or eroded (Kester et al., 1983). Therefore, this practice may also be considered partial dilution.

1.2.   PAST AND PRESENT PRACTICES

In Europe, three dumpsites with depths of 4000 m have been used for disposal of wastes at sea (Fig. 1.2a); two of the sites were used for industrial wastes (one of them was also used for sewage sludge disposal), and a third site received low-level nuclear wastes. The Oslo Commission reports the types and quantities of wastes dumped in the Oslo Convention area, which includes several shallow-water dump sites in the North and Baltic Seas, in addition to the deepwater dumpsites (Oslo Commission, 1983). For instance, in 1981 the Federal Republic of Germany (FRG) dumped 1.5×10^4 t of sewage sludge, Denmark discharged 5300 t of liquid industrial wastes, and the United Kingdom dumped 99 t of solid industrial wastes at deepwater dumpsites (Fig. 1.2a) (Oslo Commission, 1984).

Dumping of low-level nuclear wastes was carried out by member countries of the Nuclear Energy Agency (NEA) up to 1982, but no dumping occurred in 1983 (Curtis, 1984). Table 1.2 shows the dumping information up to the year 1981. The NEA follows the requirements adopted by the International Maritime Organization (formerly the Inter-Governmental Maritime Consultative Organization) (Nuclear Energy Agency–Organisation for Economic Co-Operation and Development, 1983).

Four deep-ocean sites have received industrial and sewage wastes generated in the United States: Deepwater Dumpsite (DWD)-106, located 196 km southeast of New York City (Fig. 1.2b); a site 70 km north of Arecibo, Puerto Rico (Fig. 1.2c); and two sites in the Gulf of Mexico (not shown), one 220 km south of Galveston,

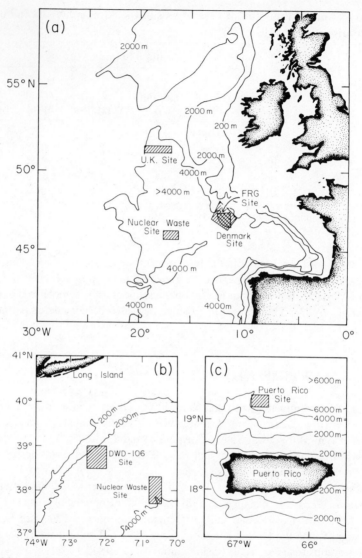

Figure 1.2. Deepwater dumpsites: (a) United Kingdom and Denmark industrial waste sites, Federal Republic of Germany sewage sludge dumpsite and nuclear waste site in the eastern Atlantic Ocean; (b) United States Deepwater Dumpsite-106 and nuclear waste site; Puerto Rico industrial waste dumpsite.

Texas, and the other 90 km south of the mouth of the Mississippi River. Also shown in Fig. 1.2b is the currently inactive 3800-m site, which received low-level nuclear wastes during 1957–1959 (Hagen, 1983). Dumping at the Gulf of Mexico sites ended in 1978, and the Puerto Rico site has not been used since 1981 (O'Connor, 1983). The amounts of materials dumped at these sites and on the continental shelf of the New York Bight are summarized in Table 1.3. The amount of material taken

Table 1.2.   Ocean Dumping of Low-level Radioactive Wastes by European Countries

Year	Dumpsite			Weight (t)	Radioactivity (10^{12} Bq) α	$\beta + \gamma$	$^3H^a$
1949	48°30'N,	13°00'W		9	0.00	0.04	
1950	49 50	02	18	350	0.07	0.74	
1951	49 50	02	18	320	0.04	0.67	
	55 20	11	20	33	0.04	0.19	
1952	49 50	02	18	530	0.07	1.1	
1953	55 08	12	10	57	0.07	0.07	
	49 50	02	18	760	0.37	1.4	
1954	49 50	02	18	1,100	0.85	2.0	
1955	49 50	02	18	1,200	1.3	1.6	
	32 37	14	05	1,500	0.44	1.2	
1956	49 50	02	18	1,000	1.6	1.2	
1957	49 50	02	18	1,500	4.0	6.0	
	32 42	19	30	4,400	35	30	
1958	32 42	19	30	2,700	26	40	
	49 50	02	18	1,000	2.1	2.1	
1959	49 50	02	18	1,200	0.15	2.7	
1960	49 50	02	18	2,600	2.7	8.1	
1961	49 50	02	18	2,000	0.74	11	
	32 38	20	05	4,400	21	60	
1962	46 27	06	10	250	0.63	6.0	
	49 50	02	18	1,400	0.19	2.8	
1963	49 50	02	18	1,500	0.11	1.6	
	45 27	06	16	5,800	14	260	
1964	45 27	06	36	4,400	16	560	
1965	48 15	13	15	1,800	4.2	510	
1966	48 15	13	15	1,000	2.9	91	
1967	42 50	14	30	11,000	9.3	280	
1968	48 20	13	16	3,200	27	2800	
1969	49 05	17	05	9,200	19	810	
1970	48 19	13	15	1,700	8.6	750	
1971	46 15	17	25	4,000	23	410	
1972	46 15	17	25	4,100	25	800	
1973	46 15	17	25	4,400	27	470	
1974	46 15	17	25	2,300	15	3700	
1975	46 15	17	25	4,500	29	2200	(1,100)
1976	46 15	17	25	6,800	33	2000	(780)
1977	46 00	16	45	5,600	35	2800	(1,200)
1978	46 00	16	45	8,000	41	2900	(1,300)
1979	46 00	16	45	5,400	52	3100	(1,600)
1980	46 00	16	45	8,400	69	6100	(3,600)
1981	46 00	16	45	9,400	78	5700	(2,800)

Source: Adapted from Mitchell (1983).
^{a}The ^3H data are available only since 1975. Since ^3H is a β emitter, it is also included in the column for β and γ emitters.

9

Table 1.3. Ocean Dumping under United States Permit[a]

| Disposal Site | Waste Type | Quantity (10^3 t) | | | | |
		1978	1979	1980	1981	1982
Deep Sea						
Deepwater Dumpsite-106	Industrial	730	560	510	250	190
	Coal ash[b]	0	0	2	0	0
	Sewage sludge	70	82	47	20	38
Puerto Rico Site	Industrial	360	330	360	240	0
Gulf of Mexico	Industrial	1	0	0	0	0
Nearshore						
New York Bight	Industrial	1800	2000	2400	1800	830
	Sewage sludge[c]	5500	6400	7300	6700	7600

[a]Source: U.S. Environmental Protection Agency (1981) and P. Anderson (personal communication); excludes dredged material.

[b]Deepwater Dumpsite-106 is being investigated as a potential site for disposal of coal ash (Duedall et al., 1985).

[c]Except for 5.4×10^4 t of sludge from Camden, New Jersey, in 1978, these quantities represent digestor cleanout, the material obtained upon periodic cleaning of sewage sludge digestors. Sludge from these digestors is dumped routinely in the New York Bight.

to the DWD-106 site decreased 3.5-fold from 1978 to 1982. Therefore, in quantity, the dumping on the continental shelf off the east coast of the United States greatly exceeds deep-sea dumping.

Ocean disposal of dredged material is much greater than the input of other wastes on a mass basis. In the United States, for example, 6×10^7 t of dredged material was placed in the ocean during 1980 (U.S. Army Corps of Engineers, 1982). Of that total, 41% was placed at sites within 5.5 km of the shoreline; this, according to U.S. law, is not considered ocean dumping. The remaining 59% was distributed among 23 ocean dumpsites, all but one of which were on the continental shelf. The only deepwater dumpsite for dredged material is south of Honolulu, Hawaii, where there is no continental shelf (Chave and Miller, 1983); 6.4×10^5 m^3 of dredged material was disposed of in 1977 at a depth of 410 m.

The practice of at-sea incineration of halogenated hydrocarbons and some other toxic organic compounds was begun in the North Sea by the FRG in 1969 (Chapters 2 and 6). At-sea incineration has been used occasionally by the United States on a limited basis (Kamlet, 1981). With properly designed and carefully operated equipment, destruction efficiencies >99.95% can be achieved by incineration. After CO_2 and H_2O are taken into account, the primary constituent of the stack gases is HCl, which is readily absorbed and neutralized by the surface layer of the ocean without discernible deleterious effects (Kamlet, 1981; Chapters 3 and 4 of this volume). Currently the amount of material incinerated at sea (primarily in the North Sea) is about $(1.2–1.6) \times 10^5$ t y^{-1} (Chapter 2).

Duedall et al. (1983) summarized all the 1976–1979 ocean dumping permits issued by the 46 member nations to the International Convention on the Prevention of Marine Pollution by Dumping Wastes and Other Matter, commonly known as the London Dumping Convention (Inter-Governmental Maritime Consultative Organization, 1976). Except for the United States permits, none include dumping at depths greater than 200 m; omitted from this consideration were the contained low-level radioactive wastes dumped by the United Kingdom and other European countries at the NEA dumpsite in the northeastern Atlantic Ocean (Table 1.2) (Park et al., 1983).

We are uncertain as to the extent of recent or past unreported instances of deep-ocean disposal of obsolete ships, munitions, and other military material (Fig. 1.3). However, there is an important example of a most unwise use of a region on the continental shelf off California as a munitions dumpsite (Hood and McRoy, 1971). This is a region of known phosphorite deposits. The Collier Carbon and Chemical

Figure 1.3. Disposal of obsolete ships and munitions.

Corporation, operating on a lease with the U.S. Government, had to abandon efforts to mine the phosphorite because of the hazards from unexploded shells disposed of on the phosphorite deposit.

1.3. DUMPING INTO SURFACE WATERS IN THE DEEP SEA

In many respects, the dumping of wastes into the wakes of moving ships or barges is the same whether over the deep sea or the continental shelf. For instance, Csanady (1981) modelled the initial dispersion of industrial wastes dumped at the DWD-106 site in terms of the rate of discharge, the depth of the mixed layer, and turbulent mixing perpendicular to the axis of the plume. The fact that one of the data sets used to develop the model was actually obtained in shallow water was inconsequential because vertical mixing was limited by a seasonal pycnocline at about 20-m depth. As long as wastes remain in the upper mixed layer, their physical behavior is independent of the total depth of the water column.

Wastes routinely dumped at deep ocean dumpsites have been aqueous solutions or dilute suspensions with densities in the range of 1.01–1.15 g cm^{-3} (Csanady, 1981; Kester et al., 1981; Brooks et al., 1983), dumped at a rate of about 10^2 m^3 km^{-1}, so that initial dilutions exceed 10^3 times and the diluted wastes become neutrally buoyant. Their subsequent dispersion occurs in the mixed layer. During winter months, when a seasonal pycnocline is absent, these wastes have been detected at depths down to 100 m (Mukherji and Kester, 1983). These depths are above the permanent pycnocline of the deep ocean, but the wastes could have reached the seafloor on most continental shelves.

Because waste disposal occurs mainly in the upper layers of the ocean, most attempts to measure biological responses to deep ocean disposal have emphasized near-surface/planktonic organisms. This differs from the continental shelf studies that emphasize benthic organisms (Bascom et al., 1980; Stanford et al., 1981). MacLean (1981) found no histological evidence of damage to euphausiids; Murphy et al. (1983) observed short-term, small-scale shifts in phytoplankton species composition in waste plumes; Capuzzo and Lancaster (Chapter 11) found a loss of zooplankton fecundity in a waste plume; Fay and Wastler (Chapter 4) used plankton as a biological indicator, but found no effects of an at-sea incineration plume.

1.4. CHARACTERISTICS DISTINGUISHING THE DEEP SEA FROM THE COASTAL OCEAN

1.4.1. Physical Characteristics

The major physical difference between deep sea and coastal ocean waste disposal is the extent of dilution before waste components reach the seafloor, where they can accumulate. Other things being equal, wastes dumped over the deep ocean will

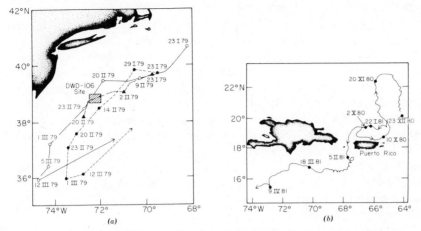

Figure 1.4 Trajectories of drogue buoys from ocean dumpsites tracked by satellite: (a) Deepwater Dumpsite-106 (Bisagni, 1981), and (b) Puerto Rico dumpsite (Williams, 1981).

result in more widespread but lower concentrations of contaminants in the sediment than if the disposal occurs on the continental shelf.

Rates of initial dilution in surface waters may be the same in coastal regions and in the deep ocean. Horizontal turbulent diffusion coefficients depend on wind speed (Csanady, 1981), which obviously does not depend on the depth of the water column. Wastes will be carried away from the site of discharge in regions of strong currents, whereas wastes will accumulate in areas of weak currents. Deepwater Dumpsite-106, for example, lies in an area where wastes tend to be carried southwest and eventually into the Gulf Stream (Fig. 1.4a). In contrast, the Puerto Rico dumpsite is in an area of less continual advection (Fig. 1.4b). These site-specific characteristics must be considered in both deepwater and coastal regions.

The rate of horizontal mixing decreases below the surface layer, due to the lack of direct forcing by winds. Ewart and Bendiner (1981) found that patches of dye placed at depths of 300 and 1000 m in the Pacific Ocean were dispersed horizontally at a rate consistent with a diffusion velocity of 0.1 cm s^{-1}, which is 10 times slower than would be expected in the mixed layer of the ocean (Okubo and Pritchard, 1969). Computation of eddy kinetic energy from current meter records (a measure of the current variations about the mean) showed deeper water to be less energetic in the 500- to 2000-m depth range than in the upper 100 m at a site in the northwestern Atlantic Ocean (Webster, 1969). Schmitz et al. (1982) found that the deep ocean was more energetic in the vicinity of the strong western boundary currents than in other areas. Consequently, when a waste is placed in the surface waters of the ocean, it will be mixed and advected at a fairly rapid rate. As the waste penetrates into the deep ocean, mixing and advection will continue, but at a slower rate. The actual rates of these processes will vary with location in the ocean (Chapter 17).

There are a number of mechanisms by which wastes can enter the deep ocean from the surface layer. The presence of the usual vertical density gradient greatly slows turbulent mixing into the deep sea. An engineered delivery system, such as a pipe extending beneath the pycnocline (Brooks et al., 1982) or short-lived containers, could be used to inject a waste directly into the deep ocean. Particulate settling of waste components can transfer material from the surface to the deep ocean within a short time. One mechanism applies only to wastes with a density greater than seawater and released in such a way that a descending mass is formed. Such a mass will sink at a rate determined by its initial density until it has entrained enough seawater to become neutrally buoyant. At that depth it then becomes subject to passive mixing, with individual waste particles settling at their intrinsic velocities. Koh and Chang (1973) modelled this process mathematically, and found that the depth of penetration is strongly dependent on the vertical density gradient of the water column. Discharging waste in this manner could transfer the waste into or through pycnoclines.

The only waste that has been dumped *en masse,* other than contained wastes, is dredged material, which descends to the seafloor after being dumped in relatively shallow water. One deep ocean disposal experiment, a spot-dumping of fly ash, failed to reveal more than traces of the ash in the upper 100 m of the water column, implying that it may have penetrated into or beneath the permanent pycnocline (Rose et al., 1985). Kupferman et al. (1982) estimated that if radioactively contaminated soil were dumped at DWD-106 under certain conditions, a mass could form and descend to 250 m, where it would spread out in the permanent pycnocline. In order for waste masses to spread at the pycnocline, specific conditions of waste properties, discharge procedures, and water column stratification are required. If a waste spreads at the pycnocline, it would undergo more dispersion before ultimately reaching the seafloor than would waste dumped as a coherent mass over continental shelves.

Most wastes dumped at deep ocean sites have been subjected to mixing in the surface waters immediately following discharge. Descent of components of these wastes requires that they exist as, or become associated with, particles with fall velocities $>10^{-2}$ cm s^{-1}. The magnitude of this critical velocity depends on the depth of the mixed layer and on the vertical turbulence within it (Lerman, 1979). In general, slow-settling particles (10^{-3} cm s^{-1}) will be retained in the surface layer by vertical mixing. Particles falling at $<10^{-2}$ cm s^{-1} will take years to reach the deep-sea floor; they will be subject to extensive horizontal displacement even if this gravitational descent is not inhibited by vertical mixing. A Stokes' settling velocity of 10 m d^{-1} corresponds to that of a quartz sphere (density 2.5 g cm^{-3}) about 10 μm in diameter. Proportionately less dense or smaller particles will not reach the deep-sea floor by gravity alone. Examples of such nonsettling particles include clay, fine silt, and substantial portions of sewage sludge (Faisst, 1981). For these wastes to enter the deep sea after initial dispersion in the surface waters requires some process that will increase their fall velocity. Similarly, all dissolved waste components must be incorporated into falling particles if they are to be removed from the surface layer within a reasonably short period.

Fine particles can collide and adhere to one another, forming a flocculant particle with fall velocity greater than that of the initial particles. The importance of this process in determining the initial behavior of sewage sludge has been considered by Morel and Schiff (1980) and by Hunt (1982). Morgan and Lovorn (Chapter 13) model this process for particulate discharges associated with manganese nodule mining and processing. Rates of flocculation depend on the turbulence and the particle concentration in the water column, both of which increase the frequency of collisions among particles. The loss of hydrous iron oxide particles in a stratified water column reflects flocculation when the rate of iron removal from the water is second-order with respect to its concentration (Chapter 15). Quantitative application of flocculation models to actual waste disposal operations requires more theoretical development, particularly with regard to the early stages of discharge, where concentrations and induced turbulence are relatively large. it would appear, however, that as horizontal dispersion proceeds and concentrations decrease, the rate of particle flocculation will decrease.

Osterberg et al. (1963) suggested that incorporation of contaminants into zooplankton fecal material provides the fast sinking particles required to penetrate rapidly into the deep ocean. In recent years this idea has been developed in considerable detail. A number of elements (Cherry et al., 1978) and xenobiotic (synthetic organic) compounds (Elder and Fowler, 1977) have been found in fecal material. Settling rates of fecal pellets depend on the type of organisms producing them (Small et al., 1979; Capuzzo and Lancaster, 1981). The rate of collection of organic material (not solely fecal pellets) in sediment traps below the surface layer varies roughly in proportion to the rate of primary productivity in the surface water (Deuser et al., 1981; Knauer and Martin, 1981).

Biologically packaged elements or organic material may not fall directly to the seafloor. Vertical profiles of some nutrients and trace metals in the deep ocean often show mid-depth maxima, indicating that there has been biological removal from the surface followed by regeneration at depth (Fig. 1.5a). Falling particles either break up into very slowly settling particles or components within the particles become dissolved and released to the aqueous phase. Rates of mass settling to the deep-sea floor, determined from sediment trap measurements, are on the order of a few mg cm^{-2} y^{-1} (Rowe and Gardner, 1979; Brewer et al., 1980), corresponding to sedimentation rates of fractions of a millimeter per year. Possible alteration of this mass flux and its effect on organisms is an important issue for considerations of oceanic waste disposal.

Flocculation and biological packaging can occur over the continental shelf as well as in the deep sea. Flocculation is of great importance in controlling the distribution of river-borne material as it enters the ocean (Sholkovitz, 1978). Biological productivity is generally much higher on the continental shelf than in the deep sea; thus, one would expect that the role of biological packaging and transfer of material would be greater on the shelf also. Solid–liquid phase exchange processes play a major role relative to biological removal when resuspended particle concentrations are high.

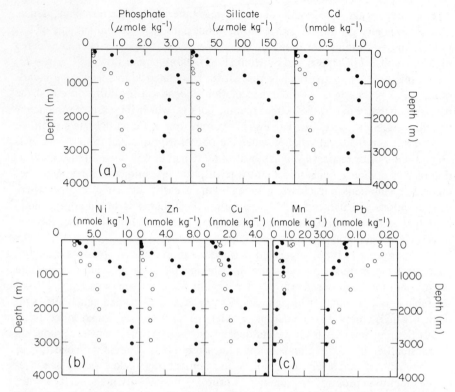

Figure 1.5. Nutrient and metal profiles in the North Atlantic and North Pacific Oceans (adapted from Bruland and Franks, 1983 with permission of Plenum Press). The North Atlantic data (○) are from 34°15′ N, 66°17′W; the North Pacific data (•) are from 32°41′ N, 145°00′W.

1.4.2. Chemical Characteristics

Elemental components of wastes that are often of environmental concern also occur naturally in seawater and in atmospheric particles. Bruland and Franks (1983) found that in the western North Atlantic surface waters, concentrations of Mn, Ni, Cu, Zn, and Cd are greater at a shelf water station than in the open ocean by factors of 9, 3, 3, 40, and 100, respectively. Conversely, they found deepwater concentrations of Mn, Ni, Cu, Zn, and Cd to be 0.3, 2, 2, 28, and 140 times greater than surface water concentrations. The difference between surface and deepwater concentrations is greater in the Pacific than in the Atlantic Ocean (Bruland, 1980) (Fig. 1.5), probably due to the longer recirculation time of the Pacific. Similarly, Boyle et al. (1981) reported higher Cu concentrations in coastal waters than in the surface of the open ocean. In general, coastal waters and deep oceanic waters are regions of relatively high metal concentrations, whereas surface oceanic waters tend to have low concentrations of metals. Mercury in the northwestern Atlantic Ocean shows systematic variations that are consistent with this generalization in the upper 1000 m, and it also shows hydrographically and biologically controlled variations (Mukherji and Kester, 1979; Fitzgerald et al., 1984). The distributions of many of these metals show water column gradients and maxima that are similar to those of phosphate (Fig. 1.5), nitrate (not shown), and silicate (Fig. 1.5).

Two metals, Mn and Pb, have lower concentrations in the deep ocean than in the surface waters (Fig. 1.5) (Landing and Bruland, 1980; Schaule and Patterson, 1981). The chemistry of Mn favors its existence as a solid in aerated seawater, so it is not readily remobilized at depth in the ocean. The distribution of Pb has probably been influenced by worldwide emissions into the atmosphere and oceans, causing it to have surface concentrations greater than would be maintained by natural geochemical cycles.

The atmosphere is an important source for elements entering the ocean. The atmosphere receives input from windblown dust, seasalt spray, crustal degassing, volcanic activity, biological activity, and human sources. Salomons and Forstner (1984) have estimated the atmospheric emissions of trace elements from both natural sources and industrial sources (Table 1.1). The metals Cd, Cu, Ni, Pb, and Zn enter the atmosphere from industrial activity at rates of 7300, 5.6×10^4, 4.7×10^4, 4.5×10^5, and 3.1×10^5 t y^{-1}, respectively, which are several times greater than those of natural sources. These metals are deposited in the ocean at rates that exceed natural sedimentation (U.S. National Academy of Sciences, 1978).

Oceanic distributions of organic compounds associated with anthropogenic activity, such as polychlorinated biphenyls (PCBs) and polyaromatic hydrocarbons (PAHs), have not been studied in great detail in oceanic waters. In the North Atlantic Ocean, Harvey and Steinhauer (1976a) showed that surface concentrations of PCBs near the coast are about 10 times greater than in the open ocean. deLappe et al. (1980) found that U.S. coastal waters contain <1 μg kg^{-1} of total hydrocarbons and <1 ng kg^{-1} of PCBs. Data are not available for the variation of these substances with depth in oceanic waters, but high concentrations of PCBs [4.5–38 mg kg^{-1} (dry wt)] have been found in fecal pellets from euphausiids (Elder and Fowler, 1977). The highly chlorinated PCB isomers that are adsorbed strongly onto surfaces may show little remobilization from descending particles.

The composition of sediments provides further evidence for the chemical differences between continental shelf and deep-sea environments. The concentrations of many elements are higher in deep-sea sediments than in continental shelf sediments (Riley and Chester, 1971). To some extent this difference is due to the dilution of these elements by large quantities of terrigenous material on the continental shelves. But the differences are also related to the fact that deep-sea sediments are usually fine-grained particles with large surface area, compared to continental shelf sediments. Consequently, water–sediment exchange processes are likely to be greater for deep-sea sediments than for shelf sediments.

Xenobiotic compounds are less concentrated in deep-sea sediments than in coastal sediments. Harvey and Steinhauer (1976b) found PCB concentrations of ~ 1 ng g^{-1} at the surface of deep-sea sediments. Data of Laflamme and Hites (1978) indicate PAH concentrations of 50 ng g^{-1} in deep-sea sediments, and about 10 times higher concentrations in coastal sediments. These generalizations about the difference in trace components of deep-sea and coastal sediments do not reflect the regional variations that occur due to differences in sediment grain size, surface properties, or proximity to sources of contamination or geochemical activity.

1.4.3. Biological Characteristics

An important difference between the deep ocean and the coastal regions is the lower productivity and biomass in the deep ocean. Ryther (1969) concluded that the theoretical yield of seafood from the deep sea should be small because surface primary productivity in oceanic waters (~ 50 g m^{-2} of carbon per year) is only about 10% of that on the continental shelves. The more complex food web connecting phytoplankton and fish in oceanic waters implies a lower efficiency of carbon transfer to the trophic levels used by humans and may also contribute to lower biomass at high trophic levels. An inverse relationship exists between depth and benthic biomass (Rowe et al., 1982). Between the surface and seafloor of the deep ocean there exists a diverse array of pelagic organisms that are of ecological, scientific, and aesthetic value, but their biomass is not sufficient to justify commercial exploitation. As an example, rattails (grenadiers), mainly *Coryphaenoides armatus,* have a biomass of about 0.2 g (wet wt) m^{-2} on the Tufts Abyssal Plain in the northeastern Pacific Ocean (Mullin and Gomez, 1981). Other biological characteristics of the deep ocean are extremely slow growth rates, long generation times, small population size, low fecundity, limited dispersal, and low recruitment rates (Grassle, 1977; Sanders, 1979), suggesting that recovery rates following perturbations in the deep sea may be quite slow. The abundance of benthic organisms per unit area is much lower in the deep sea than in coastal regions, but the diversity of species is higher (Rex, 1981). Deep sea communities in general appear to comprise species with broad geographic ranges at certain depths; however, only limited information is available on distributional patterns in the world's oceans, dispersal capabilities of deep-sea species, and the biotic interactions that are important in structuring deep-sea communities. These limitations must be considered in an evaluation of waste impact on the deep-sea benthos.

Low productivity in the surface water of the deep ocean results from the loss of nutrients by vertical transfer to below the pycnocline. Wherever the nutrient-rich water from intermediate depths in the ocean returns to the euphotic zone, as in the upwelling regions off Peru and off the west coast of Africa and North America, extraordinarily high levels of productivity can occur. Newly upwelled water contains not only moderate concentrations of nutrients, but also elevated concentrations of metals that have been regenerated along with the nutrients. Barber and Ryther (1969) found that chelating agents had to be added to recently upwelled waters before phytoplankton could achieve high production rates. These and other observations have demonstrated the importance of metal speciation on biological response. In the case of Cu, there is a good correlation between the concentration of free metal ions and the inhibition of phytoplankton growth (Sunda and Guillard, 1976). Evidently, natural mechanisms condition upwelled water so that it can support high levels of productivity. These mechanisms may involve the complexation of inhibitory metals by phytoplankton exudates (Morel and Morel-Laurens, 1983), or the mixing of upwelled waters with coastal waters containing relatively high concentrations of Mn (Huntsman and Sunda, 1981) or Fe (Morel and Morel-Laurens, 1983) to mitigate the suppressive effects of other metals. Continental shelf waters are highly productive, despite the amount of Cu and Zn which could be toxic to phytoplankton, indicating that complexation mechanisms may exist in the coastal waters. Many observations of natural complexing agents in coastal waters confirm this expectation (Huizenga and Kester, 1983; Sunda and Ferguson, 1983).

The degradation rates of organic matter vary greatly between the continental shelf and the deep ocean. On the continental shelf the organic matter that penetrates the pycnocline from primary production is regenerated primarily in the benthic region; this process appears to occur rapidly enough that each year's production is degraded without much residual undegraded organic matter remaining in the sediment. In the deep sea this degradation process occurs much more slowly. There is considerable evidence that the rate of oxygen consumption decreases nearly exponentially with depth (Kester, 1975). Low oxygen consumption may reflect both low standing stock of macro- and meibenthos as well as low rates of bacterial action.

If degradable organic wastes are placed in the deep sea, consideration must be given to the possibility that the rates of oxygen consumption may be increased, thereby altering the natural balance between the prevailing oxygen consumption rate and the oxygen renewal rate of the deep and intermediate depth regions of the ocean. While free-living bacteria have not been found to significantly mineralize organic substrates placed in deepwater or deep sediments Jannasch and Wirsen, 1982; Jannasch et al., 1971), relatively fast-growing (when substrate is provided) bacteria have been found in association with deep-sea animals (Yayanos et al., 1979; Deming and Colwell, 1981). Deming (1983) found that bacteria associated with fecal pellets descending onto the seafloor are capable of relatively rapid utilization of organic matter.

There is evidence that if degradable organic matter is initially dispersed in the surface layer of the ocean, only a small portion of it will reach the seafloor. Knauer and Martin (1981) found that the flux of carbon to sediment traps at a depth of 500 m was only 4% of the carbon fixed by productivity in the overlying waters. Rowe and Gardner (1979) found that material obtained by sediment traps near the seafloor contained 4–6% (by wt) organic carbon, whereas the underlying surface sediments contained ~1% (by wt) organic carbon. Organisms utilize very effectively whatever organic carbon reaches them. In effect, the coastal waters and the deep ocean function as a septic system for mineralizing organic compounds. In such a consideration it becomes important to know the extent the added waste alters the natural degradation processes.

In contrast to disposal in coastal regions, the most significant differences in biological responses to waste disposal in the deep sea would be slower recovery rates of deep-sea benthos and limited capacity for detoxification of xenobiotic compounds. Grassle (1977) demonstrated that deep-sea sediments were only slowly recolonized after perturbations, with only 10% of the normal benthic community having recolonized initially azoic sediment trays within 2 y. Faster recovery times have been observed in coastal regions (Swartz et al., 1980).

It is possible that deep ocean disposal of wastes could, on a limited scale, lead to drastic changes in benthic community structure, and recovery rates following cessation of disposal operations may be quite long. From both a sedimentological and an ecological point of view, such an effect could be perceived as being similar to natural episodic events on the continental margins, where large fluxes of sediment are deposited by turbidity currents, but the temporal and spatial scales of recovery may differ by orders of magnitude.

Xenobiotic compounds occur in relatively low concentrations in deep-sea water or sediments. Increasing water column or sedimentary concentrations of these compounds could cause increases in body burdens of the compounds among deep-sea organisms. There is evidence that, like their shallow-water and terrestrial counterparts, deep-sea organisms have the metabolic capacity to transform PAHs to excretable products (Stegeman, 1983). Intermediate compounds produced in this biotransformation process are the agents responsible for the parent compound's toxicity. As yet, too little is known about the process in shallow-water or terrestrial animals to relate measured body burdens to effects on individuals or populations. It is therefore unknown whether deep-sea organisms are uniquely sensitive to xenobiotic compound contamination.

1.4.4. Geological Characteristics

The primary geological characteristic that distinguishes the deep sea from the coastal ocean is topography. Some parts of the deep seabed are irregular due to the presence of subduction zones, mid-ocean ridges, fracture zones, and seamounts; while large, flat abyssal plains exist at some other parts (Fig. 1.6). Some of these features, such as the subduction zones, mid-ocean ridges, and the fracture zones, undergo displacement during continental drift, volcanic activity, and seafloor spreading. In the coastal ocean the continental shelf is the principal topographic feature. The shelf may be considered an extension of the continent. The shelf is not featureless, however. Submarine canyons, which cut across the continental shelf and are often found near large river mouths, have steep walls and are observed to extend into the continental slope and rise (Shepard, 1977). Such canyons become areas for transport of material, both natural and anthropogenic, and also for rapid movement of larger amounts of sediment in the form of turbidity currents that reshape the canyon and seafloor. These are areas of instability (Ryan and Farre, 1983) and therefore may not be suitable for the disposal of wastes which require permanent disposal at a specific location.

A majority of the solid wastes from ocean dumping via ships and barges takes place on the continental shelf. This activity has affected the bottom topography (Palmer and Gross, 1979). Coal waste deposits in United Kingdom waters have resulted in an uneven bottom in fishing zones to such an extent that trawler nets are damaged (Eagle et al., 1979). In the United States dredged material disposal occurring in the New York Bight apex has produced a 6- to 8-m mound of material

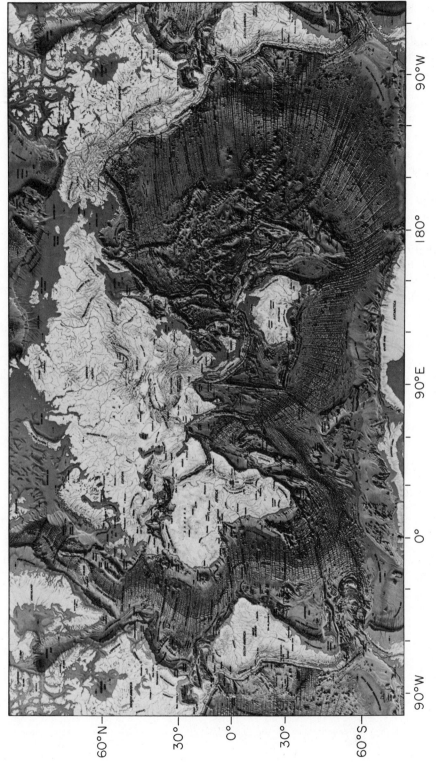

Figure 1.6. The floor of the oceans (Copyright ©, 1980, Marie Tharp). Illustration courtesy of Marie Tharp.

21

(Dayal et al., 1983) on the seafloor, affecting water circulation; it may interfere with future commerce, due to the shallowing of a potential navigable waterway when deeper-draft vessels are needed.

The composition of sediments is important when considering the fate of wastes, because some sediments have the capacity to sorb certain materials through ion exchange processes. This consideration is most advanced in the area of nuclear waste disposal at sea. McVey et al. (1983) have shown in laboratory studies that ^{137}Cs and ^{239}Pu can be contained within the deep-sea sediment, due to their adsorption on clays.

Knowledge of sedimentation rates and processes in the ocean is also important when considering the fate of wastes disposed of in the ocean. Because wastes entering the ocean are often in the form of particulate material, we can use our understanding of the behavior of natural particles as a guide in learning about the behavior of waste material. Sedimentation rates in the open ocean vary considerably, but are generally orders of magnitude smaller than those measured in the coastal areas. In the Indian and Pacific Oceans, for example, sediment accumulates at a rate of 0.1–0.5 mg cm^{-2} y^{-1} (Lisitzin, 1972); the majority of this material is biogenic in origin. For an extreme comparison, sediment accumulation rates >2 g cm^{-2} y^{-1} have been reported on the Mississippi Delta (Trefry and Presley, 1982).

In coastal areas, the principal source of sediment is the streams and rivers that empty into the ocean; rivers in the regions of India and China contribute the majority, about 6×10^9 t y^{-1}, of suspended matter to the ocean (Fig. 1.7). Suspended matter can act as a trap for contaminants. River-borne sediment deposited in the coastal region can be resuspended, transported, and redeposited by a combination of physical and biological processes, and the sedimentation rate will be the net

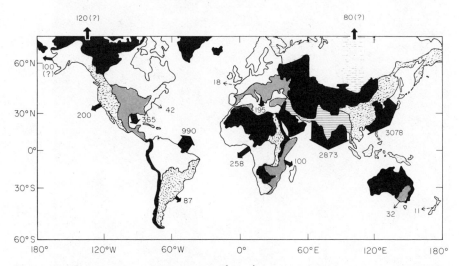

Figure 1.7. Discharge of suspended matter (10^6 t y^{-1}) from major rivers of the world (Milliman, 1981). Each shaded area represents one drainage area. solid areas represent areas where drainage information is unavailable.

effect of all these processes. We are unable to predict the processes responsible for the transport of this material to the open ocean. Knowledge of the processes responsible for slow accumulation rates of solids to the deep-sea floor will be advanced through research using sediment traps.

Bishop and Hollister (1974) suggested that certain abyssal-clay regions of the deep seafloor be considered as potential disposal sites, especially for high-level radioactive wastes. Heath et al. (1983) list the scientific reasons to explore the use of such sites: (1) they are far from seismically and tectonically active lithospheric plate boundaries; (2) they are far from active or young volcanoes; (3) they contain thick layers of very uniform fine-grained clays; (4) they are devoid of natural resources likely to be exploited in the foreseeable future; (5) the geologic and oceanographic processes governing the deposition of sediments in abyssal-clay regions are well understood and have remained unchanged during past oceanic and climatic changes; and (6) they have sedimentary records of tens of millions of years of slow, uninterrupted deposition of fine-grained clay, which supports predictions of the future stability. Abyssal-clay regions may prove to be important for the waste management of the future generations, not only for high-level radioactive wastes but also other highly toxic wastes.

1.5. CLOSING REMARKS

The two prevailing oceanographic features of the ocean in mid-latitudes are the permanent pycnocline, often around 100 m in depth, which separates the surface mixing zone and the deep water, and the oxygen minimum zone at several hundred meters deep. These two features are of important consideration when the deep ocean is to be used as a waste repository.

The surface mixing zone has been used to disperse and dilute industrial and sewage wastes. As the amount of the wastes increases, the capacity of the mixing zone to accommodate the wastes safely must not be surpassed. To develop a safe disposal method, biological and physical cycles of the ocean must be considered simultaneously.

The oxygen minimum zone is created by biochemical oxidation in the ocean, coupled with deep-sea water replenishment from the high latitudes. Cold, saline water sinks at the polar seas; its initial oxygen concentration is high (100% saturation with respect to the atmospheric oxygen content). As this water travels above the deep-sea floor toward lower latitudes it loses some of its oxygen content, but still contains more oxygen than the oxygen minimum zone. The oxygen reservoir below the oxygen minimum zone is very large but is renewed very slowly; Stuiver et al. (1983) give the residence time of deepwater for the Atlantic, Indian, and Pacific Oceans to be 175, 230, and 560 y, respectively. Since on a mole basis there is about 100 times more oxygen in the deep ocean than there is carbon fixed by photosynthesis on the earth's surface in one year, it is unlikely that oxygen-consuming wastes could ever be discharged in sufficient volume to materially alter oxygen concentrations on an oceanic scale. Nevertheless, given the slow rate of oxygen renewal, it is important to consider effects on oxygen concentration before adopting any particular waste disposal strategy.

Some parts of the deep-sea floor may be suitable for disposal of wastes. As human population and its ancillary industrial activity increase in the future, we should continue to explore and identify the most geologically suitable portion of the earth's surface for waste disposal. Because of the distance from human activity, the seafloor, especially the sediment beneath the deep-sea floor, might effectively isolate and contain dangerous material.

ACKNOWLEDGMENTS

We thank W. G. Nelson and J. G. Windsor, Jr., of the Florida Institute of Technology for reviewing this chapter. We also thank T. D. Bewig and E. M. Main for editorial assistance. This work was supported by National Ocean Service, U.S. National Oceanic and Atmospheric Administration. Opinions expressed are the authors' and do not necessarily reflect U.S. Government policy.

REFERENCES

Barber, R. T., and J. H. Ryther. 1969. Oceanic chelators: factors affecting primary production in the Cromwell Current upwelling. *Journal of Experimental Marine Biology and Ecology,* **3,** 191–199.

Bascom, W., and the Staff of SCCWRP. 1980. The effects of sludge disposal in Santa Monica Bay. *In:* Coastal Water Research Project Biennial Report for 1979–1980. Southern California Coastal Water Research Project, Long Beach, California, pp. 197–234.

Bisagni, J. J. 1981. Lagrangian measures of near-surface waters at the 106 mile dumpsite. NOAA Technical Memo OMPA-11. National Oceanic and Atmospheric Administration, Boulder, Colorado, 23 pp.

Bishop, W. P., and C. D. Hollister. 1974. Seabed disposal—where to look. *Nuclear Technology,* **24,** 245–443.

Boyle, E. A., S. S. Huested, and S. P. Jones. 1981. On the distribution of copper, nickel, and cadmium in the surface waters of the North Atlantic and North Pacific Ocean. *Journal of Geophysical Research,* **86,** 8048–8066.

Brewer, P. G., Y. Nozaki, D. W. Spencer, and A. P. Fleer. 1980. Sediment trap experiment in the deep North Atlantic: isotopic and elemental fluxes. *Journal of Marine Research,* **38,** 703–728.

Brooks, J. M., D. A. Weisenburg, G. Bodennec, and T. C. Sauer, Jr. 1983. Volatile organic wastes at the Puerto Rico dumpsite. *In:* Wastes in the Ocean, Vol. 1: Industrial and Sewage Wastes in the Ocean, I. W. Duedall, B. H. Ketchum, P. K. Park, and D. R. Kester (Eds.). Wiley-Interscience, New York, pp. 171–198.

Brooks, N. H., R. G. Arnold, R. C. Y. Koh, G. A. Jackson, and W. K. Faisst. 1982. Deep Ocean Disposal of Sewage Sludge off Orange County, California: A Research Plan. EQL Report No. 21, Environmental Quality Laboratory, California Institute of Technology, Pasadena, California, 101 pp. plus 2 appendices.

Bruland, K. W. 1980. Oceanographic distributions of cadmium, zinc, nickel, and copper in the North Pacific. *Earth and Planetary Science Letters,* **147,** 176–178.

Bruland, K. W., and R. P. Franks. 1983. Mn, Ni, Cu, Zn, and Cd in the western north Atlantic. *In:* Trace Metals in Sea Water, C. S. Wong, E. Boyle, K. W. Bruland, J. D. Burton, and E. D. Goldberg (Eds.). Plenum Press, New York, pp. 395–414.

Capuzzo, J. M., and B. A. Lancaster. 1981. The effects of pollutants on marine zooplankton at Deep Water Dumpsite 106: Preliminary findings. *In:* Ocean Dumping of Industrial Wastes, B. H. Ketchum, D. R. Kester, and P. K. Park (Eds.). Plenum Press, New York, pp. 411–419.

Chave, K. E., and J. N. Miller. 1983. Pearl Harbor dredged-material disposal. *In:* Wastes in the Ocean, Vol. 2: Dredged-Material Disposal in the Ocean, D. R. Kester, B. H. Ketchum, I. W. Duedall, and P. K. Park (Eds.). Wiley-Interscience, New York, pp. 91–98.

Cherry, R. D., J. J. W. Higgo, and S. W. Fowler. 1978. Zooplankton fecal pellets and element residence times in the ocean. *Nature,* **274,** 246–248.

Csanady, G. T. 1981. An analysis of dumpsite diffusion experiments. *In:* Ocean Dumping of Industrial Wastes, B. H. Ketchum, D. R. Kester, and P. K. Park (Eds.). Plenum Press, New York, pp. 109–129.

Curtis, C. E. 1984. Radwaste disposal risks assessed at LDC meeting. *Oceanus,* 27(2), 68–71.

Dayal, R., M. G. Heaton, M. Fuhrmann, and I. W. Duedall. 1983. A geochemical study of the dredged-material deposit in the New York Bight. *In:* Wastes in the Ocean, Vol. 2: Dredged-Material Disposal in the Ocean, D. R. Kester, B. H. Ketchum, I. W. Duedall, and P. K. Park (Eds.). Wiley-Interscience, New York, pp. 123–149.

deLappe, B. W., R. W. Risebrough, A. M. Springer, T. T. Schmidt, J. C. Shropshire, E. F. Letterman, and J. R. Payne. 1980. The sampling and measurement of hydrocarbons in natural waters. *In:* Hydrocarbons and Halogenated Hydrocarbons in the Aquatic Environment, B. K. Afghan and D. Mackay (Eds.). Plenum Press, New York, pp. 29–68.

Deming, J. W. 1983. Evidence for wide-spread occurrence of barophilic bacteria at abyssal depths in the Bay of Biscay. Abstract 1467, Annual Meeting of American Society for Microbiology, New Orleans, Louisiana.

Deming, J. W., and R. R. Colwell. 1981. Barophilic bacteria associated with deep-sea animals. *Biological Sciences,* **31,** 507–511.

Deuser, W. G., E. H. Ross, and R. F. Anderson. 1981. Seasonality in the supply of sediment to the deep Sargasso Sea and implications for the rapid transfer of matter to the deep ocean. *Deep-Sea Research,* **28,** 495–505.

Duedall, I. W., B. H. Ketchum, P. K. Park, and D. R. Kester (Eds.). 1983. Global inputs, characteristics, and fates of ocean-dumped industrial and sewage wastes: an overview. *In:* Wastes in the Ocean, Vol. 1: Industrial and Sewage Wastes in the Ocean. Wiley-Interscience, New York, pp. 3–45.

Duedall, I. W., D. R. Kester, P. K. Park, and B. H. Ketchum (Eds.). 1985. Wastes in the Ocean, Vol. 4: Energy Wastes in the Ocean. Wiley-Interscience, New York, xxx pp.

Eagle, R. A., P. A. Hardiman, M. G. Norton, R. S. Nunny, and M. S. Rolfe. 1979. The Field Assessment of Effects of Dumping Wastes at Sea: 5. The Disposal of Solid Wastes off the North-East Coast of England. Fisheries Research Technical Report No. 51, Directorate of Fisheries Research, Ministry of Agriculture, Fisheries and Food, Lowestoft, United Kingdom, 34 pp.

Elder, D. L., and S. W. Fowler. 1977. Polychlorinated biphenyls: penetration into the deep ocean by zooplankton fecal pellet transport. *Science,* **197,** 459–461.

Ewart, T. E., and W. P. Bendiner. 1981. An observation of the horizontal and vertical diffusion of a passive tracer in the deep ocean. *Journal of Geophysical Research,* **86,** 10974–10982.

Faisst, W. K. 1981. Characterization of particles in digested sewage sludge. *In:* Particulates in Water: Characteristics, Fates, Effects, and Removal, C. Kavanaugh and J. O. Leckie (Eds.). Advances in Chemistry Series No. 189, American Chemical Society, Washington, D.C., 259–282 pp.

Fitzgerald, W. F., G. A. Gill, and J. P. Kim. 1984. An equatorial Pacific Ocean source of atmospheric mercury. *Science,* **224,** 597–599.

Grassle, J. F. 1977. Slow recolonization of deep-sea sediment. *Nature,* **265,** 618–619.

Hagen, A. A. 1983. History of low-level radioactive waste disposal in the sea. *In:* Wastes in the Ocean, Vol. 3: Radioactive Wastes and the Ocean, P. K. Park, D. R. Kester, I. W. Duedall, and B. H. Ketchum (Eds.). Wiley-Interscience, New York, pp. 47–64.

Harvey, G. R., and W. G. Steinhauer. 1976a. Biogeochemistry of PCB and DDT in the North Atlantic. *In:* Environmental Biogeochemistry, Vol. 1, J. P. Nraigu (Ed.). Ann Arbor Science, Ann Arbor, Michigan, pp. 203–221.

Harvey, G. R., and W. G. Steinhauer. 1976b. Transport pathways of polychlorinated biphenyls in Atlantic water. *Journal of Marine Research,* **34,** 561–575.

Heath, G. R., C. D. Hollister, D. R. Anderson, and M. Leinen. 1983. Why consider subseabed disposal of high-level nuclear wastes? *In:* Wastes in the Ocean, Vol. 3: Radioactive Wastes and the Ocean, P. K. Park, D. R. Kester, I. W. Duedall, and B. H. Ketchum (Eds.). Wiley-Interscience, New York, pp. 303–325.

Hood, D. W., and C. P. McRoy. 1971. Use of the ocean. *In:* Impingement of Man on the Oceans, D. W. Hood (Ed.). Wiley-Interscience, New York, pp. 667–698.

Huizenga, D. L., and D. R. Kester. 1983. The distribution of total and electrochemically available copper in the northwestern Atlantic Ocean. *Marine Chemistry,* **13,** 281–291.

Hunt, J. R. 1982. Particle dynamics in seawater: implications for predicting the fate of discharged particles. *Environmental Science and Technology,* **16,** 303–309.

Huntsman, S. A., and W. G. Sunda. 1981. The role of trace metals in regulating phytoplankton growth with emphasis on Fe, Mn, and Cu. *In:* The Physiological Ecology of Phytoplankton, I. Morris (Ed.). Blackwell, Oxford, United Kingdom, pp. 285–328.

Inter-Governmental Maritime Consultative Organization (IMCO). 1976. Inter-Governmental Conference on the Convention on the Dumping of Wastes at Sea (London, 30 October–13 November 1971). Final Act of the Conference with Technical Memorandum and Resolution adopted by the Conference and Convention on the Prevention of Marine Pollution by Dumping of Wastes and Other Matter. Inter-Governmental Maritime Consultative Organization, London, 36 pp. plus amendments (Publication No. 76.14E), 6 pp.

IMCO. 1981. Convention on the Prevention of Marine Pollution by Dumping of Wastes and Other Matter, 1972. Reports of permits issued for dumping in 1979. LDC.2/Circ. 64 (30 April 1981), Inter-Governmental Maritime Consultative Organization, London, 26 pp.

Jackson, G. A. 1982. Sludge disposal in southern California basins. *Environmental Science and Technology*, **16**, 746–757.

Jannasch, H. W., and C. O. Wirsen. 1982. Microbial activities in undercompressed and decompressed deep-seawater samples. *Applied Environmental Microbiology*, **43**, 1116–1124.

Jannasch, H. W., K. Eimhjellen, C. O. Wirsen, and A. Farmanfarmaian. 1971. Microbial degradation of organic matter in the deep sea. *Science*, **171**, 672–675.

Kamlet, K. S. 1981. Ocean disposal of organochlorine wastes by at-sea incineration. *In:* Ocean Dumping of Industrial Wastes, B. H. Ketchum, D. R. Kester, and P. K. Park (Eds.). Plenum Press, New York, pp. 295–314.

Kester, D. R. 1975. Dissolved gases other than CO_2. *In:* Chemical Oceanography, vol. 1, 2nd edition, J. P. Riley and G. Skirrow (Eds.). Academic Press, London, pp. 497–556. 556.

Kester, D. R., R. C. Hittinger, and P. Mukherji. 1981. Transition and heavy metals associated with acid-iron waste disposal at Deep Water Dumpsite 106. *In:* Ocean Dumping of Industrial Wastes, B. H. Ketchum, D. R. Kester, and P. K. Park (Eds.). Plenum Press, New York, pp. 215–232.

Kester, D. R., B. H. Ketchum, I. W. Duedall, and P. K. Park. 1983. The problem of dredged-material disposal. *In:* Wastes in the Ocean, Vol. 2: Dredged-Material Disposal in the Ocean, D. R. Kester, B. H. Ketchum, I. W. Duedall, and P. K. Park (Eds.). Wiley-Interscience, New York, pp. 3–27.

Ketchum, B. H., D. R. Kester, and P. K. Park (Eds.). 1981. Ocean Dumping of Industrial Wastes. Plenum Press, New York, 525 pp.

Knauer, G. A., and J. H. Martin. 1981. Primary production and carbon-nitrogen fluxes in the upper 1,500 m of the northwest Pacific. *Limnology and Oceanography*, **26**, 181–186.

Koh, R. C. Y., and Y. C. Chang. 1973. Mathematical Model for Barged Ocean Disposal of Wastes. EPA-660/2-73-029, Office of Research and Development, U.S. Environmental Protection Agency, Washington, D.C., 595 pp.

Kupferman, S. L., D. R. Anderson, L. H. Brush, L. S. Gomez, J. C. Laul, and L. E. Shepard. 1982. Ocean FUSRAP: Feasibility of Ocean Disposal of Materials from the Formerly Utilized Sites Remedial Action Program (FUSRAP). Paper presented at Waste Management '82 (March 1982) Tucson, Arizona. Sandia National Laboratories, Albuquerque, New Mexico, 15 pp.

Laflamme, R. E., and R. A. Hites. 1978. The global distribution of polycyclic aromatic hydrocarbons in recent sediments. *Geochimica et Cosmochimica Acta*, **42**, 289–303.

Landing, W. M., and K. W. Bruland. 1980. Manganese in the north Pacific. *Earth and Planetary Science Letters*, **49**, 45–56.

Lerman, A. 1979. Geochemical Processes Water and Sediment Environments. Wiley-Interscience, New York, 481 pp.

Lisitzin, A. P. 1972. Sedimentation in the World Ocean. Special Publication No. 17, Society of Economic Paleontologists and Mineralogists, Tulsa, Oklahoma, 218 pp.

MacLean, S. A. 1981. Focal Gill Melanization in Euphausids: Summarization of Field Studies. Unpublished Report, Submitted to the Office of Marine Pollution Assessment, U.S. National Oceanic and Atmospheric Administration, Rockville, Maryland, 11 pp.

McVey, D. R., K. L. Erickson, and W. E. Segfried, Jr. 1983. Thermal, chemical, and mass transport processes induced in abyssal sediments by the emplacement of nuclear wastes: experimental and modelling results. *In:* Wastes in the Ocean, Vol. 3: Radioactive Wastes and the Ocean, P. K. Park, D. R. Kester, I. W. Duedall, and B. H. Ketchum (Eds.). Wiley-Interscience, New York, pp. 359–388.

Milliman, J. D. 1981. Transfer of river-borne particulate material to the oceans. *In:* River Inputs to Ocean Systems, J.-M. Martin, J. D. Burton, and D. Eisma (Eds.). Proceedings of a SCOR/ACMRR/ECOR/IAHS/UNESCO/CMG/IABO/IAPSO Review and Workshop, (26–30 March 1979). Italy United Nations, New York, pp. 5–12.

Mitchell, N. T. 1983. History of dumping and description of waste. *In:* Interim Oceanographic Description of the North-East Atlantic Site for the Disposal of Low-Level Radioactive Waste, P. A. Gurbutt, and R. R. Dickson (Eds.). Nuclear Energy Agency Organisation for Economic Co-Operation and Development, Paris, pp. 8–12.

Morel, F. M. M., and N. M. L. Morel-Laurens. 1983. Trace metals and plankton in the oceans: facts and speculations. *In:* Trace Metals in Sea Water, C. S. Wong, E. Boyle, K. W. Bruland, J. D. Burton, and E. D. Goldberg (Eds.). Plenum Press, New York, pp. 841–869.

Morel, F. M. M., and S. L. Schiff. 1980. Geochemistry of Municipal Waste in Coastal Waters. Report No. 259, Department of Civil Engineering, Massachusetts Institute of Technology, Cambridge, Massachusetts, 205 pp.

Mukherji, P., and D. R. Kester. 1979. Mercury distribution in the Gulf Stream. *Science,* **204,** 64–66.

Mukherji, P., and D. R. Kester. 1983. Acid-iron disposal experiments in summer and winter at Deepwater Dumpsite-106. *In:* Wastes in the Ocean, Vol. 1: Industrial and Sewage Wastes in the Ocean, I. W. Duedall, B. H. Ketchum, P. K. Park, and D. R. Kester (Eds.). Wiley-Interscience, New York, pp. 141–155.

Mullin, M. M., and L. S. Gomez (Eds.). 1981. Biological and Related Chemical Research Concerning Subseabed Disposal of High-Level Nuclear Waste: Report of a Workshop (12–16 January 1981), Jackson Hole, Wyoming. Report SAND81-00122, Sandia National Laboratories, Albuquerque, New Mexico, 43 pp.

Murphy, L. S., E. M. Haugen, and J. F. Brown. 1983. Phytoplankton: comparison of laboratory bioassay and field measurements. *In:* Wastes in the Ocean, Vol. 1: Industrial and Sewage Wastes in the Ocean, I. W. Duedall, B. H. Ketchum, P. K. Park, and D. R. Kester (Eds.). Wiley-Interscience, New York, pp. 219–233.

Nuclear Energy Agency–Organisation for Economic Co-Operation and Development. 1983. Decision of the OECD Council of the 22nd of July 1977 Establishing a Multilateral Consultation and Surveillance Mechanism for Sea Dumping of Radioactive Waste. Nuclear Energy Agency–Organisation for Economic Co-Operation and Development, Paris, 29 pp.

O'Connor, T. P. 1983. Assessment of Ocean Dumping North of Puerto Rico. Technical Memorandum NOS 28, National Ocean Service, U.S. National Oceanic and Atmospheric Administration, Rockville, Maryland, 119 pp.

Okubo, A., and R. W. Pritchard. 1969. Summary of our Present Knowledge of Physical Processes of Mixing in the Ocean and Coastal Waters and a Set of Practical Guidelines for the Application of Nuclear Safety Evaluations of the Use of Nuclear Power Sources in the Sea. Report NYO-3109-40 (U.S. Atomic Energy Commission Reference) and Reference 69-1 Chesapeake Bay Institute, The Johns Hopkins University, Baltimore, Maryland, 159 pp.

Oslo Commission. 1983. Ninth Meeting of the Oslo Commission, Berlin: 15–17 June 1983. OSCOM 9/5/2-E (English), Oslo Commission, London, 4 pp. plus tables.

Oslo Commission. 1984. Eighth Annual Report. Oslo Commission, London, 210 pp.

Osterberg, C., A. G. Carey, Jr., and H. Curl, Jr. 1963. Acceleration of sinking rates of radionuclides in the ocean. *Nature*, **200**, 1276–1277.

Palmer, H. D., and M. G. Gross (Eds.). 1979. Ocean Dumping and Marine Pollution: Geological Aspect of Waste Disposal. Dowden, Hutchinson & Ross, Stroudsburg, Pennsylvania, 268 pp.

Park, P. K., D. R. Kester, I. W. Duedall, and B. H. Ketchum (Eds.). 1983. Wastes in the Ocean, Vol. 3: Radioactive Wastes and the Ocean. Wiley-Interscience, New York, 505 pp.

Rex, M. A. 1981. Community Structure in the deep-sea benthos. *Annual Review of Ecology and Systematics*, **12**, 331–353.

Riley, J. P., and R. Chester. 1971. Introduction to Marine Chemistry. Academic Press, London, 465 pp.

Rose, C. D., T. J. Ward, and V. E. dePass. 1985. Ecological assessment for coal fly ash dumped at Deepwater Dumpsite-106. *In:* Wastes in the Ocean, Vol. 4: Energy Wastes in the Ocean, I. W. Duedall, D. R. Kester, P. K. Park, and B. H. Ketchum (Eds.). Wiley-Interscience, New York, pp. xxx–xxx.

Rowe, G. T., and W. D. Gardner. 1979. Sedimentation rates in the slope water of the northwest Atlantic Ocean measured directly in sediment traps. *Journal of Marine Research*, **37**, 581–600.

Rowe, G. T., P. T. Polloni, and R. L. Haedrich. 1982. The deep-sea macrobenthos on the continental margin of the northwest Atlantic Ocean. *Deep-Sea Research*, **29**, 257–278.

Ryan, W. B. F., and J. A. Farre. 1983. Potential of radioactive and other waste disposals on the continental margin by natural dispersal processes. *In:* Wastes in the Ocean, Vol. 3: Radioactive Wastes and the Ocean, P. K. Park, D. R. Kester, I. W. Duedall, and B. H. Ketchum (Eds.). Wiley-Interscience, New York, pp. 215–236.

Ryther, J. H. 1969. Photosynthesis and fish production in the sea. *Science*, **166**, 72–76.

Salomons, W., and V. Forstner. 1984. Metals in the Hydrocycle. Springer-Verlag, Berlin, 349 pp.

Sanders, H. L. 1979. Evolutionary ecology and life-history patterns in the deep sea. *Sarsia*, **64**, 1–7.

Schaule, B. K., and C. C. Patterson. 1981. Lead concentrations in the northeast Pacific: evidence for global anthropogenic perturbations. *Earth and Planetary Science Letters*, **54**, 97–116.

Schmitz, W. J., Jr., P. P. Niiler, R. L. Bernstein, and W. R. Holland. 1982. Recent long-term moored instrument observations in the western north Pacific. *Journal of Geophysical Research*, **87**, 9425–9440.

Swartz, R. C., W. A. DeBeu, F. A. Cole, and L. C. Bensten. 1980. Recovery of the macrobenthos at a dredge site in Yaquina Bay, Oregon. *In:* Contaminants and Sediments, Vol. 2: Analysis, Chemistry, Biology, R. A. Baker (Ed.). Ann Arbor Science, Ann Arbor, Michigan, pp. 391–408.

Shepard, F. P. 1977. Geological Oceanography: Evolution of Coasts, Continental Margins, & the Deep-Sea Floor. Crane, Russak & Company, New York, 214 pp.

Sholkovitz, E. R. 1978. The flocculation of dissolved Fe, Mn, Al, Cu, Ni, Co, and Cd during estuarine mixing. *Earth and Planetary Science Letters,* **41,** 77–86.

Small, L. F., S. W. Fowler, and M. Y. Unlu. 1979. Sinking rates of natural copepod fecal pellets. *Marine Biology,* **51,** 233–241.

Stanford, H. M., J. S. O'Connor, and R. L. Swanson. 1981. The effects of ocean dumping on the New York Bight ecosystem. *In:* Ocean Dumping of Industrial Wastes, B. H. Ketchum, D. R. Kester, and P. K. Park (Eds.). Plenum Press, New York, pp. 53–86.

Stegeman, J. J. 1983. Hepatic microsomal monooxygenase activity and the biotransformation of hydrocarbons in deep benthic fish from the western North Atlantic. *Canadian Journal of Fisheries and Aquatic Science,* **40**(Supplement 2), 78–85.

Stuvier, M., P. D. Quay, and H. G. Ostlund. 1983. Abyssal water carbon-14 distribution and the age of the world ocean. *Science,* **219,** 849–851.

Sunda, W. G., and R. L. Ferguson. 1983. Sensitivity of natural bacterial communities to additions of copper and cupric ion activity: a bioassay of copper complexation in seawater. *In:* Trace Metals in Sea Water, C. S. Wong, E. A. Boyle, K. W. Bruland, J. D. Burton, and E. D. Goldberg (Eds.). Plenum Press, New York, pp. 871–891.

Sunda, W. G., and R. R. L. Guillard. 1976. The relationship between cupric ion activity and the toxicity of copper to phytoplankton. *Journal of Marine Research,* **34,** 511–529.

Trefry, J. H., and B. J. Presley. 1982. Manganese fluxes from Mississippi Delta sediments. *Geochimica et Cosmochimica Acta,* **46,** 1715–1726.

U.S. Army Corps of Engineers. 1982. 1980 Report to Congress on Administration of Ocean Dumping Activities. Water Resources Support Center Pamphlet 82-P1, U.S. Army Corps of Engineers, Fort Belvoir, Virginia, 41 pp.

U.S. Environmental Protection Agency. 1981. Annual Report to Congress, January–December 1980, on the Administration of the Marine Protection, Research and Sanctuaries Act of 1972 as Amended (Public Law 92-532) and Implementation of the International Ocean Dumping Convention. U.S. Environmental Protection Agency, Washington, D.C., 33 pp.

U.S. National Academy of Sciences. 1978. The Tropospheric Transport of Pollutants and Other Substances to the Oceans. Prepared for the Workshop on Tropospheric Transport of Pollutants to the Ocean Steering Committee, Ocean Sciences Board, Assembly of Mathematical and Physical Sciences, National Research Council. U.S. National Academy of Sciences, Washington, D.C., 243 pp.

Webster, F. 1969. Vertical profiles of horizontal ocean current. *Deep-Sea Research,* **16,** 85–98.

Williams, W. G. 1981. Lagrangian measurements in the fall and winter of mesoscale circulation north of Puerto Rico and transport through the Mona Passage. Final Report under NOAA Contract NA-81-RAA-02 to Clearwater Consultants, Inc., Boston, Massachusetts, 34 pp. plus appendices.

Yayanos, A. A., A. S. Dietz, and R. Van Boxtel. 1979. Isolation of a deep-sea barophilic bacterium and some of its growth characteristics. *Science,* **205,** 808–810.

PART II: INCINERATION AT SEA

2

DEVELOPMENT OF INTERNATIONAL CONTROLS FOR INCINERATION AT SEA

Manfred K. Nauke

Environmental Division
International Maritime Organization
London, United Kingdom

Abstract		**34**
2.1.	**Introduction**	**34**
2.2.	**Prevention of Marine Pollution by Incineration at Sea**	**38**
	2.2.1. Control of the Incinerator System	38
	2.2.2. Control over the Nature of Wastes Incinerated	40
	2.2.3. Selection of Incineration Sites	41
	2.2.4. General Controls on the Vessel and Its Operation	43
	2.2.5. Monitoring and Notification Provisions	43
2.3.	**Action Taken by the London Dumping Convention**	**44**
2.4.	**Action Taken by the Regional Conventions**	**46**
2.5.	**Safety Requirements of Incineration Ships**	**46**
2.6.	**Research**	**48**
2.7.	**Future Development**	**49**
References		**50**

ABSTRACT

Since 1966 incineration of organochlorine substances at sea has been investigated and used as a means of waste disposal. Six ships have been developed for incineration at sea. Conditions have been established that provide a combustion efficiency of at least 99.95% for organochlorine compounds. The important factors in incinerating these wastes are maintaining a flame temperature of 1250°C, providing a residence time of at least 1 s in the incineration furnace, and maintaining a 3% surplus of oxygen in the flame. International agreements through the Oslo Commission and the Convention for the Prevention of Marine Pollution by Dumping of Wastes and Other Matter (London Dumping Convention) have led to the formulation of mandatory regulations and technical guidelines for incineration at sea. Most of the at-sea incineration of wastes has occurred in the southern portion of the North Sea and to a limited extent in the Gulf of Mexico. No environmental impacts as a result of incineration at sea have been identified. Improvements could be made in automated monitoring of at-sea incineration operations.

2.1. INTRODUCTION

Modern technological society produces large amounts of industrial wastes. A relatively high proportion of these wastes is produced by the organochemical manufacturing industry. For example, in 1981 the organochemical industry of the United States produced 127×10^6 t of organic chemicals (Paige et al., 1978), of which 18×10^6 t are organochlorines. About 550,000 t of organochlorine wastes result from this production, which by using modern technology can be recycled to an extent of 60–70% (Barniske, 1980). The remaining 165,000–220,000 t have to be deposited on land or at sea, or have to be destroyed by incineration. In addition, large amounts of wastes containing halogenated hydrocarbons result from the use of industrial solvents. These wastes often consist of complex mixtures of organohalogen and non-organohalogen compounds that are difficult to reprocess.

The main methods of disposal of organohalogen wastes are by depositing wastes in specific geological formations or by destroying them by incineration. In order to destroy organohalogen wastes completely by incineration, three conditions have to be met: (1) temperatures of more than 900°C must be maintained; (2) the residence time of the wastes in the incinerator must be long enough to reach a complete oxidation of the wastes; and (3) sufficient air must be available for complete combustion.

There are some incineration facilities on land that are able to burn solid and liquid organohalogen wastes with very high destruction efficiencies. During the destruction process the waste components are transformed into inorganic products, which mainly consist of CO_2, HCl, and H_2O. Other components such as nitrogen oxides (NO_x) and sulfur oxides (SO_x) might be present in minor quantities for some wastes. Depending on the chlorine content of the waste, the HCl content in the stack gases can reach values of up to 160 g m^{-3} under one atmosphere. In general

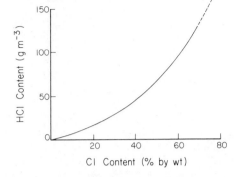

Figure 2.1. The combustion of chlorinated hydrocarbons with various contents of chlorine and resulting contents of hydrochloric acid in stack gas (after Barniske, 1980).

the chlorine content of chlorinated hydrocarbon wastes is between 60 and 70% (by wt). This means that the emission products have hydrochloric acid concentrations between 90 and 125 mg m^{-3} (Fig. 2.1).

National regulations in many countries have established threshold limit values for HCl of 5 mg m^{-3} and stack emissions of incineration facilities of 100 mg m^{-3} (Federal Republic of Germany; Technical Guidelines for Air Quality, T. A. Luft, 1974). This means that scrubbing systems have to be used with incineration systems.

Under certain conditions (lower temperatures, high excess of air, and deficiency of water vapor) small amounts of Cl$_2$ are produced by the reaction:

$$4 \text{ HCl} + \text{O}_2 \rightleftharpoons 2 \text{ H}_2\text{O} + 2 \text{ Cl}_2$$

For scrubbing processes designed to remove combustion products, mainly hydrochloric acids, particulates, and small amounts of unburned wastes, alkaline solutions such as sodium hydroxide or calcium hydroxide are used. The wastewater will contain salts (NaCl or CaCl$_2$) and soluble combustion products, as well as residual amounts of the alkaline materials and suspended particulates. Some pilot studies have been carried out for the recovery of the HCl. However, this practice cannot compete economically with other industrial sources of HCl.

Scrubbing systems have been installed at some smaller incineration plants. Many of these are confronted with problems caused by the corrosion of cooling systems, particle filter systems, and parts of the scrubbing installations. A schematic view of an incineration facility for burning solid and liquid industrial wastes is shown in Fig. 2.2. After continually encountering corrosion problems in its scrubbing devices, a small company in the Federal Republic of Germany (FRG) specializing in the construction of incineration facilities proposed in the late 1960s that these problems might be avoided if incineration were carried out at sea, without scrubbing systems. After consulting marine chemists and meteorologists, who concluded that the amount of HCl coming from an incineration ship would be absorbed readily by the sea, planning started for the first incineration vessel, *M/T Matthias I.*

The environmental administrations in the FRG very strongly supported the idea of burning organochlorine wastes at sea because: (1) many problems had been

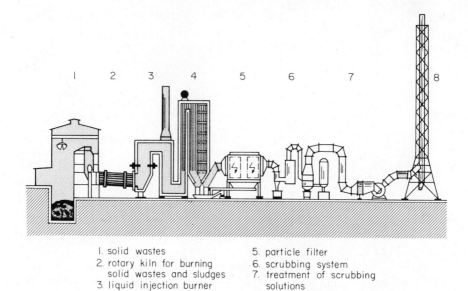

1. solid wastes
2. rotary kiln for burning
   solid wastes and sludges
3. liquid injection burner
   and after burner
4. cooling system

5. particle filter
6. scrubbing system
7. treatment of scrubbing
   solutions
8. stack (100 m)

Figure 2.2.   Land-based incineration facility for burning solid and liquid chemical wastes.

encountered with the treatment and disposal of scrubbing solutions and sludges; and (2) it was felt that the development of large-scale collecting and incineration systems for organohalogen wastes could provide a better-controlled, better-monitored, and more economical procedure than alternative methods.

At that time many problems had been encountered with the disposal of so-called EDC tars (wastes from vinyl chloride manufacture), which contain more than 200 different organochlorine compounds. The dumping of these residues at sea resulted in fish mortality in the wake of the dumping vessel. This impact was one of the factors leading to the development of the 1972 Oslo Convention. The first incineration ship, *M/T Matthias I,* was a modified small chemical tanker of 438 gross tons that went into service in 1969. The incineration market was increasing, and in the early 1970s three incineration ships, *Matthias I* and *Matthias II* (both under the flag of the FRG) and the *M/T Vulcanus* (under the flag of Singapore), operated in the North Sea. They burned wastes from the FRG, the Netherlands, France, and the United Kingdom.

During the 1970s a series of international and regional conventions were formulated to address policies concerning the disposal of wastes in the marine environment (Park and O'Connor, 1981). At that time the texts of the Oslo Convention and the London Dumping Convention (LDC) were being prepared, and the representatives of some countries participating in the negotiations proposed that internationally agreed provisions and criteria on the control of incineration operations should be developed. Others, however, emphasized that incineration at sea should be regarded as a provisional method only, and that by developing agreed standards such methods would be officially recognized and approved. Accordingly, the Oslo Convention and the LDC, the texts of which were finalized in 1972, did not take into account this method of disposal at sea. The signatory parties to the LDC agreed (contrary to the parties to the Oslo Convention) to include in the definition of "dumping" the disposal of matter at sea derived from the treatment of wastes or other matter on vessels, aircraft, platforms or structures, thus facilitating further consideration of this subject within the framework of the LDC.

Later, when one of the two incineration companies initiated operations in the Mediterranean Sea to burn chemical wastes loaded in Italian and French ports, France proposed that special provisions be considered within the LDC and the Oslo Convention to prevent marine and atmospheric pollution from incineration operations at sea. Accordingly, in 1976, a resolution of the First Consultative Meeting of Contracting Parties to the London Dumping Convention requested the Secretary General of the Inter-Governmental Maritime Consultative Organization (IMCO), now known as the International Maritime Organization (IMO), to convene a meeting of experts to prepare special provisions on incineration at sea for consideration at the Second Consultative Meeting (IMCO, 1972). Similar action was undertaken within the framework of the Oslo Convention.

From 1974 to 1977 the United States conducted several tests of incineration at sea using the *Vulcanus*. The environmental studies and regulatory decisions related to those tests in the Gulf of Mexico and the Pacific Ocean are summarized by Kamlet (1981) and in Chapter 3.

In the spring of 1977, a group of experts met in Paris to prepare for the Oslo Commission a code of practice for the prevention of marine pollution by incineration at sea. One week later a similar group, this time expanded by experts from Canada and the United States, met in London to consider technical guidelines on incineration at sea for the Second Consultative Meeting of Contracting Parties to the London Dumping Convention.

Fortunately, at the time these meetings were held, the results of the first comprehensive investigations made on board the incineration vessels *Matthias I*, *Matthias II*, and *Vulcanus* by scientists from the United States, France, and The Netherlands were available, as well as preliminary results of test burnings carried out in 1976 on board the most recent incineration ship, *Matthias III*.

Taking into account the experiences with land-based incineration facilities, and after consideration of the results of the studies carried out on board the incineration vessels, the experts from the contracting parties to the LDC and Oslo Convention concluded that organohalogen wastes could be burned in shipboard incinerators with destruction efficiencies of at least 99.9%, if the following conditions were met: (1) flame temperature of at least 1250°C, (2) a residence time of 1 s in the furnace, and (3) an oxygen surplus of more than 3% in the flame.

The experience gained since 1969 with the incineration of liquid organochlorine wastes at sea very clearly indicated that these conditions could be met easily by adjusting the flow rates of the waste, the supporting fuel oil, and the air. It also was found that the geometry of the burner is an important factor for ensuring homogenous conditions. The funnel-type ovens used on board the incineration ship

Vulcanus (and later on board the incineration ship *Vesta*) showed certain advantages over the open-cup type ovens used by the *Matthias* ships (Fig. 2.3) by keeping homogeneous temperature conditions inside the combustion chamber (Compaan, 1980). The results of these studies very clearly demonstrated that no adverse ecological effects were evident if the incineration operation was carried out properly.

The experts considered that the presence of CO in detectable quantities in the combustion gases would indicate incompleteness of combustion. It was therefore agreed that the CO and CO_2 concentrations in the combustion gases should be used as a parameter for determining combustion efficiency.

Another factor that was given high priority was the use of appropriate control and recording systems on board the incineration vessels. It was felt essential that temperatures, the waste and air feed to the incinerator, and the CO and CO_2 concentrations in the combustion gases should be monitored and recorded continuously.

The experts made an attempt to include all these factors, together with criteria for the selection of incineration sites and provisions regarding the loading and transport of the wastes and the disposal of residues, in the technical guidelines on the prevention of marine pollution by incineration at sea.

Accordingly, the technical guidelines prepared by the group of experts in 1977 covered a wide range of technical and regulatory aspects, including: (1) specifications, control, and approval of the incinerator systems; (2) control over the nature of wastes incinerated; (3) selection of incineration sites; (4) general controls on the vessel and its operation; (5) monitoring and recording devices; and (6) notification procedures of incineration activities.

2.2. PREVENTION OF MARINE POLLUTION BY INCINERATION AT SEA

2.2.1. Control of Incinerator Systems

First of all the experts agreed that any requirements should refer to "marine incineration facilities," with this term including vessels, platforms, or other manufactured structures operating for the purpose of incineration at sea (that is, deliberate combustion of wastes for the purpose of their thermal destruction). Activities incidental to the normal operation of vessels and platforms were considered to be outside the scope of the LDC.

It then was agreed that any marine incineration facility—ship or platform—before starting its first operation, must be approved by a contracting party (country) to the LDC. To this effect, an initial survey must be made, including tests showing combustion and destruction efficiencies $>99.9\%$. These tests are to be based on measurements of concentrations of CO and CO_2 (for the determination of the combustion efficiency) and of unburned halogenated organic compounds (for the determination of the destruction efficiency) in the stack gases. In addition, measure-

MT MATTHIAS II

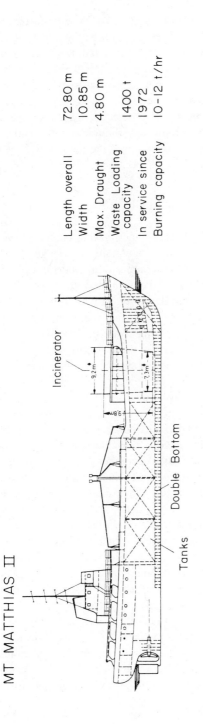

Length overall	72.80 m
Width	10.85 m
Max. Draught	4.80 m
Waste Loading capacity	1400 t
In service since	1972
Burning capacity	10–12 t/hr

MT VESTA

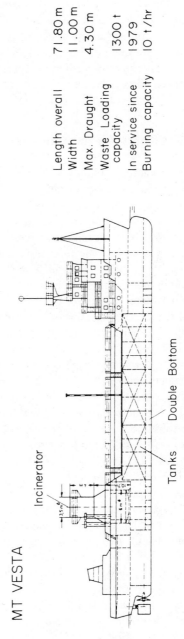

Length overall	71.80 m
Width	11.00 m
Max. Draught	4.30 m
Waste Loading capacity	1300 t
In service since	1979
Burning capacity	10 t/hr

Figure 2.3. Two incineration ships of similar size but with different positions and types of incinerators: cup-shaped oven on M/T *Matthias II* at bow section, funnel-shaped oven on M/T *Vesta* at after section of ship.

ments of the oxygen concentration of the stack gases have to be carried out. Other points that need to be approved by national authorities are the siting and type of temperature measuring devices; the gas sampling system, including probe locations, analytical devices, and the manner of recording; the automatic shut-off system that will shut down the whole system if the temperature drops below approved minimum temperatures; and devices for controlling the feed rates to the incinerator of wastes and fuel oil. Such a survey subsequently is to be carried out once every 2 y to ensure that the incinerator continues to comply with the relevant provisions. Additional surveys have to be made after any modification of the incineration system.

2.2.2. Control over the Nature of Wastes Incinerated

In order to adjust fuel and waste rate to the incinerator and to avoid complications during the incineration operation it is essential to have a certain knowledge of the following properties of the wastes to be incinerated: composition, calorific values, flash point, vapor pressure, ash content, solids in suspension, and viscosity.

Accordingly, information on these parameters has to be provided by the producer of the waste. The regulatory authorities are interested mainly in the composition of the organohalogens in the waste. Also, being aware that metals usually present in the waste will be emitted as small particles into the atmosphere and will eventually enter the marine environment, the authorities should require a complete list of the metal concentrations, particularly those regulated by the conventions.

When preparing the technical guidelines, it was obvious that all experience gained at that stage was related to the burning of relatively simple and low-molecular-weight organochlorine wastes. Doubts were expressed about the efficiency of the combustion of polychlorinated biphenyls (PCBs), polychlorinated triphenyls (PCTs), tetrachlorodibenzo-*p*-dioxin (TCDD), dichlorodiphenyl trichloroethane (DDT), and hexachlorobenzene. It was agreed that when incineration of one of these substances at sea was proposed, as well as any other substance over which doubts exist with regard to its combustion efficiency, a detailed survey with intensive stack monitoring will have to be carried out prior to the issue of a permit.

There are two main sources of organohalogen wastes for incineration at sea: (1) wastes derived from individual production processes of chemical manufacturers and (2) wastes collected from many small companies and laboratories which either produce smaller amounts of wastes or which have to dispose of spent solvents. Examples of the two types are illustrated in excerpts taken from two permits issued for incineration at sea by the contracting parties (Tables 2.1, 2.2, and 2.3). The composition of wastes from individual production processes is relatively precise, whereas the composition of mixtures of wastes stemming from many companies is very difficult to determine. It should be noted, however, that efforts have been made to determine the inorganic components that are listed in the Annexes (given in Park and O'Connor, 1981) to the LDC.

**Table 2.1. Principal Organic and
Inorganic Components of Waste Incinerated
at Sea from a Single Industrial Source[a]**

Component	Maximum Amount
Alcohols	60 (% by vol)
Ketones	33
Carbonic acids	33
Diethylene ether	10
Ethyl acetate	8
Tetrahydrofuran	6
Dioxane	1
Pyridine	4
Dimethylformamide	3
Acetonitrile	2
Cyclohexane	5
Cyclohexanol	5
Arachin oil	1
Mineral oil	1
Triethylamine	1
Other aromatic hydrocarbons	16
Other aliphatic hydrocarbons	5
Steroids	0.5 (wt %)
Aluminum	0.8
Copper	0.3 (mg liter^{-1})
Nickel	0.4
Chromium	0.6

[a]Components of the waste were derived from the production of vinyl chloride and vinylidene chloride. Adapted from IMCO (1979).

2.2.3. Selection of Incineration Sites

Although ecological effects of incineration at sea have either not yet been demonstrated or have been shown to be temporary, it was agreed that incineration operations should be avoided in particularly sensitive sea areas such as fish breeding or nursery grounds and in areas with high productivity or important fish stocks. Sites with good oceanic dispersion characteristics would be more favorable than those with little current or turbulence. Incineration vessels attract sea birds and migrating birds. In selecting an incineration site, migratory routes, particularly of birds, but also of mammals and other organisms, should be avoided.

The atmospheric dispersion of a proposed area is of particular interest. Information on wind speed, air and seawater temperatures, and frequency and altitude of inversions will be needed for an evaluation of atmospheric stability. The geo-

Table 2.2.   Various Wastes Collected for an Incineration at Sea from a Variety of Industrial Sources[a]

1. Chlorinated hydrocarbons with synthetic resins.
2. Chlorinated hydrocarbons from the production of cosmetics.
3. Chlorinated hydrocarbons from the cleaning of textiles.
4. Chlorinated hydrocarbons from misproductions.
5. Chlorinated liquid residues from the production of pesticides.
6. Color and lacquer residues contaminated by chlorinated hydrocarbons.
7. Dichlorophenols.
8. Liquid wastes from laboratories with chlorinated hydrocarbons.
9. Oils containing chlorinated hydrocarbons.
10. Oil dispersion with chlorinated hydrocarbons.
11. Sewage sludge with chlorinated hydrocarbons.
12. Solvents with chlorinated hydrocarbons from mechanical cleaning methods.
13. Solvents with chlorinated hydrocarbons from the production of pharmaceuticals and from chemical experiments.
14. Solvents with chlorinated hydrocarbons from the cleaning of tanks.

[a]Adapted from IMCO (1979).

graphical situation, particularly the distance from inhabited or recreational areas, and the prevailing wind direction should be given due attention. It has been shown that a long-range transport of combustion gases under stable atmospheric conditions may lead to an irritating odor in coastal areas (GESAMP, 1982).

Furthermore, a number of technical considerations should be noted. Incineration of a waste load generally takes a few days, depending on the capacity of the vessel. Periods of bad weather may force interruption of the incineration process and may

Table 2.3.   Inorganic Components Determined in a Representative Sample of the Wastes[a]

Metal	Concentration (mg kg^{-1})
Mercury	—
Cadmium	0.3–1.6
Arsenic	1.6–3.0
Lead	1.4–2.9
Copper	0.4–1.1
Zinc	1.5–2.8
Beryllium	—
Chromium	0.84–11.3
Nickel	9.7–12.8
Vanadium	—
Iron	8.5–16.0

[a]Adapted from IMCO (1979).

under certain conditions involve an increased risk for the incineration vessel. High-sea conditions that make incineration impossible are related to high wind speeds, insufficient water depth, and wind fetch. Bottom topography, water depth, and the presence of submarine cables and pipelines may be important for anchoring.

Finally, incineration should not hinder other uses of the sea. The presence of a combustion plume close to shipping lanes or areas with oil or gas exploration and exploitation is undesirable. The conflicts with other activities such as fishing and sand and gravel extraction should be considered in selecting an incineration site.

2.2.4. General Controls on the Vessel and Its Operation

Several operational factors must be considered during at-sea incineration. One is the disposal of residues from the burning of solid wastes. Another is the broadcasting of regular radio warnings during the period of incineration at sea. The bright light produced by incineration at night can attract or confuse other vessels. The loading, storage, and transport of wastes, either in packages or in bulk, must be in compliance with the relevant IMO standards and regulations.

In this connection, attention is drawn to two points:

1. Several experiments at sea have been carried out to burn solid wastes containing organohalogen compounds. National authorities, however, have been very reluctant to issue licenses for the burning of solid wastes, mainly because it was felt that an appropriate control mechanism regarding the feed rate of such wastes to the oven was not yet available. The technical guidelines, however, have been prepared in such a way that all types of wastes, liquids and solids, as well as organohalogen and non-organohalogen wastes, are covered.

2. Incineration ships carrying liquid wastes to the incineration site must have a valid certificate of fitness as required under the IMO Code for the Construction and Equipment of Ships Carrying Dangerous Chemicals in Bulk. This so-called Bulk Chemical Code contains lists of chemicals and allocates specific requirements for carrying these chemicals. Three different types of ships have been classified in the code, depending on the spaces between double bottoms and double hulls. All incineration ships that have so far been in operation were or are type 2 chemical tankers. Accordingly, each incineration ship leaving a port for an incineration operation must have a certificate of fitness as a type 2 chemical tanker regarding loading and safe transport of chemical wastes, a certificate by which the performance of the incineration system is approved, and a permit for the incineration of specific wastes in an area selected by the issuing authority. Recently the IMO began to consider specific standards for incineration vessels mainly from the point of view of safety to humans during loading and transport of the wastes (Chapter 5).

2.2.5. Monitoring and Notification Provisions

All parameters essential for the complete destruction of wastes by incineration, such as temperatures and the concentrations of O_2, CO, and CO_2 in the combustion gases, have to be recorded at least once every 15 min. In addition, records of the ship's course, speed, and time have to be kept as a safeguard to ensure that incineration takes place at an approved site. This is currently done by automatic cameras that photograph the control panel once every 15 min. The photographs are sent to the national authorities that issued the incineration permit.

The Secretariat of the London Dumping Convention (IMO) shall be informed of each permit that has been issued by a contracting party in a form agreed by the consultative meeting of contracting parties.

2.3. ACTION TAKEN BY THE LONDON DUMPING CONVENTION

The technical guidelines on incineration at sea were adopted by the Second Consultative Meeting of Contracting Parties to the London Dumping Convention in late 1977. Several contracting parties, however, recognizing that the technical guidelines were only recommendations, emphasized that a binding legal instrument should be developed. It was therefore agreed that incineration experts, together with legal experts, should consider the preparation of a legal instrument.

The third consultative meeting in October 1978, following consideration of a proposal by its experts, adopted amendments to the Annexes to the LDC including, by an addendum to Annex I, regulations for the control of incineration at sea (IMCO, 1978). These regulations were prepared by compiling those parts of the technical guidelines that could be implemented on a mandatory basis, while others that were considered to be recommendations remained in the technical guidelines. It was recognized that all the provisions that remained in the technical guidelines had been prepared on the basis of existing scientific knowledge of the incineration processes, in particular with regard to the burning of liquid organochlorine wastes, and that in the light of scientific work and technical development, these provisions would have to be kept under review as the results of further research and investigations became available. The mandatory regulations, on the other hand, reflect those requirements that were thought to be of a basic nature and therefore less dependent of further technological and scientific development regarding incineration techniques and types of wastes burned at sea. A comparative list of the main mandatory provisions and recommendations that have to be applied or taken into account if organohalogen wastes and pesticides and their by-products are incinerated at sea is given in Table 2.4.

For the different types of wastes that might be burned at sea the requirements differ to a certain extent. For wastes that do not contain organohalogen compounds or pesticides, the national authorities control the incineration as seems appropriate to them. A summary of the requirements for the issue of permits for incineration is given in Table 2.5. The issue of a special permit for the incineration of crude oil, fuel oil, and LDC Annex II substances has been queried several times since the technical guidelines were adopted. For clarification it should be pointed out that when preparing the technical guidelines it was felt that waste oil containing Annex I substances might be considered by incineration operators as fuel for burn-

Table 2.4. Main Mandatory Provisions and Recommendations for the Incineration of Organohalogen Wastes and Pesticides and Their By-Products at Sea

Regulations on Incineration (Mandatory)	Technical Guidelines on Incineration (Recommendations)
1. Survey and approval of incineration system (test of destruction and combustion efficiencies, approval of measuring and sampling devices).	1. IMO certificate of fitness for ship.
2. Flame temperatures above 1250°C.	2. Pilot studies for potentially toxic wastes (for example, PCBs, PCTs, TCDD, BHC, and DDT).
3. Combustion efficiency: $\{(C_{CO_2} - C_{CO})/C_{CO_2}\}\,100 = 99.95 \pm 0.05\%$	3. Loading and storage.
4. No black smoke when incinerating wastes.	4. Disposal of residues.
5. No flames above plane of stack.	5. Shutoff system when combustion temperature drops to 1200°C.
6. Site selection criteria in addition to Annex III of the LDC.	6. Minimum 3% excess oxygen (= 20% excess air) in stack gas.
7. Recording of temperatures, CO and CO_2 concentrations, and feed rates of wastes and fuel.	7. Residence time of 1 s at 1250°C.
8. Notification (general).	8. Metallic Annex I residue contents should be in trace amounts, as defined for dumping.
	9. Regular radio warnings, provisions for the prevention of hazards to other vessels.
	10. Recording of feed rates of air and O_2 and recording of meteorological conditions.
	11. Notification (details).

Table 2.5. Requirements for the Issue of Permits for Incineration of Wastes at Sea

Substance	Permit Type	Regulations	Technical Guidelines
Organohalogen compounds Pesticides and by-products	Special	All provisions of the regulations to be applied	All provisions of the technical guidelines to be taken into full account
Crude oil and fuel oil taken on board for the purpose of disposal LDC Annex II substances (without pesticides)	Special	Control to the satisfaction of contracting parties, taking into account: All applicable provisions of regulations in Parts I and II	All applicable provisions of the technical guidelines
All other substances	General	Same as above	Same as above

ing other wastes with low calorific values, thus leading to uncontrolled emissions of potentially harmful substances into the marine environment.

2.4. ACTION TAKEN BY THE REGIONAL CONVENTIONS

Most incineration operations have so far been carried out in the southern North Sea. Proposals brought forward by an incineration company to incinerate organo-halogen wastes in the Mediterranean Sea and by planning groups to incinerate household wastes and garbage in that area were considered by the contracting parties to the Barcelona Convention, who agreed that no incineration shall be carried out in their convention area.

The Oslo Commission agreed that a separate legal instrument on incineration should be developed within the framework of the Oslo Convention, taking into account the specific regional conditions, in particular of the North Sea area. The draft text of the requirements is in general very similar to that of the London Dumping Convention regulations on the control of incineration at sea, except that the contracting parties of the Oslo Convention have agreed to meet before 1 January 1990 to establish a final date for the termination of incineration at sea in the Oslo Convention area. In addition, the draft rules on incineration at sea considered by the Oslo Commission are more restrictive in terms of the substances and materials that may be the subject of an incineration permit. Only organohalogen compounds and pesticides and their by-products will be permitted for incineration at sea by the contracting parties to the Oslo Convention. However, the Oslo rules also provide for the situation where any other substance may be incinerated at sea provided that a prior consultation procedure is followed. These rules on incineration at sea, which will form a new Annex IV to the Oslo Convention, are subject to formal adoption by members of the Oslo Convention. As of June 1984 the new Annex IV, which was opened for signature on 2 March 1983, had been ratified by Denmark, Norway, and Sweden.

2.5. SAFETY REQUIREMENTS OF INCINERATION SHIPS

As yet five vessels have been in operation as incineration ships (Table 2.6). Four of these ships are reconstructed cargo ships and tankers. The classification societies for ships, in the absence of any specific standards for incineration ships, agreed that for the time being the requirements for IMO ship type 2 should be fulfilled for transport of organohalogen wastes.

The IMO Subcommittee on Bulk Chemicals, noting that the establishment of specific requirements for incineration ships was necessary, agreed that an additional chapter should be included in the Bulk Chemical Codes, containing suitable design criteria, construction standards, and other safety measures for ships transporting wastes for incineration at sea. The Maritime Safety Committee of the IMO in June 1983 adopted a new chapter to the codes, concerning requirements for ships

Table 2.6. Ships Used for Incineration of Wastes at Sea

Ship	Operator[a]	Period of Service	Length (m)	Beam (m)	Gross Tons	Number of Ovens	Number of Burners per Oven	Burning Capacity (t h⁻¹)	(t y⁻¹)	Cargo Tanks Number	Total size (m³)
Matthias I	1	1969–1976			438	1	6	3–6	15,000	6	550
Matthias II	1	1972–1984	72.8	10.9	999	1	8	10–12	60,000	12	1,200
Matthias III	2	1976–1977	176.5	21.5	12,636	1	20	20–40	150,000	9	15,000
Vulcanus	3	1973–present	102.0	14.4	3,098	2	3	20–25	100,000	15	3,500
Vulcanus II	4	1983–present	93.6			3					
Vesta	5	1979–present	71.8	11.0	999	1	3	10	50,000	8	1,400

[a]Operators: (1) Industrie-Anlagen-Verwaltungsgesellschaft OberYrsel-Weisskirchen mbH, FRG; (2) Wulf GmbH and So. KG, Essen, FRG; (3) Ocean Combustion Services BV, Rotterdam, The Netherlands; (4) Waste Management Inc., Oak Brook, Illinois, USA; (5) Lehnkering AG, Duisburg, FRG.

engaged in the incineration of liquid chemical wastes at sea. A draft chapter is currently under consideration by the subcommittee, which specifies in particular tank type, cargo segregation, accommodation spaces, location of the incinerator, piping arrangements, venting systems, vapor detection, electrical systems, fire protection, overflow control, and protection of personnel.

2.6. RESEARCH

Investigations of performance of at-sea incineration systems began in 1969 with the *Matthias I*. The experience that had been gained with land-based incineration systems was not sufficient to allow immediate practice of incineration under the relatively rough conditions at sea. Many experiments had to be carried out with regard to the type of insulation bricks to be used in open ovens at sea as well as to the size and shape of the ovens in relation to the stability of the vessel. The cup-shaped ovens used by the *Matthias* ships (Fig. 2.3) have been shown to lead to better stability of the ship in rough sea conditions, whereas the funnel-type oven developed by the operator of the *Vulcanus* has the advantage that the combustion zone is better controlled and is maintained at a more homogeneous temperature (Compaan, 1980).

Five years after the first incineration at sea by the *Matthias I,* two other incineration ships, *Matthias II* and *Vulcanus,* also were burning wastes. The administrations concerned with these operations promoted research not only in the performance of incineration systems and the combustibility of certain types of wastes, but also in the effects of combustion products on the marine environment. This work was promoted by the national authorities of The Netherlands, the United States, and France. Later, when discussions started on the preparation of the technical guidelines on the control of incineration at sea, some efforts were also made toward the development and testing of control and monitoring devices such as flow meters, sampling systems, gas analytical equipment, and temperature measuring systems.

During the consideration of a suitable legal instrument for the control of incineration at sea it became quite obvious that not all contracting parties to the conventions would fully and wholeheartedly support the disposal of organohalogen wastes at sea by means of incineration. The arguments centered around the questions related to the ultimate fate of the stack gases, in particular the behavior and distribution of the flue gas and emission products. These arguments stem from the very serious problems many countries have with acid rain. Sweden, for example, spends 40 million dollars per year to treat lakes and streams that are affected by acidic emission products, 75% of which originate in England and the European continent (Anonymous, 1981). The FRG, aware that two of the three ships currently operating are flying its flag, promoted further research in 1979 related to the impact of emissions from incineration vessels on the marine environment, as well as the distribution of flue gas and its various components under different meteorological conditions in the North Sea.

All investigations carried out so far have shown that: (1) organochlorine wastes can be destroyed by incineration at sea with efficiencies >99.95%; (2) the three incineration vessels, *Matthias II, Vulcanus,* and *Vesta,* which for the time being operate mainly in the southern North Sea, fulfill the requirements set out in the regulations on the control of incineration at sea; and (3) no adverse effects on the marine environment which could be due to incineration at sea have ever been found.

Further research will be necessary as new types of wastes such as nonchlorine organohalogens are proposed for incineration. Furthermore, good results can be achieved only if the incineration system is operated in a proper manner; additional work should be initiated concerning the improvement of control and recording systems. The currently used control system consists of photographing all the relevant gauges and indicators of the control panel every 15 min. The checking of hundreds of photographs after each incineration operation is very time consuming and could certainly be made more efficient by using digital recording techniques with computer processing to detect any abnormalities.

The use of incineration corridors or incineration lanes across the oceans was proposed by incineration operators. In 1977 the representatives of various countries felt that the control and surveillance systems had not yet been sufficiently developed to guarantee proper monitoring far away from the coast to assure that no organohalogen wastes would bypass the incineration system and enter the sea directly by discharges from the vessel. The concept of crossing the oceans and at the same time burning wastes has therefore not been used, although from an environmental point of view this approach should be given preference to an approach based on the use of incineration sites of limited size and near the coast.

2.7. FUTURE DEVELOPMENT

For the time being three incineration ships burn about 120,000–160,000 t of organohalogen wastes per year in the southern North Sea at a site 120 km off the coast. The site has been selected by the Oslo Commission as a common incineration site for the contracting parties to the Oslo Convention (1972). Incineration in the North Sea may, however, by terminated in 1990, due to the policy adopted by the Oslo Commission to phase out any disposal of industrial wastes in its Convention area.

The provisions of the Helsinki Convention (1974) exclude incineration in the Baltic Sea area. The contracting parties to the Barcelona Convention (1976) decided that incineration of wastes shall by prohibited in the Mediterranean Sea. Accordingly, any future incineration activities beyond the present decade will be carried out in open ocean rather than in enclosed or semi-enclosed regions such as the North Sea, the Baltic Sea and the Mediterranean Sea. It can be assumed that there will be a continued demand for burning wastes at sea, especially for hazardous wastes containing PCBs or TCDD, or wastes that create problems in scrubbing systems.

The effective implementation of international conventions planned or already developed for the protection of the total environment will make it difficult or impossible for many waste producers to continue their current practices of waste disposal. A certain percentage of these wastes will be difficult or impossible to recycle, and those wastes have to be destroyed by incineration, either on land or at sea. A decision as to which of these two means is preferable depends on many factors, such as transport and energy costs, the kind and type of emission standards to be maintained at land incineration systems, the availability on land of disposal areas for scrubbing sludges, and the treatment facilities for scrubbing wastes. Considerable progress has been made in the international control of incineration at sea; this approach is likely to play a role in the future disposal of combustible wastes globally.

REFERENCES

Anonymous. 1981. Acid rain is Sweden's most serious environmental problem. *World Environment Report,* **7,1**.

Barcelona Convention. 1976. Convention for the Protection of the Mediterranean Sea Against Pollution and Protocol for the Protection of the Mediterranean Sea by Dumping from Ships and Aircraft. *International Legal Materials,* **15,** 290–318.

Barniske, L. 1980. Technische Gesichtspunkte bei der Verbrennung von Chlorkohlenwasserstoff-Abfällen. *In:* Hüll and Abfall Beihefte, Vol. 17. Erich Schmidt Verlag, Berlin, pp. 47–56.

Compaan, H., 1980. Incineration of Chemicals at Sea. Number CL80/86, Organization for Industrial Research, TNO, Delft, The Netherlands, 30 pp.

GESAMP (United Nations Joint Group of Experts on the Scientific Aspects of Marine Pollution). 1982. Reports and Studies No. 16, Scientific Criteria for the Selection of Waste Disposal Sites at Sea. International Maritime Organization, London, 60 pp.

Helsinki Convention. 1974. Convention on the Protection of the Marine Environment of the Baltic Sea Area. *International Legal Materials,* **13,** 546–590.

Inter-Governmental Maritime Consultative Organization (IMCO). 1972. Inter-Governmental Conference on the Convention on the Dumping of Wastes at Sea (London, 30 October–13 November 1971). Final Act of the Conference with Technical Memorandum and Resolution adopted by the Conference and Convention on the Prevention of Marine Pollution by Dumping of Wastes and Other Matter, plus 1978 and 1980 amendments (1982 Edition). Inter-Governmental Maritime Consultative Organization, London, 31 pp. plus Amendments, 6 pp.

IMCO. 1978. Report of the Third Consultative Meeting of Contracting Parties to the Convention on the Prevention of Marine Pollution by Dumping of Wastes and Other Matter, 9–13 October 1978. IMCO Doc. LDC III/12 (24 October), *reprinted in International Legal Materials,* **18,** 817–826 (1979). Inter-Governmental Maritime Consultative Organization, London.

IMCO. 1979. Notification of Special Permits Issued for Incineration of Wastes at Sea. Inter-Governmental Consultative Organization, London.

Kamlet, K. S. 1981. Ocean disposal of organochlorine wastes by at-sea incineration. *In:*

Ocean Dumping of Industrial Wastes, B. H. Ketchum, D. R. Kester, and P. K. Park (Eds.). Plenum Press, New York, pp. 295–314.

Luft, T. A., 1974. Technische Anleitung zur Reinhaltung der Luft of 28 August 1974. Gemeinsames Ministerialblatt, Ausgabe A, p. 425.

Olso Convention. 1972. Convention for the Prevention of Marine Pollution by Dumping from Ships and Aircraft. *International Legal Materials,* **11,** 262–266.

Paige, S. F., L. B. Baboolal, H. J. Fisher, K. H. Scheyer, A. M. Shaugh, R. L. Tan, and C. F. Thorne, 1978. Environmental Assessment: At Sea and Land-Based Incineration of Organochlorine Wastes. EPA-600/2-78-087, U.S. Environmental Protection Agency, Washington, D.C., 68 pp.

Park, P. K., and T. P. O'Connor. 1981. Ocean dumping research: historical and international development. *In:* Ocean Dumping of Industrial Wastes, B. H. Ketchum, D. R. Kester, and P. K. Park (Eds.). Plenum Press, New York, pp. 3–23.

3

RESEARCH ON AT-SEA INCINERATION IN THE UNITED STATES

Donald G. Ackerman, Jr., and Ronald A. Venezia

Radian Corporation
Research Triangle Park, North Carolina

Abstract		**54**
3.1.	**Introduction**	**54**
3.2.	**At-Sea Incineration**	**55**
	3.2.1. International Controls	55
	3.2.2. National Controls	55
	3.2.3. Typical Wastes	56
	3.2.4. The *M/T Vulcanus I*	57
3.3.	**At-Sea Incineration Studies in the United States**	**58**
	3.3.1. Chlorinated Hydrocarbon Incineration	58
	3.3.2. Herbicide Orange Incineration	60
	3.3.3. Flow Rate Measurement Instruments	64
	3.3.4. The Second Research Incineration of Polychlorinated Biphenyls	64
	3.3.5. Testing of the *M/T Vulcanus II*	66
	3.3.6. Related Operational Studies	67
	3.3.7. Environmental Impact	68
3.4.	**Conclusions**	**69**
References		**69**

ABSTRACT

Research on oceanic incineration in the United States started in 1974 when the U.S. Environmental Protection Agency (EPA) sanctioned the incineration of four shiploads, about 16,800 t, of organochlorine wastes at an incineration site 305 km southeast of Galveston, Texas. The wastes, burned by the incineration ship *M/T Vulcanus I,* consisted primarily of trichloropropane, trichloroethane, and dichloroethane. Extensive stack gas testing and marine monitoring projects were undertaken to measure the effectiveness of the incinerators and the effects of the emissions on the marine environment. There have been three other major research test programs sponsored by the EPA, during which stack gas sampling and marine monitoring were performed. These were burns of organochlorine waste in 1977, three shiploads of Herbicide Orange in 1977, and a research burn of wastes containing polychlorinated biphenyls in 1983. Each of these test programs is described in this chapter. Results of the stack gas sampling have all shown that the incinerators on the *Vulcanus I* and *Vulcanus II* can be operated at destruction efficiencies in excess of the international requirement of 99.9% and better than U.S. regulatory requirements of 99.99% for hazardous wastes and 99.9999% for PCBs. The two marine monitoring programs have shown no detectable organochlorine compounds in samples of seawater and biota in the area of plume touchdown, and no difference in pH, chlorinity, and trace metals between samples of seawater in control and plume touchdown areas.

3.1. INTRODUCTION

Incineration is a well-developed and, from an engineering perspective, a well-understood technology that can provide an optimum solution to the disposal of combustible wastes by reducing the large waste volumes to nontoxic gases and residual amounts of solids and liquids. Incineration is particularly attractive for the disposal of hazardous organic wastes because it provides ultimate destruction. Emissions from the proper burning of such wastes pose a minimal long-term ecological burden.

Incineration has long been practiced on land, but incineration at sea, on board specially designed vessels, is a relatively recent development. The technology was first used in Europe, where organochlorine industrial wastes have been routinely incinerated at sea since 1969 (Chapter 2). At-sea incineration has been carried out on board six vessels (*M/T Matthias I, Matthias II, Matthias III, Vulcanus I, Vulcanus II,* and *Vesta*), all of which were designed and constructed in Europe. Only the *Vulcanus I, Vulcanus II,* and *Vesta* are currently operating.

At-sea incineration has not been a routine practice in U.S. waters, but there is growing interest, which may lead to routine operations. Waste Management, Inc., of Oak Brook, Illinois, recently purchased the *Vulcanus I,* constructed the *Vulcanus II,* and obtained research permits for at-sea incineration of liquid polychlorinated biphenyl (PCB) wastes. Also, At-Sea Incineration, Inc., of Greenwich, Connecticut, will operate at least one U.S. Flag incineration vessel.

Considerable research has been performed on the environmental effects of at-sea incineration of hazardous wastes, particularly organochlorine wastes. Research activities to date have emphasized monitoring, sampling, and analysis of stack gas emissions. Other activities have included studies for designating at-sea incineration sites, preparation of environmental impact statements, observation of incinerator ship testing in Europe, regulatory analyses, and preliminary design and design evaluations of ships and structures for at-sea incineration in U.S. waters. This research, both American and European, indicates that at-sea incineration is competitive with other disposal methods and can be performed without adverse environmental effects when conducted in accordance with international regulations. This chapter describes research on oceanic incineration performed in U.S. waters and efforts to develop this technology in the United States.

3.2. AT-SEA INCINERATION

3.2.1. International Controls

The Convention on the Prevention of Marine Pollution by Dumping of Wastes and Other Matter, commonly known as the London Dumping Convention (LDC), was negotiated in London in November 1972 and came into force in August 1975 (U.S. Department of State and U.S. Environmental Protection Agency, 1979). Under the LDC, participating nations, including the United States, agreed to regulate all oceanic dumping of wastes through national administrative authorities. Dumping is defined as any deliberate disposal at sea of wastes or other matter from vessels, aircraft, platforms, or other man-made structures. Participating nations are required to maintain records concerning the nature and quantities of material which they permit to be dumped and the circumstances of such dumping. This information must be reported periodically to the International Maritime Organization (IMO), the organization responsible for administration of the LDC.

In 1978, at the Third Consultative Meeting of the Contracting Parties to the LDC, the Contracting Parties adopted by consensus the Resolution on Incineration at Sea, which includes amendments to the Annexes of the LDC and Regulations for the Control of Incineration of Wastes and Other Matter At Sea. The new regulations require approval of incineration systems aboard ships by appropriate national authorities, specify requirements for operation of incinerator and installation of recording devices, and require periodic inspections and testing to ensure continued operations within the legal requirements (Chapter 2).

3.2.2. National Controls

Under the Marine Protection, Research, and Sanctuaries Act of 1972, as amended in 1977 (U.S. Congress, 1977), the U.S. Environmental Protection Agency (EPA) is the federal agency primarily responsible for regulating ocean dumping. The U.S. Coast Guard has lead agency responsibility for vessel and port safety. The EPA (1981a) considers at-sea incineration a form of dumping and has published regulations governing ocean dumping. These regulations also adopt international standards as the minimum in U.S. waters. Several of the more important requirements are:

1. A system of surveys (initial and biennial) to measure and certify performance of vessels.
2. A system for permits established by each signatory party.
3. A provision for special studies if the combustibility of a waste is in doubt.
4. Criteria for designating incineration sites.
5. Minimum flame temperature of 1250°C.
6. Minimum combustion efficiency of 99.95 ± 0.05%.
7. Minimum waste destruction efficiency of 99.9%.

3.2.3. Typical Wastes

Industrial wastes best suited for at-sea incineration are liquid organic chemicals. Certain organic solids may also be candidates because they may be soluble or dispersed in liquid waste or fuel oil. Wastes may be wet, emulsified in water, or even contain aqueous layers. Wastes burned at sea have been almost exclusively organochlorine compounds because they are more costly to dispose of on land. Other classes of substances such as hydrocarbons or oxygenated organic compounds (for example, alcohols, aldehydes, acids, and esters) are typically disposed of on land. There is no reason, however, to exclude those compounds from incineration at sea if they are combustible and do not contain any prohibited matter.

The major difference between at-sea and land-based incineration is that the combustion products go directly from the incinerator into the marine environment. When the wastes are organochlorine compounds, the major products of the combustion process are CO_2, H_2O, and HCl. Not having to treat the combustion effluent (for example, scrub HCl) reduces capital and operating expenses significantly (Shih et al., 1978). Minor constituents of the stack effluent are trace levels of unburned waste and organic compounds produced during combustion. Metals that may be present in the waste will appear as particulate matter, mainly in the form of oxides, in the effluent gases. Phosphorus, sulfur, and nitrogen in the waste will appear as P_2O_5, SO_x, and NO_x. Other species (for example, CO, H_2, and Cl_2) will be present at low levels (10^{-8}–10^{-5} mole fraction).

In general, wastes with high inorganic substance content are not suitable for at-sea incineration. Because inorganic substances are not destroyed by incineration, they enter the marine environment dispersed but undestroyed. Consequently, the inorganic substance content of a combustible waste needs to be determined, and the suitability of the waste for incineration needs to be evaluated in terms of direct ocean dumping criteria. If the waste contains concentrations of a heavy metal that, after allowance for dispersal, would lead to prohibition of direct dumping, at-sea incineration of the waste would also be prohibited.

3.2.4. The *M/T Vulcanus I*

All but one test reported in this chapter were performed aboard the *Vulcanus I;* the additional test was performed aboard the *Vulcanus II.* The incinerators on these two vessels are virtually identical, so only the *Vulcanus I* is described. The incinerator on the *Vesta* is virtually identical to those on the *Vulcanus I* and *Vulcanus II.* Instrumentation for controlling and monitoring the incineration process on the *Vulcanus I* has been continually upgraded. Sections 3.3.5 and 3.3.6 of this chapter provide the most up-to-date discussion of this technology.

In 1972 the *Vulcanus I,* originally a cargo ship, was converted to a chemical tanker fitted with two large incinerators at the stern. The *Vulcanus I* has 15 cargo tanks with a waste loading capacity of 3503 m^3 and an overall tonnage of 4768 t. The vessel meets all applicable requirements of the International Maritime Organization (IMO) concerning transport of dangerous cargo by tanker. There are generally 18 crew members: twelve people operate the vessel and 6 operate the incinerators.

Waste is burned in two identical, refractory-lined incinerators. Each incinerator consists of two main sections, a combustion chamber and a stack, through which the combusting gases pass sequentially. This dual chamber configuration provides a calculated residence time of 1 s at flame temperatures between 1300 and 1500°C.

Combustion air is supplied by large fixed-speed blowers with a rated maximum capacity of 90,000 m^3 h^{-1} for each incinerator. Adjustable vanes in the combustion air supply system control air feed rate. Calculations based on emission rates of major stack gas components indicate that combustion air flow rate is normally about 70% of rated capacity. There is, however, no instrumentation to monitor the volume of air flow.

Liquid wastes are fed to the incinerators by electrically driven metering pumps. Upstream of each burner supply pump is a grinder, which reduces solids in the waste to a slurry that can be pumped. The grinders also act as mixing pumps by recirculating waste to the cargo tanks.

Three rotary cup burners are located at the same level on the periphery of each incinerator, near its base. The burners are of a concentric design and deliver waste or fuel oil through a central tube to atomization nozzles, where the liquid meets high-velocity air delivered through an annulus. Three-way valves on each incinerator burner provide either waste feed, fuel-oil feed, or a shutoff condition. Waste and fuel oil cannot be fed into a burner simultaneously; however, alternate burners could be operated with fuel and waste to achieve high combustion temperature, if necessary, depending on the relative heat contents of the fuel oil and waste. Waste feed rates are determined by flow meters or by measuring the time required to empty cargo tanks of known volumes of waste. Maximum waste feed rate is 12.5 t h^{-1} per incinerator.

Temperatures during operation of the incinerators are measured by two platinum–platinum/10% rhodium thermocouples in each incinerator. Each pair is located in a well opposite one of the burners. One thermocouple, called the controller, is located 1.3 cm from the inside surface of the refractory lining, and provides temperature information to the automatic waste shutoff system. A second thermocouple, ~4 cm from the inner surface of the firebrick, is referred to as the indicator because it provides temperature information to two panels: one in the incinerator control room and the other on the bridge. The bridge panel (which also indicates the day, month, and time that the waste pumps are operating, and the ship's location from DECCA navigational instrumentation) may be sealed and the displays photographed every 15 min for a permanent record.

3.3. AT-SEA INCINERATION STUDIES IN THE UNITED STATES

3.3.1. Chlorinated Hydrocarbon Incineration

The first officially sanctioned at-sea incineration in the United States was performed aboard the *Vulcanus I* between October 1974 and January 1975 (Wastler et al., 1975). The incineration occurred at a site designated by the EPA in the Gulf of Mexico, 305 km southeast of Galveston, Texas. The 4770 km^2 incineration site was beyond the continental shelf, in water depths ranging from 914 to 1829 m, outside all major shipping lanes, and beyond commercial fishing and shrimping grounds. During incineration operations, the *Vulcanus I* was required to be within the site and downwind of any vessel other than those engaged in environmental monitoring.

The wastes were a mixture of chlorinated hydrocarbons predominated by trichloropropane, trichloroethane, and dichloroethane resulting from the production of glycerine, vinyl chloride, epichlorohydrin, and epoxy resins at the Shell Chemical Company manufacturing complex in Deer Park, Texas. Elemental composition was 63% chlorine, 29% carbon, 4% hydrogen, 4% oxygen, and traces (subparts per million) of heavy metals.

Four shiploads, totalling 16,800 t, were burned. The first two shiploads were burned under research permits; the remaining shiploads were burned under interim permits. Wastes were fed at an average of 21.2 t h^{-1} during the first research burn and 24.5 t h^{-1} during the second. Flame temperature, as measured by optical pyrometer, ranged from 1310 to 1610°C. Waste destruction efficiencies ranged from 99.92 to 99.98% and averaged 99.95% (Badley et al., 1975; Wastler et al., 1975).

The EPA coordinated an extensive monitoring and surveillance effort during the two research burns. Stack gas was sampled for HCl and unburned waste components with a system consisting of a water-cooled Vycor® probe (Corning Glass Works, Corning, New York), a 21-m long by 0.63-cm wide ($\frac{1}{4}$-inch diameter), thin-walled Teflon® line, two water-filled impingers to absorb HCl and water-soluble organic compounds, an impinger with sodium arsenate solution for determining Cl$_2$, and an impinger filled with isopropanol to collect water for analysis of insoluble organic compounds. A bypass in the train directed the sample gas to a hydrocarbon analyzer (flame ionization detector) for measurement of low-molecular-weight hydrocarbons. Concentrations of CO, O_2, and CO_2 were also measured.

During the first research burn, a scientific team, largely from the EPA, was aboard the *R/V Oregon II,* a research vessel owned and operated by the U.S. National Oceanic and Atmospheric Administration. The *Oregon II* made two cruises. The first cruise, at the start of the research burn, emphasized identifying the plume and sampling to measure its impact on the ocean. The second cruise was at the end of the burn, and more extensive sampling was performed to identify any long-term impacts. An HCl monitor was used partially to map the incinerator plume. Complete mapping could not be performed because with only one monitor simultaneous measurements could not be made at several altitudes in the plume (Wastler et al., 1975).

During the second research burn, an aircraft from the EPA's National Environmental Research Center at Las Vegas, Nevada, made cross-wind and axial passes through the plume during the first 3 d (Wastler et al., 1975). Three monitoring instruments were employed: a condensation nuclei monitor, a Geomet Model 401 chemiluminescence monitor (Geomet, Inc., Pomona, California) for HCl, and Dohrmann Model C-200-B coulometer (Dohrmann Division, Envirotech Corp., Santa Clara, California), used as the primary standard for calibrating and as a backup to the chemiluminescence monitor. Air samples were also taken in Tedlar® (E.I. duPont de Nemours, Wilmington, Delaware) bags for analysis of HCl. During both burns, the *R/V Orca,* a 30-m long oceanographic research vessel, collected numerous seawater samples for measurement of pH, chlorinity, organochlorines, and trace metals (As, Cd, Cr, Cu, Pb, Hg, Ni, and Zn).

Data collected on concentrations of HCl and condensation nuclei showed that the top of the plume trailed horizontally from the *Vulcanus I* stack at an angle of about 20°, reached a maximum altitude of 850 m above sea level, and fanned out horizontally to a width of about 1200 m at a distance of 2400 m downwind from the stack. Analysis of the seawater samples showed no detectable amount of organochlorine compounds and no changes in pH, chlorinity, or trace metal concentrations (Wastler et al., 1975).

The second at-sea incineration in U.S. waters took place during March and April 1977. Approximately 16,000 t of organochlorine wastes from the Shell Chemical Company manufacturing plant in Deer Park, Texas, were destroyed aboard the *Vulcanus I* in four shiploads (Venezia, 1978). The first burn was extensively tested (Clausen et al., 1977).

A 4.6-m long, stainless steel-jacketed, water-cooled sampling probe was developed for the Shell waste burns. Combustion effluent passed through a central quartz liner and was cooled from 1000°C at the inlet to 150°C at the outlet by independently controllable flows of seawater and a water–air mixture. The probe, mounted on the starboard incinerator, was used by remote control, and several points were sampled along one traverse diameter, in accordance with the EPA Method 1 (U.S. EPA, 1976a).

The heated Teflon line (1 cm in diameter) carried combustion effluent sample gas from the traversing probe to a tee from which other heated Teflon lines led to an EPA Source Assessment Sampling System (Aerotherm Corporation, Mountain View, California) and to an on-line monitoring system. The sampling train (Lentzen et al., 1978) consisted of a heated particle filter, an organic vapor sorbent trap containing XAD-2 resin (Rohm and Haas, Philadelphia, Pennsylvania), two impingers containing silica gel to absorb water vapor, a pump, and a dry gas meter. The sampling train was operated at 85–110 liter min^{-1}. The sampling train and control module for the traversing probe were on the observation deck, the topmost deck forward of the funnel and above the bridge.

On-line combustion gas monitoring employed the following instruments (Beckman Instruments, Inc., Fullerton, California): Model 315A for CO (nondispersive infrared, NDIR), Model 315B for CO_2 (NDIR), Model 108A for hydrocarbons (flame ionization), and Model 742 for O_2 (electrochemical). A modified Beckman gas conditioner was used to cool, filter, and dry the sample gas for distribution to the instruments. A soda lime trap was used to remove HCl from the sample gas to the O_2 instrument. Sample gas to the hydrocarbon analyzer was not conditioned.

A standard 6 m × 2.4 m × 2.4 m shipping container was modified as a portable laboratory to house the on-line monitoring instruments and to serve as the operations room for the sampling team. The portable laboratory was mounted atop a second shipping container, which housed supplies and spare equipment.

On-line monitoring was performed simultaneously with stack sampling. It was found that wall effects on combustion effluent composition were negligible at probe insertion depths > 15 cm past the inner wall of the incinerator. Stack samples acquired with the sampling train were analyzed for specific Shell waste constituents and other organic species potentially present.

Approximately 4100 t of Shell waste were burned at an average rate of 22 t h^{-1} and at an average flame temperature of 1535°C (from optical pyrometer measurements). Trace levels of known waste constituents (for example, trichloropropane at 0.1–0.6 mg m^{-3}) were found in the stack gas samples. Destruction efficiencies ranged from 99.92 to 99.98%, which is better than the 99.9% required by the permit. Results of the monitoring program are presented in Table 3.1. They are comparable to those measured during testing of land-based incinerators (Ackerman et al., 1978a).

3.3.2. Herbicide Orange Incineration

From July to September 1977, U.S. Air Force stocks of Herbicide Orange were burned aboard the *Vulcanus I* at an incineration site in the Pacific Ocean, ~322 km west of Johnston Atoll. Three shiploads, totalling 10,400 t, were burned under research (first load) and special permits (second and third loads). The Herbicide Orange consisted of an equivolume mixture of the n-butyl esters of 2,4-dichlorophenoxyacetic acid (2,4-D) and 2,4,5-trichlorophenoxyacetic acid (2,4,5-T). Because the Herbicide Orange was contaminated with ~1 μg g^{-1} of the highly toxic compound 2,3,7,8-tetrachlorodibenzo-*p*-dioxin (TCDD), the EPA imposed an extensive monitoring protocol. Oceanic monitoring activities are described by Ack-

Table 3.1.   Waste Characteristics and Results of the Second Shell Waste Burn[a]

Characteristic	Value
Heat content (kcal kg^{-1})	2500–3860
Flash point (°C)	38
Density at 25°C (g cm^{-3})	1.2–1.35
Chlorine content (%)	60–70
Composition (%)	
trichloropropane	25–35
trichloroethane	15–25
dichloroethane	15–25
dichlorobutane	0–4
tetrachloropropylether	2–6
tetrachloroethane	20–30
other chorinated hydrocarbons	0–25
Combustion efficiency (%)	99.92–99.98
Total hydrocarbon destruction efficiency (%)	99.991–99.997
Chlorinated hydrocarbon destruction efficiency (%)	99.92–99.98

[a]Adapted from Clausen et al. (1977).

erman et al. (1978b); monitoring activities on Johnston Atoll are described by Thomas et al. (1978).

During the Herbicide Orange burns, combustion effluent was sampled using three probes. Two probes (one in each stack) were installed to divert continuous samples through a 1-cm outside diameter, heated Teflon lines to an on-line monitoring system. These probes, 122 cm × 1.24 cm high-temperature alumina with 1.6-mm-thick walls, did not require external cooling and were fixed in place, extending about 38 cm past the inside wall. The third probe was the same as that developed for the Shell waste burns (Clausen et al., 1977). Capable of traversing the starboard stack, it diverted a representative portion of the combustion effluent to two different sampling trains. Sample points were located along one traverse diameter by EPA Method 1 (U.S. EPA, 1976a).

One of the two stack sampling trains was a benzene impinger train. It had been previously tested by the U.S. Air Force Occupational and Environmental Health Laboratory and proven effective for sampling 2,4-D, 2,4,5-T, and TCDD (U.S. Air Force, 1974). It was the primary train for collecting samples for analysis of TCDD. The benzene impinger train, operated at a flow rate of 2–3 liter min^{-1}, consisted of six Greenburg-Smith impingers, a pump, and a dry gas meter. The first two impingers were modified by adding coarse quartz frits to the ends of the nozzles, and each was filled with 350 ml of benzene. The next two impingers, without Greenburg-Smith impactor nozzles, were two-thirds filled with activated charcoal to remove benzene. The fifth impinger contained 240 ml of 30% (wt per vol) NaOH to absorb HCl. The sixth impinger contained silica gel, which was used to remove H_2O from the gas stream. Because of the rapid degradation of TCDD by ultraviolet radiation, the benzene impingers were wrapped in aluminum foil.

The second stack sampling train was an EPA Method 5 train (U.S. EPA, 1976a), modified by eliminating the particle filter and incorporating an organic vapor sorbent trap. This train was used to collect samples for analysis of other organic compounds potentially present in the combustion effluent. This train also provided redundant samples for TCDD analyses if the benzene impinger samples were lost or destroyed. This train, operated at about 20 liter min^{-1}, consisted of a water-jacketed organic vapor sorbent trap containing XAD-2 resin, an empty impinger to collect condensate from the sorbent trap, two impingers containing measured amounts of 10% (wt per vol) NaOH to absorb HCl, another empty impinger, an impinger containing silica gel to absorb water vapor, a pump, and a dry gas meter.

The on-line combustion gas monitoring system, rebuilt for the Herbicide Orange tests, was housed in the portable laboratory developed for the second Shell waste burn, and consisted of a duplicate set of the following Beckman instruments: Model 865 for CO (NDIR), Model 864 for CO_2 (NDIR), Model 402 for hydrocarbons (flame ionization), and Model 742 for O_2 (electrochemical). There were two modified Beckman gas conditioners to cool and dry the sample gas for distribution to the instruments. The plumbing for the on-line monitoring system was designed so that either stack could be monitored by either set of instruments, although both stacks could not be monitored simultaneously. Additionally, on-line monitoring could be performed independently of stack sampling.

Because TCDD is an extremely toxic compound, a comprehensive personnel protection plan was incorporated in the permits granted to incinerate Herbicide Orange. A boundary-isolation method was selected as most likely to minimize exposure and least likely to hinder work of personnel on board. Under this method, certain areas (pump and incinerator rooms and main deck) were designated as potentially contaminated, and other areas (living quarters, bridge, galley, and mess hall) were designated as uncontaminated. In order to prevent herbicide from being carried into uncontaminated areas, personnel wore disposable coveralls and shoe covers in potentially contaminated areas. When leaving these areas, personnel removed the disposable clothing, showered, and put on normal work clothing.

In order to determine compliance with the personnel protection plan, an extensive sampling and monitoring program was instituted. A gas chromatograph was installed, based on a Shimadzu 6AMPFE(s) instrument with one electron capture and two flame ionization detectors, a linear temperature programmer, recorder, data processor, and isolation transformer (Shimadzu Corp., Tokyo, Japan). Electron capture detection was used exclusively because of its greater sensitivity to chlorinated hydrocarbons. These instruments were installed in the portable laboratory.

Boundaries between areas designated as uncontaminated and potentially contaminated were sampled daily during incinerator operations to determine whether herbicide was being carried into areas of the ship designated as uncontaminated.

This sampling consisted of wiping surfaces with filter paper discs, extracting the discs with benzene, and analyzing the extract for 2,4-D and 2,4,5-T. If those compounds were found in an area designated as uncontaminated, that area was cleaned and sampled until 2,4-D and 2,4,5-T were undetectable. Samples from one benzene impinger from each stack sampling test were analyzed to obtain direct verification of at least 99.9% destruction efficiency for 2,4-D and 2,4,5-T. Also, samples of workspace air were taken with gas sampling syringes and analyzed on board for 2,4-D and 2,4,5-T.

Work space air monitors were placed in the dining, pump, and incinerator rooms and the portable laboratory. These samples used tubes filled with Chromosorb 102® (Johns-Manville, Denver, Colorado) to trap organic vapors. The tubes were changed every 12 h during the first burn and every 24 h during the second and third burns. After each burn, selected tubes were analyzed on Johnston Atoll for 2,4-D and 2,4,5-T.

Table 3.2 summarizes the results of the sampling program. Destruction efficiencies of 2,4-D and 2,4,5-T were >99.999% (neither 2,4-D nor 2,4,5-T was detected in any gas sample). Destruction efficiencies for TCDD ranged from >99.98 to >99.99%. Combustion efficiencies ranged from 99.96 to 99.98% (Ackerman et al., 1978b).

Analyses of workspace air monitor tubes showed that the 8-h threshold limit value of 10 mg m^{-3} for 2,4-D plus 2,4,5-T was more than one order of magnitude

Table 3.2. Waste Characteristics and Results of the Herbicide Orange Burn

Characteristic	Value
Heat content (kcal kg^{-1})	5570[a]
Flash point (°C)	146[a]
Density at 25°C (g cm^{-3})	1.275–1.295[a]
Chlorine content (%)	~30[a]
Composition (%)	
2,4-D (n-butyl esters of 2,4-dichlorophenoxyacetic acid)	~50[a]
2,4,5-T (n-butyl esters of 2,4,5-trichlorophenoxyacetic acid)	~50[a]·
TCDD (μg g^{-1})	1.9[a]
Combustion efficiency (%)	99.98–99.99[b]
Total hydrocarbon destruction efficiency (%)	99.98–99.99[b]
Herbicide Orange destruction efficiency (%)	>99.999[b]
TCDD destruction efficiency (%)	>99.98->99.99[b]

[a]Value from U.S. Air Force (1974).
[b]Value from Ackerman et al. (1978b).

greater than concentrations of those compounds in the pump and incinerator rooms and 3–4 orders of magnitude greater than concentrations in the dining rooms and the portable laboratory (Thomas et al., 1978).

3.3.3. Flow Rate Measurement Instruments

As part of its continuing support of the development of international regulations and guidelines for at-sea incineration, the EPA sponsored a study to evaluate various types of liquid flow rate measurement instruments and to design a combustion gas monitoring system that could be readily operated and maintained by the crew of an incineration ship. This study culminated with testing on board the *Vulcanus I* in the North Sea during November 1978–January 1979 (Ackerman et al., 1979). Two different types of flow meters, operating on different principles (vortex shedding and ultrasonic), were operated without difficulty while three shiploads of waste were burned. The ultrasonic flow meter was judged preferable to the vortex shedding flow meter because the former was mounted externally to waste pipes, whereas the latter must be mounted internally and is thus exposed to the waste. The online gas monitoring instrumentation operated satisfactorily and with minimal operator attention.

3.3.4. The Second Research Incineration of Polychlorinated Biphenyls

During August 1982, the *Vulcanus I* burned a shipload (3507 t) of waste containing polychlorinated biphenyls (PCBs), chlorobenzenes (CBs), and ultratrace levels of 2,3,7,8-tetrachlorodibenzofuran (2,3,7,8-TCDF) at the Gulf of Mexico Ocean Incineration Site under a research permit from the EPA (Ackerman et al., 1983a). Combustion gases were sampled with the train mandated for testing land-based incinerators for emissions of PCBs (Beard and Schaum, 1978). The train, a modified EPA Method 5, consisted of the following components: water-cooled, quartz-lined probe; heat-traced Teflon transfer line; three modified Greenburg-Smith impingers; a trap containing Florisil as a sorbent; a water-jacketed trap containing XAD-2 as a sorbent; and three additional Greenburg-Smith impingers. The first two impingers contained organic-free distilled, deionized water. The last impinger contained a weighed amount of indicating silica gel.

Ten tests were performed, each consisting of the acquisition of a sample of stack gas and a sample of waste accumulated over the duration of the test. Sampling procedures were in accordance with EPA Method 5 except that sampling was conducted at a fixed point 1 m from the inner wall of the stack. Sampling was performed at a fixed point rather than by dual-diameter traverse because the stack gas exits at a temperature of about 1000°C. Thus, organic compounds of interest were expected to be in the gas phase rather than sorbed onto any particulate matter in the stack gas. Because the flow region is turbulent (Re $\simeq$ 200,000), the stack gas is well mixed. For these reasons, sampling did not have to be isokinetic along two-diameter traverses. Nominal flow rates were 17 liter min^{-1}, and nominal durations were 2 h.

Air in the dining and incineration control rooms was sampled to determine whether PCBs were present. Selected areas of deck surface were sampled with filter paper to detect whether contamination was occurring, and these samples were analyzed on board to determine the effectiveness of the health and safety plan. Pertinent process-related data, such as wall temperatures and concentrations of CO, CO_2, and O_2 in the combustion gases, were acquired from the vessel's Chief Engineer.

Samples of air from the dining and incinerator rooms showed no detectable levels of PCBs and CBs. Combustion efficiency averaged 99.99%. Averages of other process-related incineration parameters were: waste feed rate, 6.22 t h^{-1} per incinerator; wall temperature, 1303°C; concentration of O_2, 10.1%; concentration of CO_2, 9.1%; concentration of CO, 8 ppm; excess air, 95%; and waste residence time, 1.1 s.

Samples from six of the ten tests were analyzed. No PCB, CB, or TCDF was detected in any of the stack gas samples. Average destruction efficiencies for these compounds are given in Table 3.3. Samples of stack gas and waste were analyzed for tetrachlorodibenzo-p-dioxins (TCDDs). These were not found in any sample. It was not possible to calculate destruction efficiencies for TCDDs because these compounds were not detected in the wastes.

Sampling of ambient air was performed before (baseline) and during the incineration (Guttman et al., 1983). This sampling was conducted using the research vessel *R/V Antelope*. Real-time monitoring of HCl ensured that the plume from the *Vulcanus I* was actually being sampled. Analyses of the baseline samples of ambient air showed no detectable PCBs or other organochlorine compounds (detection limit: 0.3 ng m^{-3}) and only traces of nonchlorinated compounds. Analyses of samples of air from the plume showed no detectable PCBs (detection limit: 0.3 ng m^{-3}) or other organochlorine compounds. Nonchlorinated organic compounds were detected in amounts higher than those observed during the baseline tests. It was theorized that these compounds were generated either by the propulsion engines or by the incineration process.

Sampling of surface water and exposure studies of selected marine organisms were also conducted before and during the incineration (TerEco Corporation, 1982).

Table 3.3. Average Destruction Efficiencies from the Incineration of Polychlorinated Biphenyls in August 1982[a]

Compound	Concentration in Waste (% by wt)	Destruction Efficiency[b] (%)
Polychlorinated biphenyls	27.49	>99.99989
Chlorobenzenes	6.87	>99.99993
Tetrachlorodibenzofurans	4.8×10^{-6}	>99.96

[a]Source: Ackerman et al. (1983a).
[b]The symbol (>) means that the compound was not detected in the stack gas and that the actual destruction efficiency was greater than the value given in the table.

Organisms (one species of shrimp and two species of fin fish) were placed in Pelagic Biotal Ocean Monitors (P-BOMs). During incineration operations, P-BOMs were placed in the incineration site so they would be exposed to the plume and in control areas (no exposure) outside the site.

Analyses of surface waters showed that acidity and salinity were the same in control and plume-impact areas. No Aroclor® 1254 (PCB) was detected in baseline and test samples of surface water (detection limit: 0.2 mg liter^{-1}), in the collectors placed on the P-BOMs (detection limit: 2 mg m^{-2}), in samples of neuston (detection limit: 1 ng Aroclor 1254 per m^3 of surface water), or in one of the exposed species of fish (detection limit: 0.025 mg g^{-1}). Although PCBs were detected in the other species of fish, it was found that all fish of that species were contaminated with PCBs before the testing started. The three species (fish and shrimp) were analyzed for changes in metabolic activity resulting from exposure to the plume, but no effects were found. The investigators concluded that no environmental effects of the incineration were detected.

3.3.5. Testing of the *M/T Vulcanus II*

The *Vulcanus II*, commissioned in November 1982, was tested in February 1983 (Ackerman et al., 1983b). The testing took place in the North Sea Incineration Site, an area off the coast of The Netherlands in the vicinity of 52°16′N and 03°45′E. The wastes burned resulted from the manufacture of vinyl chloride and were loaded at Norsk Hydro at Rafnes, Norway. The cargo consisted of 188 m^3 (245 t) of light-ends and 608 m^3 (797 t) of heavy-ends, a total of 796 m^3 (1042 t). Light-ends and heavy-ends were loaded into separate tanks. (Light-ends and heavy-ends are terms for lower and higher boiling distillate fractions.)

Combustion gases were sampled with a Volatile Organic Sampling Train developed by the EPA for other combustion sources (Jungclaus and Gorman, 1982). The sampling train consisted of the following components: inlet valve, two water-coated condensers, sorbent trap containing Tenax® (Alltech Associates, Inc., Deerfield, Illinois) condensate flask, water-cooled condenser, sorbent trap containing Tenax and activated charcoal (GW 20/50; Calgon Corporation, Pittsburgh, Pennsylvania), flasks containing indicating silica gel, and a meter box. A quartz-lined, stainless steel-jacketed, water-cooled probe was used to cool the sampled stack gas and was connected to the train by a heat-traced Teflon line. A chilled mixture of antifreeze and water was circulated through the condenser to maintain the gas entering the traps at or below 20°C. Sampling was conducted at a fixed point 40 cm past the inner wall of the stack.

Four tests were performed. A test consisted of pumping stack gas through six pairs of traps, one pair at a time. The sampling rate was nominally 1 liter min^{-1}, and each pair was exposed for 20 min. With leak-tests before and after each change of traps, a test took about 3.5 h. During each test, one time-composited sample of each of the two wastes was taken. Pertinent process-related data were acquired from computer printouts maintained by the Chief Engineer and the navigational log maintained by the Master of the *Vulcanus II*. The information includes temperature in the incinerators; feed rates of waste and air; concentrations of CO_2, CO, and O_2 in the stack gas; and ambient temperature, pressure, and humidity.

Five compounds present in the wastes were selected as principal organic hazardous constituents, and all samples of stack gas and waste were analyzed for them. Immediately before analyses, each trap was spiked with a known amount of an internal standard. Analytical procedures and instrumental conditions for the gas chromatograph-mass spectrometer (GC-MS) used were similar to those of EPA Method 624 (U.S. EPA, 1979). Contents of a trap were thermally desorbed individually into a Method 624 trap contained in a purge-and-trap apparatus, and contents of the Method 624 trap were then thermally desorbed into the GC-MS.

Combustion efficiencies averaged 99.98%. Averages of other process-related parameters were: feed rate of light-ends, 5.92 t h^{-1} (one incinerator); feed rate of heavy-ends, 9.88 t h^{-1} (one incinerator); wall temperature, 1166°C; outlet temperature, 1038°C; concentration of O_2, 10.6%; concentration of CO_2, 9.6%; concentration of CO, 22 ppm; excess air, 103%; and residence time, 1.1 s. Destruction efficiencies for the five primary organic hazardous constituents are presented in Table 3.4. It can be seen that the destruction efficiencies exceed the land-based standard of 99.99%. Carbon tetrachloride and chloroform are, respectively, the fourth and tenth hardest-to-destroy compounds in the EPA's hierarchy of incinerability. Since they were present at concentrations of 20.5 and 26.1%, respectively, this waste presented a considerable challenge to the incineration system.

3.3.6. Related Operational Studies

In addition to actual monitoring of at-sea incineration operations, the EPA has sponsored a variety of other activities. Major activities have been the preparation of environmental impact statements (EISs) related to the designation of at-sea incineration sites. The Gulf of Mexico site (where the two Shell waste incinerations occurred) was designated in 1976 (U.S. EPA, 1976b). An EIS for the North Atlantic site has been prepared (U.S. EPA, 1981b). The U.S. Department of State and the EPA (1979) published an EIS in support of adopting amendments to Annexes I and II of the LDC.

Table 3.4.   Destruction Efficiencies from the Test of the *M/T Vulcanus II*[a]

Compound	Concentration in Waste (% by wt)	Destruction Efficiency[b] (%)
1,1-dichloroethane	6.8	99.99994
1,2-dichloroethane	7.8	99.99996
1,1,2-trichloroethane	38.9	>99.999995
Chloroform	26.1	99.9996
Carbon tetrachloride	20.5	99.998

[a]Source: Ackerman et al. (1983b).
[b]The symbol (>) means that the compound was not detected in the stack gas and that the actual destruction efficiency was greater than the value given in the table.

In support of the EIS for the North Atlantic incineration site, the EPA had a contractor prepare an environmental assessment comparing at-sea and land-based incineration (Paige et al., 1978). A related study compared costs and environmental impacts associated with disposal of liquid organochlorine wastes by land-based incineration, at-sea incineration, and chlorinolysis (Shih et al., 1978). These studies indicated that the environmental impacts from all three disposal options were minimal under normal conditions and that at-sea incineration was the least costly option.

A fourth major research activity was the offshore platform hazardous waste incineration system project. Chevron U.S.A., Inc., offered to transfer an offshore oil platform to the federal government. The platform is in the Gulf of Mexico, ~ 100 km south of Mobile Point, Louisiana, and 120 km east of North Pass, Louisiana. A conceptual design project was performed (Corey et al., 1980), and an EIS has been prepared (Andis et al., 1982).

The U.S. Department of Commerce has been working toward a U.S. Flag incineration ship (U.S. Department of Commerce, 1976). In support of these efforts, the EPA sponsored a brief study of the environmental impacts that could result from the adoption of international standards regulating at-sea incineration (Fisher, 1978). The EPA and the U.S. Department of Commerce recently sponsored an updating of the chemical waste incineration ship project (Johnson et al., 1980; U.S. EPA et al., 1980).

3.3.7. Environmental Impact

The effects of at-sea incineration on the marine environment have been measured directly and estimated from plume dispersion modelling. When organochlorine wastes are burned, the HCl content of the stack gas and its effects on birds and on marine organisms in the vicinity of a plume are of obvious concern. For the first Shell waste burns, a plume dispersion model predicted a maximum HCl concentration of 3.1 ml liter^{-1} (TerEco Corporation, 1975). This is below the threshold limit value of 5 ml liter^{-1} (American Conference of Governmental and Industrial Hygienists, 1979). Actual measurements of HCl in the plume ranged from 0.01 to 7.25 ml liter^{-1}.

Because of its buffering capacity, seawater is capable of neutralizing 80 g of HCl per m^3. It was also calculated from the plume dispersion modelling that the seawater HCl concentration at plume impact would be 197 mg liter^{-1}. This contribution would not be detected by a pH change because of the ocean's buffering capacity, and the corresponding increases in chloride ion concentration would be negligible compared with the 19 g kg^{-1} chloride background of the ocean.

During the first Shell waste burn, water samples taken in the vicinity of the plume showed no significant differences in pH, chlorinity, or copper (the most abundant heavy metal in the waste) from samples taken in control areas. Organochlorine residues were not detected at the 0.5 mg g^{-1} level (Wastler et al., 1975). A similar lack of measurable effects was observed during the second research burn of PCBs (TerErco Corporation, 1982; Guttman et al., 1983).

Analyses of the phytoplankton and zooplankton samples for chlorophyll *a* and adenosine triphosphate showed no obvious or subtle adverse impacts. Fish exposed at the point of plume touchdown were also analyzed. An increase in activity of the liver enzyme system involved in metabolism of chemicals foreign to the organism (cytochrome P-450) was noted, indicating that the fish were exposed to foreign chemicals. However, when the exposed fish were left in clean water for a few days, the enzyme activity returned to that of the control fish (Wastler et al., 1975). No effects on marine biota were observed during the second research burn of PCBs (TerEco Corporation, 1982).

3.4. CONCLUSIONS

Wastler et al. (1975) concluded from the results of the first Shell waste burns that no adverse environmental effects were noted, that at-sea incineration of the Shell waste was compatible with the intent of the Marine Protection, Research, and Sanctuaries Act, Public Law 92-532, and that at-sea incineration was a viable disposal method that should be considered with other methods, including direct disposal in the ocean, disposal on land, and land-based incineration.

Incineration offers the most satisfactory route for disposal of organochlorine wastes (Venezia, 1978). Aside from the fact that this method converts the waste into relatively simple products, it is important to note that, under the proper conditions, the process can be made self-sustaining, essentially free of environmentally unacceptable by-products, and independent of treatment of the effluent combustion products. Incineration at sea has several unique advantages:

1. Acquisition of fixed land sites is not required.
2. Treatment of the effluent gases from the process is not required because the main pollutant remaining, HCl, can be spread over broad areas of the ocean and thus diluted to acceptable below-background levels.
3. Generation and subsequent disposal of solid wastes (such as scrubber solids) are avoided.
4. Incineration can be carried out in remote, uninhabited areas under favorable atmospheric conditions.

REFERENCES

Ackerman, D. G., J. W. Adams, J. F. Clausen, N. J. Cunningham, E. H. Dohnert, A. Grant, J. C. Harris, R. J. Johnson, P. L. Levins, C. C. Shih, J. L. Stauffer, K. E. Thrun, R. F. Tobias, L. R. Woodland, and C. A. Zee. 1978a. Destroying Chemical Wastes in Commercial Scale Incinerators, Final Report Phase II. Report to the Office of Solid Waste, U.S. Environmental Protection Agency. No. PB 278816/2WP, National Technical Information Service, Springfield, Virginia, 121 pp.

Ackerman, D. G., H. J. Fisher, R. J. Johnson, R. F. Maddalone, B. J. Matthews, E. L. Moon, K. H. Scheyer, C. C. Shih, and R. F. Tobias. 1978b. At-Sea Incineration of Herbicide Orange Onboard the *M/T Vulcanus*. EPA-600/2-78-086, U.S. Environmental Protection Agency, Research Triangle Park, North Carolina, 273 pp.

Ackerman, D. G., R. J. Johnson, E. L. Moon, A. E. Samsonov, and K. H. Scheyer. 1979. At-Sea Incineration: Evaluation of Wasteflow and Combustion Gas Monitoring Instrumentation Onboard the *M/T Vulcanus*. EPA-600/2-79-137, U.S. Environmental Protection Agency, Research Triangle Park, North Carolina, 286 pp.

Ackerman, D. G., J. F. McGaughey, and D. E. Wagoner. 1983a. At-Sea Incineration of PCB-Containing Wastes Onboard the *M/T Vulcanus*. EPA-600/7-83-024, U.S. Environmental Protection Agency, Research Triangle Park, North Carolina, 286 pp.

Ackerman, D. G., R. G. Beimer, and J. F. McGaughey. 1983b. Incineration of Volatile Organic Compounds by the *M/T Vulcanus II*. Report to Chemical Waste Management, Inc., Oak Brook, Illinois. Energy and Environmental Division, TRW Incorporated, Redondo Beach, California, 134 pp.

American Conference of Governmental and Industrial Hygienists. 1979. TLVS. Threshold Limit Values for Chemical Substances and Physical Agents in the Workroom Environment with Intended Changes for 1979. American Conference of Governmental and Industrial Hygienists, Cincinnati, Ohio, 94 pp.

Andis, J. D., C. A. Atkinson, M. E. Drehsen, D. A. Kiefer, T. L. Sarro, S. J. Sheffield, G. R. Van Dyke, P. J. Weller, and S. D. Wolf. 1982. Final Environmental Impact Statement for the Offshore Platform Hazardous Waste Incineration Facility, Vol. 1. Prepared for Hazardous Response Support Division and Criteria and Standards Division, U.S. Environmental Protection Agency, Washington, D.C., 122 pp.

Badley, J. H., A. Telfer, and E. M. Fredericks. 1975. At-Sea Incineration of Shell Chemical Organic Chloride Waste. Technical Progress Report BRC-Corp 13-75-1, Shell Development Company, Bellaire Research Center, Houston, Texas, 80 pp.

Beard, J. H., III, and J. Schaum. 1978. Sampling Methods and Analytical Procedures Manual for PCB Disposal: Interim Report. Office of Solid Waste, U.S. Environmental Protection Agency, Washington, D.C., 119 pp.

Clausen, J. F., H. J. Fisher, R. J. Johnson, E. L. Moon, C. C. Shih, R. F. Tobias, and C. A. Zee. 1977. At-Sea Incineration of Organochlorine Wastes Onboard the *M/T Vulcanus*. EPA-600/2-77-196, U.S. Environmental Protection Agency, Research Triangle Park, North Carolina, 95 pp.

Corey, R. J., G. G. Engleman, F. E. Flynn, R. J. Johnson, E. L. Moon, T. L. Sarro, R. L. Tan, S. L. Unger, P. J. Weller, and C. A. Zee. 1980. Offshore Platform Hazardous Waste Incineration Feasibility Study. Phase I: Conceptual Design. Contract No. 68-02-2613, Industrial Environmental Research Laboratory, U.S. Environmental Protection Agency, Research Triangle Park, North Carolina, 255 pp.

Fisher, H. J. 1978. At-Sea Incineration of Organochlorine Wastes. Environmental Aspects and Impacts of Adopting International Regulatory Standards. EPA Contract No. 68-02-2165, Industrial Environmental Research Laboratory, U.S. Environmental Protection Agency, Research Triangle Park, North Carolina, 26 pp.

Guttman, M. A., N. W. Flynn, and R. F. Shokes. 1983. Ambient Air Monitoring of the August 1982 *M/T Vulcanus* PCB Incineration at the Gulf of Mexico Designated Site. Office of Water, U.S. Environmental Protection Agency, Washington, D.C., 87 pp.

Johnson, R. J., D. G. Ackerman, J. L. Anastasi, C. L. Crawford, B. Jackson, and C. A. Zee. 1980. Design Recommendations for a Shipboard At-Sea Hazardous Waste Incineration System. EPA Contract No. 68-03-2560, Industrial Environmental Research Laboratory, U.S. Environmental Protection Agency, Cincinnati, Ohio, 98 pp.

Jungclaus, G., and P. Gorman. 1982. Evaluation of a Volatile Organic Sampling Train (VOST). Draft Final Report. Contract No. 68-01-5915, Office of Research and Development, Research Triangle Park, North Carolina, and Office of Solid Waste, U.S. Environmental Protection Agency, Washington, D.C., 56 pp.

Lentzen, D. E., D. E. Wagoner, E. D. Estes, and W. F. Gutknecht. 1978. IERL-RTP Procedures Manual: Level I Environmental Assessment, 2nd Edition. EPA-600/7-78-201, U.S. Environmental Protection Agency, Washington, D.C., 277 pp.

Paige, S. F., L. B. Baboolal, H. J. Fisher, K. H. Scheyer, A. M. Shaug, R. L. Tan, and C. F. Thorne. 1978. Environmental Assessment: At-Sea and Land-Based Incineration of Organochlorine Wastes. EPA-600/2-78-087, U.S. Environmental Protection Agency, Washington, D.C., 68 pp.

Shih, C. C., J. E. Cotter, D. Dean, S. F. Paige, E. P. Pulaski, and C. F. Thorne. 1978. Comparative Cost Analysis and Environmental Assessment for Disposal of Organochlorine Wastes. EPA-600/2-78-190, U.S. Environmental Protection Agency, Washington, D.C., 129 pp.

TerEco Corporation. 1975. A Report on the Philadelphia Dumpsite and Shell Incineration Monitorings. TerEco Corporation, College Station, Texas, 255 pp.

TerEco Corporation. 1982. Biological Monitoring of PCB Incineration in the Gulf of Mexico. Office of Water, U.S. Environmental Protection Agency, Washington, D.C., 56 pp.

Thomas, T. J., D. P. Brown, J. Harrington, T. Stafford, L. Toft, and B. Vigon. 1978. Land-Based Environmental Monitoring at Johnston Island—Disposal of Herbicide Orange. Report No. OEHL TR-78-87, submitted to U.S. Air Force Occupational and Environmental Health Laboratory, Brooks Air Force Base, Texas, 323 pp.

U.S. Air Force. 1974. Final Environmental Statement for Disposition of Orange Herbicide by Incineration. U.S. Department of Defense, Washington, D.C., 855 pp.

U.S. Congress. 1977. An Act to Amend the Marine Protection, Research and Sanctuaries Act of 1972. Public Law 95-153, 91 stat. 1255, Washington, D.C.

U.S. Department of Commerce. 1976. Final Environmental Impact Statement. Maritime Administration Chemical Waste Incinerator Ship Project, Vol. 1. Document No. MA-EIS-7302-76-041F, U.S. Maritime Administration, Washington, D.C., 386 pp.

U.S. Department of State and U.S. Environmental Protection Agency. 1979. Final Environmental Impact Statement for the Incineration of Wastes at Sea Under the 1972 Ocean Dumping Convention. Office of Environmental Affairs, U.S. Department of State, Washington, D.C., 336 pp.

U.S. Environmental Protection Agency (EPA). 1976a. Proposed amendments to reference methods. *Federal Register* (8 June), **44,** 23060–23083.

U.S EPA. 1976b. Final Environmental Impact Statement. Designation of Site in the Gulf of Mexico for Incineration of Chemical Wastes. Oil and Special Materials Control Division, Washington, D.C., 126 pp.

U.S. EPA. 1979. Guidelines establishing test procedures for the analysis of pollutants. Method 624—purgeables. *Federal Register* (3 December), **44,** 69464–69575.

U.S. EPA. 1981a. Subchapter H—Navigable Waters. Code of Federal Regulations, Title 40, Parts 220-231, 87 pp.

U.S. EPA. 1981b. Final Environmental Impact Statement (EIS) for North Atlantic Inciner-ation Site Designation. Report No. EPA 440/5-82-025, Oil and Special Materials Con-trol Division, U.S. Environmental Protection Agency, Washington, D.C., 396 pp.

U.S. EPA et al. 1980. Report of the Interagency Ad Hoc Work Group for the Chemical Waste Incinerator Ship Program. Joint report by U.S. Environmental Protection Agency, U.S. Department of Commerce—Maritime Administration, U.S. Department of Trans-portation—National Bureau of Standards, Washington, D.C., 243 pp.

Venezia, R. A. 1978. Incineration At-Sea of Organochlorine Wastes. Paper Presented at the 2nd Conference of the Environment, Paris, 11 pp.

Wastler, T. A., C. K. Offutt, C. K. Fitzsimmons, and P. E. Des Rosiers. 1975. Disposal of Organochlorine Wastes by Incineration at Sea. EPA-430/9-75-014, U.S. Environmental Protection Agency, Washington, D.C., 238 pp.

4

OCEAN INCINERATION: CONTAMINANT LOADING AND MONITORING

Roger R. Fay

Department of Oceanography
Texas A&M University
College Station, Texas

T. A. Wastler

Marine Protection Branch
U.S. Environmental Protection Agency
Washington, D.C.

Abstract	**74**
4.1. Introduction	**74**
4.1.1. United States Applications	75
4.1.2. Future Waste Disposal Requirements	76
4.2. Previous Research Results	**77**
4.3. Monitoring Needs and Future Incineration	**80**
4.3.1. Site-Related Problems	84
4.3.2. Nature and Mode of Contaminant Input	85
4.3.3. Realistic Indicators of Impact	86
4.4. Conclusions	**87**
Acknowledgments	**87**
References	**88**

ABSTRACT

Incinerations of Shell Chemical Company's organochlorine wastes in 1974–1975 and in 1977, and an incineration of Herbicide Orange in 1978 were studied. Stack gas monitoring showed combustion efficiencies >99.9% during the burns. The major component of concern in stack emissions is HCl, but the emission plume from the first organochlorine burn did not cause a significant change in either chlorinity or pH of surface seawater. Similarly, organochlorine and trace metal concentrations in the plume water did not vary from that of the control station (below the detection limit of 0.5 ng g^{-1} organohalogens). No differences were observed in chlorophyll and adenosine triphosphate concentrations, or cell counts of phytoplankton in plume and control areas. Phytoplankton and zooplankton samples were also examined for their accumulation of organochlorines and trace metals, but no elevations attributable to incineration could be detected. However, ambient levels of organochlorines (presumed to originate from tar balls) caused considerable variation in the observed concentrations in zooplankton. A device and attendant methodologies for conducting *in situ* bioassay and bioaccumulation studies under realistic field conditions were developed. During the 1977 organochlorine burn, phytoplankton, a zooplankter, a bivalve, and fish were exposed to the incinerator emissions in the *in situ* device, and the organisms' responses to the emissions were measured through a number of sublethal indicators (adenylate energy charge, histopathological aberrations, and enzyme activity). Biomass and bioaccumulation of contaminants were also measured. No apparent effect due to incineration was noted.

4.1. INTRODUCTION

The problem of how to dispose of unwanted pesticides, herbicides, and organochlorine wastes has been recognized for some time. In the United States of America, prior to the passage of the Marine Protection, Research, and Sanctuaries Act (MPRSA) in 1972 (U.S. Congress, 1972), these substances were commonly dumped directly into the sea at approved ocean disposal sites. With the prohibition of such practices by the MPRSA, and later by international agreement [Convention on the Prevention of Marine Pollution by Dumping of Wastes and Other Matter (commonly called the London Dumping Convention) adopted in 1975], alternative technologies had to be employed. In the United States during the early 1970s, disposal methods primarily included direct ocean disposal, land-based incineration, deepwell injection, and landfill. The additional technology of at-sea incineration, however, was being developed in Europe. Initial efforts in 1969 by a German company using the *M/T Matthias I*, a small tanker fitted with an incinerator, showed the technical feasibility of at-sea incineration of organochlorine wastes.

Since 1969 ocean incineration has continued to be a preferred method of disposal for organohalogen wastes in European waters. In 1979 170,000 t of organohalogen wastes were incinerated at the designated site in the North Sea by the three operating incineration ships (Chapter 2).

4.1.1. United States Applications

In October 1974 the first at-sea incineration in U.S. waters was conducted in the Gulf of Mexico under the auspices of the U.S. Environmental Protection Agency (EPA). Monitoring of this event, as well as other U.S. incinerations that have occurred to date, provides the technical basis for concluding that at-sea incineration is a viable alternative to other means of disposal. Based on the belief that at-sea incineration is an acceptable means of ocean disposal of certain types of hazardous materials, the EPA has designated one ocean disposal site in the Gulf of Mexico for at-sea incineration and is presently in the process of designating additional sites elsewhere. International acceptance of the feasibility of at-sea incineration is exemplified by the fact that recently adopted amendments to the London Dumping Convention regulations permit at-sea incineration of certain types of materials that had previously been banned from ocean disposal (IMCO, 1976).

In compliance with EPA requirements, the Shell Chemical Company facility in Deer Park, Texas, suspended conventional ocean dumping of organochlorine wastes when their permit, which expired in November 1973, was not renewed. The search for environmentally acceptable methods of disposing of their waste led Shell Chemical Company to at-sea incineration, which had been used by European industry and had been evaluated and endorsed by European regulatory bodies and the scientific community (Chapter 2). In October 1974, a public hearing was held in Houston, Texas, in response to Shell Chemical Company's application for a permit to incinerate organochlorine waste in the Gulf of Mexico. As a result of the hearing, Shell Chemical Company was granted a research permit for at-sea incineration of 4200 t (one shipload) of organochlorine wastes.

The first at-sea incineration operations conducted in United States waters were performed aboard the *M/T Vulcanus I* in the Gulf of Mexico between October 1974 and January 1975. The first two burns (4200 t each) were conducted under EPA research permits; the second two burns (4200 t each) were conducted under EPA special permits. The wastes, which had resulted from the production of glycerin, vinyl chloride, epichlorohydrin, and epoxy resins, were a mixture of organochlorines with trichloropropane, trichloroethane, and dichloroethane predominating. Combustion efficiencies (the percentage of hydrocarbons destroyed) ranged between 99.92 and 99.98%. In accordance with permit conditions, a substantial monitoring effort was undertaken. Following review of the results, the EPA concluded that the incineration resulted in no significant adverse effects on the environment (Wastler et al., 1975).

The second at-sea incineration operation occurred during March and April 1977. Under an EPA special permit, ~ 16,800 t (four shiploads) of Shell Chemical Company's wastes were burned aboard the *Vulcanus I* in the Gulf of Mexico. Waste material was similar to that incinerated during the first organochlorine burns. Combustion efficiency was 99.95%. Again, monitoring studies concluded that there were no significant adverse effects on the environment (Clausen et al., 1977; Pequegnat et al., 1978).

The third at-sea incineration consisted of three shiploads (10,400 t) of Herbicide

Orange from the U.S. Air Force. The incineration was carried out during July–September 1977 on the *Vulcanus I* at a designated area in the Pacific, ~300 km west of Johnston Atoll. The first burn was carried out under an EPA research permit and the remaining two were under a special permit. The Herbicide Orange consisted of an approximate 50-50 mixture (by volume) of the *n*-butyl esters of 2,4-dichlorophenoxyacetic acid (2,4-D) and 2,4,5-trichlorophenoxyacetic acid (2,4,5-T). Certain lots of the herbicide contained the contaminant 2,3,7,8-tetrachlorodibenzo-*p*-dioxin (TCDD). The TCDD concentration in the entire stock of herbicide ranged from 0 to 47 μg g^{-1}, and averaged 1.9 μg g^{-1}. Because of the extremely high toxicity of TCDD, special precautions were placed in effect during all loading and operating procedures on the ship. Results showed that destruction efficiencies for 2,4-D and 2,4,5-T were >99.999%, and that the destruction efficiency of TCDD was >99.93%. All requirements of the EPA permits were met (Ackerman et al., 1978).

4.1.2.   Future Waste Disposal Requirements

The amounts and kinds of wastes available for incineration at sea will influence the need for and the nature of a monitoring program. As past incinerations in the United States have been on a specialized need basis, the monitoring and research efforts conducted in conjunction with these incinerations were designed to answer specific questions regarding the behavior of the emissions or the environmental effects of a relatively limited input of contaminants. If incineration is to be continued on a larger scale or on a continual basis, it is likely that monitoring efforts will have to consider the increased contaminant loading.

Estimates of the amounts of wastes produced in the United States that are suitable for ocean incineration are given in Table 4.1. It is significant to note that not only do the wastes increase threefold from 1977 to 1989, but that the 1983 yearly figure for oganochlorine wastes (6.06 $\times$ 10^5 t) is almost 14 times greater than the

Table 4.1.   Estimates of U.S. Organic Chemical and Organic Waste Production, 1977–1989[a]

Substance	Quantity Produced (10^5 t)		
	1977	1983[b]	1989[b]
Total organic chemical production	934	1440	2010
Total organic waste	23	42.5	63.5
Total organochlorine production	133	205	287
Total organochlorine waste	3.28	6.06	9.07

[a]Source: U.S. Department of State and EPA (1979).
[b]Projected.

total wastes incinerated at sea by the United States to date (Shell Chemical Company wastes in 1974–1975 and 1977, and Herbicide Orange in 1977). Thus, if ocean incineration is to play a significant role in the disposal of organic and organochlorine wastes produced in the United States, the frequency of incineration and hence the amount of incineration emissions entering the marine environment will increase dramatically. This potential increase raises two questions in regard to monitoring effects. First, since initial monitoring efforts have not shown significant short-term effects on the marine environment at the incineration site, does it follow that, although the rate of emissions will remain unchanged, an increase in the duration of emissions (increasing the number of burns per year) will similarly be without significant adverse effects on the marine environment? Second, considering the nature of contaminant introduction to the environment (low-level, widely dispersed, and over a relatively long period) and the nature of the receiving environment (low productivity, extremely deep), do traditional methods of monitoring effects stand a reasonable chance of elucidating causal relationships resultant from at-sea incineration?

4.2. PREVIOUS RESEARCH RESULTS

The toxic chemical wastes suitable for ocean incineration produce emissions consisting primarily of acid (usually HCl), carbon dioxide, and water when subject to high-temperature incineration. Shipboard incinerators are designed to oxidize >99.9% of the waste material. Thus, unburned wastes are introduced into the environment at very low concentrations. From analyses of data collected during the incineration of organochlorine wastes at the Gulf of Mexico incineration site, Wastler et al. (1975) concluded that constituents of the airborne emissions which may pose a potential threat to the marine environment are limited to HCl, the major component of the incineration plume; any organochlorines not destroyed during incineration, where combustion efficiency is >99.9%; and heavy metals, which are present in the waste in trace concentrations. Thus, for at-sea incineration in a generic sense, potentially adverse ecological impacts may arise from the introduction of acid into the atmosphere and subsequently onto the ocean surface, and the introduction of unburned contaminants (organohalogens and heavy metals) into the ocean, with possible direct effect on organisms or introduction into the food web.

The waste composition and incineration products for the organochlorine wastes incinerated in the Gulf of Mexico and the results of the research efforts provide the initial data base from which future decisions regarding at-sea incineration can be made. The major components and elemental analysis of the wastes which were incinerated during two research burns in 1974 are presented in Table 4.2. Based on a tank capacity of 3503 m^3 and a waste density of 1.3 g cm^{-3}, the mass of the waste components per shipload was calculated. Using the nominal 99.9% combustion efficiency, the minimum required in the permit for this waste, residual amounts of contaminants which may affect the ocean can be calculated. Actual measured combustion efficiencies were found to range between 99.92 and 99.98% (Badley et

Table 4.2.   Composition of Organic Chloride Wastes Incinerated in the Gulf of Mexico in 1974[a]

	Research Burn 1		Research Burn 2	
Component	Composition (% by wt)	Shipload (t)	Composition (% by wt)	Shipload (t)
Major				
1,2,3-trichloropropane	23	1230	28	1280
tetrachloropropyl ether	6	270	6	270
1,2-dichloroethane	11	500	10	460
1,1,2-trichloroethane	13	592	13	592
dichlorobutanes and heavier	11	500	10	460
dichloropropenes and lighter	9	910	22	1000
allyl chloride	3	140	3	140
dichlorohydrins	9	410	8	360
Elemental				
carbon	29	1320	29.3	1330
hydrogen	4	180	4.1	190
oxygen	4	180	3.7	170
chlorine	63	2870	63.5	2890
Metal	$(mg\ kg^{-1})$	(kg)	$(mg\ kg^{-1})$	(kg)
copper	0.51	2.32	1.1	5.01
chromium	0.33	1.50	0.1	0.45
nickel	0.25	1.14	0.3	1.36
zinc	0.14	0.64	0.3	1.36
lead	0.05	0.23	0.06	0.27
cadmium	0.0014	0.006	0.001	0.005
arsenic	<0.01	<0.045	<0.01	<0.045
mercury	<0.001	<0.005	<0.002	<0.009
Density	$1.30\,(g\,cm^{-3})$		$1.29\,(g\,cm^{-3})$	

[a]Adapted from Badley et al. (1975). Each research burn totaled 4200 t.

al., 1975). For 1,2,3-trichloropropane, the waste component in greatest abundance, an average of 1.25×10^3 kg per shipload remains uncombusted. With combustion consuming 25 t of waste per hour, the time required to burn a shipload, and hence to disperse this 1.25×10^3 kg of trichloropropane, is approximately 8 d. During this time the contaminants are dispersed locally through the atmosphere before coming into contact with the ocean surface. Thus, at the point of contact with the ocean, the contaminants have undergone tremendous dilution.

Organochlorine concentrations of water samples collected where the plume impacts the sea surface and from control areas were measured during the first research burn by gas chromatography-mass spectrometry. Concentrations in both areas were indistinguishable, being below the limit of detection (TerEco Corporation, 1974, 1975; U.S. EPA, 1974).

In the case of metals, which are not destroyed by combustion, the input per shipload would be extremely low (Table 4.2.). Ranging from grams to kilograms of metals per shipload, the metal input constitutes on the order of 0.1% of the current metal input to Deepwater Dumpsite-106 off New York (Bisagni et al., 1977).

On the first and second research burns, concentrations of metals contained in the waste were measured in water samples from fallout and control areas. Although random variation in concentration was observed, no significant differences were detected between samples from affected and control areas (U.S. EPA, 1974; TerEco Corporation, 1975).

The acid generated during incineration may also be considered a contaminant. Again the organochlorine waste incinerated in the Gulf of Mexico will serve as the example. Stoichiometric calculations for these wastes, which contain 63% chlorine, show that 4700 g of HCl per second would be introduced into the atmosphere if waste was burned at a rate of 25 t h^{-1} (Shain, 1974; U.S. EPA, 1974). Field monitoring of the emissions showed that downwind sea level concentrations of HCl were generally in the range of 1–2 μg g^{-1}, and that a lens of maximum atmospheric concentration (1–5 μg g^{-1}) was located approximately 400–500 m downwind of the incineration vessel at an altitude of 120–250 m (U.S. EPA, 1976). The U.S. Department of Labor standard allows 8 h d^{-1} exposure to 5 μg g^{-1} HCl (Mattern, 1975); the odor detection limit is 1 μg g^{-1}.

During periods of light precipitation the addition of this acid to the sea surface would be the greatest. For comparison with existing practice, consider the acid-waste site located in the Atlantic Ocean, about 72 km southeast of Delaware Bay. Acid wastes (3.8 $\times$ 10^3 m^3 h^{-1}) are discharged directly from a barge over an 11–15 km stretch. The waste was reported to have a pH of 0.01 or less (Champ, 1973). The permit had allowed for the discharge of 7.57 $\times$ 10^4 m^3 per month. For convenience in calculation assume the pH to be 0.0, or 1 mole of acid per liter. Each barge load of acid waste contained 3.8 $\times$ 10^6 moles of acid, which was discharged in 1 h. For incineration producing 4700 g of HCl s^{-1}, 85 $\times$ 10^6 moles of acid are produced per shipload (4.6 $\times$ 10^5 moles of HCl h^{-1}). With an effective wind velocity of 5 m s^{-1} across the incinerator stacks, the ocean surface fallout area would be 22 $\times$ 10^6 m^2 during each hour of incineration (U.S. EPA, 1976). Contrast this to the 7.4 $\times$ 10^5 m^2 site into which the acid wastes were dumped during 1968–1977.

Field studies have shown local perturbations in the pH of seawater following acid-waste discharges, but that neutralization occurs 1–4 h after discharge. Even with this measurable change in pH, no substantial changes in the marine life of the area were detected (Champ, 1973). Extensive field monitoring of waste burns in the Gulf of Mexico have not detected any change in pH, alkalinity, or chlorinity of surface waters directly in the fallout plume (TerEco Corporation, 1974, 1975). Thus, the effects of the acid from incineration on seawater and marine life are negligible in comparison to acid wastes, and in fact have been undetectable in the field.

Biological indicators examined during the research burns of Shell organochlorines included phytoplankton species and abundance counts, chlorophyll a biomass determinations, planktonic adenosine triphosphate (ATP) determinations, and zooplankton species and abundance counts (TerEco Corporation, 1974, 1975; U.S. EPA, 1974). None of these indicators demonstrated a difference between affected and control areas. It was noted, however, that the very low values for plankton counts, ATP, and chlorophyll tended to obfuscate possible differences which might have been more readily discerned in more abundantly populated areas.

Phytoplankton and zooplankton tows for bioaccumulation analyses were also made in affected and control areas. Phytoplankton samples collected in this manner exhibited organochlorine concentrations of 3 μg g^{-1} (the detection limit for the sample size provided). No differences were noted between control and affected area samples (TerEco Corporation, 1975). Similarly, no differences were noted in copper or zinc concentrations in the phytoplankton from the two areas. It should be noted, however, that these phytoplankton and zooplankton samples were collected during the initial period of combustion during the second research burn.

Zooplankton samples were examined for organochlorine concentration in two phases. The solid phase showed no difference in concentration between affected and control areas. The liquid phase exhibited variable concentrations ranging from 0.2 to 2 μg g^{-1}. Control area concentrations were not consistently lower than those from affected areas, and the wide variability was attributed to the inevitable, but variable, presence of tar balls in the samples (Wastler et al., 1975).

4.3. MONITORING NEEDS AND FUTURE INCINERATION

Impacts on the marine environment that result from the incineration of many types of organohalogen wastes can be estimated by drawing upon extensive studies of the disposal site and surrounding environs, and intensive monitoring during incinerations of similar substances at other incineration sites. In many cases such comparisons indicate that elaborate site monitoring plans involving intensive sampling of the site and surrounding environs are not only unnecessary, but in practice they hold little chance for discerning causal relationships. Such is the case for a waste material recently considered for ocean incineration. The waste is 9.5×10^5 liters of DDT, which is to be disposed of by the Defense Property Disposal Service of the U.S. Department of Defense (Defense Logistics Agency, 1980). Many parallels can be drawn from the Shell organochlorine wastes incinerated in 1974 and 1977 and the DDT stocks requiring final disposal.

The Shell wastes are similar to DDT in that both are organochlorines with a chlorine content of ~65%. However, they differ in that eight shiploads of organochlorine wastes were incinerated, whereas the DDT incineration would require only $\frac{1}{4}$ shipload. Furthermore, the organochlorine wastes were 100% organochlorines, but the DDT waste is only about 18% DDT in a kerosene base. Thus, the concentration and total amount of the component of greatest concern is far less for the proposed incineration of DDT.

For the incineration of DDT in a kerosene solvent, emission constituents which may be of concern in the marine environment are HCl (hydrogen chloride exhausted from the stacks which, combined with water, forms hydrochloric acid) and any DDT not destroyed during incineration. The two emission products vary significantly from each other in their rates of formation and their subsequent effect on the environment. Hydrogen chloride is emitted at approximately 1040 kg h^{-1}, whereas unburned DDT is estimated in the worst case to be only 1.8 kg h^{-1}.

At a feed rate of 10 t h^{-1} of 18% DDT in kerosene with 150% excess air, 1040 kg h^{-1} (2.90 kg s^{-1}) HCl will be emitted. By contrast, stoichiometric calculations for the organochlorine waste previously burned in the Gulf of Mexico estimated that 4.7 and 3.8 kg s^{-1} of HCl would be emitted at feed rates of 25 and 20 t h^{-1}, respectively, for that waste (U.S. EPA, 1976). Aerial monitoring of these emissions demonstrated the lens of maximum atmospheric concentration of HCl (1–5 μg g^{-1}) to be at elevations of 120–250 m above sea surface at a downwind distance of 400–500 m. Sea surface monitoring showed the downwind HCl concentrations on the order of 1–2 ppm, with a one-time maximum of 7.3 ppm (U.S. EPA, 1976).

Monitoring of surface seawater pH and chlorinity was conducted for the organochlorine waste incinerations (HCl emissions of 3800–4700 g s^{-1}). No significant change in pH or chlorinity was observed between upwind and downwind (exposed to plume) areas (U.S. EPA, 1976). Thus, by comparison of HCl emission rates for DDT incineration with those for previously burned organochlorines, no effect on the atmosphere or seawater could reasonably be expected due to HCl emissions.

The amount of unburned DDT is a function of the destruction efficiency of incineration, and the rate of DDT emissions depends both on the destruction efficiency and the rate of feed into the incinerators. Destruction efficiencies >99.99% have been measured for DDT at temperatures of 1000°C and higher (Carnes and Oberacher, 1976). Moreover, *Vulcanus I* operators state that destruction efficiencies >99.99% can easily be met. Permit requirements for previous ocean incinerations have specified a minimum destruction efficiency of 99.9%.

Although the *Vulcanus I* has the capacity for a feed rate of 25 t h^{-1}, operators have indicated that because of the high energy content of the DDT–kerosene mixture a feed rate of approximately 10 t h^{-1} would be sufficient to sustain the temperature required for 99.99% destruction. Higher feed rates would result in excessively high temperatures, which would damage the incinerators. The conditions for estimating DDT emissions to the environment are summarized in Table 4.3.

From the foregoing calculations and conditions it is estimated that 17 kg (probable case) to 170 kg (worst case) of DDT will be released to the environment at the incineration site. The fate and effects of this DDT cannot be precisely defined because of the variability of the controlling factors such as atmospheric dispersion and transport, flux of DDT from the air to the sea, mixing and dilution in seawater, and the rate of scavenging of DDT by particulates in the ocean. In lieu of such an

**Table 4.3.   Estimated Incineration Conditions for
At-Sea Incineration of Surplus DDT in a Kerosene Base**

Mixture of DDT and kerosene	9.5×10^5 liter; 8.4×10^5 kg
Total DDT	1.5×10^5 kg
Feed rate	10 t h^{-1} (1.8 t h^{-1} for DDT)
Destrucion efficiency	99.99% (worst case, 99.9%)
DDT emission	0.18 kg h^{-1} (worst case, 1.8 kg h^{-1})
Time required for incineration	84 h

approximation it seems appropriate to consider various worst-case scenarios concerning the input of the residual DDT into the marine environment. Similarly, the input of DDT into the atmosphere can be evaluated by comparison to past applications of DDT.

As a worst-case scenario, consider that all of the DDT emissions are transferred to the seawater via exchange at the surface or through scavenging by rainfall, and for the purpose of calculation assume that the DDT is confined to the boundaries of the incineration site. The incineration site has an area of 49 km^2. Expected DDT concentrations in the water column resultant from the worst and probable destruction efficiencies for three assumed mixing depths are shown in Table 4.4.

Even with these most environmentally conservative assumptions (no mixing outside site boundaries and all emissions absorbed in the sea) the most probable resultant concentration in the short term, 0.35–3.5 ng liter $^{-1}$, is quite low. The average DDT concentration for Gulf of Mexico waters (based on 34 samples) is estimated to be 0.6 ng liter^{-1} (Giam et al., 1976). Thus, the theoretical increase anticipated for the Gulf of Mexico incineration site only ranges from approximately 0.5 to 6 times the estimated ambient concentration. If further mixing beyond the site boundary and a less than 100% transfer to the sea are acknowledged, then the increase in DDT over ambient levels becomes negligible.

**Table 4.4.   Expected Maximum DDT
Concentrations in Surface Waters as a
Result of At-Sea Incineration of DDT**

	DDT Concentration (10^{-9} g liter^{-1})	
Depth (m)	Probable Case[a]	Worst Case[b]
1[c]	3.5	35
10[c]	0.35	3.5
75[c,d]	0.047	0.47

[a]The DDT destruction efficiency is assumed to be 99.99%.
[b]The DDT destruction efficiency is assumed to be 99.9%.
[c]Uniform mixing from the sea surface to the depth given is assumed.
[d]Approximate depth of the surface mixed layer in the Gulf of Mexico.

To further elucidate the magnitude of this DDT input into the Gulf of Mexico waters, two other sources are considered: annual flux from the Mississippi River and from the atmosphere. It is estimated that the Mississippi River (DDT concentration of 0.5 ng liter^{-1}) contributes 1.2×10^3 kg of DDT to the Gulf of Mexico each year. Similarly, the atmospheric concentration (1.7 ng m^{-3}) contributes 1.5×10^3 kg y^{-1} through rainfall (Atlas, 1979). River and rainfall annual contributions being approximately equal are each 8 times greater than the worst-case input at 99.9% destruction efficiency and 80 times greater than the probable input at 99.99% destruction efficiency.

With such a high atmospheric flux relative to the incineration emissions, one might expect that, were the emissions to remain in the atmosphere, the incineration would not have a measurable effect on the atmospheric burden of DDT. For the calculation of ambient atmospheric DDT burden, 0.04 ng m^{-3} is used as the mean concentration for the Gulf of Mexico (Giam et al., 1976). For the column of air over the incineration site (4.9×10^9 m^2) the height of the troposphere is assumed to be 6.5 km. Thus, the ambient DDT burden in the atmosphere over the incineration site is calculated to be 1.3 kg of DDT. Calculation of the same parameter for the entire Gulf of Mexico (1.6×10^6 km^2) shows an atmospheric burden of 420 kg. Although the probable emission (17 kg) is 10 times greater than the instantaneous ambient burden, and the worst case exceeds the instantaneous ambient burden over the site by 100-fold, the whole Gulf of Mexico ambient atmospheric burden is 1.5 times the worst-case emission. While this may seem significant, it must be remembered that the flux of DDT is from the atmosphere to the sea, and that the residence time for chlorinated hydrocarbons in the atmosphere is 0.05–0.3 y (18–110 d) (Bidleman et al., 1976). Thus, although the atmospheric increase may seem relatively important in the short term, the long-term significance must be in the context of elevating the seawater concentration.

In evaluating the significance of this input of DDT to the atmosphere it is necessary to evaluate the significance of this input not only in comparison to ambient concentrations, but also in the context of prior uses. The DDT spraying during 1945–1958 by the U.S. Department of Agriculture amounted to 4.3×10^6 kg. As late as 1974, $>4.5 \times 10^4$ kg of DDT were sprayed over northwestern pine forests for tussock moth control (Orgill et al., 1974), and 1.05×10^8 kg y^{-1} are estimated to be used annually worldwide for malaria mosquito and cotton insect control (Goldberg, 1975). By comparison, the incineration emissions of 17 kg DDT for a probable case and 170 kg DDT for the worst case seem negligible.

Thus, the introduction of DDT residues into the environment would not be expected to result in a measurable increase in DDT concentrations beyond the very short term. The expected addition of DDT ($\sim$0.18 kg h^{-1}) represents only about 50% of the DDT estimated to be present in Gulf of Mexico waters equal in area to the incineration site and extending to a depth of 10 m. Dilution, both through vertical and horizontal mixing, will rapidly return locally elevated DDT concentrations to ambient levels. The input of DDT to this area of low productivity is also small in comparison to other DDT inputs to the Gulf. The DDT inputs from the Mississippi River and rainfall each are 8 times greater per year than the one-time, worst-case input of DDT from the proposed incineration (assuming only a 99.9% destruction efficiency producing a total 170 kg DDT). With respect to probable emissions (99.99% destruction efficiency) these other sources each exceed the incineration input by 80-fold. Thus, the DDT emissions resultant from the at-sea incineration of these liquid DDT stocks may be considered as a negligible input into the Gulf of Mexico ecosystems.

From such examination of probable contaminant input it seems readily evident that, for one-time incinerations such as that considered for restricted pesticide stocks of DDT or the herbicide Silvex® (Dow Chemical), monitoring efforts which are limited to ensuring ≥ 99.9% destruction efficiency are adequate protection for the marine environment. As we have seen, these one-time incinerations do not result in appreciable increases in pollutant loads to the marine environment. However, if ocean incineration were to be employed on a regular or continual basis for the disposal of organic wastes, the emissions to the marine environment would assume greater significance, as would the need for definitive effects monitoring. It is this need to provide more realistic information on the impacts from ocean incineration which should be addressed in future monitoring efforts. Major impediments to definitive monitoring efforts may be grouped as site-related problems, those related to the nature and mode of input of the waste, and problems involving realistic indicators of impact.

4.3.1. Site-Related Problems

In the United States, ocean incineration is permitted only at designated sites which have been chosen to minimize the incineration's impact on the environment. These sites have been, and probably will continue to be, in open ocean locations at least 160 km offshore and in water depths ranging to thousands of meters. The characteristics that make these sites desirable from the standpoint of minimizing environmental impact also contribute to the difficulty of effects monitoring. The water depths and distances offshore are so large as to require sampling efforts on an oceanographic scale (as opposed to many of the monitoring efforts conducted nearshore from small boats and ships with limited overnight capacity). In addition to obvious cost factors which will affect the economy of data acquisition, the length of time required to obtain samples in these depths and over such a great area will limit the number of samples and replicates, as well as influence the degree of correlation if control and affected area comparisons are to be made.

In addition to the logistics problems, biological and chemical characteristics of the site contribute more significant obstacles. The low productivity in the water column makes characterization of the resident populations imprecise. Not only are sufficient data generally lacking for a description of biotic components found therein, but populations are characterized by high variability in abundance and compositional characteristics. The presence or absence of rare or occasional species has a much more pronounced effect on the perceived population character in areas of low productivity or low biomass. In areas where populations are characterized by few numbers and low biomass, the difficulty in discerning natural spatial and temporal variations from those induced by anthropogenic effects is very great.

Food webs in the open ocean are often characterized by considerable spatial separation. Bioaccumulation studies in the field are fraught with enough difficulty and ambiguity without adding further uncertainty arising from trophic levels separated by hundreds of meters vertically and hundreds of kilometers laterally.

Finally, the absence of a nonmotile or sedentary biological community at the affected site remains a large obstacle to implementation of traditional effects monitoring efforts. Compositional changes in the benthic populations have most often been utilized in effects monitoring in shallow waters or where the contaminants or their effects were known to reach the seafloor (for example, New York or Philadelphia's sewage sludge sites, or any of the dredged material disposal sites). With water depths of more than 1000 m at ocean incineration sites, a direct effect from the airborne emissions on the benthos at or even surrounding the site seems implausible. Thus, with the benthos so far removed physically from the incineration contaminant inputs, and without a sessile or sedentary biological population within immediate range of the incineration products, monitoring efforts attempting to elucidate impact through compositional changes in the biota appear futile.

4.3.2. Nature and Mode of Contaminant Input

The contaminants from a single burn, either combustion by-products or residual uncombusted waste, are minimal when taken in the context of amounts of similar wastes disposed of, or occurring through indirect processes, in the ocean. However, continual ocean incineration would result in significant contaminant input. What distinguishes ocean incineration waste products from a monitoring perspective is the fact that they are introduced to the marine environment at a low rate and over a very large area. For example, from proposed DDT incineration 1040 kg of HCl per hour and 0.18 kg of DDT per hour would be emitted to the atmosphere during a burn. However, unlike direct ocean disposal, these contaminants would be dispersed over a large area before contact with the sea surface. If, indeed, all contaminants were transferred to the seawater immediately following emission, dispersion in the plume alone would result in their spread over an instantaneous area of ~ 3 km^2. Moreover, permit requirements stipulate that an effective windspeed of 5 m s^{-1} must be maintained over the incinerator stack, thereby greatly increasing the total area exposed to low concentration emissions (estimated to be 22×10^6 m^2 per hour of incineration). With contaminants entering the sea at such low concentrations and over such a broad area, it is extremely difficult to determine a central source of the contamination. It is also difficult to trace incineration emissions entering the seawater or to track their movements. Whereas sewage sludge and dredged material may be identified and traced by their texture, anthropogenic artifacts, or other easily recognizable features, no such tracers are inherent to the process of ocean incineration.

4.3.3. Realistic Indicators of Impact

Because of the aforementioned difficulties associated with the incineration site and emission contaminants, as well as the difficulty of simulating receiving environment conditions in the laboratory, it seems unlikely that answers to the question of ocean incineration fate and effects will be forthcoming through traditional methods of field study. As a step toward providing a means for measuring effects of ocean incineration on the biota of the incineration site and surrounding environs, the EPA sponsored a program of study to develop a method and indicators for effects monitoring at ocean incineration sites (TerEco Corporation, 1977; Pequegnat et al., 1978, 1979, 1980). These devices, called Biotal Ocean Monitors (BOMs), have since been employed in many other ocean disposal applications, including sewage sludge, dredged material, salt dome brine, and spilled oil. However, they are particularly well suited for the low-level, dispersed contamination characteristic of ocean incineration sites.

The BOM is a device for conducting *in situ* bioassays at the incineration site and simultaneously at an unaffected control area. What makes the BOM unique is that actual conditions of exposure and dilution of the contaminants are incorporated into the test, and sublethal indicators of stress are used to quantify impact over a relatively short time. By conducting the test in the field, organisms are exposed to realistic concentrations and dilution rates of the waste. The use of synoptic controls allows for direct comparison with responses in unaffected areas. Sublethal indicators of stress are needed in order to gauge chronic impacts. As expected, and as demonstrated in initial monitorings, acute impacts, indicated by mortality of the organisms, are not likely to occur from ocean incineration, at least in the short term, and are less likely to be documented.

The use of sublethal indicators for detection of chronic stress has been restricted in these studies to histopathological abberations, inhibition or activation of certain enzyme systems, and the adenylate energy charge. These studies with the BOM examined the response of several enzyme systems (ATPase, catalase, and cytochrome P-420 and P-450) in a number of marine organisms (*Fundulus grandis, Mytilus edulis, Mercenaria mercenaria, Crassostrea virginica,* and *Penaeus setiferus*) to a variety of pollutant types (ocean incineration, dredged material, sewage sludge, brine discharge, and spilled oil). Adenylate energy charge ratio has also been measured in a number of those species and in *Palaemonetes pugio* and *Mydisopsis bahia.* Body burdens (bioaccumulation) of heavy metals, hydrocarbons, chlorinated hydrocarbons, and PCBs have also been measured in the same organisms for which the chronic stress indicators had been measured. The BOM information is given in TerEco Corporation (1977, 1979, 1980), Pequegnat et al. (1978, 1979, 1980), and Pequegnat and Wastler (1980).

Many other physiological indicators may be appropriate for use in the BOMs; however, consideration should be given to those factors which are of essence to incineration effects monitoring. The indicator should be responsive to the approximate concentration of contaminants and duration of exposure which would be encountered in the field. This causal relationship should be established and quantified through laboratory testing prior to application of the techniques in the field. The organisms employed should be representative or typical of those encountered at the incineration site. A case may be made for incorporating a standard organism in the field tests for use in comparison to other wastes, sites, and impacts, but conducting field bioassays exclusively with organisms foreign to the incineration site lends little to the realism of the test or to the understanding of actual incineration effects. Finally, consideration should be given to the complexity of the analytical procedure. If the monitoring efforts are going to be fully valuable as a management tool, the procedures employed must be adaptable to routine analysis, and the data derived should be quantitative and readily reproducible.

4.4. CONCLUSIONS

The incineration of organic and organochloride wastes at sea has been shown to be an environmentally sound method for destruction and disposal of wastes that are difficult or unsafe to dispose of at land-based facilities. The emission of contaminants from the incineration process on a one-time basis has been shown to have no long- or short-term effects on the marine environment, as long as destruction efficiencies $\geq 99.9\%$ are attained. Monitoring efforts in response to a significant increase in ocean incineration activity should consider the limitations on monitoring imposed by the incineration site characteristics and the nature of waste introduction. Field confirmation of cause-and-effect relationships, established through laboratory testing utilizing a number of sublethal indicators of chronic stress, is a possible means for impact elucidation, both on a short-term and cumulative basis. The Biotal Ocean Monitor (BOM) system is proposed as a first step in that direction.

ACKNOWLEDGMENTS

Through contractual support to a number of projects, several agencies and groups have contributed to the research efforts which helped formulate the ideas and thoughts expressed in this chapter: the U.S. Environmental Protection Agency (Contract Nos. 74-202-10, 68-01-2893, 68-01-2829, and 68-01-4797), Shell Chemical Company (Houston, Texas), Defense Logistics Agency of the Defense Property Disposal Service (Battle Creek, Michigan), U.S. Army Corps of Engineers, New York District, and Waterways Experiment Station (Vicksburg, Mississippi). Colleagues at TerEco Corporation, with whom initial ocean incineration monitoring concepts and practice began, also deserve special recognition for their contributions; specifically, W. E. Pequegnat, E. A. Kennedy, B. M. James, G. Duthu, and A. D. Fredericks.

REFERENCES

Ackerman, D. G., H. J. Fisher, R. J. Johnson, R. F. Maddalone, B. J. Matthews, E. L. Moon, K. H. Scheyer, C. C. Shih, and R. F. Robias. 1978. At Sea Incineration of Herbicide Orange Onboard the *M/T Vulcanus*. Environmental Protection Technology Series Report EPA 600/2-78-086, U.S. Environmental Protection Agency, Washington, D.C., 263 pp.

Atlas, E. L. 1979. Synthetic organics in the Gulf of Mexico—a review. *In:* NOAA Workshop on the Gulf of Mexico (1–5 October), Miami, Florida. U.S. National Oceanic and Atmospheric Administration, Miami, Florida, unpaginated.

Badley, J. H., A. Telfer, and E. M. Fredricks. 1975. At-Sea Incineration of Shell Chemical Organic Chloride Waste, Stack Monitoring Aboard the *M/T Vulcanus*. Technical Progress Report BRC-CORP 13-75-F, Shell Development, Bellaire Research Center, Houston, Texas, 38 pp. plus appendixes.

Bidleman, T. F., C. P. Rice, and C. E. Olney. 1976. High molecular weight chlorinated hydrocarbons in the air and sea: Rates and mechanisms of air/sea transfer. *In:* Marine Pollutant Transfer, H. L. Windom and R. A. Duce (Eds.). Lexington Books, Lexington, Massachusetts, pp. 323–351.

Bisagni, J. J., S. W. Congdon, and K. A. Hausknecht. 1977. A summary of the input of industrial waste chemicals at Deepwater Dumpsite 106 during 1974 and 1975. *In:* Baseline Report of Environmental Conditions in Deepwater Dumpsite 106, Vol. 3. NOAA Dumpsite Evaluation Report 77-1, U.S. National Oceanic and Atmospheric Administration, Rockville, Maryland, pp. 487–497.

Carnes, R. A., and D. A. Oberacher. 1976. Pesticide incineration. News of Environmental Research in Cincinnati Office of Research and Development, U.S. Environmental Protection Agency, Washington, D.C., 4 pp.

Champ, M. A. 1973. Operation SAMS: Sludge Acid Monitoring Survey. CERES Program Publication No. 1, Center for Earth Resources and Environmental Studies, The American University, Washington, D.C., 169 pp.

Clausen, J. F., H. J. Fisher, R. J. Johnson, E. L. Moon, C. C. Shih, R. F. Tobias, and C. A. Zee. 1977. At Sea Incineration of Organochlorine Wastes Onboard the *M/T Vulcanus*. Technical Series Report EPA-600/2-77-196, U.S. Environmental Protection Agency, Washington, D.C., 88 pp.

Defense Logistics Agency, Defense Property Disposal Service. 1980. Draft Environmental Impact Statement for the Safe Collection, Transportation, and Final Disposal of U.S. Department of Defense Stocks of DDT. Defense Logistics Agency, Defense Property Disposal Service, Battle Creek, Michigan, 177 pp. plus appendices.

Giam, C. S., H. S. Chan, and G. S. Neff. 1976. Concentration and fluxes of phthalates, DDTs, and PCBs to the Gulf of Mexico. *In:* Marine Pollutant Transfer, H. L. Windom and R. A. Duce, (Eds.). Lexington Books, Lexington, Massachusetts, pp. 375–386.

Goldberg, E. D. 1975. Synthetic organohalides in the sea. *Proceedings of the Royal Society of London,* **189**(B), 277–289.

Inter-Governmental Maritime Consultative Organization (IMCO). 1976. Inter-Governmental Conference on the Convention on the Dumping of Waste at Sea (London, 30 October–13 November 1971). Final Act of the Conference and Convention on the Prevention of Marine Pollution by Dumping of Wastes and Other Matter. (Publication No.

76.14E), Inter-Governmental Maritime Consultative Organization, London, 36 pp. plus amendments, 6 pp.

Mattern, R. V. 1975. Shell Chemical Company—Application for a Special Permit for Ocean Incineration, 23 April 1975. Regional Administrator, U.S. Environmental Protection Agency Region VI, Dallas, Texas, unpaginated.

Orgill, M. M., M. R. Peterson, and G. A. Setinel. 1974. Some initial measurements of DDT resuspension and translocation from Pacific Northwest forests. BNWL-SA-5126, Battelle Pacific Northwest Laboratories, Richland, Washington, 30 pp.

Pequegnat, W. E., and T. A. Wastler. 1980. Field bioassays for early detection of chronic impact of chemical wastes upon marine organisms. *Helgölander Meeresuntersuchungen*, **33**, 531–545.

Pequegnat, W. E., B. M. James, E. A. Kennedy, A. D. Fredericks, and R. R. Fay. 1978. Development and Application of Biotal Ocean Monitor Systems to Studies of the Impacts of Ocean Dumping. Contracts 68-01-2893 and 68-01-4797, Technical Report to U.S. Environmental Protection Agency, Washington, D.C., 143 pp.

Pequegnat, W. E., B. M. James, E. A. Kennedy, A. D. Fredericks, R. R. Fay, and F. G. Hubbard. 1979. Application of the Biotal Ocean Monitor System to a Preliminary Study of the Impacts of Ocean Dumping of Dredged Material in the New York Bight. Contract No. 68-01-4797, Technical Report to U.S. Army Engineer Waterways Experiment Station, Vicksburg, Mississippi, 76 pp.

Pequegnat, W. E., R. R. Fay, and T. A. Wastler. 1980. Combined field–laboratory method for chronic impact detection in marine organisms and its application to dredged material disposal. *In:* Estuarine and Wetland Processes, P. Hamilton and K. B. MacDonald (Eds.). Plenum Press, New York, pp. 631–648.

Shain, S. A. 1974. Public Statement at U.S. Environmental Protection Agency Public Hearing, 4 October 1974, Houston, Texas.

TerEco Corporation. 1974. A Field Monitoring Study of the Effects of Organic Chloride Waste Incineration on the Marine Environment in the Northern Gulf of Mexico. Report submitted to Shell Chemical Company, Houston, Texas. TerEco Corporation, College Station, Texas, 50 pp.

TerEco Corporation. 1975. Sea-Level Monitoring of the Incineration of Organic Chloride Waste by *M/T Vulcanus* in the Northern Gulf of Mexico. Contract 68-01-2829, U.S. Environmental Protection Agency, Washington, D.C., 39 pp.

TerEco Corporation. 1977. A Report on the Philadelphia Dumpsite and Shell Incineration Monitorings, for Public Law 92-532, Marine Protection, Research, and Sanctuaries Act of 1972. Report to the Marine Protection Branch, U.S. Environmental Protection Agency, Washington, D.C., 60 pp.

TerEco Corporation. 1979. Design, Fabrication, and Testing of Biotal Ocean Monitors for *in situ* Determination of Pollution Impacts. Technical Report to Marine Protection Branch, U.S. Environmental Protection Agency, Washington, D.C., 85 pp.

TerEco Corporation. 1980. Application of the Biotal Ocean Monitor System to a Study of the Impacts of Ocean Dumping of Dredged Material in the New York Bight. Technical Report to New York District Corps of Engineers, 94 pp.

U.S. Congress. 1972. Marine Protection, Research, and Sanctuaries Act of 1972. Public Law 92-532, 86 Stat. 1052, Washington, D.C.

U.S. Department of State and U.S. Environmental Protection Agency. 1979. Final Environmental Impact Statement for the Incineration of Wastes at Sea under the 1972 Ocean Dumping Convention. U.S. Department of State and U.S. Environmental Protection Agency, Washington, D.C., 176 pp.

U.S. Environmental Protection Agency (EPA). 1974. Preliminary Technical Report on Incineration of Organochlorine Wastes in the Gulf of Mexico. Oil and Special Materials Control Division, U.S. Environmental Protection Agency, Washington, D.C., 225 pp.

U.S. EPA. 1976. Designation of a Site in the Gulf of Mexico for Incineration of Chemical Wastes. Final Environmental Impact Statement. U.S. Environmental Protection Agency, Washington, D.C., 97 pp.

Wastler, T. A., C. K. Offutt, C. K. Fitzsimmons, and P. E. Des Rosiers. 1975. Disposal of Organochlorine Wastes by Incineration at Sea. EPA-430/9-75-014, Division of Oil and Special Materials Control, Office of Water and Hazardous Materials, U.S. Environmental Protection Agency, Washington, D.C., 227 pp.

5

METHODS TO DETERMINE HYDROGEN CHLORIDE IN INCINERATION SHIP PLUMES

Claus Weitkamp

Institut für Physik
GKSS-Forschungszentrum GmbH
Geesthacht, Federal Republic of Germany

Abstract   **92**

5.1. Introduction   **92**

5.2. Purpose of Measurements of HCl in the Marine Atmosphere   **93**

5.3. Methods for Determination of HCl *In-Situ*   **97**

    5.3.1. Gas Scrubbing and Cl⁻ Assay with Mercury Nitrate and
            Diphenylcarbazone   97
    5.3.2. Derivative Spectroscopy with a Diode Laser   97
    5.3.3. Derivatization with Gas Chromatography   99

**5.4. Remote Assay of HCl with a Differential Absorption and
Scattering Lidar**   **99**

    5.4.1. Principle of Operation   99
    5.4.2. Apparatus   101

5.5. Performance Data   **103**

    5.5.1. Local Measurement Systems   103
    5.5.2. Lidar Performance   104

5.6. Results and Discussion   **105**

**5.7. MODIS: A Mathematical Model for the Propagation of Air
Pollutants**   **107**

5.7.1. Description of the Model   108
5.7.2. Performance and Results   109

5.8. Summary   **111**

Acknowledgments   **112**

References   **113**

ABSTRACT

Three methods of *in situ* measurement and a lidar system for the remote detection
of HCl in the plume of incineration ships are described. Filtering and scrubbing
the sample air through distilled water with subsequent analysis for Cl^- ions with
$Hg(NO_3)_2$ and diphenylcarbazone, and derivative formation of HCl from the samples with 7-oxabicyclo-(4,1,0)-heptane followed by gas chromatography of the reaction product (which was not used in the present investigation) are both off-line
methods, whereas derivative spectroscopy with a diode laser is a direct-reading or
on-line method of HCl assay. The remote detection system is an infrared differential absorption and scattering lidar using the $P_2(3)$ and $P_2(5)$ lines from a DF
laser. Results obtained include a slow decrease of the HCl concentration by diffusion, an HCl lifetime on the order of 1 h, negligible ($<5\%$) attachment of the
gaseous HCl to aerosols, and very rapid washout of the gas by rain. Also described
is a mathematical model for the simulation of air pollution propagation that relies
on the integration of the transport equations for the moments of the concentration
with respect to a horizontal line transverse to the main wind direction, rather than
the concentrations themselves. The code MODIS appears to have all properties
necessary for the description of the HCl concentration in the plume of incineration
ships.

5.1. INTRODUCTION

Chlorinated hydrocarbons are used extensively in a great variety of chemical, physical, and other industrial processes. A considerable amount of these substances is
residue from the production of industrial chemical products or is used as a solvent
that cannot be recycled economically for further use. Quantities on the order of
100,000 t of organochloride waste are produced annually in each of the major west
and central European countries.

Only a small part of this waste is in solid form and amenable to disposal in decommissioned salt mines or other underground sites. Most of the waste is in the liquid state and is usually not allowed in this kind of waste dumpsite because of the danger of leakage from containers and evaporation and formation of flammable or explosive gas mixtures. Deep-well disposal, the pumping of the liquid into porous rock formations 700–900 m underground, is an expensive procedure, and the discussion about the environmental effects of this means of disposal is not closed. Some of the compounds are known to produce mutations, birth defects, cancer, and various acute toxic effects in animals and humans, and the environmentally safe disposal of this type of waste continues to pose considerable problems.

The method of chlorinated hydrocarbon disposal having minimal known effects on the biosphere is destruction by incineration. The combustion gases contain large quantities of water vapor and CO_2 (normally not considered pollutants), little SO_2, and very little NO, NO_2, and CO (Clausen et al., 1977). But practically all of the original chlorine is converted to hydrogen chloride, which with water forms hydrochloric acid. Airborne HCl produces irritation of the eyes and respiratory tract in animals and humans in concentrations > 5 μl liter^{-1}, and severe corrosion of buildings and weather-exposed metal structures (such as automobiles) even at small concentrations. Land-based incinerators that are likely to produce HCl are therefore equipped with scrubbers that remove the HCl from the incineration gases. Because of its high chlorine content, however, organochlorine waste cannot be treated economically by this technique. On the other hand, no harmful effects have been observed if HCl in the concentrations that occur in waste incineration is added to seawater (Paige et al., 1978). The relatively large concentrations of bicarbonate and carbonate ions in seawater provide an effective buffer for additions of HCl.

5.2. PURPOSE OF MEASUREMENTS OF HCl IN THE MARINE ATMOSPHERE

Large-scale incineration of organochlorine waste started in 1969 on board the *M/T Matthias I* (Wulf, 1972). The annual amount of incinerated material was 4000 t. Five additional ships were subsequently commissioned for waste incineration, and three of these (*M/T Vulcanus I, M/T Vulcanus II,* and *M/T Vesta*) are still in operation. Annual incineration rates gradually increased to about 100,000 t in 1974 (Fabian, 1979) and have remained at this level.

Incineration took place at various sites in the Atlantic Ocean and the North Sea, and the bulk of the material was incinerated in an area 37 km off the coast of The Netherlands in the English Channel (Fig. 5.1). Although no quantitative measurements were made, actual HCl concentrations in Dutch cities seem to have occasionally been considerably higher than predicted (Weikard, 1978). In 1979 this incineration area was closed and a new area located farther north, near Dogger Bank, about half-way between Helgoland (Federal Republic of Germany) and the city of Hull (United Kingdom), was approved. The new area is more than 100 km

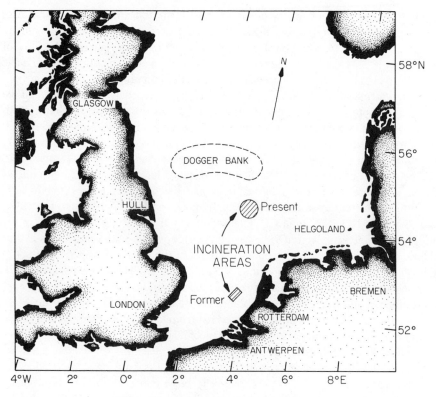

Figure 5.1.   Incineration sites in the North Sea.

from the nearest shore (Fig. 5.1). The HCl carried by the prevailing west and southwest winds does not reach any coast before at least 300 km over water, and no noticeable HCl concentrations in the onshore winds have been reported by the surrounding countries.

It takes an incineration vessel about 22 h to steam from Antwerpen, Belgium, to the new incineration area. In addition to the time and fuel consumption, the relatively large distance to the loading ports also increases the proportion of maintenance and downtime of the ships. This effort can be undertaken, if necessary, to avoid intolerably large HCl concentrations on land, but it would be preferable to avoid these large distances when weather conditions provide sufficient dispersion of the HCl. An investigation of HCl concentration in the plume under different weather conditions is needed. This could be done by accumulating a large body of experimental data to obtain statistically relevant measurements for all possible combinations of weather conditions. An alternative and probably simpler approach is to determine the parameters for the different processes responsible for the degradation of the pollutant. A relatively few measured concentration profiles could be compared with results of calculated concentration distributions obtained from the actual meteorological data via mathematical diffusion models. Even if the individual coefficients governing processes such as washout, rainout, aerosol formation, aerosol attachment, dry deposition, and chemical degradation cannot be assessed individually, it may suffice to determine certain combinations necessary for the predictive use of the diffusion models.

Both local and remote measurements are valuable for this purpose. Local measurements made in the plume at different distances downwind from the incineration ship can be useful for determining the degradation of HCl, particularly if the ratio method is used (Breeding et al., 1976). This method can be used when the source emits another substance well-mixed with the HCl, so that this substance is subject to the same diffusion coefficient α, but with a degradation coefficient negligible in comparison with the degradation coefficient of the HCl. The decrease in concentration of this inert component, c_i, is thus solely determined by diffusion, whereas the concentration decrease of the reactive species, c_r, is caused by both diffusion and degradation:

$$\frac{dc_i}{dt} = u \frac{dc_i}{dx} = -\alpha c_i \qquad\qquad 1$$

$$\frac{dc_r}{dt} = u \frac{dc_r}{dx} = -(\alpha + \beta)\, c_r \qquad\qquad 2$$

where u and x are the wind speed and distance from the source. Equations 1 and 2 are easily integrated, and the degradation coefficient β can be determined from measurements of the concentrations c_{i1}, c_{i2}, c_{r1}, c_{r2} of the inert and reactive species at distances x_1 and x_2 as

$$\beta = -\frac{u}{x_2 - x_1} \ln \frac{(c_{r2} - c_{r\infty})/(c_{r1} - c_{r\infty})}{(c_{i2} - c_{i\infty})/(c_{i1} - c_{i\infty})} \qquad\qquad 3$$

where $c_{i\infty}$ and $c_{r\infty}$ are the concentrations at infinite distance, or background concentrations. Instead of β the lifetime $\tau = 1/\beta$ or half-life $t_{1/2} = \tau \ln 2$ are sometimes used. If the mixing of the gases occurs at a well-defined height h, the product

$$v_{dep} = h\beta \qquad\qquad 4$$

which is usually given in cm s^{-1} and called deposition velocity turns out to be a useful quantity.

In practice the ratio method is not without problems because it is not easy to find a suitable reference substance. In the combustion of organochlorine waste, gases that are produced at sufficiently constant rates are CO_2 and H_2O (Clausen et al., 1977), but because of the considerable background level of both gases, unrealistically high measurement accuracies would be required. Emission rates of CO and undestroyed hydrocarbons (CH_x) are both linked to the combustion efficiency and are much less constant than the former two gases, but the main shortcoming for their use as a reference is their small concentration in the combustion gases. The occurrence of NO and NO_2 (often referred to as NO_x) is related to the combustion temperature and thus is indirectly linked to the combustion efficiency. Al-

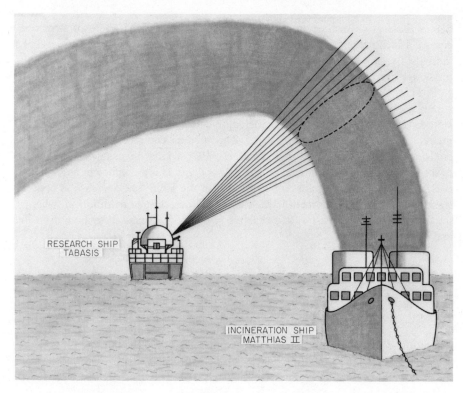

Figure 5.2.   Plume measurement on a downwind course.

though probably no more constant than that of CO or CH_x, the concentrations of nitrogen oxides are larger than that of CO and CH_x by about one order of magnitude, and NO_x appear to be the combustion gases that minimize reference gas problems.

It is evident that the remote measurements, although generally much less sensitive and requiring greater experimental effort, are able to yield three-dimensional concentration data and offer the possibility of investigating processes that cannot be inferred from sea-level measurements alone. It is thus possible to measure the extent of a combustion gas plume and to verify or determine such features as Gaussian width parameters and effective stack heights. For the more advanced models that take source and sink terms into consideration, remote measurements offer the possibility of determining some of the coefficients that describe these processes. The normal procedure will be that of taking cross sections through the plume (schematically represented in Fig. 5.2) at different distances from the incineration ship, integrating the measured concentrations over the cross sections of the plume, and deducing from the integrated concentrations the total degradation coefficient, β. Each of the components of β can itself be a function of the weather parameters. How well the individual components can be determined, how results from local and remote measurements must be combined for their determination, and whether there is a practical need for their individual assessment remains to be investigated.

5.3. METHODS FOR *IN-SITU* DETERMINATION OF HCl

Of the numerous methods of HCl determination that are given in textbooks on gas analysis and pollution detection (for example, see Sittig, 1974) very few fulfill the requirements of sensitivity and selectivity necessary for our objective. One of these methods, gas scrubbing and wet chemical analysis for Cl⁻, was adapted to our particular needs. Because of the relatively long collection time required by this technique, a faster, but less sensitive method using laser light absorption was developed. A third method developed elsewhere (Vierkorn-Rudolph et al., 1979) and based on gas chromatography also might be useful.

5.3.1. Gas Scrubbing and Cl⁻ Assay with Mercury Nitrate and Diphenylcarbazone

Sample gas is drawn through 30 ml of distilled water at a flow rate of 550 liter h^{-1} in specially designed Teflon® scrubbers (Lenhard and Schindler, 1981). The aerosols are removed from the air stream by 0.45 μm pore size Teflon membrane filters in front of the absorption flasks. The filter deposits are then dissolved in distilled water. Chlorine determination in both the filter and the gas solution is performed with acidic mercury nitrate according to the reaction

$$x_0\, Hg^{2+} + x\, Cl^- \longrightarrow \frac{x}{2}\, HgCl_2 + \left(x_0 - \frac{x}{2}\right) Hg^{2+} \qquad 5$$

The concentration of the deep-blue reaction product of diphenylcarbazone with the remaining Hg^{2+} ions allows the determination of $(x_0 - x/2)$ and, hence, the chloride ion contents, x. The Na^+ ions are measured by atomic absorption spectrophotometry. By comparison of the Cl^- and Na^+ values in the gas and filter fractions the gaseous HCl, HCl attached to aerosols, and NaCl aerosol can be determined separately.

5.3.2. Derivative Spectroscopy with a Diode Laser

If the intensity I of a laser beam that has passed through a gas volume of length l containing absorbing molecules of particle number density n and absorption cross section σ differs only little from the intensity I_0 of the incident beam, Beer's law can be written as

$$I(\nu) = I_0 e^{-nl\sigma(\nu)} \simeq I_0[1 - nl\sigma(\nu)] \qquad 6$$

By suitable choice of the spectral region, σ can be made to depend strongly on the wavelength λ or wave number $\nu = 1/\lambda$. A diode laser can be tuned to the maximum

ν_0 of an absorption line and modulated sinusoidally around ν_0 according to

$$\nu = \nu_0 + a \sin (\omega t) \qquad\qquad 7$$

Expanding equation 6 into a Taylor series around ν_0 and neglecting cubic and higher terms, we get

$$\frac{I(\nu)}{I(\nu_0)} = 1 - nl\sigma(\nu_0) - nl \frac{d\sigma}{d\nu}(\nu_0)\, a \sin (\omega t) - \frac{1}{4} nl \frac{d^2\sigma}{d\nu^2}(\nu_0)\, a^2 [1 - \cos (2\omega t)] \qquad 8$$

This means that the intensity variation of the laser beam at the modulation frequency ω is proportional to the number density n of the absorbing molecules and the derivative of the absorption cross section σ with wave number. This latter quantity goes through zero at the absorption maximum. The signal at frequency ω is therefore not suited for the measurement itself, but it can be used to advantage for stabilization of the laser frequency by regulating the diode current through a feedback loop that keeps the signal at ω equal to zero. At two times the modulation frequency, the amplitude modulation of the transmitted beam is proportional to the concentration and the second derivative of the absorption cross section; the 2ω signal is therefore a sensitive measure of the particle concentration.

The apparatus (Pokrowsky and Herrmann, 1984) is shown schematically in Fig. 5.3. The essential part is an LS3 double-beam diode laser spectrophotometer (Laser

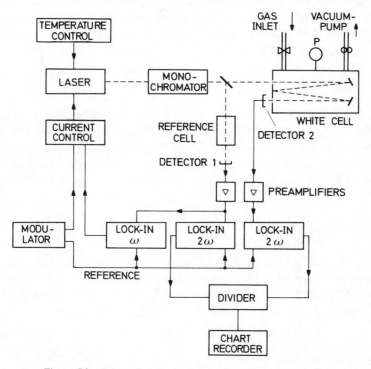

Figure 5.3.   Schematics of a diode laser derivative spectrometer.

Analytics, Bedford, Massachusetts) with 1-m White cell for the sample gas. The pressure in the sample cell is kept at 100 mbar. At this pressure the narrowing of the line width eliminates any sensitivity of the device to other gases and allows the amplitude of the laser frequency modulation to be kept small. This provision is important because a residual amplitude modulation with frequency modulation of the laser may appear like an absorption signal and limit the sensitivity of the detection scheme. A 60-mm single-pass cell filled with 1% HCl in nitrogen at 100 mbar is used as a reference. It serves simultaneously for the locking of the laser frequency to the HCl absorption line maximum and the calibration of the system from the second harmonic of the reference signal. The simple relation

$$n_s = n_r \frac{S_s I_r R_r l_r}{S_r I_s R_s l_s} \qquad\qquad 9$$

where S, I, R, and l are the second harmonic signals, beam powers incident on the detectors, detector responsivities, and optical pathlengths, respectively, is only applicable when saturation effects do not occur in the signal or in the reference channel. The former condition is usually fulfilled to good accuracy, but not the latter. A nonlinear calibration procedure, described in more detail elsewhere (Weitkamp, 1984), is therefore required.

5.3.3. Derivatization with Gas Chromatography

Derivatization with subsequent gas chromatography is a very promising method for this kind of application because of its high sensitivity (Vierkorn-Rudolph et al., 1979). The method is based on the reaction of HCl with 7-oxabicyclo-(4,1,0)-heptane and gas chromatographic separation and detection of the reaction product, 2-chlorocyclohexanol. Sample air is collected in glass tubes of 2.5 cm^3 volume; in the laboratory the HCl is washed out either directly with an acetone-7-oxabicyclo-(4,1,0)-heptane solution or with water with subsequent derivative formation and extraction of the product with trichloromethane. In the gas chromatographic step, best results have been obtained with a separation column 6 m long $\times$ 4 mm inside diameter, packed with 3–5% Carbowax 20 M (Union Carbide) on Chromosorb WHP (80/100 mesh), and a flame ionization detector. We have not employed this method in our studies to date.

5.4. REMOTE ASSAY OF HCl WITH A DIFFERENTIAL ABSORPTION AND SCATTERING LIDAR

5.4.1. Principle of Operation

If a short, powerful pulse of laser radiation is transmitted to the atmosphere, a small fraction of the light is scattered back in the direction of the transmitter and can be detected with a sensitive receiver system. The scattering is caused mainly by solid and liquid aerosol particles. The intensity of the backscattered light there-fore varies greatly with weather conditions. To compensate for this effect, a second pulse is transmitted at a slightly different wavelength. Wavelengths are chosen such that the signal wavelength λ_1 is strongly absorbed by the gas of interest, but the reference wavelength λ_0 is not (Fig. 5.4). The power received by the detector at each of the two wavelengths is a function of time or of distance x to the point of measurement, as the light travels back and forth at a velocity very nearly equal to the speed of light:

$$P(x, \lambda_i) = P_0(\lambda_i) \frac{c\tau}{2} A \, \epsilon \, F(x) \, \beta_\pi(x) \frac{1}{x^2} \exp\left\{ - \int_0^x 2[\alpha(\xi, \lambda_i) + \beta(\xi)]d\xi \right\}$$

$$(i = 0, 1)$$ 10

where P_0 is the average power of the transmitted pulse, τ is the pulse duration, and A and ϵ are the detector area and efficiency. F is a factor that takes into account both the incomplete overlap of the transmitted beam with the detector field of view and the partial blocking of radiation from short distances purposely introduced to flatten the lidar signal (Harms et al., 1978; Harms, 1979). β_π is the backscatter, β is the total scattering, and α is the absorption coefficient; α, β_π, and β may vary with distance x or ξ, and α is also strongly wavelength-dependent. Using equation 10 for the two wavelengths λ_0 and λ_1, and introducing the specific absorption coefficient

$$\alpha^* = \frac{\alpha}{p}$$ 11

we immediately obtain the partial pressure

$$p(x) = \frac{1}{2[\alpha^*(\lambda_1) - \alpha^*(\lambda_0)]} \frac{d}{dx} \ln \frac{P(\lambda_0, x)}{P(\lambda_1, x)}$$ 12

and the volume concentration

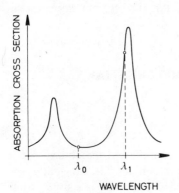

Figure 5.4. Choice of lidar signal (λ_1) and reference wavelength (λ_0).

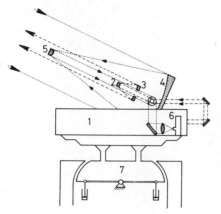

Figure 5.5. Schematic drawing of optical part of lidar system: 1 = laser; 2, 3 = transmitter telescope; 4, 5 = receiver telescope; 6 = detector and liquid nitrogen dewar; and 7 = stabilized platform. Transmitted beam is dashed; received light path is dotted.

$$c(x) = \frac{p(x)}{P_{\text{total}}} \qquad\qquad 13$$

of the gas of interest. The partial pressure and concentration are thus given as a product of two factors, the first of which contains only the specific absorption coefficients at the two wavelengths λ_0 and λ_1, which are constant for a given total pressure and temperature, whereas the second contains only the measured lidar signals. The system thus does not need any further calibration provided the absorption coefficients are known.

5.4.2. Apparatus

The experimental setup is shown schematically in Fig. 5.5. The laser is a pulsed deuterium fluoride (DF) laser (Model 203-2, Lumonics, Kanata, Ontario). The $P_2(3)$ line of DF, which is strongly absorbed by HC1, is used as the signal line and the $P_2(5)$ DF line provides reference. The laser beam is expanded fourfold to reduce the beam divergence to 0.25 mrad, and transmitted into the atmosphere. Backscattered light is collected by a 50-cm diameter, afocal Cassegrain telescope and measured by a 1-mm diameter indium antimonide detector cooled to liquid nitrogen temperature. For variation of the zenith angle the beam is coupled into the transmitter and out of the receiver telescope through the elevation axis. The optical part of the setup is mounted on a stabilized platform that actively compensates yaw, pitch, and roll movements of the ship. This is necessary for the reduction of the single-shot statistical error by accumulation of signals from several laser shots, and very helpful in the systematic measurement of cross sections through a plume. The acquisition, storage, reduction, and visual display of the data, and most of the hardware control, are performed by a small computer (LSI-11, Digital Equipment Corporation, Marlborough, Massachusetts). For weather protection the whole apparatus is covered by a small dome on the quarterdeck of the *R/V Tabasis*. The essential data of the lidar system are summarized in Table 5.1.

Table 5.1. Physical Characteristics of the Differential Absorption and Scattering Lidar for Depth-Resolved Measurements of HCl

Property	Signal	Reference
Laser	Df, pulsed	
Line	$P_2(3)$	$P_2(5)$
Wavelength	3.6363 μm	3.6983 μm
Pulse energy	10 mJ	30 mJ
HCl absorption coefficient	5.64 cm^{-1} atm^{-1}	0.02 cm^{-1} atm^{-1}
Pulse duration	300 ns	
Repetition frequency	1 Hz	
Wavelength selection	Grating	
Receiver optics	50 cm afocal Cassegrain	
Detector	InSb 1 mm diameter liquid N$_2$-cooled	
Compression of signal dynamics	Geometric	
Transmitter-receiver geometry	Noncoaxial	
Amplifier bandwidth	500 kHz to 2 MHz	

5.5. PERFORMANCE DATA

5.5.1. Local Measurement Systems

Most of the local measurements were obtained using the filter and scrubber setup with off-line analysis for Cl^- and Na^+ ions by wet chemical and atomic absorption spectrophotometer (AAS) analysis. The efficiency of the scrubbers and filters, determined by drawing the air sample through several identical devices in series and comparing the contents of consecutive components, was 85% for the dissolution of gaseous HCl in water and $\geq 95\%$ for the retention of NaCl aerosol on the filters. Whereas the figures for HCl gas were obtained from laboratory measurements, the data for NaCl were determined on-site to minimize effects of the size distribution of the aerosol. When one of the filters with NaCl aerosol was additionally exposed to gaseous HCl, $<1\%$ of the HCl was adsorbed by the filter and its deposit. Only at concentrations >1 μl HCl per liter air could a change in the Na^+ to Cl^- ratio be observed in the filter deposit. The sensitivity of the method increases with collection time. Typical values are 1 nl HCl per liter air for 1 h sampling and 100 nl liter^{-1} for a 1 min run. Another great advantage of the system is the compact construction of the sampling device, which eliminates all problems with long intake pipes, particularly in connection with a gas as reactive as HCl. In fact, sampling was performed on the flying bridge of the *Tabasis* in all but the roughest weather conditions.

The sensitivity of the derivative spectrometer obeyed the $1/f^{1/2}$ law, where f is the detection bandwidth, down to f values of about 1 Hz, which is the lowest reasonable bandwidth if the instantaneous concentrations are of interest. The absolute sensitivity was slightly better than 20 ml liter^{-1}Hz$^{1/2}$. This value applies to an effective optical length of the White cell of 64 m, very close to the theoretical optimum (Pokrowsky, 1981) for the 98.42% reflectivity of the mirrors at the wavelengths used. The laser was operated at the $P(6)$ absorption line of $H^{35}Cl$ near 3.634 μm. This line was chosen because a laser diode happened to be available for this wavelength. An increase in sensitivity by more than a factor of two is possible if a more intense absorption line is utilized. An investigation to determine the main source of noise showed that the vibrations and the pitch and roll movements of the ship accounted for most of the signal noise; the measured overall sensitivity as given above is indeed a rather conservative value for this type of device.

For a comparison, parallel measurements with the scrubber/wet chemical assay system were made. Samples were taken for about 30 min, and the derivative spectrometer recorder readout was averaged over this time. Results are given in Table 5.2. With an estimated error of $\pm 15\%$ for the wet chemical and $\pm 10\%$ for the diode laser measurement, the agreement is excellent.

Only one other system of comparable sensitivity appears to be available for on-line assay of HCl, the bromide-bromate method (Gregory and Moyer, 1977). It is based on the reaction of the H^+ ions with a sodium bromide–sodium bromate mixture applied as a coating to the inner wall of a tube. The resulting free bromine

**Table 5.2.   Comparison of HCl Concentrations Measured in the Same
Sample Gas Volume by Wet Chemical and Diode Laser Spectrometric Assay**

			Measured Average HCl Concentration	
Date	Time (h)	Air Volume (liters)	Wet Chemical (nl liter^{-1})	Diode Laser (nl liter^{-1})
21 May 1982	13:00–13:38	300	116	128
25 May 1982	20:00–20:20	160	659	700

is measured by chemiluminescent oxidation of luminol. This detection scheme is
quite sensitive, but considerably slower than the derivative spectrometer. The main
advantage of the laser system over the bromide-bromate method, however, is its
specificity. No response to Cl_2, NO_x, CO_2, and SO_2 was detected, a property particularly valuable for the measurement of HCl in combustion gases. Also, the diode
laser system can be operated continuously without the need for regular shutdown
for maintenance or replenishment of chemical reagents.

5.5.2.   Lidar Performance

The first experiment to test the lidar system took place in 1980 in the new incineration area southeast of the Dogger Bank (Fig. 5.1). This first test was very successful. Occasionally, however, in those portions of the plume that showed dense
cloud formation and which produced huge backscatter signals rapid temporal and
spatial variation of the cloud structures introduced large errors into the differential
lidar signal. This effect was later almost completely eliminated by shortening the
interval between the signal and reference pulse to 200 ns.

The actual performance data summarized in Table 5.3 are for average weather
conditions (visibility $\simeq 9$ km). Hazy weather improves the measurement conditions, whereas exceptionally clear weather results in smaller backscatter signals
and reduced performance. The sensitivity, depth resolution, and number of laser
shots are not independent of each other. The depth resolution can be improved by
almost a factor of two if a faster amplifier is used; the faster amplifier produces
more noise, and noisier signals either require the accumulation of a larger number
of shots or result in decreased sensitivity. The range, defined as that stretch of
distances for which the other data are met or exceeded, also depends on weather
conditions, although not as directly as the other parameters. The region of maximum overlap of the laser beam with the detector field of view and, hence, the
distance of maximum return signal can be adjusted via the intersection angle of
the transmitter and receiver axes. The long-distance limit of the range is due to the
small power of the return signals (equation 10). The short-distance limit is given
by small transmitter-receiver overlap and also by residual electromagnetic inter-

Table 5.3. Performance of HCl Differential Absorption and Scattering Lidar

Property	Value
Sensitivity	0.3 μl HCl per liter air
Depth resolution	75–100 m
Number of shots required	15–150 pulse pairs
Duration of measurement	15–150 s
Minimum distance	100–500 m
Maximum range	500–2000 m
Interference from:	
CO_2	± 5.6 nl liter^{-1} for 0.314 ml liter^{-1}[a]
CH_4	$+5.0$ nl liter^{-1} for 2 μl liter^{-1}[a]
H_2	$+4.2$ nl liter^{-1} for 23.8 ml liter^{-1}[b]
N_2	± 1.5 nl liter^{-1} for 780 ml liter^{-1}[a]

[a]Natural abundance.
[b]Corresponding to 100% relative humidity at 20°C and atmospheric pressure.

action of the 60 kV laser ignition pulses with the detection electronics that handle signal amplitudes in the nW range.

The interference of normal tropospheric concentrations of CO_2, CH_4, H_2O, and N_2 with the HCl to be measured is <2% of the HCl detection limit, and thus negligible. The $\pm$ sign for CO_2 and N_2 in Table 5.3 indicates that the magnitude of the cross section is unknown and that its upper limit may apply to the signal or to the reference line, thus producing either a positive or negative error in the HCl concentration. The + sign for CH_4 and H_2O means that the cross section is larger for the signal line, and the presence of the gas produces a positive error in the concentration of HCl. The effects of SO_2, N_2O, NO, NO_2, CO, Cl_2 and H_2S in the stack gases were negligible. The complexity of the absorption spectra increases and the peak cross section of the lines decreases with increasing molecular weight. Consequently, the numerous hydrocarbons from the original waste or from compounds formed during incineration which are present in very small amounts are extremely unlikely to produce either positive or negative interference, although such an interference can in principle not be totally ruled out.

5.6. RESULTS AND DISCUSSION

Although the primary goal of the experiments presented in this chapter was to field test the different systems, systematic data were obtained also.

Only a few lidar measurements were made in those parts of the plume which showed dense clouds of condensed water vapor. The maximum value of 15 μl HCl per liter of air measured in such a plume at a distance of about 500 m from the incineration ship therefore may not be representative of all types of plumes and all possible weather conditions.

The early lidar measurements were made either in visually transparent plumes or in the transparent periphery of otherwise opaque plumes. Concentrations in the periphery were always <5 μl liter^{-1} beyond 500 m from the ship. On the other hand, the decrease of the concentrations with increasing distance from the incineration ship was often quite small. Figure 5.6 shows the results of a series of measurements for distances up to 1.8 km. The same qualitative behavior was observed for longer distances as well, and occasionally a value close to 1 μl liter^{-1} was detected 27 km downwind from the incineration ship. On one occasion a plume could be traced to a distance of 11 km, with maximum concentration of 1.5 μl liter^{-1}; at 13 km the concentration was 1 μl liter^{-1}; at 15 km it had decreased to the detection limit of 0.5 μl liter^{-1}. No variation of the concentration with height was detected. With a lidar range of about 800 m and an elevation angle of 45°, the vertical profile appeared constant to a height of at least 500 m. We have no expla-

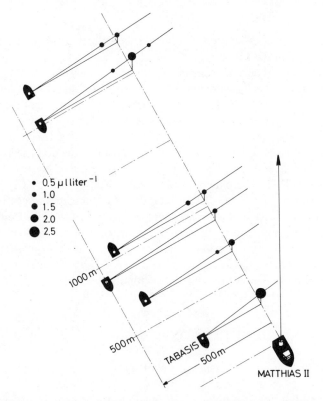

Figure 5.6. Lidar measurements of HCl concentrations in the plume of the *M/T Matthias II*. Data were taken on 1 November 1980, 15:30 to 16:10 Greenwich Mean Time; the wind speed was 13 m s^{-1}.

nation of this result other than that the plume had penetrated into an upwelling mass of air. This was probably due to the instability of the air mass, which caused vertical mixing to a height of up to 500 m.

The normally small decrease in concentration in the center of the plume with distance from the ships was totally reversed under conditions of precipitation. Even in light rain maximum concentrations at distances of 1000–1500 m never exceeded 1 μl liter^{-1}, and they decreased to below the detection limit of then 0.5 μl liter^{-1} beyond 1500 m from the incineration ship.

Surprisingly, the lidar measurements, which only register gaseous HCl, account for about 95% of the total HCl; the local measurements in the plume have shown that $<5\%$ of the HCl is attached to aerosols during the weather conditions investigated. Another interesting result of local measurements in the plume is an HCl lifetime of 1 h. This value was obtained from two 30-min measurements 6 km apart, at a wind speed of 7 m s^{-1}, with c_1, c_2, c_∞ (equation 3) of 23, 15, and 10, and 82, 25, and 0.3 nl liter^{-1} for NO$_x$ and HCl, respectively (Lenhard and Schindler, 1981). This lifetime is much shorter than the 54 h value of Kritz and Rancher (1980) and closer to the 8 h result of Chesselet et al. (1972) for HCl deposition over continental areas. However, it is of the correct order of magnitude if compared to the corresponding values of 10–20 h found for SO$_2$. The budget of inorganic tropospheric chlorine that can be deduced from this result is consistent with the small concentrations of HCl found in background samples and the relatively large Cl$^-$ concentrations measured in Atlantic Ocean rainwater (Lenhard and Schindler, 1981).

5.7. MODIS: A MATHEMATICAL MODEL FOR THE PROPAGATION OF AIR POLLUTANTS

The propagation of air pollutants is usually described by Gaussian models. These models have been very successful for the diffusion of stable gases or particulates emitted at a constant rate by a localized source over land. Gaussian models are phenomenologic in nature and based on a large body of experimental material accumulated by meteorologists over many years. They are therefore often referred to as statistical models. Gaussian models, however, cannot be used to advantage for more complicated situations such as time-dependent emissions, reactive species, or diffusion in the marine atmosphere, for which the current relations of model parameters with atmospheric stability classification are not valid. In these cases a more general approach is required, consisting in the solution of transport equations with the appropriate boundary and initial conditions. In this section we will describe a diffusion model called MODIS, developed at our institute. It provides an illustration of the use of the measured HCl concentrations in the marine atmosphere. More detailed information on this and other models is available in Dunst (1980); Carmichael et al. (1980); and Eppel et al. (1980, 1981).

5.7.1   Description of the Model

The change in the concentration c of the substance of interest is given by the sum of five terms:

$$\frac{\partial c}{\partial t} = q - \vec{\nabla}(c\vec{U}) - \vec{\nabla}(c\vec{V}) + \vec{\nabla}K\,\vec{\nabla}c - Rc \qquad 14$$

where the first term on the right-hand side describes the sources, the second the change by horizontal advection, the third by vertical advection, the fourth the change by turbulent exchange, and the fifth the decrease by chemical reactions. Let the Cartesian coordinates x, y, z be chosen such that the x axis is the main wind direction, y is the transverse, and z the vertical coordinate. The concentrations $c(x, y, z, t)$ and the source term $q(x, y, z, t)$ are scalars; the horizontal wind velocity $\vec{U} = (u,v,0)$ and the vertical wind velocity $\vec{V} = (0,0,-v_s)$ are vectors; and

$$K = \begin{pmatrix} K_{xx} K_{xy} K_{xz} \\ K_{yx} K_{yy} K_{yz} \\ K_{zx} K_{zy} K_{zz} \end{pmatrix}$$

is the turbulent exchange tensor. R is the removal constant, and $\vec{\nabla} = (\partial/\partial x, \partial/\partial y, \partial/\partial z)$ is the gradient vector.

The boundary conditions for the integration volume of the solution of the differential equation 14 are $c = 0$ at the upwind boundary, c is continuous at the downwind boundary, c is continuous at the top ($z = H$), and

$$\left[v_s + \left(K_{xz} + K_{yz} + K_{zz} \right) \frac{\partial}{\partial z} \right] c = v_{\text{dep}}\, c \qquad 15$$

at the bottom, where v_{dep} is the deposition velocity mentioned earlier.

For the elements of the turbulent exchange tensor, it is obvious that with the choice of the coordinates as described, K_{xx} is totally unimportant and can be neglected, except perhaps in the case of a very brief release of material, which then may acquire some finite width in the main wind direction by turbulent diffusion. The situation is not so clear for the nondiagonal elements of K. Numerical tests have shown, however, that for stationary situations the error made by neglecting the nondiagonal terms is unimportant, and it has become current practice to only retain two elements of the K tensor, namely the diagonal elements $K_{yy} \equiv K_y$ and $K_{zz} \equiv K_z$.

Let us now consider the quantities

$$c^{(n)}(x, z, t) = \int_{-\infty}^{\infty} c(x,y,z,t)\, y^n\, dy \qquad n = 0,1,2 \qquad 16$$

and likewise $q^{(n)}(x,z,t)$; we call $c^{(n)}$ and $q^{(n)}$ the nth moment of c and q with respect to the y axis. The moments $c^{(n)}$ have a concrete meaning; it follows from equation 16 that

$$c^{(0)} = Q, \ \frac{c^{(1)}}{c^{(0)}} = y_0, \ \frac{c^{(2)}}{c^{(0)}} - \left(\frac{c^{(1)}}{c^{(0)}}\right)^2 = \sigma_y^2 \qquad\qquad 17$$

that is, that the moment $c^{(0)}$ is equal to the total concentration $Q(x,z)$ along a line parallel to the y axis, or area of the c versus y distribution, the first moment determines the center of gravity $y_0 = y_0 (x,z)$ of that distribution, and the second its width $\sigma_y = \sigma_y (x,z)$.

Equation 14, which is valid for c, is also valid for the moments of c. The resulting moment equations are then solved using discrete element techniques. The vertical solution area is covered with a rectangular grid that need not be equidistant. Spatial derivatives in the diffusive terms and the convective term associated with the sink velocity v_s are approximated by central differences, whereas the convection in the x direction is treated by upstream differencing. This different treatment of the x and z convection is justified by the fact that the vertical motion is usually dominated by diffusion, and the horizontal by advection. The result is an equation system for the moment values at the grid points (x_i, z_i) that is first-order in time and can be integrated using a fourth-order Runge-Kutta scheme. The use of moment-reduced equations is motivated by practical arguments because only three two-dimensional equations, instead of one three-dimensional equation, must be solved for each grid point, which allows enormous savings in computer time and cost. The resulting moment distributions from which the concentration field is constructed were chosen to give the model MODIS its name.

5.7.2 Performance and Results

The model has been tested for its dependence on mesh size of the coordinate grid, boundary conditions, input parameters such as removal constant and sink velocity, influence of crosswind magnitude, relative importance of advective and convective diffusion, and influence of the Coriolis force. For the boundaries it was found that the results depend critically on the deposition velocity, so the lower boundary condition (equation 15) is essential for correct results of the bottom concentrations. At the upper boundary, restrictions narrower than that of a continuous change of the concentration may lead to the occurrence of unphysical phenomena. Variations of the sink velocity and removal constant produce the correct changes in the results. Crosswind velocities (v) can get as high as 50% of the main wind velocity (u), with the error of the resulting concentrations remaining below 10%. The Coriolis force produces the correct deviation of the center line of the plume from the direction of the surface wind. The most critical process is the interplay between advective and convective diffusion expressed numerically by the Peclet number $P_\Delta = u\Delta x/K_z$, which relates the horizontal velocity (u) with the vertical diagonal element (K_z) of the exchange tensor and the grid resolution in the x direction, Δx. The finite P_Δ values are believed to represent the main limitation of the model. Comparisons have also been made with Gaussian models where applicable, with good agreement of the results. The program is equipped with a variety of flux-profile relations for the determination of vertical diffusion coefficients; stable to neutral weather conditions can thus be covered.

As an example, the result of an instationary problem that could not be tackled with Gaussian models is given (Eppel et al., 1980). A sudden puff of material is released 150 m above ground, 2.5 km downwind from the center of the coordinate system at time $t = 0$. As mentioned previously the simplification $K_x = 0$ must be dropped for this case, and components of K were chosen to be $K_x = K_y = 6.0$ m^2 s^{-1}, $K_z = 1.5$ m^2 s^{-1}, with the nondiagonal elements equal to zero. No transverse wind ($v = 0$), no sink and deposition velocity ($v_s = v_{dep} = 0$), and no degradation of the material ($R = 0$) were considered.

Figure 5.7 shows the distribution of the zeroth moment (the integrated concentration in the y direction) in the x-z plane at 6-min intervals. The concentrations themselves are inferred from similar representations of the distributions of the first and second moment. It is obvious that the concentrations decrease faster than the zeroth moments due to the increase of the second moments, or distribution widths, with time.

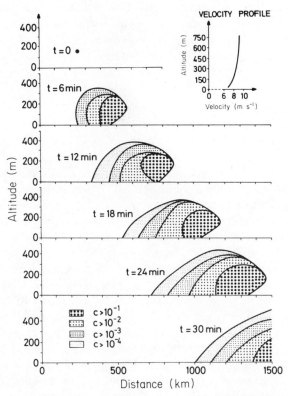

Figure 5.7. Results of the simulation of an instant puff at time $t = 0$ with the diffusion model MODIS. Boundaries between dotted areas are isolines of the integrated concentrations along parallel horizontal lines perpendicular to the main wind direction.

In the comparison with results of other models, the results of MODIS are re-markably accurate. The restrictions that must be obeyed to attain this goal are not very severe. There is good reason to believe that the fit of calculated to measured concentration distributions with MODIS will yield valuable information about hith-erto quantitatively unknown parameters if correct meteorological data are available.

5.8. SUMMARY

At-sea incineration of chlorinated hydrocarbon waste is currently considered the least harmful method of destruction and disposal of these substances with respect to effects on the environment. Hydrogen chloride, the only major combustion prod-uct that is not a constituent of the natural atmosphere, is a relatively mild poison to mammals in concentrations below the ppm level and for short exposures, but larger concentrations or prolonged exposure can be dangerous to plants, animals, and humans, and produces severe corrosion of equipment and buildings. The HCl is neutralized as soon as it reaches the surface of the sea; even massive HCl de-posits have shown to produce effects on seawater pH that are comparable to the natural diurnal variations.

Although incineration of organochlorides has become a routine procedure, little is known about the HCl distribution in the marine atmosphere or the parameters that describe HCl removal by chemical reactions and by processes such as dry deposition, aerosol attachment, and precipitation. Nor have successful applications of diffusion models to the description of the HCl dilution (as opposed to removal) been reported; this may partly be due to the different incineration and meteorolog-ical stability conditions at sea as compared to those on land. Undoubtedly, more advanced theories of plume dispersion that rely less on the phenomenological as-sessment of parameters than do current Gaussian models will be helpful in the prediction of HCl concentrations under varying weather situations.

Prerequisites for the measurement of the concentration of HCl in the plume of incineration ships are detection techniques that are sensitive, fast, accurate, free from interferences by other compounds, and that lend themselves to measurements in three dimensions. No single procedure can to date fulfill all of these require-ments, but it seems promising to test existing methods and to develop new methods for quantitative HCl assay, which in combination might provide the necessary in-formation.

A very sensitive method of HCl determination is the absorption of the gas in water-filled scrubbers and determination of the Cl^- ions by colorimetry with acidic mercury nitrate and diphenylcarbazone. The addition of filters in front of the scrub-bers allows the removal of particulates and the separate analysis of HCl attached to the aerosols. The Cl^- originating from sea salt is accounted for by Na^+ assay via AAS. The sensitivity and discrimination power of the method are sufficient for the determination of the natural HCl background. Typical collection time is 30 min.

A time constant of this magnitude is usually not tolerable. A new method for the assay of HCl was therefore developed that is based on the absorption of infrared radiation from a tunable diode laser. The laser radiation passes through 64 m of effective path length of the sample gas. Extreme specificity is obtained by operating the sample cell at reduced pressure; actually, no interference by any of the more abundant gases from the incineration process or the atmosphere was found. For minimum signal-to-noise ratio and maximum sensitivity the laser wavelength is modulated around the center of the absorption line, and the second derivative of the absorption signal is measured. At a time constant of 1 s the sensitivity reached during the first field tests is 20 nl liter^{-1}.

An off-line method similar to scrubbing-colorimetry is derivatization of sample air with 7-oxabicyclo-(4,1,0)-heptane followed by gas chromatography of the reaction product, 2-chlorocyclohexanol. The method is sensitive and specific, but was not field-tested in the present investigation.

None of the three systems described is suitable for systematic measurements of HCl above the mast top of the ship in which they are installed. Therefore, a lidar system was designed that allows space-resolved remote concentration measurements. The lidar uses the technique of differential absorption and scattering, which consists of the emission of a short pulse of laser radiation and collection and analysis of the backscattered light. The information on the concentration as a function of distance is evaluated from the intensity of the return signal as a function of time or, more precisely, the ratio of the lidar returns at two wavelengths, one of which is strongly absorbed by the gas of interest, whereas the other serves as a reference for the elimination of atmospheric absorption and backscatter fluctuations. This technique also eliminates effects like variation of the laser pulse power and changes in mirror reflectivity. As infrared light at wavelengths around 3.5 μm from a DF laser is used, the device is safe for human eyes.

The mathematical models used include both state-of-the-art Gaussian descriptions and a more advanced plume simulation model called MODIS. In the latter the moments of the unknown concentration distributions with respect to the transverse coordinate are determined by numerical integration of the transport equation in a vertical plane parallel to the main flow direction. The complete three-dimensional distribution is then reconstructed from the moment distributions. The technique allows the consideration of volume and surface sinks, shear wind situations, and time-dependent meteorological parameters. For the numerical treatment of the moment equations discrete-element techniques are applied.

ACKNOWLEDGMENTS

This work would not have been completed without continuous encouragement by W. Michaelis and the contributions of R. Baumgart, H.-J. Heinrich, W. Herrmann, S. Köhler, and P. Pokrowsky. Free use was made of the results of discussions with K. Bächmann, D. Eppel, and U. Lenhard. The author also wishes to acknowledge the gift of the stabilized platform by the German Federal Navy, and the excellent cooperation of the captain and crew of the *Tabasis*.

REFERENCES

Breeding, R. J., H. B. Klonis, J. P. Lodge, Jr., J. B. Pate, D. C. Sheesley, T. R. Englert, and D. R. Sears. 1976. Measurement of atmospheric pollutants in the St. Louis area. *Atmospheric Environment*, **10**, 181–194.

Carmichael, G. R., D. K. Yang, and C. Lin. 1980. A numerical technique for the investigation of the transport and dry deposition of chemically reactive pollutants. *Atmospheric Environment*, **14**, 1433–1438.

Chesselet, R., J. Morelli, and P. Buat-Menard. 1972. Some aspects of the geochemistry of marine aerosols. *In:* The Changing Chemistry of the Oceans, D. Dyrssen and D. Jagner (Eds.). Wiley-Interscience, New York, pp. 93–114.

Clausen, J. F., H. J. Fisher, R. J. Johnson, E. L. Moon, C. C. Shih, R F. Tobias, and C. A. Zee. 1977. At-sea incineration of organochlorine wastes onboard the *M/T Vulcanus*. EPA-600/2-77-196, Office of Research and Development, U.S. Environmental Protection Agency, Washington, D.C., 88 pp.

Dunst, M. 1980. Ergebnisse von Modellrechnungen zur Ausbreitung von Stoffbeimengungen in der planetarischen Grenzschicht. *Zeitschrift für Meteorologie*, **30**, 47–59.

Eppel, D., J. Häuser, and A. Müller. 1980. Three-dimensional simulation model MODIS for the propagation of air-pollutants. Fifth International Clean Air Congress (20–26 October 1980), Buenos Aires, Argentina. Report GKSS 80/E/56, GKSS-Forschungszentrum Geesthacht, Federal Republic of Germany, 14 pp.

Eppel, D., J. Häuser, H. Lohse, and F. Tanzer. 1981. Pollutant dispersion in the Ekman layer using moment-reduced transport equations. Twelfth International Technical Meeting (ITM) on Air Pollution Modeling and its Applications (25–28 August 1981), Menlo Park, California, 14 pp.

Fabian, H. W. 1979. Verbrennung chlorierter Kohlenwasserstoffe. *Umwelt*, **9** No. 1, 12–17.

Gregory, G. L., and R. H. Moyer. 1977. Evaluation of a hydrogen chloride detector for environmental monitoring. *Review of Scientific Instruments*, **48**, 1464–1468.

Harms, J. 1979. Lidar return signals for coaxial and noncoaxial systems with central obstruction. 1979. *Applied Optics*, **18**, 1559–1566.

Harms, J., W. Lahmann, and C. Weitkamp. 1978. Geometrical compression of lidar return signals. *Applied Optics*, **17**, 1131–1135.

Kritz, M. A., and J. Rancher. 1980. Circulation of Na, Cl, and Br in the tropical marine atmosphere. *Journal of Geophysical Research*, **85**, 1633–1639.

Lenhard, U., and R. N. Schindler. 1981. Measurements of natural and anthropogenic hydrogen chloride on the North Sea. *In:* Third International Association of Meteorology and Atmospheric Physics, Third Scientific Assembly (17–28 August 1981), Hamburg, Federal Republic of Germany. National Center for Atmospheric Research, Boulder, Colorado, p. 89.

Paige, S. F., L. B. Baboolal, H. J. Fisher, K. H. Scheyer, A. M. Shaug, R. L. Tan, and C. F. Thorne. 1978. Environmental Assessment: At-Sea and Land-Based Incineration of

Organochlorine Wastes. EPA-600/2-78-087, Office of Research and Development, U.S. Environmental Protection Agency, Washington, D.C., 107 pp.

Pokrowsky, P. 1981. Bestimmung von Absorptionsquerschnitten atmosphärischer Schadgase im Infrarotbereich. Dissertation, Universität Hamburg, Federal Republic of Germany, 80 pp.

Pokrowsky, P., and W. Herrmann. 1984. Sensitive detection of hydrogen chloride by derivative spectroscopy with a diode laser. *Optical Engineering*, **23,** 88–91.

Sittig, M. 1974. Pollution Detection and Monitoring Handbook. Noyes Data Corporation, Park Ridge, New Jersey, and London, England, 401 pp.

Vierkorn-Rudolph, B., M. Savelsberg, and K. Bächmann. 1979. Determination of trace amounts of hydrogen chloride by derivatization with epoxides and gas chromatographic separation. *Journal of Chromatography*, **186,** 219–226.

Weikard, J. 1978. Prognose von HCl-Immissionen bei der Verbrennung chlorhaltiger organischer Rückstände auf See. Bayer Leverkusen Report, 16 November 1978, 3 pp.

Weitkamp, C. 1984. Calibration of diode-laser second-derivative modulation spectrometry with a reference cell. *Applied Optics*, **23,** 83–86.

Wulf, H. 1972. Verbrennung auf See bis Windstärke 9. Beseitigung von chlorierten Kohlenwasserstoffen. *Umwelt*, **2** No. 3, 48–49.

6

INCINERATION AT SEA: EXPERIENCE GAINED WITH THE M/T VESTA

Wilfried Lankes

Lehnkering AG,
Duisburg, Federal Republic of Germany

Abstract		**116**
6.1.	**European Development of Incineration Practice at Sea**	**116**
	6.1.1. Legal Basis	116
	6.1.2. Incineration Ships in Operation	116
	6.1.3. Materials Destroyed by Incineration at Sea	117
6.2.	**The Incineration Ship *M/T Vesta***	**118**
	6.2.1. The Decision to Build the Ship	118
	6.2.2. Technical Specifications	118
	6.2.3. Incineration Equipment	119
	6.2.4. Control Instruments	119
6.3.	**Practical Experience with the *M/T Vesta***	**120**
	6.3.1. Incineration Efficiency and Destructive Performance	120
	6.3.2. Shipboard Air Quality Measurements	120
6.4.	**Environmental Consequences of Incineration at Sea**	**121**
Acknowledgments		**122**
References		**122**

ABSTRACT

Incineration at sea has been used in the North Sea to dispose of chlorinated hydrocarbons since 1969. The company Lehnkering AG designed and built the incineration vessel *M/T Vesta* and has operated it within the jurisdiction of the Federal Republic of Germany since 1979. The vessel has a number of specialized features for the reliable and safe destruction of combustible wastes. Measurements of emissions after incineration show a combustion efficiency of 99.90–99.95%. A series of air quality measurements were made aboard the vessel to assure safe working conditions for the crew. Incineration of combustible wastes at sea offers several advantages over land-based incineration, without causing measurable impact on the marine environment.

6.1. EUROPEAN DEVELOPMENT OF INCINERATION PRACTICE AT SEA

6.1.1. Legal Basis

Incineration ships have been operating in Europe since 1969, mainly in the southern part of the North Sea. Their main purpose is to incinerate chlorinated hydrocarbon wastes which are not suitable for reuse. In the Federal Republic of Germany (FRG), incineration practice at sea is controlled by the Law for the Prevention of Ocean Pollution due to the Dumping of Wastes from Ships and Aircraft, dated 11 February 1977 (Bundesgesetzblatt II, 1977). Article 2 of this law states that explicit permission must be obtained from the national licensing authority, the German Hydrographic Institute, for the dumping and incineration of wastes or other matter on the high seas. The German federal law is based on the international agreements under the Oslo Convention and the Convention for the Prevention of Pollution by Dumping of Wastes and Other Matter, also known as the London Dumping Convention, both of which have concluded regulations and technical guidelines governing the incineration of wastes at sea (Chapter 2).

6.1.2. Incineration Ships in Operation

Since 1969, a total of five incineration ships have been put into service worldwide, three of which, the *M/T Matthias II*, the *M/T Vulcanus*, and the *M/T Vesta*, are still operating. The *Matthias II* is a rebuilt freighter; the *Vulcanus* is a rebuilt tanker. The *Vesta*, which was commissioned in 1979, was designed and built as an incineration ship (Fig. 6.1).

An estimate of the quantities of chlorinated hydrocarbon wastes that have been incinerated in the North Sea since 1969 is given in Fig. 6.2. The information provided in this chapter is based on the technical details of the experience gained with the incineration ship *Vesta*.

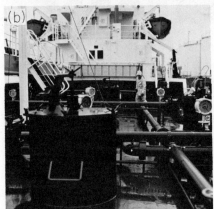
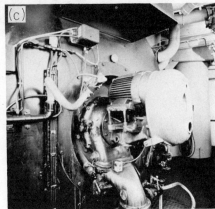

Figure 6.1. (a) The incineration vessel *M/T Vesta*; (b) gangway between fore and aft parts of the vessel; and (c) combustion chamber.

6.1.3. Materials Destroyed by Incineration at Sea

The materials that have so far been incinerated at sea consist mainly of liquid chlorinated hydrocarbon wastes resulting from the production and utilization of chlorinated hydrocarbons. The annual production in the FRG of approximately 3.4×10^6 t results in by-products and residues of $(1.8-2.4) \times 10^5$ t y^{-1}. About 60–70% of this is reutilized; the remainder must be disposed of as waste. The use of chlorinated hydrocarbons as solvents results in additional residues. The total yield of liquid and sludge-type chlorinated hydrocarbon wastes in the FRG is estimated at $(1.2-1.5) \times 10^5$ t y^{-1}. The chlorine proportion of these wastes averages 60–70% (Barniske, 1980).

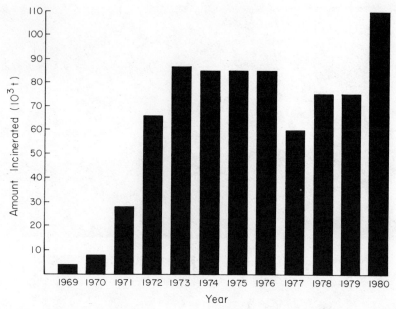

Figure 6.2. Amount of chlorinated hydrocarbon wastes incinerated in the North Sea during 1969–1980. Data from Fabian (1977) and the author's calculations.

6.2. THE INCINERATION SHIP *M/T VESTA*

6.2.1. The Decision to Build the Ship

With the coming into force in the FRG in 1977 of the Law for the Prevention of Ocean Pollution due to the Dumping of Wastes from Ships and Aircraft, the requirements concerning incineration at sea by the federal government were considerably strengthened. There was, however, an increasing demand for incineration at sea. In 1978 the company Lehnkering AG, in light of the strict requirements with regard to the performance and control of the incineration system and the safety of the ships and personnel, decided to design and build a new ship which fulfills all the regulatory specifications, rather than to modify an existing vessel. This was carried out in cooperation with waste producers, specialists in furnace construction, experts on waste incineration at sea, and the responsible environmental and marine licensing authorities of the FRG.

6.2.2. Technical Specifications

The coastal motor tanker *Vesta* was commissioned on 21 May 1979 (Fig. 6.1a,b). After comprehensive trials on the high seas, the ship was awarded the classification GL 100 A 4 M + MC 16/24, and fulfills the International Maritime Organization regulations for a type II chemical tanker. The classification number is internationally used, and means that the ship has the highest standard for a sea-going vessel;

MC 16/24 means that machine control is obligatory only 8 h d^{-1}. Incineration at anchor can be carried out at wind forces of up to 8–10 on the Beaufort scale. The ventilation of the operating rooms in the stern is effected by three separate systems, namely: machine and ventilator rooms, furnace room with furnace control room (Fig. 6.1c), and pump room. A radial ventilator rated at 25,000 m^3 h^{-1} is installed in the forecastle area for the first two systems. The air circulation channels to the stern also serve as a gangway between the fore and aft parts of the ship. The ship is equipped with nine loading tanks for liquid waste materials, with a total tank volume of 1100 m^3. This corresponds to a liquid load of 1265–1430 t, with an average density of 1.15–1.30 t m^{-3}. A tank for 34 m^3 of additional fuel is installed in the double floor of the furnace area; additional fuel can also be transported in the loading tanks. Filling level indicators and overfilling safety contacts in each loading tank exclude accidental spillage of the waste liquids. The pipe layout and the circuit guarantee that the liquid waste materials taken on board can only be incinerated and disposed of via the incineration equipment. It is impossible to discharge the liquid into the sea. The *Vesta* is a double-hull construction, in which ballast tanks are installed between the loading tanks and the outer walls and bottom of the ship. The arrangement and size of the ballast tanks permit trim and stability balancing in any loading case that may occur.

6.2.3 Incineration Equipment

The incineration facility comprises an 11-m high combustion chamber with a lower diameter of 6 m, equipped with three rotary atomizing burners (Fig. 6.1c). The combustion chamber, with a total weight of 150 t, is lined with a special refractory material suitable for high operating temperatures. In order to protect the monolithic type of construction of the refractory lining from damage, the entire chamber has been elastically mounted in rollers. This absorbs the shocks and vibrations caused by sea swell. Rotary atomizers were selected since, due to their design, they are capable of producing extremely short flames with combustion efficiencies >99.9%.

Optimization of incineration also necessitates a furnace geometry suitable for the burner equipment, which then guarantees the high temperature level. Further constructive measures ensure that high turbulence, which improves mixing, is prevalent in the combustion chamber. The incineration performance of the facility is ~10 t h^{-1}, depending on the calorific value of the materials incinerated. In order to ensure good regulation of the firing equipment, each burner is equipped with a dosing facility adjustable within the range up to 1:5. The dosing facilities are connected in series with homogenizers, which reduce the solid materials present in the waste to a size suitable for processing. The burners are capable of efficiently atomizing wastes containing impurities with a grain size of up to 3 mm.

6.2.4. Control Instruments

The temperature of the inner furnace wall is continuously measured at three points; temperature is measurable up to 1600°C. If the temperature drops below 1100°C at any measuring point, the supply of waste materials is halted by an automatic shut-off device. The facility is provided with a release thermostat, which permits incineration of wastes at 1200°C. Furthermore, the facility is equipped with a radiation pyrometer with a measuring range of 900–1600°C. If the content of oxygen in the exhaust chamber drops below 3% (by vol), an alarm signal is given. The incineration facility is electronically interlocked in such a way that it can only be started up if the ventilators for the machine room and the furnace operating room are in operation.

Every 15 min a recording camera photographs the readings of the navigation instruments, the measurements of furnace temperatures, the operational status of the waste pumps currently in operation, and the ship's position. The flue gases leaving the incinerator are regularly analyzed for oxygen, carbon dioxide, and carbon monoxide concentrations. These values are also registered by the recording camera. At the end of each voyage, the operational information monitored is submitted to the licensing authorities, enabling them to determine the incineration efficiencies and the position of the ship during the entire operation.

6.3. PRACTICAL EXPERIENCE WITH THE *M/T VESTA*

6.3.1. Incineration Efficiency and Destructive Performance

In 1980 the Rheinisch-Westfaelischer Technischer Ueberwachungsverein, Essen (Technical Surveillance Authority), carried out, at the request of the Umweltbundesamt (Federal Office for Environmental Protection), extensive examinations of incineration efficiency and destructive performance during the incineration of selected waste materials on the *Vesta*. The emission concentrations of carbon monoxide, carbon dioxide, oxygen, nitric oxides, total organic compounds (reported as carbon), chloride compounds (reported as Cl), and bromide compounds were determined. The measurements of carbon dioxide and carbon monoxide in the exhaust were carried out to establish incineration efficiency. The calculations made using the results of these measurements showed that incineration efficiencies of 99.90–99.95% are attained.

Destructive performance was calculated by using the mass ratio of the uncombusted components contained in the exhaust air to the corresponding components in the initial materials (wastes). The following components of the wastes and exhaust gases were measured to establish destruction efficiencies: benzene and chlorinated benzenes such as chlorobenzene, dichlorobenzene, hexachlorobenzene; and hexachlorobutadiene. The results showed that the destructive performance averaged over the incineration period (15–22 September 1979) was between 99.90 and 99.95% (Lützke et al., 1980).

6.3.2. Shipboard Air Quality Measurements

During the forty-eighth voyage of the *Vesta*, from 27 to 31 May 1981, concentration measurements of the room air in the individual work stations were carried out.

Constant source measurements were made in the pump room for the evaluation of pump emissions, and in the furnace room to determine the room air concentration. Two individuals carried pocket pumps to establish personal exposure during a 6-h duty period. In addition, measurements were continued over a 12-h period in the furnace control room (measuring control room), where the operating staff generally work. The results of the measurements are summarized as follows:

1. Qualitative correlations existed between the waste components and the relevant air samples.
2. The results of 78 person-specific measurements of various substances showed 55 below the analytical detection limit; all values were below the ppm range $(0.01–0.2 \ \mu g \ g^{-1})$.
3. In the furnace room, the room air concentration was at the detection limit of $0.01 \ \mu g \ g^{-1}$.
4. Concentrations $< \mu g \ g^{-1}$ were found in the pump room.
5. The actual concentration values were clearly below the maximum work station concentration values. The operating and living quarters therefore fulfill the requirements for land-based chemical factories (Bayer AG, 1981).

6.4. ENVIRONMENTAL CONSEQUENCES OF INCINERATION AT SEA

The basic difference between incineration practice on land and at sea lies in the fact that no exhaust air purification systems are used at sea, whereas incineration plants on land utilize extensive facilities for flue gas purification. This means, among other things, that the costs for incineration on land are higher than at sea. At present the costs for incineration at sea are approximately DM (Deutsche Mark)150–180 (50–59 dollars) per ton.

Seawater offers high absorptive capacities for the inorganic chlorides produced during incineration, and therefore, considered from an ecological and economic point of view, may at present be regarded as the best solution for the disposal of halogenated hydrocarbon wastes, provided that the specified incineration and destruction efficiencies are maintained. Evaluation of the environmental impact of incineration at sea has led many experts to consider this as the best present-day disposal method. In relation to other methods available, this method has been shown to have the lowest negative effect on the environment.

The *Vesta* was designed in cooperation with waste producers, licensing authorities, and ship-owners; furthermore, experience gained with earlier incineration ships was taken into consideration. The *Vesta* therefore corresponds to the latest state of knowledge and technology and fulfills all legal requirements. It is, however, desirable that international cooperation regarding the registration and disposal of halogenated hydrocarbons should be improved with a view to controlling the disposal of these chemical wastes in such a manner that the lowest possible burden to the environment is caused by their destruction.

ACKNOWLEDGMENTS

The author wishes to thank W. Lange, Technical Director of the Lehnkering AG, Duisburg, who contributed greatly to the construction of the *Vesta,* for his help in compiling the report and for reading the manuscript. In addition, the author received valuable assistance in the assessment and evaluation of the incineration and destruction results from H. W. Fabian, Bayer AG, and K. Hilger, Haniel Umweltschutz GmbH.

REFERENCES

Barniske, L. 1980. Technische Gesichtspunkte bei der Verbrennung von Chlorkohlenwasserstoffabfällen. Beihefte zu Müll and Abfall, Nummer 17, Abfallbeseitigung auf See, p. 47 ff.

Bayer AG. 1981. Verbrennung von chlorierten Kohlenwasserstoffen auf See. Raumluft- und Arbeitsplatzkonzentrationen auf dem Verbrennungsschiff "Vesta" der Firma Lehnkering AG, Unpublished report dated 27 July 1981, unpaginated.

Bukndesgesetzblatt II, S.165, von 11. Februas 1977 (Federal Law Sheet).

Fabian, H., 1977. Beseitigungmethoden für chlorierte Kohlenwasserstoff-Abfälle. Vortrag am 04.10.1977 in der TU Berlin (5. Abfallwirtschaftliches Seminar).

Lützke, K., K.-D. Hoffman, W. Guse, 1980. Untersuchungen zum Verbrennungswirkungsgrad und zur Vernichtungsleistung bei der Verbrennung von ausgewählten Abfallstoffen auf einem Verbrennungsschiff. Research report 19-104 04 149, Rheinisch-Westfälischer Technischer Überwachungsverein e.V., Essen, 79 pp.

PART III: INDUSTRIAL WASTES:
Modelling, Microcosms, and Biological Effects.

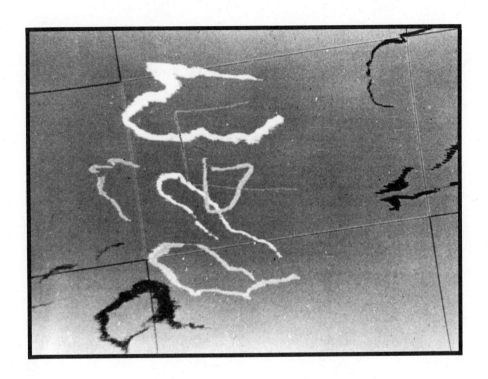

7

A THREE-DIMENSIONAL NUMERICAL DISPERSION MODEL FOR ACID-IRON WASTE DISPOSAL

Robin Robertson and Malcolm L. Spaulding

Department of Ocean Engineering
University of Rhode Island
Kingston, Rhode Island

Abstract		**126**
7.1.	**Introduction**	**126**
7.2	**Model Description**	**128**
	7.2.1. Governing Equations	128
	7.2.2. Solution Procedure	129
	7.2.2a. Eulerian Step	129
	7.2.2b. Lagrangian Step	130
7.3.	**Description of Study Area**	**131**
7.4.	**Results**	**132**
	7.4.1. Base Case	133
	7.4.2. Sensitivity Studies	135
	7.4.3. Warm Core Ring-Induced Dispersion	137
7.5.	**Conclusions**	**141**

Ms. Robertson's present address: Areté Associates, Van Nuys, California.

Acknowledgments   143

References   143

ABSTRACT

A three-dimensional numerical model has been developed to predict the dispersion
of suspended and particulate acid-iron waste; the model uses marker particles to
statistically define the waste and a hybrid Eulerian-Lagrangian solution procedure
to solve the three-dimensional convective diffusion equation. The model was previously validated against analytic solutions for point waste releases in uniform and
sheared flow fields, and its computational characteristics were determined. The
model was applied to predict the dispersion of acid-iron waste at Deepwater
Dumpsite-106, assuming a 10-km long, 10-m thick, 40-m wide plume as the initial
waste configuration. A series of sensitivity simulations with varying turbulent diffusion coefficients and current shear rates performed with the model indicates that
vertical current shear coupled with vertical diffusion is more important in determining dilution than horizontal diffusion. A simulation of plume dilution for waste
discharged in the center of a stationary warm core ring shows that the ring-induced
vertical shear substantially increases dilution over the unsheared flow fields. Dilution to background level is estimated at a minimum of 15 d for this highly idealized
ring simulation. Although the modelling approach presented here is capable of
handling most of the complexities of oceanic dispersion, the critical unknowns are
an accurate spatial and temporal definition of the current field and its turbulent
transport properties.

7.1.   INTRODUCTION

With an ultimate goal of understanding the ecological implications of disposing of
wastes in the ocean, an extensive effort has been undertaken to predict the dispersion of these materials in coastal and continental shelf waters (Johnson, 1974).
This effort is probably best summarized in a comprehensive barge disposal model
developed by Koh and Chang (1973). These investigators assembled individual processes into a model system to address the disposal of barged wastes, dredged material, and sewage sludge by several disposal procedures to include wake discharge,
point dumping, and diffuser discharge. Although the potential of this modelling
approach to predict the fate of the waste seemed excellent, actual operational experience indicated that the model system was difficult to use from a computational
viewpoint, and that a large number of derived (not directly measurable) coefficients

were necessary for reasonable predictive capability. In the case of the acid-iron waste discharge here, the problems were compounded by a lack of detailed definition of the current field and information on particulate and floc formation rate and size distribution as the waste reacts with seawater.

In recent years the problem of estimating dilution rates and their time scales has been addressed because of its importance in understanding the environmental consequences of waste disposal in the ocean. Using data collected from the acid-iron waste dumping at Deepwater Dumpsite (DWD)-106 by Kohn and Rowe (1981), Bisagni (1977a, 1977b), Frye and Williams (1977a, 1977b), and Orr and Hess (1978), Csanady (1981) performed a very thorough analysis of the various field data sets integrated with several simple dispersion model estimates (Csanady, 1973) to gain insight into the key mechanisms controlling the dilution rates. From this analysis and simple modelling results, Csanady concluded:

1. Waste dilution occurs in two phases: rapid dispersion in the wake of the barge followed by slower dispersion due to naturally occurring mean shear and turbulence.
2. Horizontal dispersion in the upper 10–20 m of the stratified water column is controlled mainly by mean shear-vertical mixing interaction.
3. Extrapolation of an effective diffusivity increasing in direct proportion to time provides a reasonable estimate of diffusion over several days.

Simpson et al. (1979) investigated solutions to a simple diffusion equation using both constant and variable eddy diffusivities as well as variable diffusion velocities. In agreement with Csanady (1981), they concluded that these simple models give a first-order estimate of plume dilution rates, but raised questions about the validity of these models for longer time periods.

Both Simpson et al. (1979) and Csanady (1981) provide a basis for estimating dispersion for the acid-iron waste plume and represent an important first step in understanding the key processes governing plume dynamics. Remaining important unanswered questions regarding the waste plume behavior are:

1. What are the roles of eddies, horizontal shear, wind, and thermally induced vertical mixing in determining the long-term (greater than 1–2 d) dilution rates for the acid-iron waste plume?
2. Does particulate and floc formation, which occurs as the waste reacts with seawater, alter the waste transport?
3. Are cross-pycnocline mixing rates important to predicting dilution of industrial wastes?

It is the goal of this work to develop and apply a three-dimensional numerical dispersion model to address some of these questions.

7.2. MODEL DESCRIPTION

7.2.1. Governing Equations

The incompressible ensemble time-averaged three-dimensional mass transport equation for turbulent flow with negatively buoyant particles can be written as:

$$\frac{\partial c}{\partial t} + \frac{\partial uc}{\partial x} + \frac{\partial vc}{\partial y} + \frac{\partial wc}{\partial z}$$

$$= \frac{\partial}{\partial x}\left(D_x \frac{\partial c}{\partial x}\right) + \frac{\partial}{\partial y}\left(D_y \frac{\partial c}{\partial y}\right) + \frac{\partial}{\partial z}\left(D_z \frac{\partial c}{\partial z}\right) - w_s \frac{\partial c}{\partial z} \quad 1$$

where u, v, and w are the mean turbulent flow velocities, c is the concentration of the material of interest, D_x, D_y, and D_z are the turbulent diffusion coefficients in the x, y, and z directions, respectively, and w_s is the asymptotic settling velocity. It has been assumed that the particle settling velocity is independent of time and space but is dependent on particle diameter, and that the suspended material is dilute within the flow field. Hence, interparticle forces are not considered.

For the purposes of application to the acid-iron waste dispersion problem, it has been assumed that the flow field may be determined either from field observations or a model of the current structure (analytic or numerical) and that the turbulent diffusion coefficients are specified either theoretically or empirically.

It is common practice to simplify equation 1 through dimensional reduction and assuming simple flow fields and constant dispersion coefficients in order to obtain an analytic solution for the problem of interest (Csanady, 1973). If one desires to study more complicated flow fields and dispersive behavior, however, it is often necessary to develop numerical solutions to the mass transport equation. Finite difference and finite element solution algorithms have been developed for this purpose (Gordon and Spaulding, 1974), but both suffer from length- and time-scale-dependent numerical dispersion, severely depressed concentrations upstream of point waste load sources, difficulty in handling scale-dependent diffusion, and extensive computational requirements for simulating dispersion of an effluent containing a variety of particle sizes and density characteristics.

These difficulties may be overcome by reformulating the mass transport equation and solving the resulting equation using an Eulerian-Lagrangian particle-in-cell solution procedure. Following Sklarew (1970), equation 1 can be written in flux conservative form to yield:

$$\frac{\partial c}{\partial t} + \frac{\partial}{\partial x}\left(u - \frac{D_x}{c}\frac{\partial c}{\partial x}\right)c + \frac{\partial}{\partial y}\left(v - \frac{D_y}{c}\frac{\partial c}{\partial y}\right)c$$

$$+ \frac{\partial}{\partial z}\left(w + w_s - \frac{D_z}{c}\frac{\partial c}{\partial z}\right)c = 0 \quad 2$$

Defining the diffusive velocities u_D, v_D, w_D in the x, y and z directions as:

$$u_D = -\frac{D_x}{c}\frac{\partial c}{\partial x}$$

$$v_D = -\frac{D_y}{c}\frac{\partial c}{\partial y} \qquad\qquad 3$$

$$w_D = -\frac{D_z}{c}\frac{\partial c}{\partial z}$$

and the pseudo total velocities (the sum of the advective and diffusive velocities) as:

$$u_T = u_D + u$$

$$v_T = v_D + v \qquad\qquad 4$$

$$w_T = w_D + w + w_s$$

Equation 2 can be written as:

$$\frac{\partial c}{\partial t} + \frac{\partial}{\partial x}\left(u_T c\right) + \frac{\partial}{\partial y}\left(v_T c\right) + \frac{\partial}{\partial z}\left(w_T c\right) = 0 \qquad\qquad 5$$

Physically, this reformulation states that a particle is advected with the mean motion of the fluid field and diffused with a velocity proportional to the concentration gradient immediately surrounding the particle.

7.2.2. Solution Procedure

The solution to the pseudo velocity equations is accomplished by a Lagrangian-marker-particle-in-Eulerian-cell technique, utilizing Sklarew's total pseudo flux method (Sklarew, 1970; Spaulding, 1976; Pavish, 1976). The scheme employs a space-staggered three-dimensional Eulerian grid system composed of equal-volume rectangular cells. Concentrations are defined at the center of the cells and the advection velocities, u, v, and w, and the diffusion velocities, u_D, v_D, and w_D are defined at the center of the respective cell faces. Marker particles placed inside the Eulerian grid, which statistically represent the pollutant cloud, are defined by their individual Lagrangian coordinates and their mass and settling characteristics. A time cycle of the method can be divided into an Eulerian and Lagrangian step.

7.2.2a. Eulerian Step

At the beginning of each time step, the concentrations, defined at the center of each cell, are used to calculate the diffusion velocities, defined at the center of the cell faces (equation 3). Using a space-centered finite difference approximation, these diffusion velocities are calculated throughout the three-dimensional space and then added to the externally supplied advection velocities, also defined at the grid faces, to yield the pseudo total velocities, u_T, v_T, and w_T.

7.2.2b. Lagrangian Step

Following the calculation of the pseudo total velocities in the Eulerian grid, each marker particle is advected by the velocity field from time t to $t + \Delta t$. Particle advection is performed by a simple explicit procedure using a bilinear weighting scheme to interpolate velocities for particles inside the grids. Selection of an appropriate time increment or step is based on a simple advective transfer limit; that is, a particle cannot be advected more than one-half a grid space (Δx) in a time step, (i.e. $u\Delta t < \Delta x/2$).

The Lagrangian step contains the options of allowing selective expansion of the Eulerian grid system with the diffusive growth of the marker particle cloud and selective translation of the grid with the mean motion of the advected cloud in any of the three spatial dimensions. Incorporation of this procedure permits maximum resolution of the marker particle concentration field with a minimum number of computational grids and allows waste plume dilutions to be followed over many orders of magnitude. These expansion and translation procedures are particularly useful for simulating instantaneous point releases in horizontally unbounded flow situations.

The final segment of the Lagrangian step is the calculation of the new concentration field from the new particle positions. Using the mass assigned to each particle and a volume the size of one Eulerian grid cell, a concentration can be determined by simple partitioning of a particle's mass to surrounding grids. This mass-sharing procedure is repeated for each particle in the field to calculate the total concentration distribution.

The spatial and temporal evolution of the waste cloud is then determined by repeating the computational procedure. Note that new environmental information such as current field definition, sources of release, and vertical stratification can be input at each time step of the simulation.

The waste is usually specified by its spatial and temporal source strength and by the particle size–density distribution of the material or particle settling velocities. Using this latter information and any chemical reactions that might modify the waste composition, estimates of particle settling rates can be determined. The source strength is normally given by a Gaussian distribution of marker particles across the plume, with appropriate longitudinal and vertical dimensions to characterize the waste discharge dynamics. Timing of particle release defines the temporal behavior of the source strength. For an instantaneous release all particles begin at the same time, whereas for a time-dependent source the particles are released according to a defined schedule.

A more detailed presentation of the numerical solution procedure is given by Pavish (1976). This chapter presents the validation of the model procedure against analytic solutions for advection and diffusion of instantaneous and continuous releases of waste in bounded and unbounded, shear and unsheared flow fields. A detailed presentation on computational aspects of the procedure is included.

7.3. DESCRIPTION OF STUDY AREA

The study area, shown in Fig. 7.1, is located in the New York Bight, 195 km southeast of Ambrose Light Tower. The water depth in this area ranges from 1500 to 2700 m. The water column structure at DWD-106 has two general forms corresponding to the summer and winter seasons. The water column above the permanent thermocline is stratified from May to October and is nearly isothermal from October to May. The permanent thermocline is usually located between 100 and 200 m depth; a seasonal thermocline is located between 10 and 40 m in the summer season. During May to October, warm slope water is present above the seasonal thermocline and a layer of weak thermal gradients is present between the seasonal and permanent thermoclines. Occasionally, in the winter months, October to May, thermal inversions occur when cool shelf water moves over the warmer, high-salinity slope water.

The mean current in this region is generally southwesterly at <0.25 m s^{-1} and tends to be parallel to the isobaths. Drogue measurements by Bisagni (1981a, 1981b, 1981c) show a slight shear in the vertical direction with the velocity increasing with depth. Velocity directions below 10 m depth are often 180° out of phase with Ekman predictions. J. Bisagni (personal communication) suggests the presence of a return flow in the deeper layers driven by mass conservation to account for the velocity increases and direction changes with depth.

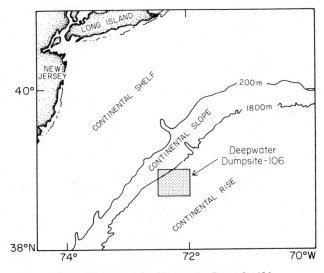

Figure 7.1.   Location of Deepwater Dumpsite-106.

Warm core rings formed from the Gulf Stream often pass through the study area. At these times the current structure of the area is completely overridden by the velocity structure of the ring. The velocity structure used to represent the ring is characterized by a maximum velocity at the ring's radius, with the velocities outside the ring core decreasing exponentially with radial distance (G. Flierl, personal communication). The warm core rings range from 60 to 80 km in radius and generally travel southwest with the mean current of the region and approximately parallel to the isobaths (Mizenko and Chamberlin, 1981).

7.4. RESULTS

A series of simulations using the modelling methodology presented in Section 7.2.2 was performed to investigate the dispersion behavior of the acid-iron waste discharge. Table 7.1 gives a detailed list of all simulations performed, noting the specific conditions for each case.

Table 7.1. Acid Iron Waste Simulation Cases

Case[a]	Dispersion Coefficient ($m^2 s^{-1}$) Horizontal	Vertical[b]	Current Field	Thermocline Depth (m)	Length of Simulation (h)	Current Shear (s^{-1})
1	30.0	0.0100 0.0010	None	18	530	0
2	3.0	0.0100 0.0010	None	18	24	0
3	1.0	0.0100 0.0010	None	18	24	0
4	0.3	0.0100 0.0010	None	18	24	0
5	30.0	0.0010 0.0001	None	18	30	0
6	30.0	0.0100 0.0010	None	150	30	0
7	1.0	0.0100 0.0010	None	18	30	0.001
8	1.0	0.0100 0.0010	None	18	30	0.010
9	30.0	0.0100	Warm core ring	None	90	Ring induced
10	3.0	0.0100	Warm core ring	None	90	Ring induced

[a]Initial conditions for all cases: waste plume 10 km long, 10 m thick, and 40 m wide; uniform distribution in length and depth and Gaussian in width ($\sigma = 7$ m).
[b]The second parameter for the vertical dispersion coefficient applies to the region below the thermocline.

7.4.1 Base Case

In order to define a frame of reference for the sensitivity studies on velocity shear and dispersion rates, and the effects of a warm core ring, a base case was selected using typical estimates for all parameters. Following the analysis of Csanady (1981) on mixing within the barge wake, and the general pattern of acid-iron disposal (Simpson et al., 1979), the initial waste plume was specified as 10 km long, 10 m thick, and 40 m wide, with the waste neutrally buoyant in the water column. The initial distributions were assumed to be uniform in length and depth, but Gaussian in width, with a standard deviation of 7 m. It was further assumed that the entire plume was instantly discharged.

The advective velocity field was assumed to be zero because a uniform steady current field makes no contribution to dilution, and detailed current data are not available for DWD-106. The seasonal thermocline, typical for stratified conditions, was set at 18 m by specifying a vertical diffusivity of 0.01 m^2 s^{-1} in the upper 18 m of the water column and 0.001 m^2 s^{-1} at all other depths. The horizontal eddy diffusivity in both the along- and cross-shelf directions was specified as 30 m^2 s^{-1} (Fischer, 1980). This value includes the shear, vertical diffusion correction and hence represents an effective horizontal dispersion rate. This value for horizontal dispersion was estimated by Fischer (1980) for midshelf waters and nonstratified conditions, and it is therefore a likely maximum value for the stratified conditions simulated here.

Using the preceding data as input and 2000 marker particles to define the acid-iron release, a simulation of the spreading waste cloud was performed. The model grid system was set to resolve the initial waste plume and was allowed to expand as the simulation proceeded. To assist in visualizing the spreading dynamics, a series of spatial plots has been prepared, documenting the time-dependent distribution of particles. Figure 7.2 shows the plane, side, and end views of the waste particle distribution for various times after the discharge event. The time for each plot is selected to show the evolution of the waste cloud. In each of these plots, all particles are projected onto a single plane.

The principle direction of dispersion is in the cross-plume direction. Calculation of the cross-plume width standard deviation as a function of time shows the square root behavior displaying rapid initial and much slower subsequent growth. Along-plume axis dispersion is extremely small. The confinement of vertical waste transport is also clearly evident, with particles reaching the seasonal thermocline depth of 18 m within 1.25 h after the release and being effectively trapped there.

Figure 7.3 shows the dilution versus time plot for this simulation, with the dilution defined as the maximum concentration at time $t = 0$ divided by the maximum concentration at the time of interest. Total waste dilution can be estimated by multiplying the value in Fig. 7.3 by a wake discharge dilution factor of 5000 (Csanady, 1981).

This model agrees with previous studies (Simpson et al., 1979; Csanady, 1981) in predicting extremely rapid dilution shortly after the release (a factor of 100 in 1.5 h) and much slower dispersion at later times (a factor of 6 in the next 30 h).

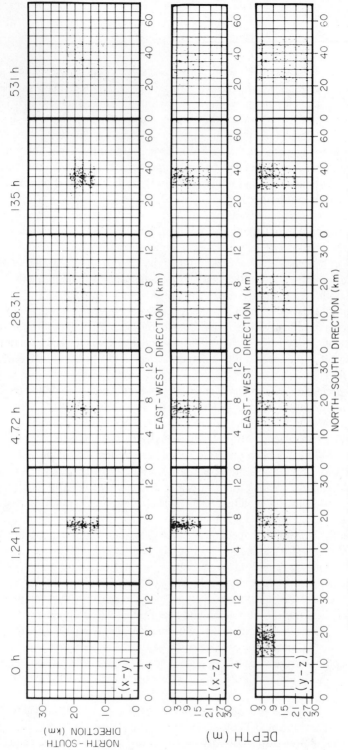

Figure 7.2. Spatial distribution of waste tracer particles over 531 h. The distributions shown are in the *x–y*, *x–z*, and *y–z* planes at six times after a dump. Based on case number 1 (see Table 7.1).

134

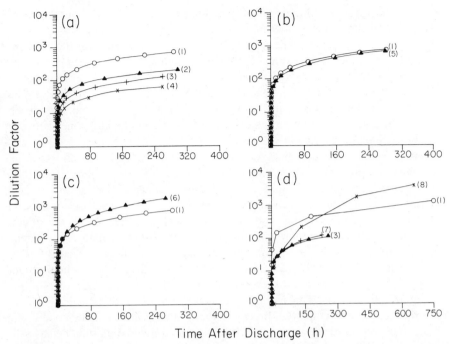

Figure 7.3. Variation of the dilution factor with time. Variations shown are associated with changes in (a) horizontal diffusion coefficient, (b) vertical diffusion coefficient, (c) thermocline depth, and (d) vertical current shear. The numbers in parentheses refer to case numbers listed in Table 7.1.

This is clearly a result of the sharp initial concentration gradients in the cross-plume direction coupled with the assumption of constant horizontal dispersion coefficients. Similarly, for times following the discharges, a close inspection of the model predictions shows that only the cross-plume dispersion rate is important because only in the cross-plume direction are the concentration gradients significant.

7.4.2. Sensitivity Studies

A series of simulations was performed to investigate the sensitivity of dilution to (1) the selection of horizontal and vertical diffusion coefficients, (2) the location of the thermocline, and (3) the vertical current shear. All simulations began with the same initial conditions as the base case. Figure 7.3a shows the influence of varying the horizontal dispersion coefficient over a range that is typical for the study region (Yudelson, 1967; Okubo, 1971; Csanady, 1973; Ichiye et at., 1981). Although the behavior is similar at very early times, the increased dilution caused by the increased horizontal dispersion coefficient is clearly evident at times > 1 h.

The effect on dilution that would be caused by a change in the vertical diffusion coefficient by one order of magnitude is shown in Fig. 7.3b. Since the initial waste release is uniform in the upper 10 m, and cross-plume dispersion dominates the dilution behavior, little effect is noted. The higher dilution for the larger value of vertical diffusion becomes noticeable 2 h after the dump, but the cases appear to converge with time. This result can be explained by the presence of the effective diffusion floor at the 18 m seasonal thermocline depth.

The presence of the seasonal thermocline obviously has a strong influence in preventing vertical mixing of the waste. This effect can be seen clearly in Fig. 7.3c for depths typical of the seasonal (18 m) and permanent (150 m) thermoclines. With a deeper diffusion floor, dilution is significantly higher, and the difference between the two thermocline cases increases with time.

Vertical shear in the flow field, coupled with vertical diffusion, is an important mechanism for predicting waste dilution in the ocean (Csanady, 1966, 1973, 1981; Fischer, 1980) and in many cases is more important than horizontal diffusion in determining waste spreading. Since most simplified waste dispersion models do not incorporate sufficient detail in the current field to accurately define this effect, it is common practice to employ a modification of Elder's (1959) approach, whereby the horizontal diffusivity is modified to account for this shear vertical diffusion mechanism. Fischer (1980) has performed this analysis for the Mid-Atlantic Bight region, looking at horizontal dispersion rates generated by density gradients, currents, tides, and storms. This modified horizontal diffusivity, often called horizontal dispersion, is then employed directly in these simplified dispersion models. Although this procedure allows the models to estimate observed dilution behavior, it also tends to obscure the details of the mixing process.

Since the present modelling approach can readily handle complex flow fields, a series of simulations has been performed to investigate the effects of the current vertical shear–vertical diffusion interaction on dilution. Figure 7.3d shows the dilution time plot for horizontal and vertical diffusivities fixed at 1 and 0.01 $m^2 s^{-1}$, respectively, and vertical shear rates ranging from 0.0 to 0.01 s^{-1}. These are reasonable estimates of the shear in the upper water column (Fischer, 1980).

At small shear rates the dilution is only slightly higher than the nonsheared case. At larger shear rates (0.01 s^{-1}), the dilution is substantially higher. In fact, the highly sheared plume shows dilutions higher than the unsheared base case after about 20 h, even though the base case horizontal dispersion coefficient is 30 times greater. The precise location of this crossover point is strongly dependent on current shear rate and vertical diffusivity. The important point is that modest amounts of vertical current shear coupled with typical vertical diffusivities can readily explain the wide range of horizontal dispersion rates reported in the literature, and are key processes in determining acid-iron waste plume dilution.

Several simulations of acid-iron dispersion using settling velocities and particulate size distributions based on laboratory experiments without particle flocculation and aggregation (D. Kester, personal communication) showed no difference in dilution rates compared to simulations where the waste is neutrally buoyant. This result can be explained by the extremely slow settling rates of the waste compared to the vertical diffusion rate.

In this study, we did not attempt to present all possible combinations of diffusivity and current shear variations. The temporal and spatial variations of these parameters were ignored to simplify the analysis. Hence, comparison of these dilution plots with field observations should consider the complexity of the ocean compared to our model. This analysis nevertheless suggests that accurate measurements of vertical current shear and vertical diffusivity will permit more accurate dilution rate prediction than is possible using estimates of effective horizontal diffusivity because the physics underlying the dispersion processes can be taken into account.

7.4.3. Warm Core Ring-Induced Dispersion

Since warm core rings are often present in the study region (Mizenko and Chamberlin, 1981), and given that the horizontal and vertical shears present in a ring are likely to have substantial effects on the dilution rates of an acid-iron plume, a simulation was performed for a waste plume dumped in a warm core ring. Following G. R. Flierl's (personal communication) model, the stream function for these rings is given by:

$$\varphi = V_0 r_0 \frac{1.5 - r^2}{2r_0^2} F(z) \qquad \text{for} \quad r < r_0$$

or
6

$$\varphi = V_0 r_0 e^{(1 - r/r_0)} F(z) \qquad \text{for} \quad r \geq r_0$$

where V_0 is the maximum tangential velocity (0.8–1 m s^{-1}), r_0 the radius of maximum velocity (60–80 km) and φ is the stream function at location r. The stream function can be differentiated with respect to the angle ω and radius r to obtain equations for the velocities, V_θ and V_r, in the ω and r directions, respectively:

$$V_\omega = V_0 \frac{r}{r_0} F(z) \qquad \text{for} \quad r < r_0$$

$$V_r = 0$$

7

$$V_\omega = V_0 e^{(1 - r/r_0)} F(z) \qquad \text{for} \quad r \geq r_0$$

$$V_r = 0$$

The position of the ring center is specified to move in a general southwesterly direction at a rate of approximately 0.05 m s^{-1} (Olson, 1980). The function $F(z)$ defines the vertical variation of the horizontal velocities (Fig. 7.4). Figure 7.5 shows the horizontal velocity structure at the surface. The thermocline structure of the ring was assumed to be similar to that of cold core rings (Backus et al., 1981), with both the seasonal and permanent thermoclines being displaced past 250 m, the maximum depth modelled.

A simulation was performed with the 10-km discharge centered in the middle of the ring. This initial release maximizes the vertical shear effects on the acid-iron waste plume compared to a release along a circumferential arc, and it is equivalent

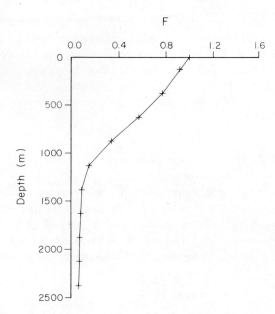

Figure 7.4. Vertical structure function, *F,* for a warm core ring model (G. Flierl, personal communication).

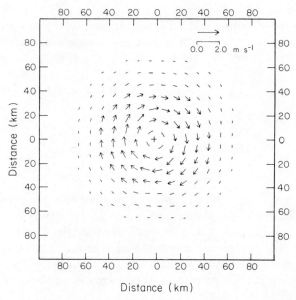

Figure 7.5. Horizontal velocity structure at the surface for a warm core ring model (G. Flierl, personal communication).

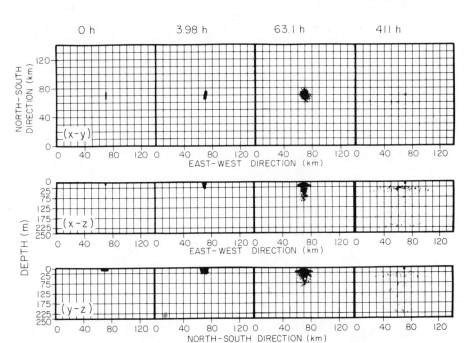

Figure 7.6. Spatial distribution of waste tracer particles. The distributions shown are in the x-y, x-z, and y-z planes at four times after a dump. Based on case number 9 (see Table 7.1).

to a radially directed release at a larger radius within the ring core because the shear rates do not change greatly with radius. The acid-iron discharge has the same initial conditions as the base case. The horizontal and vertical diffusion coefficients are specified as 301.0 and 0.01 m^2 s^{-1}, respectively.

Figure 7.6 shows the temporal evolution of the discharge in three spatial views. The shear effects of the warm core ring are clearly noted with the initial narrow line release changing into a cylindrical shape after 60 h. Since the ring structure also displaces the seasonal and permanent thermoclines, the penetration of the waste into the water column is evident. No thermocline was employed in the simulation. Figure 7.7 shows a temporal series of transects through the waste plume concentration maximum. The approximate Gaussian shape of the distribution is clearly evident at all times.

Careful inspection of the concentration ordinate reveals the dilution of the acid-iron waste concentration maximum. Figure 7.8 shows similar temporal transects in the vertical direction. The uniform distribution in the vertical direction specified at the beginning of the simulation is evident. The dominance of horizontal diffusion during the first few minutes is also noted, with the vertical distribution remaining well mixed. After 0.16 h, a vertical structure is present as the waste material diffuses downward into the water column. At much later times, this vertical gradient decreases in magnitude and the rate of change in dilution decreases.

Figure 7.9 shows the dilution plot for the ring simulation. As in the base case,

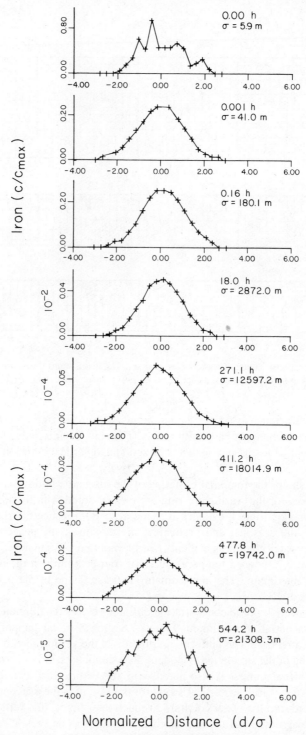

Figure 7.7. Horizontal transects at waste plume concentration versus time. Note that the time and standard deviation, σ, are shown in the upper right hand corner of each plot, and that the concentrations

there is rapid initial dilution followed by decreasing dilution rates. The increased dilution due to the presence of the ring is obvious. A second ring simulation was performed with a horizontal diffusivity of 3 m^2 s^{-1}. This decrease in horizontal mixing reduces the dilution significantly. The approximate time for the waste to be diluted to background levels (10^7) for the ring cases are 4 and 8 d for the 30 and 3 m^2 s^{-1} horizontal diffusivities, respectively, and 20 d for the base case. The 30 m^2 s^{-1} horizontal diffusivity (Fischer, 1980) value is likely to be too high because it already includes corrections for vertical current shear. A ring discharge scenario across the edge of the ring is likely to have higher dilution rates because of the added contribution from horizontal shear; thus, these predictions are expected to be intermediate times to reach background concentrations.

This simple ring-induced dispersion simulation shows some of the impacts on dilution that might occur if an acid-iron waste plume were trapped inside a ring. The ring advection rate has been eliminated in this simulation, due to time step considerations in the model. A far more striking case could have been to position the release at the edge of the ring, where there are also strong horizontal shears. This case was attempted, but required excessive computational times (estimated to be well over 20 h) and therefore was not completed.[1]

7.5. CONCLUSIONS

A three-dimensional numerical model has been developed to predict the dispersion of suspended and particulate acid-iron waste. The model scheme uses marker particles to statistically define the waste and a hybrid Eulerian-Lagrangian solution procedure to solve the three-dimensional mass transport equation. The model has been applied to predict the dilution characteristics of acid-iron waste disposal at DWD-106 under a variety of environmental conditions.

A series of sensitivity simulations suggests that horizontal and vertical current shear rates are important in determining waste plume dilution behavior, and in fact can readily explain the field observations. The accurate definition of the current field and turbulent diffusivities in both their temporal and spatial dimensions is critical to our ability to estimate the long-term dilution of the acid-iron waste.

Based on the extremely simple simulations, waste dilutions to approximate background levels (dilutions of 10^7 from the original barge conditions or 10^4 after the wake discharge) cannot be accomplished in < 15 d.

For the simple warm core ring discharge scenario studied here, the time for dilution of the waste to background levels was approximately one-half the time

[1]This case addressed by Robertson and Spaulding (1983), with the dilution time to equivalent background concentrations being reduced to slightly less than 4 days.

are reported referenced to the maximum concentration at the beginning of the simulation. The standard deviation and distances are referenced to the center of the grid. Based on case number 9 (see Table 7.1).

Iron (c/c_{max})

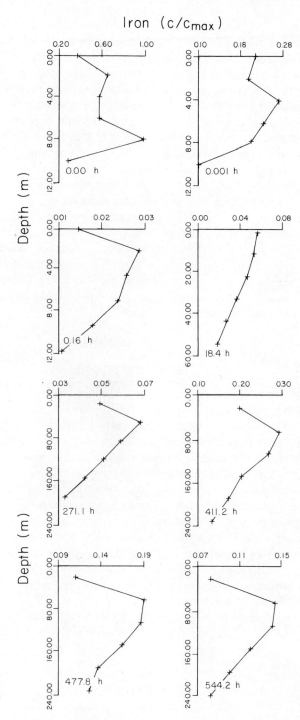

Figure 7.8. Vertical transects at waste plume concentration versus time. Based on case number 9 (see Table 7.1).

142

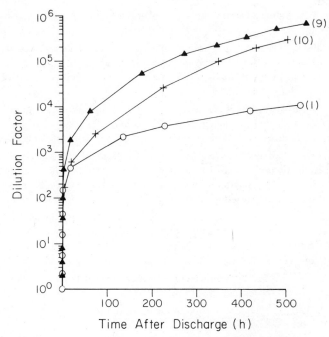

Figure 7.9. Influence of warm core ring-induced shears on dilution; the base case is included for comparison.

required for typical environmental conditions. Although additional simulations of waste discharge at the ring edge to study the effects of the horizontal current shears on dilution were attempted, excessive computational times caused the simulations to be discontinued.

ACKNOWLEDGMENTS

This work was supported by the Ocean Dumping Program, U.S. National Oceanic and Atmospheric Administration. We thank T. P. O'Connor for the overall support and P. Cornillon for providing insight into the present computer coding of the dispersion model.

REFERENCES

Backus, R. H., G. R. Flierl, D. R. Kester, D. B. Olson, P. L. Richardson, A. C. Vastano, P. H. Wiebe, and J. H. Wormuth. 1981. Gulf Stream cold-core rings: their physics, chemistry and biology. *Science*, **212**, 1091–1100.

Bisagni, J. J. 1977a. Physical Oceanography of Deepwater Dumpsite 106 February–March, 1976. Unpublished internal report, Atlantic Environmental Group, National Marine

Fisheries, U.S. National Oceanic and Atmospheric Administration, Narragansett, Rhode Island, 29 pp.

Bisagni, J. J. 1977b. The Physical Oceanography and Experimental Studies at Deepwater Dumpsite 106 During June 1976. Unpublished internal report, Atlantic Environmental Group, National Marine Fisheries, U.S. National Oceanic and Atmospheric Administration, Narragansett, Rhode Island, 44 pp.

Bisagni, J. J. 1981a. Advection of Near-Surface Waters at the 106 Mile Dumpsite. Unpublished report, Atlantic Environmental Group, National Marine Fisheries, U.S. National Oceanic and Atmospheric Administration, Narragansett, Rhode Island, 22 pp.

Bisagni, J. J. 1981b. Fall 1978 Current Measurements Near the 106 Mile Industrial Waste Site and Evaluation of a Quasi-Lagrangian Measurement Technique. Unpublished internal report, Atlantic Environmental Group, U.S. National Oceanic and Atmospheric Administration, Narragansett, Rhode Island, 25 pp.

Bisagni, J. J. 1981c. Physical oceanography studies at 106-Mile Site, July 1977. *In:* Assessment Report on the Effects of Waste Dumping in 106-Mile Ocean Waste Disposal Site. Dumpsite Evaluation Report 81-1, Office of Marine Pollution Assessment, U.S. National Oceanic and Atmospheric Administration, Boulder, Colorado, pp. 233–242.

Csanady, G. T. 1966. Accelerated diffusion in the skewed shear flow of lake currents. *Journal of Geophysical Research,* **71,** 411–420.

Csanady, G. T. 1973. Turbulent Diffusion in the Environment. D. Reidel Publishing, Dordrecht, Holland, 248 pp.

Csanady, G. T. 1981. An analysis of dumpsite diffusion experiments. *In:* Ocean Dumping of Industrial Wastes, B. H. Ketchum, D. R. Kester, and P. K. Park (Eds.). Plenum Press, New York, pp. 109–129.

Elder, J. W. 1959. The dispersion of marked fluid in turbulent shear flow. *Journal of Fluid Mechanics,* **5,** 544–560.

Fischer, H. B. 1980. Mixing processes on the Atlantic Continental Shelf, Cape Cod to Cape Hatteras. *Limnology and Oceanography,* **25,** 114–125.

Frye, D., and G. Williams. 1977a. Measurements of the Dispersion of Barged Waste Near 38°50′N Latitude and 72°15′W Longitude at the 106 Dump Site. Unpublished report, EG&G Environmental Consultants, Waltham, Massachusetts, 5 sections (paginated separately) + 3 appendices.

Frye, D., and G. Williams. 1977b. Measurements of the Dispersion of Barged Waste Water Near 38°33′N Latitude and 74°20′W Longitude. Unpublished Manuscript, EG&G Environmental Consultants, Waltham, Massachusetts, 5 sections (paginated separately).

Gordon, R. B., and M. Spaulding. 1974. A Bibliography of Numerical Models for Tidal Rivers, Estuaries, and Coastal Waters. Marine Technical Report 32, Department of Ocean Engineering, University of Rhode Island. Submitted to the National Oceanic and Atmospheric Administration, Sea Grant, 55 pp.

Ichiye, T., M. Inoue, and M. Carnes. 1981. Horizontal diffusion in ocean dumping experiments. *In:* Ocean Dumping of Industrial Wastes, B. H. Ketchum, D. R. Kester, and P. K. Park (Eds.). Plenum Press, New York, pp. 131–159.

Johnson, B. H. 1974. Investigation of Mathematical Models for the Physical Fate Prediction of Dredged Material. Technical Report D-74-2, Hydraulics Laboratory, Office of Dredged Material Research, U.S. Army Corps of Engineers, Waterways Experiment Station, Vicksburg, Mississippi, 54 pp.

Koh, R. C. Y., and Y. D. Chang. 1973. Mathematical Model for Barged Ocean Disposal of Wastes. EPA-660/2-73-029, Office of Research and Development, U.S. Environmental Protection Agency, Washington, D.C., 581 pp.

Kohn, D., and G. T. Rowe, 1981. Dispersion of two liquid industrial wastes dumped at Deep Water Dumpsite 106. *In:* Assessment Report on the Effects of Waste Dumping in the 106-Mile Ocean Waste Disposal Site. Dumpsite Evaluation Report 81-1, Office of Marine Pollution Assessment, U.S. National Oceanic and Atmospheric Administration, Boulder, Colorado, pp. 133–156.

Mizenko, D., and J. L. Chamberlin. 1981. Gulf Stream anticyclonic eddies and shelf water at 106-Mile Site during 1977. *In:* Assessment Report on the Effects of Waste Dumping in 106-Mile Ocean Waste Disposal Site. Dumpsite Evaluation Report 81-1, Office of Marine Pollution Assessment, U.S. National Oceanic and Atmospheric Administration, Boulder, Colorado, pp. 207–232.

Okubo, A. 1971. Oceanic diffusion diagrams. *Deep-Sea Research,* **18,** 789—802.

Olson, D. B. 1980. The physical oceanography of two rings observed by the cyclonic ring experiment. II. Dynamics. *Journal of Physical Oceanography,* **10,** 514–528.

Orr, M. H., and F. R. Hess. 1978. Acoustic monitoring of industrial chemical waste at Deep Water Dumpsite 106. *Journal of Geophysical Research,* **83,** 6145–6154.

Pavish, D. 1976. Development and Application of Three-Dimensional Numerical Model for Predicting Pollutant and Sediment Transport Using an Eulerian Lagrangian Marker Particle Technique. M.S. Thesis, Department of Ocean Engineering, University of Rhode Island, Kingston, Rhode Island, 209 pp.

Robertson, R. and M. Spaulding. 1983. A three dimensional numerical model of dispersion in the presence of a warm core ring. Paper presented at the American Geophysical Union Conference, Spring 1983, Baltimore, Maryland. Abstract in: *EOS,* **18,** 251.

Simpson, D. C., T. P. O'Connor, and P. K. Park. 1979. Deep Ocean Dumping of Industrial Wastes. Unpublished report, National Ocean Survey, U.S. National Oceanic and Atmospheric Administration, 42 pp.

Sklarew, R. C. 1970. A New Approach: The Grid Model of Urban Air Pollution. Paper Presented at the 63rd Annual Meeting of the Air Pollution Control Association, St. Louis, Missouri.

Spaulding, M. 1976. Numerical Modeling of Pollutant Transport Using a Lagrangian Marker Particle Cell Technique. NASA TM X-73930, Langley Research Center, U.S. National Aeronautics and Space Administration, Hampton, Virginia, 33 pp.

Yudelson, J. 1967. A Survey of Ocean Diffusion Studies and Data. Technical Memorandum 67-2, California Institute of Technology, Pasadena, California, 129 pp.

8

MOTION AND DISPERSION OF DUMPED WASTES BY LARGE-AMPLITUDE EDDIES

Glenn R. Flierl and William K. Dewar

Department of Earth, Atmospheric and Planetary Sciences
Massachusetts Institute of Technology
Cambridge, Massachusetts

Abstract	147
8.1. Introduction	148
8.2. Effects of Rings on an Isolated Patch of Material	149
8.3. Impacts of Rings on Mean Distributions and Fluxes	157
8.3.1. Circular Flow	158
8.3.2. Moving Eddies in a Channel	161
8.4. Conclusions	167
Acknowledgments	169
References	169

ABSTRACT

At deepwater waste disposal sites, the dominant currents causing material to move away from the site and disperse are the transient flows associated with mesoscale

Dr. Dewar's present address: Curriculum in Marine Sciences, 12-5 Venable Hall, The University of North Carolina, Chapel Hill, North Carolina 27514.

eddies. In the case of Deepwater Dumpsite (DWD)-106, located in the Slope Water region, several warm core rings pass through the site each year. Because of their intense surface currents (100–200 cm s^{-1}), these eddies will be a major cause of the transport and dispersal of wastes away from the site. We have calculated the effects of such strong, time-dependent, coherent flows on a patch of passive tracer. When the swirling geostrophic motions associated with the eddy or ring are larger than the translational speed of the feature, as is commonly the case, a volume of fluid is carried with the eddy as it propagates through the surrounding water. We show that smaller-scale random motions cause exchange of this fluid with the exterior, with tracer entering and exiting through a particular spot in the eddy. If the material is dumped outside the eddy, it has a fairly small probability of being mixed into the interior (except for certain regions ahead of and somewhat to the left of the feature); however, it will be displaced up to several hundred kilometers parallel to the track of the eddy by the transient currents. The repeated passage of rings through a region such as the Slope Water strongly alters the average distributions and fluxes of passive tracer material. The effects of eddies are usually characterized by an eddy diffusivity, K_e, proportional to the product of the eddy flow speeds and the length scale; however, the mixing length arguments that lead to this isotropic, homogeneous eddy diffusivity do not appear to be appropriate for rings. We solve a number of simple models and calculate the enhanced fluxes (from the Shelf Water to the Gulf Stream in the case of rings in the Slope Water) of tracer induced by strong coherent eddies. The effective diffusivity across the track of the eddies is 5–10 K, where K is the diffusivity due to smaller-scale incoherent motions such as internal gravity waves or weak mesoscale turbulence. This is quite different from the mixing length estimate K_e: it is one or two orders of magnitude smaller and it is proportional to, rather than independent of, K. However, the predicted influence of rings on the fluxes and average distributions of material is still significant.

8.1. INTRODUCTION

Disposal of waste material in the ocean is complicated by the uncertainties of the ocean currents and the lack of real understanding of either the likely trajectories and the rates of spread of a patch of contaminated oceanic water or the role of the fluctuating currents in determining the net transport of pollutants. For short time scales and nearshore problems, the dominant motions responsible for mixing are turbulence (induced by the disposal procedure itself, by winds, and by topography), tidal currents, and waves (both surface and internal). In the deep ocean, however, the strongest flows are caused by time-dependent mesoscale eddy features, with velocities of 10–20 cm s^{-1}, or the much stronger features known as rings, with currents on the order of 100 cm s^{-1} in the mixed layer. Warm core rings sweep through Deepwater Dumpsite (DWD)-106 and, because they occur every few months and are orders of magnitude more intense than the mean flows, they can dominate the patterns of waste motion, dispersal, and net transport in the Slope Water. In this chapter, the effects of rings (both individually and collectively) on tracer transport and dispersal are studied using simple models.

The conventional approach to modelling the effects of mesoscale motions such as rings on pollutant distribution uses a mixing length (or equivalent) argument to estimate an eddy diffusivity, K_e. For currents of ~ 50 cm s^{-1}, with length scales of 50 km, mixing length theory gives an eddy diffusivity of 2.5×10^8 cm^2 s^{-1}, which would lead to quite rapid spreading of material. However, in a region like the Slope Water, where the eddy field is dominated by a few very strong, coherent features, there is little justification for using the mixing length model to predict the probable motion of a patch of material or the average flux across the region.

In this chapter, mechanistic models of the motion and spread of material caused by strong ringlike features are presented. Two processes affecting the waste distribution—advection by the horizontal time-varying currents and interaction between this advection and diffusion due to weaker mesoscale eddies and internal gravity waves—are isolated in these calculations. Other processes such as vertical settling and biochemical breakdown are not discussed here.

First, the motion of a single patch of material under the influence of a strong ring is considered. As the ring hits a patch of material, it stretches the waste into a thin, tangential line about its circumference. The patch re-forms after the ring has passed, but in a distorted shape and displaced by 100–200 km. The passage of the ring, then, causes deformation of the patch, creating enhanced gradients and thereby increasing the dispersion due to the smaller-scale motions (internal waves) or weaker, incoherent eddies. In general, this process is quite anisotropic.

Second, the problem of the increased flux of material across the Slope Water caused by a series of moving Gulf Stream rings is computed. This question, in addition to its potential importance for understanding the rates of loss of pollutants from the Shelf Water or the possible impingement of material dumped in deepwater onto the shelf, is of general theoretical importance, since the role of rings in the transport of heat, salt, nutrients, and vorticity is still poorly understood. The results in this chapter suggest that when the flow is dominated by the passage of strong eddies, the mixing length estimate of eddy diffusivity is considerably larger than the actual effective diffusion coefficient, at least in the direction perpendicular to the eddy track. The flux remains proportional to the smaller-scale diffusivity, with the rings giving at most one order of magnitude enhancement.

8.2. EFFECTS OF RINGS ON AN ISOLATED PATCH OF MATERIAL

If the short-term motion (on the order of months) of dumped material is of concern, the movement and dispersal induced by mesoscale eddies must be understood. The analysis of the motion of single particles in a large amplitude Rossby wave or ringlike feature was presented by Flierl (1981). The results of this analysis will be described briefly.

When the eddy field can be represented as a sequence of highs and lows, as in a Rossby wave field (Fig. 8.1), the particles move in looping trajectories that gradually shift eastward or westward. The periods of the particles are quite variable and the Stokes' drift (the net displacement during a period divided by the period) also depends on both the initial latitude and longitude (Fig. 8.2). Since the flow is nondivergent, the area of any patch is conserved (in the absence of diffusion); however, the patch is inevitably being distorted in the direction of wave propagation because the average drift rates of the various particles are different.

Figure 8.3 shows the advective effects on a marked patch of fluid 20 km in diameter as a strong anticyclonic eddy (65 km radius) passes by. There is a strong northward displacement initially, with the circle being stretched into a 110 km × 4 km ellipse. As the ring passes the patch is left behind, with a somewhat distorted shape.

This example is not extreme. Displacements can be very large for some initial particle latitudes and can vary rapidly with north–south distance (Flierl, 1981). In Fig. 8.4, this point is illustrated by following particles set initially 150 km south of the ring track (which is due west). In this case, the patch is substantially more distorted as a result of its passage around the ring than in the previous example.

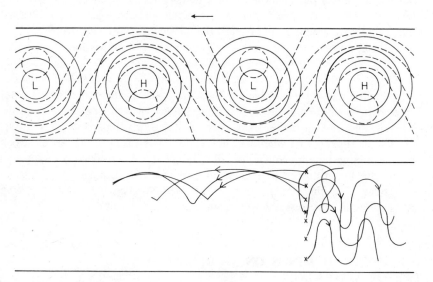

Figure 8.1. Streamfunction field, $\bar{\psi}$, for Rossby waves in a channel. The $\bar{\psi}$ is shown by solid lines; the dashed line show the streamfunction $\overline{\Psi}$ in the frame where the wave is stationary. On the lower panel are plotted the trajectories of particles started at the positions marked by x along a line of longitude within this wave field. Note the large variations in drift rate for the different particles. The trajectories have been computed for about 1.5 wave periods.

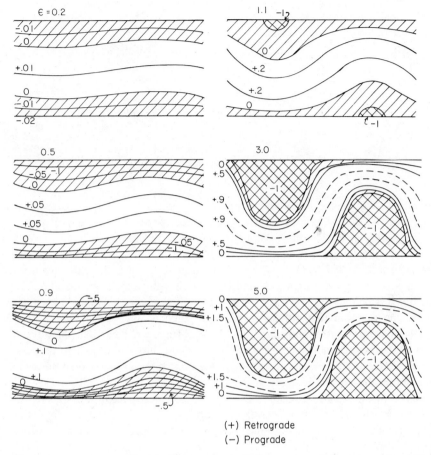

(+) Retrograde
(−) Prograde

Figure 8.2. Average east–west drift rate as a function of the initial position for particles within a Rossby wave field. The drift rate is normalized by the phase speed of the wave. The different sketches are for different ratios of the fluid speeds to the phase speed ($\epsilon = U/c$) as labeled above each set of contours.

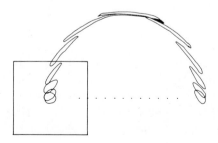

Figure 8.3. Motion and shape changes for an initially circular patch under the influence of a single strong eddy. The box is 130 km on a side and represents the diameter of the ring. The swirl speed is 5 cm s^{-1}, with the center positions marked by dots at 3-d intervals.

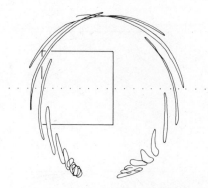

Figure 8.4. An example of patch motion when the patch is initially south of the track. See Fig 8.3 for parameters. Even more extreme cases can be found if the initial latitude is close to the streamline that approaches the stagnation point.

Interaction with successive eddies will stretch and distort the shape even further. This process occurs fairly rapidly: the time steps shown are 3-d intervals.

The purely advective effects of a ring on a patch of material suggest some insights into the spread that occurs when the waste is influenced by both advection and diffusion. As the patch is stretched out around the ring, the gradients normal to the eddy are greatly increased and cross-wise diffusion occurs rapidly. As the patch is left behind on the eastern side of the eddy, where the streamlines diverge again, the material that diffused across the patch is now spread out to greater distances in the north–south direction. It would appear, then, that the advective field of the ring cannot only enhance the transport due to the random processes, but also forces considerable anisotropy in the flux. In order to examine these ideas more fully, the effects of small-scale random motions and internal waves will be modelled by an explicit turbulent diffusivity K. The mesoscale flow associated with the ring can be described by a streamfunction $\psi\ (x,y,t)$. With these assumptions, the concentration of tracer substance $S(x,y,t)$ evolves according to the equation

$$\frac{\partial S}{\partial t} + \frac{\partial \psi}{\partial x}\frac{\partial S}{\partial y} - \frac{\partial \psi}{\partial y}\frac{\partial S}{\partial x} = K\,\nabla^2 S \qquad\qquad 1$$

One must bear in mind that this is only a valid predictor for the probability distribution of the waste and represents the ensemble-averaged effect of the internal waves and turbulence; in any single realization the substance may move quite differently. For an initial condition, assume that the tracer is released at a point x_0, y_0 so the concentration $S(x,y,t)$ at $t = 0$ is

$$S(x,y,0) = M_0\delta\ (x - x_0)\ \delta(y - y_0) \qquad\qquad 2$$

where M_0 is the total amount of substance released and δ is the Dirac delta function.

Although there is no simple analytical solution to this problem, some trends for the changes can be computed. The first is a remarkable generalization of a result by Chatwin (1974): For certain flow fields with uniform vorticity, the center of mass moves as if it were a fluid particle. The flow fields considered will be described by a streamfunction

$$\psi = a + bx + cy + \frac{1}{2}dx^2 + exy + \frac{1}{2}fy^2 \qquad\qquad 3$$

which can represent uniform flow, flow with uniform shear, flow with a stagnation point, solid body rotation or flow in elliptical patterns. Any of the coefficients a through f may be functions of time. To demonstrate that the center of mass acts as a fluid particle, consider first the location of a particle initially at (x_0, y_0). Let the Lagrangian position at time t be denoted by (ξ, η); these variables evolve according to

$$\frac{\partial \xi}{\partial t} = -\left.\frac{\partial \psi}{\partial y}\right|_{\xi,\eta,t} = -\left[c + e\xi + f\eta\right]$$

$$\frac{\partial \eta}{\partial t} = \left.\frac{\partial \psi}{\partial x}\right|_{\xi,\eta,t} = \left[b + d\xi + e\eta\right] \qquad\qquad 4$$

$$\xi|_{t=0} = x_0 \, , \, \eta\,|_{t=0} = y_0$$

The center of mass position, defined by

$$\mu_1 = \frac{1}{M_0} \int\int dx \, dy \, xS$$

$$\mu_2 = \frac{1}{M_0} \int\int dx \, dy \, yS$$

can be followed by integrating

$$\frac{\partial \mu_1}{\partial t} = \frac{1}{M_0} \int\int dx \, dy \, x \, \frac{\partial S}{\partial t}$$

$$= \frac{1}{M_0} \int\int dx \, dy \, x \, \frac{\partial}{\partial x}\left(\frac{\partial \psi}{\partial y} S\right) - \frac{1}{M_0} \int\int dx \, dy \, x \, \frac{\partial}{\partial y}\left(\frac{\partial \psi}{\partial x} S\right) \qquad 5$$

$$+ \frac{K}{M_0} \int\int dx \, dy \, x \left(\frac{\partial^2 S}{\partial x^2} + \frac{\partial^2 S}{\partial y^2}\right)$$

$$= -\frac{1}{M_0} \int\int dx \, dy \, S \, \frac{\partial \psi}{\partial y}$$

$$\frac{\partial \mu_2}{\partial t} = \frac{1}{M_0} \int\int dx \, dy \, S \, \frac{\partial \psi}{\partial x}$$

This simply states that the center of mass moves with a weighted average of the velocity field, the weighting being the concentration of material itself. For the particular flow field, equation 3, these can be simplified

$$\frac{\partial \mu_1}{\partial t} = - \frac{1}{M_0} \int \int dx \, dy \, S \left[c + ex + fy \right]$$

$$= - \left[c + e\mu_1 + f\mu_2 \right]$$

$$\frac{\partial \mu_2}{\partial t} = \left[b + d\mu_1 + e\mu_2 \right]$$

giving equations (and also initial conditions) identical to those for the fluid particle initially at (x_0, y_0) (equation 4). By further analysis of equations 2 and 3 one can show that the tracer spreads in a Gaussian shape around the center of mass with an elliptical pattern that may rotate in time.

For short times, certain properties of the concentration can be predicted for more general streamfunction fields. This can be done by assuming that S remains sharply peaked around the center of mass position (μ_1, μ_2). Under these circumstances, ψ can be Taylor-expanded so that equation 5 becomes

$$\frac{\partial \mu_1}{\partial t} = - \left\{ \frac{\partial \psi}{\partial y} \Big|_{\mu_1, \mu_2, t} + \frac{1}{2} \sum_{ij} \sigma_{ij} \frac{\partial}{\partial x_i} \frac{\partial}{\partial x_j} \frac{\partial}{\partial y} \psi \Big|_{\mu_1, \mu_2, t} + \cdots \right\}$$

$$\frac{\partial \mu_2}{\partial t} = + \left\{ \frac{\partial \psi}{\partial x} \Big|_{\mu_1, \mu_2, t} + \frac{1}{2} \sum_{ij} \sigma_{ij} \frac{\partial}{\partial x_i} \frac{\partial}{\partial x_j} \frac{\partial}{\partial x} \psi \Big|_{\mu_1, \mu_2, t} + \cdots \right\}$$

6

where i and j sum over 1 and 2 $(x_1 = x, x_2 = y)$. The second moments

$$\sigma_{ij} = \frac{1}{M_0} \int \int dx \, dy \, S \, (x_i - \mu_i) \, (x_j - \mu_j)$$

determine the deviation of the center of mass from the fluid particle position. These second moments can also be estimated by a similar procedure:

$$\frac{\partial}{\partial t} \sigma_{11} = 2K - 2 \left[\sigma_{11} \frac{\partial^2 \psi}{\partial x \partial y} + \sigma_{12} \frac{\partial^2 \psi}{\partial y^2} \right] + \cdots$$

$$\frac{\partial}{\partial t} \sigma_{12} = \sigma_{11} \frac{\partial^2 \psi}{\partial x^2} - \sigma_{22} \frac{\partial^2 \psi}{\partial y^2} + \cdots$$

7

$$\frac{\partial}{\partial t} \sigma_{22} = 2K + 2 \left[\sigma_{12} \frac{\partial^2 \psi}{\partial x^2} + \sigma_{22} \frac{\partial^2 \psi}{\partial x \partial y} \right] + \cdots$$

Here all of the derivatives of ψ are evaluated at the mean position of the patch (μ_1, μ_2).

For short times, the patch spreads isotropically

$$\sigma_{ij} \simeq 2Kt\delta_{ij}$$

Because different parts of the patch now sample different flow speeds, the effective streamfunction for the center of mass of the patch

$$\psi_{eff} = \psi + (\nabla^2 \psi) \, 2Kt \qquad\qquad 8$$

also changes in time. When the flow has constant vorticity, the gradients of the effective streamfunction are identical to those of the streamfunction itself so that, to this order, the center of mass follows a material particle. This seems to be the most general form of the theorem demonstrated above for a more specialized form of ψ.

   When the vorticity in the flow is not uniform (and the dynamics of the mesoscale almost necessitate this) the center of mass moves off the material particle track at a rate increasing with time. Figure 8.5 shows contours of the streamfunction for a strong westward-moving anticyclonic ring and the contours of the vorticity, which is proportional to the correction induced by diffusion. Figure 8.6 shows some center of mass position calculations using equation 8, which show the tendency for a patch to move outwards across the streamlines in the southeastern region of a warm, westward-moving eddy. This has been confirmed by direct numerical simulations

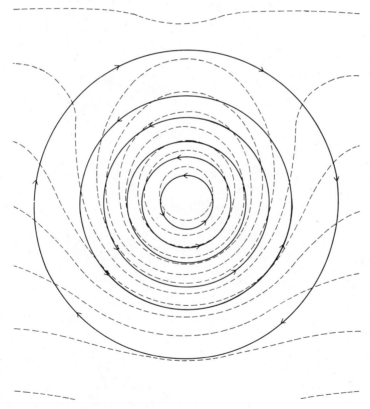

Figure 8.5.   Contours of ψ (dashed) and the vorticity (solid) for an eddy with swirl speeds of 30 cm s^{-1}. The vorticity contours show the changes in the stream function for the center of mass, with time, induced by diffusion.

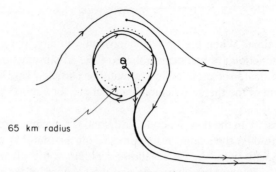

65 km radius

Figure 8.6. The motion of the center of mass for three initial locations.

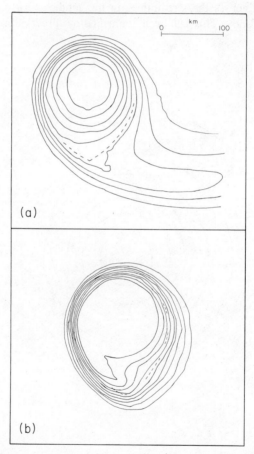

Figure 8.7. Contours showing material exiting or entering a ring. For exiting material (a), the trapped zone is filled uniformly with material; for entering material (b), the region outside the trapped zone contains tracer, and the ring has none. The main flux of material occurs near the stagnation point. The contour interval is 10% of the initial concentration.

of equation 1. Contours of S, given the initial condition that $S = 1$ within the ring and zero outside, are shown in Fig. 8.7. Note the loss of material in a tail left behind as the ring moves westward (the picture is plotted in a coordinate system moving with the ring).

In addition, the southeast quadrant is also the region where fluid appears to enter the eddy. This appearance is probably caused by fluid diffusing inwards on the eastern side and then being swirled around to the western side. This process is also illustrated in Fig. 8.7.

One could also attempt to solve equations 6 and 7 numerically in order to esti-mate the shape and size of a fluid patch; however, these calculations break down very rapidly because the moments may grow rapidly as the patch evolves, and this invalidates the assumption that the patch is small compared to the scale of the ring.

8.3 IMPACT OF RINGS ON MEAN DISTRIBUTIONS AND FLUXES

The previous section described the effect of a geostrophic eddy moving at a constant rate on a single patch of material. It is also important to compute the long-term average tracer distribution caused by boundary sources and the periodic pas-sage of rings. For the particular example of the Slope Water, with boundaries at the shelf edge and the Gulf Stream, we calculate the enhanced transport of material across the Slope Water due to the eddies. The results can be used to estimate off-the-shelf fluxes of pollutants introduced nearshore or, alternatively, fluxes from deepwater sites onto the shelf. The effects of small-scale eddies and internal waves are again modelled as an explicit turbulent diffusivity K and the larger-scale stronger rings are incorporated in detail using a model streamfunction $\psi(x,y,t)$.

The property distribution is governed by advection and diffusion

$$\frac{\partial S}{\partial t} + \frac{\partial \psi}{\partial x}\frac{\partial S}{\partial y} - \frac{\partial \psi}{\partial y}\frac{\partial S}{\partial x} = K\nabla^2 S \qquad\qquad 9$$

and specification of the boundary conditions.

In this problem, there is one important nondimensional parameter $\delta = K/UL$, where U is the characteristic fluid speed in the eddy, which characterizes the strength of the small-scale diffusion. This parameter can also be viewed as the ratio of the "real" diffusivity to the usual mixing length estimate of the eddy diffusivity $K_e = UL$. In addition, there are nondimensional ratios of various length scales (L is the domain width, γL is the domain length, and l is the eddy length scale) and $\epsilon = U/c$ (c is the propagation rate), the "steepness" of the eddy motion. The nondimensional parameter commonly used to measure the efficiency of eddy trans-port in convection problems is the Nusselt number, Nu, which is the ratio of the flux across the domain to that which would exist in a purely diffusive regime ($U = 0$). The analogous parameter will be taken as the measure of the efficiency of eddy transport in this analysis.

8.3.1. Circular Flow

There is a simple example illustrating the diffusive properties of mesoscale eddies when there are horizontally varying sources or sinks. Consider a circular domain $r \leq r_0$ with a swirling flow $\mathbf{u} = v(r)\hat{\theta}$ subjected to spatially varying boundary conditions $S(r_0, \theta) = S_0 \sin \theta$ (Fig. 8.8). The flux of material across the centerline of the circle ($y = 0$) is given by

$$F = 2 \int_0^{r_0} dr \left[-\frac{K}{r} \frac{\partial S}{\partial \theta} + vS \right] \Bigg|_{\theta=0} \qquad 10$$

First, consider the diffusive solution ($v = 0$) which, in this problem, is simply

$$S(r, \theta) = S_0 \frac{r}{r_0} \sin \theta \qquad 11$$

with a value for the flux of

$$F_{(v=0)} = -2KS_0 \qquad 12$$

When $v \neq 0$, F must be found by first solving the steady-state equation

$$\frac{v}{r} \frac{\partial S}{\partial \theta} = K \left[\frac{1}{r} \frac{\partial}{\partial r} r \frac{\partial S}{\partial r} + \frac{1}{r^2} \frac{\partial^2 S}{\partial \theta^2} \right] \qquad 13$$

and integrating equation 10 along $\theta = 0$. Even for the simplest velocity structure $v = \Omega r$ (solid-body rotation), the solution to equation 13 is complicated. The problem has been solved numerically, and contours of S are shown in Fig. 8.8 as a function of the parameter $\delta = K/\Omega r_0^2$.

In the case of weak flow $\delta \gg 1$, the solution to equation 13 is approximately

$$S = S_0 \left\{ \frac{r}{r_0} \sin \theta + \frac{1}{8\delta} \left[\frac{r^3}{r_0^3} - \frac{r}{r_0} \right] \cos \theta \right.$$

$$\left. - \frac{1}{8\delta^2} \left[\frac{r^5}{24 r_0^5} - \frac{r^3}{8 r_0^3} + \left(\frac{1}{8} - \frac{1}{24} \right) \frac{r}{r_0} \right] \sin \theta + \cdots \right\}$$

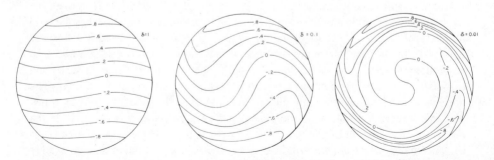

Figure 8.8.   Contours of the concentration of material S within the domain for various δ values.

and the ratio of the flux to the diffusive limit (equation 12) is

$$Nu = 1 + .01042\ \delta^{-2} \qquad\qquad 14$$

This is shown on Fig. 8.9, along with the fluxes calculated from numerical solutions to equation 13.

When the flow is very strong, $\delta \ll 1$, the equations take a boundary-layer form—in the interior of the domain $S \to 0$, with the transition between the center and the exterior occurring in a layer of width $\delta^{1/2} r_0$. This can be seen in the contours of S on Fig. 8.8 for the smaller δ values; the gradients become strong only near the wall. The approximate solution for small δ (high swirl) is

$$S = S_0 e^{(1/\sqrt{2}\delta)\ (r/r_0\ -\ 1)} \sin\left[\theta + \frac{1}{\sqrt{2}\delta}\left(\frac{r}{r_0} - 1\right)\right] \qquad\qquad 15$$

and the flux ratio is

$$Nu = \frac{1}{\sqrt{2}\delta}$$

For both of these flows, the flux across the centerline can be represented as

$$F = -\ 2kS$$

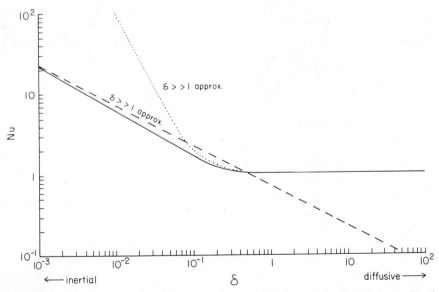

Figure 8.9.   The ratio Nu of the flux of material with and without a swirling flow when a gradient is imposed at the outer boundary. The solid line is calculated numerically and the dashed lines represent various asymptotic estimates.

where the effective diffusivity k can be written as

$$k = K + .01042 \frac{K_e^2}{K} \quad \text{(weak flow)}$$

$$k = \sqrt{\frac{K_e K}{2}} \quad \text{(strong flow)}$$

where K_e is the eddy diffusivity defined by the velocity and length scale of the flow $K_e = \Omega r_0^2$.

In most oceanographic problems, the $\delta \ll 1$ limit applies since the small-scale diffusivity K is thought to be smaller than the scale estimate of eddy diffusivity K_e. In this limit, the calculation suggests one very important result: the effective diffusivity of even a very strong eddy is not given by K_e but by the geometric mean of K_e and small-scale diffusivity K. Small-scale diffusion does not disappear from the problem (unlike three-dimensional turbulent flows), because of the boundary-layer character of the flow: the gradients of S disappear in the interior in about one turnover time (as described later) of the eddy and the gradients along the boundary only leak into the fluid because of small-scale diffusion. These anomalies are rapidly swept around the eddy by the flow so that gradients only build up over a diffusion distance $(K/\Omega)^{1/2}$; the amount of material moved across the domain is proportional to the product of the flow speed and this distance. This result has important consequences whenever the eddies remain coherent over times longer than the turnover time.

This was a case in which the eddy velocity was maximal at the boundary of the domain. If, instead, the velocity is small near the boundary, then the asymptotic dependence of the flux on the circulation speed is even weaker due to reduced swirl speeds within the boundary layer. The simplest example illustrating this phenomenon uses a velocity profile

$$V \to \alpha \left(1 - \frac{r}{r_0}\right) \quad as \quad r \to r_0$$

In this case the approximate equation when $\delta \ll 1$ is

$$\eta \frac{\partial S}{\partial \theta} + \hat{\delta} \frac{\partial^2 S}{\partial \eta^2} = 0 \qquad\qquad 16$$

where

$$\eta = \left(\frac{r}{r_0} - 1\right) \quad \text{and} \quad \hat{\delta} = \frac{K}{\alpha r_0} = \frac{K}{K_e}$$

Equation 16 has an Airy function solution with the Nusselt number given by

$$Nu = \left\{ 3^{5/6} \frac{\Gamma(2/3)}{\Gamma(1/3)} \right\} \hat{\delta}^{-1/3}$$

hence the effective diffusivity k is proportional to $(K^2 K_e)^{1/3}$. In general, this k is less than that computed in the previous problem.

8.3.2. Moving Eddies in a Channel

Consider next the fluxes across a channel induced by a train of eddies moving along the channel. For convenience, the case in which the eddies occur periodically is discussed; however, the results would probably apply to more general circumstances such as a somewhat irregular pattern of mesoscale features. If the eddies are moving steadily in the westward direction with speed $-c$ (the condition $c < 0$ is used), the streamfunction can be written

$$\psi = \psi(x - ct, y)$$

and the distribution of material likewise is given by

$$S = S(x - ct, y)$$

The advection-diffusion equation becomes

$$-c \frac{\partial S}{\partial x} + \frac{\partial \psi}{\partial x} \frac{\partial S}{\partial y} - \frac{\partial \psi}{\partial y} \frac{\partial S}{\partial x} = K\nabla^2 S$$

or (in terms of the streamfunction in a co-moving reference frame) $\Psi = \psi + cy$

$$\frac{\partial \Psi}{\partial x} \frac{\partial S}{\partial y} - \frac{\partial \Psi}{\partial y} \frac{\partial S}{\partial x} = K\nabla^2 S$$

The nondimensional form of this equation and the boundary conditions $S = 0$ at $y = 0$ and $S = S_0$ at $y = L$ are

$$\frac{\partial \Psi}{\partial x} \frac{\partial S}{\partial y} - \frac{\partial \Psi}{\partial y} \frac{\partial S}{\partial x} = \delta\nabla^2 S$$

$$\Psi = -y + \epsilon\,\psi(x, y)$$

$$\Psi(x + \gamma, y) = \Psi(x, y)$$
$$S(x + \gamma, y) = S(x, y)$$ (periodicity) 17

$$S(x, 0) = 0$$

$$S(x, 1) = 1$$

Here, the parameters

$$\delta = \frac{K}{cL}, \qquad \epsilon = \frac{U}{c}, \qquad \gamma = \frac{\text{spacing between eddies}}{\text{width of domain}}$$

measure the relative strength of diffusion to wave propagation, the advection speed compared to the translation rate and the aspect ratio of the domain. The geometry is illustrated in Fig. 8.10.

For this problem the flux across the channel

$$F = -\int_0^{\gamma L} dx \left[K \frac{\partial S}{\partial y} - \frac{\partial \Psi}{\partial x} S \right]$$

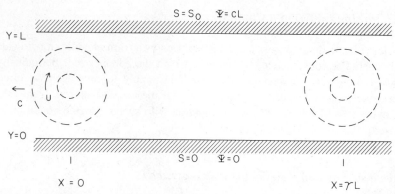

Figure 8.10. Geometry for a model problem for estimating the horizontal flux induced by the passage of a sequence of eddies.

is independent of the cross-channel dimension y and so can be calculated at either edge of the domain where the cross-channel velocity is assumed to vanish. Thus

$$F = -\int_0^{\gamma L} dx \, K \frac{\partial S}{\partial y}\bigg|_{y=L}$$

and the Nusselt number is

$$Nu = \frac{L}{\gamma L S_0} \int_0^{\gamma L} dx \frac{\partial S}{\partial y}\bigg|_{y=L}$$

which takes the simple form in nondimensional variables

$$Nu = \frac{1}{\gamma} \int_0^{\gamma} dx \frac{\partial S}{\partial y}\bigg|_{y=1} \qquad\qquad 18$$

Again, the limit of oceanographic interest occurs for small δ (that is, weak diffusion compared to advection). However, diffusion can never be altogether ignored since there is an integral constraint on the flux which comes from integrating over the area bounded by the lower wall, and a particular streamline $\Psi = \Psi_0$ (Fig. 8.11)

$$\iint_A \frac{\partial \Psi}{\partial x} \frac{\partial S}{\partial y} - \frac{\partial \Psi}{\partial y} \frac{\partial S}{\partial x} = \delta \iint_A \nabla^2 S$$

But the left-hand side vanishes so that

$$\delta \iint_A \nabla^2 S = 0$$

which can be transformed using Gauss's theorem to

$$\oint \nabla S \cdot \hat{n} \, dl = 0$$

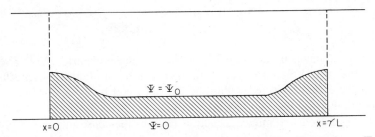

Figure 8.11. Integration domans for the cases of open $\overline{\Psi}$ contours ($\overline{\Psi} = \overline{\Psi}_0$) and closed $\overline{\Psi}$ contours ($\overline{\Psi} = 0$).

with $\hat{n}$ an outward normal unit vector. We must consider two cases. First are the streamlines which extend to the edges of the domain. Because of the periodicity in x, the foregoing integral can be reduced to

$$\int_{\Psi=\Psi 0} \nabla S \cdot \hat{n} \, dl = \int_0^\gamma dx \left.\frac{\partial S}{\partial y}\right|_{y=0} = \gamma Nu \qquad\qquad 19$$

which is constant. This holds for all open streamlines (those which intersect $x = 0$ and $x = \gamma$). Second are those closed streamlines which do not intersect the eastern or western edges. The net flux through these must be zero

$$\oint_{\Psi=\Psi 0} \nabla S \cdot \hat{n} \, dl = 0 \qquad\qquad 20$$

Even in the limit where K is small, these integral constraints cannot be ignored; in fact, they must be used to determine the solution.

Equation 17 can be solved in the $\delta \ll 1$ limit: the lowest-order approximation is

$$S = S(\Psi)$$

implying that the concentration of tracer is nearly uniform along streamlines. Applying the constraints (equations 19 and 20) gives two results. First, if there are any closed streamlines, S will be uniform within them, since

$$\nabla S = \frac{\partial S}{\partial \Psi} \nabla \Psi$$

which implies

$$0 = \oint_{\Psi=\Psi 0} \nabla S \cdot \hat{n} = \frac{\partial S}{\partial \Psi} \oint_{\Psi=\Psi 0} \nabla \Psi \cdot \hat{n}$$

The only way this can hold is if the tracer is homogenized within the closed streamline regions

$$\frac{\partial S}{\partial \Psi} = 0 \qquad\qquad 21$$

This result is analogous to the behavior seen in the previous section where for $\delta \ll 1$, the central region was uniform in concentration. In the present situation, however, the S value selected within the domain is set by the S value on the outermost closed streamline.

Second, on open streamlines, equation 19 gives the constraint on $S(\Psi)$ that

$$\left.\frac{\partial S}{\partial \Psi}\right|_{\Psi=\Psi_0} = \frac{\gamma Nu}{\displaystyle\int_{\Psi=\Psi 0} \nabla\Psi \cdot \hat{n}\, dl} = \frac{\gamma Nu}{\displaystyle\int_{\Psi=\Psi 0} |\nabla\Psi|\, dl} \qquad 22$$

This can be integrated from the lower boundary $S = 0$, $\Psi = 0$ to the upper boundary $\Psi = -1$ where S is set to one. This requirement determines the nondimensional flux of material Nu

$$Nu = \left\{ \int_0^{-1} d\Psi \left[\frac{\gamma}{\displaystyle\int_{\Psi=\Psi 0} |\nabla\Psi|\, dl} \right]^{-1} \right\} \qquad 23$$

This formula is complicated and, in general, must be computed numerically; however, some rather artificial velocity field patterns can be used to illustrate the types of behavior which can occur.

Figure 8.12 shows the start-up procedure when an eddy forms under an existing gradient of S. The fluid within the core of the eddy is wound around itself and rapidly homogenized. In addition, as the eddy moves westward, it leaves a trail of mixed fluid behind it. When the next eddy arrives, it will further mix up this fluid. The end state of this process depends critically on the presence of significant flow along the north and south channel walls.

This distinction is illustrated by calculations of the distribution of S and the Nusselt number Nu for two different model streamfunctions. Figure 8.13a shows contours of ψ and of Ψ for these two cases. In case A, the velocity is large at the boundaries of the channel (and of course is tangential at these boundaries) whereas in case B, the velocity maximum occurs in the interior and there is no eddy-induced flow at the walls. In the contours of Ψ, it can be seen that all particles are strongly influenced by the eddy in case A, whereas in case B there are some particles that are not strongly accelerated by the eddy.

The contours of S for various ϵ values (shown in Fig. 8.13b) show significant differences when ϵ is large. In case A there are still strong gradients of S within the channel in between the eddies. These are maintained by the strong diffusion that occurs when the particles are packed up against the wall north of the eddy center. However, when the eddies do not reach the wall (as in case B where Δ is the distance from the edge of the eddy to the wall), the gradients of S disappear

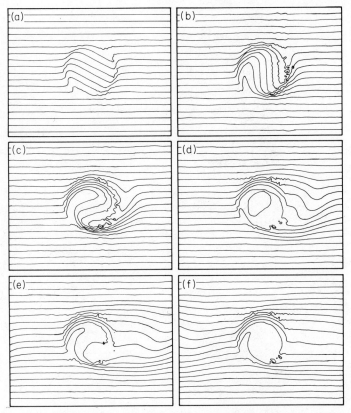

Figure 8.12. The evolution of the tracer field S when an eddy forms under an initial north–south gradient. The plots are in the frame of reference where the eddy is stationary and at time intervals of roughly $\frac{1}{8}$ of the rotation period. Note the nearly complete homogenization in the interior occuring within one rotation period shown in (f).

within the region where eddies pass so that the only gradients of S occur in narrow bands (of width Δ) to the north and south of the regions where the eddies pass. The nondimensional fluxes in the two cases

$$Nu = \frac{Q}{\gamma \ln\left(\dfrac{\gamma + Q + \epsilon}{\gamma + \epsilon}\right)} \qquad \text{(case A)}$$

$$Nu = \left\{ 2\Delta + \frac{\gamma}{Q} \ln \frac{\gamma + \epsilon(1 - 2\Delta) + Q\left(1 - \dfrac{3\Delta}{2}\right)}{\gamma + \epsilon(1 - 2\Delta)} \right\} \qquad \text{(case B)}$$

$$Q = \frac{2\epsilon(\epsilon - 1)}{\epsilon + 1}$$

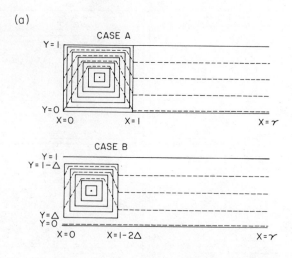

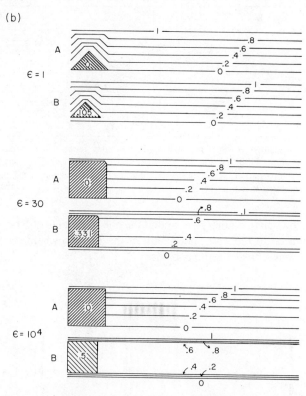

Figure 8.13. Contours of the model streamfunction in the stationary frame for two cases and of S for the two cases at various ratios of swirl speed to transitional speed ϵ. (a) The stationary reference is shown by solid lines and the moving reference is shown by dashed lines. The upper frame is for case A where the eddy has strong flow at the edge of the channel

are plotted in Fig. 8.14, showing that the flux increases as the eddy swirl speed increases, but reaches a finite limit in case B. Presumably a more realistic picture of ψ would yield results somewhere in between cases A and B.

The results of these calculations strongly suggest that rings do not greatly enhance the flux of material in the cross-channel direction perpendicular to their track). Since Nu is independent of K, the effective diffusivity

$$k = NuK$$

remains proportional to the smaller-scale diffusion rate K; furthermore, the proportionality constant Nu is not very large even for features of the strength of Gulf Stream rings ($\epsilon \sim 20$, $Nu \sim 5$–10). In the circular domain, the effective diffusivity k was smaller than the mixing length estimate K; the fluxes in the present problem are weaker yet, for the following reasons. In the circular case all streamlines are closed and the material therefore cannot be uniform along streamlines near the boundary, whereas in the channel, no streamline extends from one boundary to the other. Thus there is no diffusive boundary layer; rather, a large proportion of the flux from the wall occurs when the streamlines (relative to the ring) are packed tightly against the northern wall. This region has thickness order $1/\epsilon$, independent of K; thus the flux remains proportional to the small-scale diffusivity.

8.4. CONCLUSIONS

These simple calculations suggest the importance of considering the eddies and rings when preparing a strategy for waste disposal in the ocean. Clearly, these

$$
\Psi = \begin{cases}
\epsilon x & x < Y < 1 - x \\
\epsilon Y & y < xY < 1 - x \\
\epsilon - \epsilon x & 1 - x < Y < x \\
\epsilon - \epsilon Y & Y > xY > 1 - x \\
0 & x > 1
\end{cases}
$$

while the lower frame is for case B where there is no flow along the walls

$$
\Psi = \begin{cases}
0 & x > 1 - 2\Delta \text{ or } Y < \Delta \text{ or } Y > 1 - \Delta \\
\epsilon x & \Delta + x < Y < 1 - \Delta - x \\
\epsilon - \epsilon Y - \epsilon \Delta & Y > \Delta + x, Y > 1 - \Delta - x \\
\epsilon - \epsilon x - 2\epsilon \Delta & 1 - \Delta - x < Y < \Delta + x \\
\epsilon y - \epsilon \Delta & Y < \Delta + x, Y < 1 - \Delta - x
\end{cases}
$$

(b) Note the well-mixed regions within the eddy and the area of sharp gradients in case A and also the area which has been swept clear by the eddies in case B.

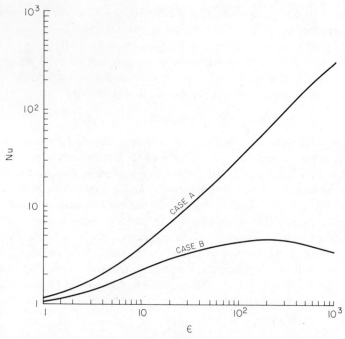

Figure 8.14. The efficiency of eddy transport compared to diffusion, *Nu*, as a function of the ratio of swirl speed to translational motion if the eddies, ϵ, for the two cases shown in Fig. 8.13.

motions will have a profound effect in determining where any particular dump will go. Displacements of several hundred kilometers may occur within a few weeks when a strong feature such as a Gulf Stream ring is near the site. The exact direction and magnitude of the eddy-induced motion depends strongly on the relative position of the dump and the ring. Furthermore, the track of the patch of water containing the waste around the ring will cause the material to be spread over quite large distances along one horizontal axis with corresponding contraction along the other. This in turn suggests that the diffusion due to smaller-scale oceanic motions will be enhanced and also become less isotropic in effect because of the influence of the energetic mesoscale motions.

However, the overall importance of the eddies, when parameterized as an effective diffusivity coefficient, is less than mixing length arguments would indicate. The material does not penetrate far into the ring when the advection is strong, so that the transport only occurs over narrow spatial regions and is not particularly large. For example, the cross-channel flux induced by rings is only 4 to 6 times that which would occur due to small-scale diffusion alone. This result has been obtained for two different cases, when the swirling flows of the eddies are a maximum at the edges of the domain and when they vanish along the walls. These results apply whenever the small-scale diffusion is weak compared to the scale estimate of the eddy diffusivity and the mesoscale flows are fairly coherent, both conditions being apparently reasonable for the deep ocean. It is possible that these conclusions may not hold when there is a broad, smooth spectrum of eddy motions from the ring scale down to the diffusion length scale $(Kt)^{1/2}$.

This calculation only applies to the transport of material perpendicular to the line of travel of the eddies. Material dumped in a ring will leak out only very slowly and thus may be transported quite far along the slope. Even for dumps outside the rings, it seems probable that the effective diffusion rate along the direction of travel may be substantially larger, since the Stokes' drifts are parallel to the line of travel.

ACKNOWLEDGMENTS

This research was supported by the Ocean Dumping Office, U.S. National Oceanic and Atmospheric Administration, grant number NA80AA-D-00057.

REFERENCES

Chatwin, P. C. 1974. The dispersion of contaminant released from instantaneous sources in laminar flow near stagnation points. *Journal of Fluid Mechanics*, **66**, 753–766.

Flierl, G. R. 1981. Particle motions in large amplitude wave fields. *Geophysical and Astrophysical Fluid Dynamics*, **18**, 39–74.

9

FATE OF OCEAN-DUMPED ACID IRON WASTE IN A STRATIFIED MICROCOSM

Mary F. Fox and Dana R. Kester

Graduate School of Oceanography
University of Rhode Island
Kingston, Rhode Island

Abstract		171
9.1.	Introduction	172
9.2.	Experimental	173
9.3.	Results	176
	9.3.1. Surface Layer Removal	176
	9.3.2. Sub-Pycnocline Accumulation and Removal	179
	9.3.3. Cross-Pycnocline Mixing	180
9.4.	Discussion	181
9.5.	Summary and Conclusions	183
Acknowledgments		184
References		184

ABSTRACT

Field studies have provided information on the short-term effects of acid iron waste disposal at a deepwater dumpsite off the coast of New Jersey. To assess the long-term effects of the acid iron waste, an experiment was conducted at the MERL, (Marine Ecosystems Research Laboratory) facility of the University of Rhode Island. The MERL tanks (2 m diameter and 5 m deep) provide planktonic ecosystems for experimental manipulation. To simulate conditions at the deepwater dumpsite, two MERL tanks were established with a 10°C temperature differential maintained between the surface and bottom layers. Acid iron waste was added to the surface layer of one of the tanks at a 10^5 dilution. The removal of iron from the surface layer of the tank and the penetration of the particulate iron through the thermocline were studied as a function of time after the waste addition. The removal of iron from the surface layer was first order with respect to iron, with a half-life of the iron concentration = 35 h. The mechanism of iron removal was gravitational settling of the iron particles and not assimilation by phytoplankton and zooplankton species exposed to acid iron waste. The results of the MERL tank experiment were consistent with field observations of an actual acid iron waste dump.

9.1. INTRODUCTION

Disposal of waste material in the ocean without detrimental effects has become an important area of marine research. For the past few years we have investigated the effects of dumping industrial wastes at a deepwater dumpsite located off the coast of New Jersey, Deepwater Dumpsite (DWD)-106 (Kester et al., 1981; Brown et al., 1983). The depth of the water column of DWD-106 is about 2000 m; therefore, the primary fate of wastes is dispersion in the water column rather than incorporation into the sediments. Acid iron waste from the production of titanium dioxide at the Du Pont Edgemoor (Delaware) facility has been dumped at DWD-106 since 1977. This liquid waste is discharged into the water column from a towed barge; there is a rapid 10^5 dilution of the waste in the wake of the barge. Subsequent oceanic mixing processes are slow and have been predicted to require weeks or months for a further 10- to 100-fold dilution of the acid iron waste plume (Csanady, 1981; Mukherji and Kester, 1983).

The chemical constituents of the acid iron waste are listed in Table 9.1. As this waste mixes with seawater, the acid is rapidly neutralized by the carbonate and borate buffers in seawater and hydrous ferric oxide precipitates. The horizontal dispersion of the waste plume has been tracked by continuous real-time measurements of elevated iron concentrations in seawater (Brown et al., 1983).

Our field studies to date have provided detailed information on the short-term fate of the acid iron waste in the marine environment, but they have not revealed the long-term effects of the waste in the ocean. Specific questions that have not been resolved include:

1. What is the ultimate fate of the acid iron waste in the ocean? Vertical profiles obtained when an acid iron waste plume was tracked for over 50 h after a dump did not show the waste beneath the seasonal thermocline. A constant horizontal diffusion velocity model applied to our field data predicted that iron con-

Table 9.1. Comparison of Chemical Properties of Du Pont Edgemoor Waste and the Seawater in Which It Will Be Discharged

Property	Waste[a]	Seawater[b]
Density (g ml^{-1})	1.15	1.02
Total dissolved solutes (g liter^{-1})	240	35
Total suspended solids (g liter^{-1})	1.5	0.001
pH	0.01	8.2
Alkalinity (equivalents liter^{-1})	−4.50	0.002
Chloride (M)	5.36	0.55
Sulfate (M)	0.0083	0.029
Hydrogen ion (M)	0.98	6×10^{-9}
Iron (M)	0.90	$<1 \times 10^{-8}$
Titanium (M)	0.063	$<1 \times 10^{-8}$
Aluminum (M)	0.063	$<1 \times 10^{-7}$
Manganese (M)	0.031	$<1 \times 10^{-8}$
Vanadium (M)	0.004	$<4 \times 10^{-8}$
Chromium (M)	0.004	$<2 \times 10^{-8}$
Lead (M)	0.0002	1.4×10^{-10}
Total organic carbon (mg liter^{-1})	960	1

[a]Based on a 10 September 1976 EPA Region III discharge permit application. From Kester et al. (1981).
[b]Data from Brewer (1975) and Wilson (1975).

centrations in the waste plume should persist at detectable limits (≥ 0.02 μmoles kg^{-1}) for several weeks after the dump. However, in our field studies we have not been able to track the waste plume for more than 1 or 2 d after a dump.

2. Are there detrimental effects on the phytoplankton and zooplankton species exposed to the chemical constituents in an acid iron waste plume for extended periods of time after a dump?

To address these questions a new approach was undertaken. An experiment was conducted at the Marine Ecosystems Research Laboratory (MERL) at the University of Rhode Island, a special facility which provides planktonic ecosystems for experimental manipulation.

9.2. EXPERIMENTAL

The MERL tanks are 2 m in diameter and 5 m deep, and contain a 30-cm layer of sediment and associated benthic organisms collected from lower Narragansett Bay, Rhode Island. The sediments did not have a direct role in our considerations of acid iron waste behavior at DWD-106, but they were important in maintaining the nutrient regeneration processes required to sustain the planktonic ecosystem. The tanks were initially filled with water ($\sim 30\%_0$ salinity, 18°C) from Narragansett

Bay, along with the prevailing population of phytoplankton and zooplankton. The tanks were not inoculated with additional plankton, and were operated as closed systems except to replenish them with water from the bay to maintain the water level in the tank.

Our field studies indicated that the pycnocline plays a major role in the behavior of the acid iron waste. Two of the MERL tanks were modified to establish a thermocline, with one serving as a control and the other as an experimental tank (Donaghay and Klos, 1985). The top 2 m of the water column was maintained at ambient temperature (18–19°C), while the bottom 2 m of water was cooled with heat exchangers to produce a 10°C temperature differential between the surface and bottom layer (Fig. 9.1). Preliminary experiments with the cooling and mixing param-

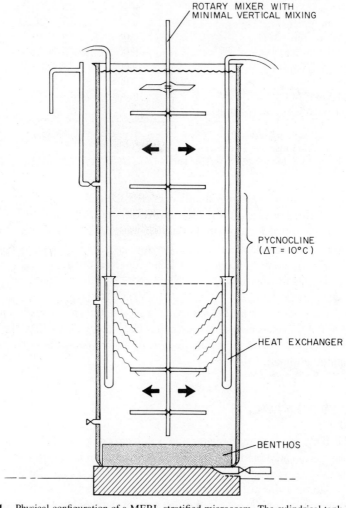

Figure 9.1. Physical configuration of a MERL stratified microcosm. The cylindrical tank is 5 m deep and 2 m in diameter. Redrawn from Donaghay and Klos (1985).

eters of the tanks established that the position and thickness of the thermocline could be altered by changing the position of the heat exchangers and the mixing bars. Throughout the course of this experiment the thickness of the thermocline was 0.5 m, with only minor fluctuations from the 10°C temperature differential between the surface and bottom layer. There were no substantial differences in the physical characteristics between the control and experimental tanks.

In order to monitor any mixing across the thermocline that could also transport acid iron waste, we added NaCl (Baker Analyzed Reagent; J. T. Baker Co., Phillipsburg, New Jersey) to the bottom layer to increase the dissolved salts by about 3‰. This NaCl also enhanced the pycnocline. Temperature and salinity profiles of the experimental and control tanks were made daily using a conductivity, salinity, and temperature probe (Model 33, Yellow Springs Instrument Co., Yellow Springs, Ohio). Discrete salinity samples of the surface and bottom water were drawn once every two weeks in both the experimental and control tanks. A detailed vertical salinity profile was made using discrete samples at the middle of the experiment in the experimental tank (Fig. 9.2). All discrete salinity samples were analyzed using an inductive salinometer.

Acid iron waste was added to the experimental MERL tank to achieve a 10^5 dilution of the waste in the surface mixed layer. This simulates the conditions observed in the field after the initially rapid dilution of the surface plume. To avoid extreme pH changes as the acid iron waste was added to the experimental tank, the waste was diluted by a factor of 100 with bay water prior to the addition to the tank. Two additions of acid iron waste were made within the first 24 h of the experiment, since an initial objective was to maintain a 10^5 dilution of the waste in the surface water for an extended period of time. However, the removal of iron from the surface layer was so rapid after each waste addition that we decided to

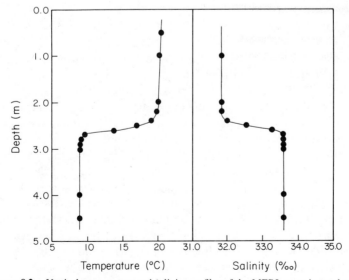

Figure 9.2. Vertical temperature and salinity profiles of the MERL experimental tank.

observe the removal process with time rather than continue with daily additions. The first two additions of waste will be referred to as the first experiment. A third waste addition was made when the iron concentration in the surface layer of the experimental tank returned to background levels (0.17 μmoles kg^{-1}); this constituted the second experiment. The walls and exposed surfaces in the experimental tank were not cleaned between the first and second experiments.

The fate of acid iron waste in the experimental tank was assessed by measuring the total iron concentration as a function of time. The water samples for chemical analyses were obtained using a Teflon® sampling tube. Water samples were siphoned directly into the sample bottle to avoid contamination. Measurements for total iron and total chromium were made by atomic absorption spectrophotometry (AAS) using a Perkin Elmer Model 5000 spectrophotometer with a graphite furnace (Perkin-Elmer Corporation, Norwalk, Connecticut). The chromium provided an additional chemical indicator of the acid iron waste. Due to the high concentration of metals, preconcentration was not necessary; the seawater sample was injected directly into a graphite furnace. The linear range of concentrations used for the direct injection analyses were: 1.0–45 ppb (0.020–0.800 μmoles kg^{-1}) for iron; 0.1–5 ppb (2.0–100 nmoles kg^{-1}) for chromium. Appropriate dilutions were made when necessary.

Total iron concentrations from the field study were determined from real-time iron measurements using a continuous flow analyzer (CFA; Scientific Instruments, Pleasantville, New York) with the colorimetric technique of Stookey (1970). Results obtained using the CFA are comparable with results obtained using AAS (Brown et al, 1983).

9.3. RESULTS

9.3.1. Surface Layer Removal

Vertical profiles of the distribution of iron at several time intervals during the second experiment were made to determine the behavior of acid iron waste in the experimental tank (Fig. 9.3). In the first profile obtained 6 h after the acid iron waste addition, the concentration of iron in the surface layer increased from a background level of 0.17 to a value of 8.1 μmoles kg^{-1}, with an accumulation of iron observed at the top of the pycnocline. Twenty hours after the waste addition the concentration of iron in the surface mixed layer decreased to 3.1 μmoles kg^{-1}, with an apparent transport of the iron maxima into the center of the thermocline. The time sequence of vertical iron profiles in the experimental tank showed a steady depletion of iron in the surface mixed layer, with the iron levels reaching background values 236 h after the waste addition. The maxima and minima in the thermocline persisted for 44 h after the dump; thereafter we observed a smooth iron gradient through the thermocline. The behavior of iron in the bottom water was complicated by the occurrence of sediment resuspension, which will be dis-

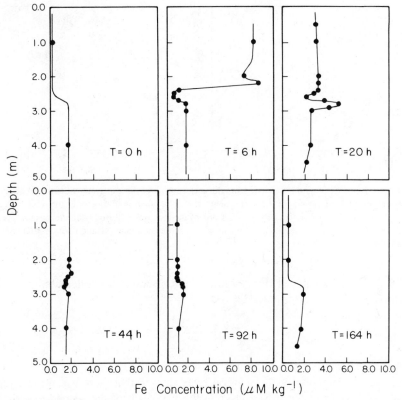

Figure 9.3. Vertical profile of the iron concentration in the MERL tank at several time intervals after waste addition during the second experiment.

cussed in detail later. However, 20 h after the waste addition, iron levels in the bottom water showed a marked increase to 2.7 μmoles kg^{-1}, with a subsequent decrease to background levels 236 h after the addition.

The removal of iron from the surface layer of the experimental tank during the first and second experiments was exponential (Fig. 9.4a) suggesting that the removal of iron from the surface mixed layer was first order with respect to iron. A first-order kinetic removal process follows the relationship:

$$\ln \left(\frac{\mathrm{Fe}_i}{\mathrm{Fe}_t}\right) = k_1 t \tag{1}$$

where Fe_i represents the initial concentration, Fe_t the concentration after time, t, and k_1 is the rate constant for the removal process. A plot of $\ln (\mathrm{Fe}_i/\mathrm{Fe}_t)$ versus time for the results of both experiments showed a linear relationship with some scatter. The rate constant for the removal process was calculated from a linear regression of the observed data using equation 1. A rate constant of 0.0205 h^{-1} was used to calculate the curve representing iron removal as a function of time

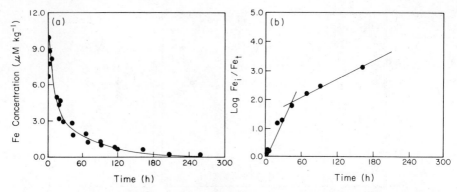

Figure 9.4. Removal of acid iron waste from the surface layer of the experimental tank: (a) depletion of total iron in the surface layer of the experimental tank as a function of time after the waste addition in the first and second experiment, and (b) first-order kinetic removal of iron from the surface layer of the experimental tank in the second experiment. Fe_i = initial iron concentration, Fe_t = iron concentration after time t.

(Fig. 9.4a). The half-life of iron, τ, in the surface water was calculated using the relationship:

$$\tau = \frac{\ln 2}{k_1} \qquad (2)$$

For these data, τ was equal to 34 h.

A closer examination of the removal rates showed that there was a more rapid removal of iron from the mixed layer in the first 50 h of the second experiment relative to the first experiment. Analysis of the results of the first experiment showed that the removal process is clearly first order with respect to iron; the half-life of iron in the surface layer is 31 h. For the second experiment the removal process was not simply first order in iron; a two-step process was indicated by the experimental data (Fig. 9.4b). Initially there was a rapid removal of iron from the mixed layer; the half-life for this removal process was 14 h. The secondary removal process was slower, with a half-life of 65 h.

The behavior of the iron floc formed after the acid iron waste addition was different in these two experiments. In the first experiment large flocculant particles of iron were observed in the surface layer; these particles grew to several millimeters within the first 36 h of the experiment. After ~36 h large particulate iron floc was not visible in the surface water, and there was a distinct increase in the clarity of the surface water. In this experiment there was minimal adsorption of iron floc on the walls and exposed surfaces of the tank. This behavior was in contrast to that observed in the second experiment. There was extensive accumulation of the iron floc on the walls and surfaces in the tank ~10 h after the acid iron waste addition. Any disturbance of the surface would dislodge the iron floc. For this reason an accurate assessment of the amount of iron on the surfaces could not be obtained from the fouling plates that were suspended in the tank for this purpose.

The iron floc particles in the surface water were not as large as those observed in the first experiment. Within 36 h after the waste addition in the second experiment the iron floc had detached from the surfaces and the clarity of the surface water was similar to that observed in the first experiment. The adsorptive loss of iron observed in the second experiment could account for the two-step iron removal process observed in that experiment.

It is not evident why the two experiments showed somewhat different results. For both experiments the same acid iron waste technique of addition was used. The differences between the two experiments were greatest during the first 10 h. Over the longer time period of the observations (100–300 h) the results were more similar. It is possible that the first experiment modified some properties of the exposed surfaces in the tank, thereby resulting in a different flocculation process during the early stages of the second experiment. A thin organic film was observed on the exposed surfaces of the tank after the first experiment, and these coated surfaces were more susceptible to the adsorption of the iron floc.

9.3.2. Sub-Pycnocline Accumulation and Removal

The iron in the bottom layer beneath the pycnocline showed a number of high concentrations that did not appear to be related to the acid iron waste. These high values may represent resuspension of bottom sediment due to the mixers or the benthic organisms, or both. Iron concentrations in the control tank varied from 600 to 1000 nmole kg^{-1} within the first 250 h of the experiment (Fig. 9.5a). These control values are consistent with the iron levels observed in the experimental tank prior to the first waste addition. At 165 h after the start of the second experiment, the control tank contained 2300 nmole kg^{-1} in the deep layer. This high value is not an analytical artifact; it occurred in three samples taken from the bottom layer. Evidently, there are processes which can occur in the sediments that can triple the iron concentration in the bottom layer of the tanks that are unrelated to the addition of acid iron waste.

An event producing high iron concentrations (1700–1800 nmole kg^{-1}) occurred in the experimental tank near the end of the first experiment (235 h after the first waste addition) and persisted into the early stage of the second experiment (1–6 h after the final addition). The results for the first experiment indicate that elevated iron concentrations observed within the first 10 h after the waste addition are not related to the vertical flux of acid iron waste from the surface layer (Fig. 9.5a). There is a two- to threefold increase in the iron levels in the bottom layer as the acid iron waste penetrates the thermocline with a subsequent decay to background levels 250 h after the addition. An anomalous high iron concentration observed after 160 h during the second experiment suggests an input of iron from bottom resuspension. However, this cannot be confirmed because of limited sampling.

This interpretation of the behavior of iron in the bottom layer can be tested by its consistency with a similar analysis of the behavior of chromium (Fig. 9.5b). The acid iron waste contains appreciable concentrations of chromium, and we can ex-

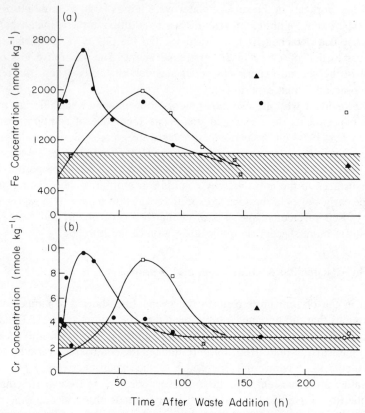

Figure 9.5. Comparison of the accumulation of Fe and Cr in the bottom layer for the (▲) control. (□) the first experiment, and (●) the second experiment.

pect that when the high iron concentrations in the bottom layer are produced by the waste, we should also find high chromium concentrations. The background chromium concentrations were in the range of 2–4 nmole kg^{-1}. Concentrations two to three times this level were observed at 40 h after waste addition in the first experiment and 20 h after addition in the second experiment. The chromium subsequently decreased to background concentrations at about the same rate as the iron concentrations. The similarity of the iron and chromium data 20–100 h after waste addition substantiates our interpretation that the waste was present in the water column beneath the pycnocline during this period. The waste subsequently diminished from the bottom layer after 60 h.

9.3.3. Cross-Pycnocline Mixing

An alternate source of iron to the bottom water of the experimental tank is from mixing of the surface and bottom water across the pycnocline. The addition of NaCl to the bottom water changed the salinity of this layer by ~3‰; this salinity difference can be used as a conservative tracer to determine the transport of iron from the surface to the bottom water. In the 480 h (20 d) period of this experiment the salinity of the bottom water of the control tank decreased from 33.71 to 33.46‰, a change of 0.25‰ in 20 d. The salinity change in the control tank for the same time period was 0.41‰. The slightly greater salinity change in the control tank was probably due to the loss of ~400 liters of water from the thermocline that resulted from a leak in a valve on the control tank midway through the experiment. The salinity of the surface water in both tanks was more variable because of the input of rainwater and loss due to evaporation; also, bay water was added to the surface layer of both tanks prior to the second experiment to maintain a constant water level in the tanks.

The salinity change with time in the experimental tank can be used to estimate the flux of iron from the surface layer to the bottom layer due to mixing across the thermocline. The change in salinity as a function of time can be determined from the slope of the regression line obtained from a plot of salinity versus time. Assuming the volume of surface water and bottom water that are exchanged across the thermocline are equal, the salinity change in the bottom water can be used to calculate the volume of surface water that must be mixed with bottom water using the relationship

$$V_m = \frac{V_b \, \Delta \, S_b}{\bar{S}_s - S_{b_i}} \tag{3}$$

Where V_m is the volume of surface water mixed with bottom water, V_b is the volume of water in the bottom layer, ΔS_b is the change in salinity in the bottom water, $\bar{S}_s$ is the average salinity of the surface water, and S_{b_i} is the initial salinity of the bottom water. Knowing the volume of surface water mixed daily into the bottom water, the loss of iron due to mixing across the thermocline can be calculated. There were deviations from linearity observed in the plot of salinity versus time. These deviations appeared to correlate with the times when large volumes of water were transferred from the tank for zooplankton sampling (~200 liters per sampling period). Assuming a linear variation of salinity change with time gives the upper limit for the flux of iron across the thermocline due to mixing. During the course of this experiment a total of 0.109 moles of iron were added to the surface layer of the experimental tank (0.057 moles in the first experiment and 0.052 moles in the second experiment). The total iron loss from the surface layer due to mixing across the pycnocline was 1.64×10^{-3} moles (0.86×10^{-3} moles of iron were lost in the first experiment and 0.78×10^{-3} moles in the second experiment). This constitutes $< 1.5\%$ loss of iron from the surface layer due to mixing.

9.4. DISCUSSION

The sequence of vertical profiles in the experimental tank can be used to construct a budget for the loss of the acid iron waste in a stratified system. The waste addition

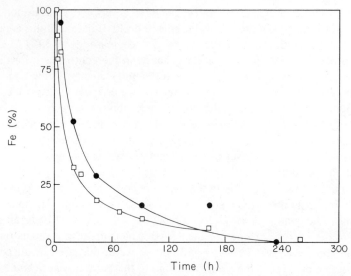

Figure 9.6. Comparison of the removal of iron from the experimental tank during the second experiment: □ = removal from the surface layer normalized to the iron concentration observed 1 h after waste addition, and ● = iron removal calculated from a mass balance of the entire tank. Iron values are expressed as a percentage of the initial values.

to the experimental tank in the second experiment contained 0.052 moles of iron. The total iron content of the water column at various times intervals during the second experiment was determined from a graphical integration of the time sequence of vertical profiles (Fig. 9.3). A mass balance of the total iron content of the water column 6 h after the waste addition accounted for 0.049 moles of Fe, or 94% of the waste added. Within the next 20 h there was a loss of ~50% of the waste from the water column (Fig. 9.6). The iron value observed 163 h after the waste addition was anomalously high; this deviation is probably due to an inaccurate estimate of the background level of iron in the bottom layer of the tank. An elevated iron level in the bottom layer suggests an input of iron from the sediments during this time period (Fig. 9.5a).

The decrease in the concentration of iron in the water column was similar to the removal of iron from the surface layer (Fig. 9.6). For this comparison the iron concentration in the surface layer was normalized to the concentration observed 1 h after the waste addition. These data suggest a first-order kinetic removal process for both the surface layer and the entire water column. The rate constant (k_1 = 0.0196 h^{-1}) and the half-life of the iron concentration (τ = 35 h) calculated from these two data sets were identical. The largest deviation appears between 10 and 50 h, when there was an accumulation of the waste in the thermocline. The similarity of these two analyses suggests that the same process is removing the acid iron waste from the bottom layer as from the surface layer. Visual observation of the particulate matter that accumulated in sediment traps suspended in the tanks below the thermocline showed that unperturbed particulate iron floc penetrated the thermocline. There was no apparent accumulation of iron in the phytoplankton and zooplankton species exposed to the acid iron waste during the experiment (P. Donaghay, personal communication). From these observations we conclude that the removal of the iron from the water column is due to gravitational settling of the particulate iron floc and not due to assimilation by organisms.

The results of the MERL study may be compared with those obtained from a field study of an acid iron waste dump at DWD-106 (Fig. 9.7). The field data were obtained on an August 1979 cruise of the *R/V Kelez*. The same acid iron waste was used in both studies, so that variation in the composition of the waste was not a factor. The acid iron waste plume was tracked in the field for 15 h; thus, the time frame for comparison of the field study and observations in the MERL tank was limited. The iron concentration from the field study and the two MERL experiments were normalized to the concentration observed 1 h after the waste addition to allow a direct comparison of the data. The removal of iron in the open ocean is faster than that observed in the tank study. This result is reasonable considering that there is both horizontal and vertical dispersion of the waste plume in the open ocean, whereas in the MERL tank there is only the vertical flux of waste in the water column. This study shows that particle removal from the mixed layer is an important factor in the decrease of acid iron waste concentration after dumping at sea.

9.5. SUMMARY AND CONCLUSIONS

The MERL study allows us to better understand the behavior of the acid iron waste in a pycnocline. In the course of the experiment we observed a depletion of iron in

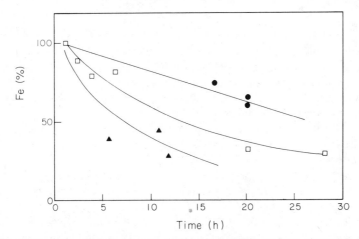

Figure 9.7. Comparison of the rate of removal of iron in the MERL tank experiment (●, first experiment; □, second experiment) and from field studies in September 1979 aboard the *R/V Kelez* (▲). The values are expressed as a percentage of the initial concentration.

the surface layer, with an accumulation at the thermocline during the first 50 h after the waste addition. The half-life of the acid iron waste in the upper layer of the tank was 35 h. The fate of the acid iron waste after penetration through the thermocline is complicated by the role of sediment resuspension. However, the high concentration of chromium in the waste can be used to differentiate iron values associated with the acid iron waste and those associated with benthic regeneration. A mass balance of the total iron content in the tank at several time intervals after the waste addition showed that the rate of iron removal from the entire water column was similar to that observed in the surface layer. Thus, the same mechanism, gravitational settling of the iron floc, is responsible for the loss of iron from the surface and bottom layers. The results of the MERL tank experiment were consistent with field studies of the actual acid iron waste dump at DWD-106. This study demonstrates the applicability of a MERL tank experiment to simulate processes that occur in the open ocean.

ACKNOWLEDGMENTS

The authors are grateful to several people for their assistance in this work: M. Pilson and C. Oviatt for their assistance with the overall design of the experiment, P. Donaghay and C. Hunt for their invaluable help with the sampling strategy and the experimental design, E. Klos for the technical design and maintenance of the stratified tanks, and D. Huizenga and W. Warren for their assistance in the trace metal sampling and analyses. This work was supported by U.S. National Oceanic and Atmospheric Administration grant NA79-AA-D00033.

REFERENCES

Brewer, P. G. 1975. Minor elements in sea water. *In:* Chemical Oceanography, Vol. 1, 2nd Edition, J. P. Riley and G. Skirrow (Eds.). Academic Press, London, pp. 415–496.

Brown, M. F., D. R. Kester, and J. M. Dowd. 1983. Automated iron measurements after acid-iron waste disposal. *In:* Wastes in the Ocean, Vol. 1: Industrial and Sewage Wastes in the Ocean, I. W. Duedall, B. H. Ketchum, D. R. Kester, and P. K. Park (Eds.). Wiley-Interscience, New York, pp. 157–169.

Csanady, G. T. 1981. An analysis of dumpsite diffusion experiments. *In:* Ocean Dumping of Industrial Wastes, B. H. Ketchum, D. R. Kester, and P. K. Park (Eds.). Plenum Press, New York, pp. 109–129.

Donaghay, P. L., and E. G. Klos. 1985. Physical, chemical and biological responses to simulated wind and tidal mixing in experimental marine ecosystems. *Marine Ecology Progress Series*, in press.

Kester, D. R., R. C. Hittinger, and P. Mukherji. 1981. Transition and heavy metals associated with acid-iron waste disposal at Deep Water Dumpsite 106. *In:* Ocean Dumping of Industrial Wastes, B. H. Ketchum, D. R. Kester, and P. K. Park (Eds.). Plenum Press, New York, pp. 215–232.

Mukherji, P., and D. R. Kester. 1983. Acid-iron dump experiments in summer and winter at Deep Water Dumpsite-106. *In:* Wastes in the Ocean, Vol. 1: Industrial and Sewage Wastes in the Ocean, I. W. Duedall, B. H. Ketchum, D. R. Kester, and P. K. Park (Eds.). Wiley-Interscience, New York, pp. 141–155.

Stookey, L. L. 1970. Ferrozine—a new spectrophotometric reagent for iron. *Analytical Chemistry,* **42,** 779–781.

Wilson, T. R. S. 1975. Salinity and the major elements of sea water. *In:* Chemical Oceanography, Vol. 1, 2nd Edition, J. P. Riley and G. Skirrow (Eds.) Academic Press, London, pp. 365–413.

10

MICROBIOLOGICAL STUDIES OF OCEAN DUMPING

Fred L. Singleton, D. Jay Grimes, Huai-Shu Xu, and Rita R. Colwell

Department of Microbiology
University of Maryland
College Park, Maryland

Abstract		**188**
10.1 Introduction		**188**
10.2. Experimental		**189**
10.2.1.	Microcosm Studies	189
10.2.2.	Field Studies	191
10.3. Results		**193**
10.3.1.	Microcosm Studies	193
	10.3.1a. *Mixed Bacterial Communities*	193
	10.3.1b. *Gnotobiotic Communities*	194
10.3.2.	Field Observations	196
	10.3.2a. *Physical and Chemical Characteristics of the Sampling Regions*	196
	10.3.2b. *Enumeration of Bacteria in Seawater*	197
	10.3.2c. *Identification of Bacteria Isolated from Seawater*	200
10.4. Discussion		**202**

Dr. Singleton's present address: Department of Biological Sciences, Old Dominion University, Norfolk, Virginia 23508.

10.5. Conclusion   205

Acknowledgments   206

References   206

Abstract

The impact of oceanic disposal of pharmaceutical wastes on the microbial flora of surface waters of the Puerto Rico dumpsite has been studied since 1979. A variety of microbiological methods have been used, including isolation and identification of marine and nonmarine aerobic, heterotrophic bacteria, and direct counting of total and active bacterial populations. The major effect of ocean dumping activities was an alteration, or restructuring, of the composition of the culturable bacterial community. In this culturable community, there was a predominance (62%) of members of the genus *Vibrio* and a decline in typical marine *Pseudomonas* spp. (< 3%). Also indicative of change in the culturable bacterial community was a high incidence of *Acinetobacter*, which comprised 29% of all isolates obtained during one research cruise. To investigate further and confirm these findings, a series of studies were carried out using laboratory microcosms designed to simulate conditions at the Puerto Rico dumpsite. Effects of addition of composite pharmaceutical waste on naturally occurring bacterial communities and on the development of species-defined bacterial communities were monitored in the microcosms by employing isolates from the dumpsite and from surrounding waters. The culturable bacteria responded to waste additions by increasing in number, proportional to amount of waste added. In species-defined communities, *Vibrio* was always dominant in the presence of pharmaceutical waste.

10.1. INTRODUCTION

As the need for disposal sites for various waste materials increases, the burden on presently designated disposal areas also increases. In recent years, the open ocean has become an increasingly attractive alternative to land disposal for an array of industrial and municipal waste materials (Park and O'Connor, 1981). The consequences of ocean dumping are not fully understood, especially with regard to the ultimate impact of such waste materials on biotic and abiotic components of the marine environment.

Effects of toxic wastes on aquatic biota have received considerable attention in the past. Very few studies have evaluated the impact of waste materials that are either nontoxic or enter the environment at concentrations below the threshold for acute toxicity. For example, effects of the release of subacute concentrations of toxic industrial wastes into the coastal marine environment of Japan were manifested in the 1960s with outbreaks of "Minamata Bay disease" (Ishikawa and Ike-gaki, 1980). Thus, wastes in the ocean can result in a dramatic series of events, or they can have more subtle effects on the ecosystem, which may be extremely difficult to detect.

The impact of ocean disposal of pharmaceutical wastes on the bacterial flora of surface waters of the Puerto Rico dumpsite has been examined and results of field studies have been reported (Peele et al., 1981; Singleton et al., 1983). In general, the findings indicate that the major, demonstrable effect was a change in the composition of the culturable bacterial community. Disposal of pharmaceutical wastes appears to be the cause, but it is possible that previously unreported characteristics of the culturable bacterial community of these waters may be involved.

The objective of this study was, therefore, to examine the causal relationship between oceanic disposal of pharmaceutical wastes and changes in the bacterial flora of surface waters of the open ocean. Two approaches were used to determine whether waste disposal activities can alter the structure and species composition of bacterial communities of surface waters within and surrounding the dumpsite. First, laboratory microecosystems (microcosms) containing natural mixed-bacterial communities or gnotobiotic bacterial communities (species-defined and composed of two species) were subjected to addition of a representative composite pharmaceutical waste sample, and the bacterial community response was monitored. Second, bacteriological survey cruises were made to evaluate and compare the natural indigenous bacterial flora of surface waters within the dumpsite and within the surrounding regions.

10.2. EXPERIMENTAL

10.2.1. Microcosm Studies

Laboratory microcosms consisted of acid dichromate-cleaned, 125-ml Erlenmeyer flasks containing 50 ml (35‰ salinity) marine salts solution (Singleton et al., 1982) supplemented with 500 μg tryptone (Difco Laboratories, Detroit, Michigan) and 5 μg yeast extract (Difco Laboratories) per liter. The microcosms were capped with cotton plugs and autoclaved at 121°C for 15 min. After cooling to room temperature (22°C), they were inoculated with appropriate bacterial strains and incubated at 25°C with constant agitation (125 RPM) for a stabilization period of 48–72 h. At designated times after stabilization, the microcosms received additions of a representative composite pharmaceutical waste sample.

The properties of pharmaceutical waste have been described by Anderson and Dewling (1981), Atlas et al. (1981), and Schwab et al. (1981). Briefly, the noteworthy chemical and physical properties of pharmaceutical waste are as follows: pH, 6.0; total organic carbon content, 42 g liter^{-1}; heavy metal content, 1.0 mg liter^{-1}; and the presence of several volatile organic compounds, including benzene, dimenthylanaline, butanol, toluene, and xylenes. Each composite waste addition was filter-sterilized by passage through a sterile, 0.2-μm membrane filter (Schleicher and Schuell, Inc., Keene, New Hampshire).

The bacterial strains employed in the gnotobiotic microcosm studies were selected from a stock culture collection of isolates, the source of which were samples collected within and surrounding the Puerto Rico dumpsite. In addition, two strains were isolated from water samples collected in the Atlantic Ocean, ~30 km offshore from Cape Henry, Virginia. The bacterial strains were selected on the basis of colonial morphology and pigmentation, so that when cultured together in a microcosm they could readily be differentiated on an agar medium (Table 10.1). In preliminary studies of the effect of composite waste on culturable bacteria, Chesapeake Bay surface water was used in the microcosms instead of the salts solution.

Bacteria used in the microcosm studies were grown in a modified Marine Broth 2216 (Difco Laboratories) prepared by adding dehydrated medium to distilled water and boiling to dissolve the ingredients. After cooling to room temperature, the broth was successively filtered through 5-, 3-, 1.2-, 0.45-, and 0.2-μm sterile nitrocellulose membrane filters (Schleicher and Schuell, Inc.). After the final filtration step, 20-ml volumes of the broth were placed into sterile 50-ml Erlenmeyer flasks and stored at room temperature (~22°C) until used.

After inoculation, the broth cultures were incubated at 25°C for 24 h, harvested by centrifugation, and washed five times with sterile, 0.2-μm-filtered marine salts solution. Following the final wash, cells were resuspended in marine salts solutions of appropriate dilution, and the absorbance (620 nm) was measured with a Spectronic® 20 spectrophotometer (Bausch and Lomb, Rochester, New York). Absorbance of cell suspensions was compared to previously prepared absorbance versus biomass curves, and an estimate of cell concentration was obtained. Appropriate dilutions of each cell suspension served as inoculum for the microcosms.

Table 10.1. Bacterial Strains Employed in Gnotobiotic Community Experiments

Collection Site	Genus	Strain	Colonial Characteristics
Puerto Rico dumpsite	Vibrio	PR-110	Large, mucoid, circular, with light pinkish-brown pigmentation
Puerto Rico dumpsite	Pseudomonas	PR-211	Transparent, moist, circular with entire edge
Puerto Rico dumpsite	Vibrio	PR-106	Smooth, moist, entire with tan pigmentation
Atlantic Ocean near Cape Henry, Virginia	Pseudomonas	AO-17	Smooth, moist, irregular, with yellow pigmentation
Atlantic Ocean near Cape Henry, Virginia	Pseudomonas	AO-66	Smooth, circular, with greenish-yellow pigmentation

Numbers of viable bacteria (bacteria culturable from the microcosms) were determined by spread-plating onto Marine Agar 2216 (MA) (Difco Laboratories). Dilutions were prepared using sterile marine salts solution. Culture plates were incubated for 7 d at 25°C, after which total colony counts and number of colony types were determined.

10.2.2. Field Studies

Two cruises were made in order to sample waters within and surrounding the dumpsite. The cruise tracklines include sample stations located north, west, and south of the dumpsite (Fig. 10.1). The cruise tracklines were selected to allow for sampling temperate and tropical waters and previously monitored locations within the dumpsite (Peele et al., 1981; Singleton et al., 1983).

A cruise in November 1980 aboard the *R/V Gyre* allowed for sampling of surface waters extending from Key West, Florida, through an area west of the dumpsite, to Puerto Rico (Fig. 10.1). Waters within and north of the Barceloneta Regional

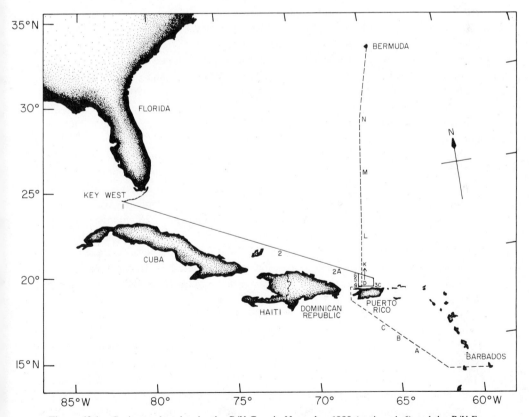

Figure 10.1. Cruise tracks taken by the *R/V Gyre* in November 1980 (stations 1–6) and the *R/V Endeavor* in June 1981 (stations A–N) to collect water samples for bacteriological and chemical analyses.

Wastewater Treatment Plant outfall plume along the northern coast of Puerto Rico were also sampled. A second cruise, aboard the *R/V Endeavor* in June 1981, was designed to collect seawater samples along a trackline from Barbados to Bermuda, including the dumpsite (Fig. 10.1).

Surface water samples were collected aseptically using a sterile Niskin® sampler (General Oceanics, Miami, Florida). All samples were subjected to bacteriological analysis immediately after collection. Most of the seawater samples were collected from depths of 1–5 m.

Numbers of culturable, aerobic, heterotrophic bacteria present in surface-water samples were determined using MA and Plate Count Agar (PCA) (Difco Laboratories). Surface-water samples were filtered, in triplicate, through sterile, 0.2-μm nitrocellulose membrane filters (GA-8; Gelman Sciences, Inc., Ann Arbor, Michigan). The filters were placed on MA and PCA plates and incubated for 7 d at 25°C before counting.

Total bacterial numbers were determined by acridine orange staining and epifluorescent microscopy (Francisco et al., 1973; Daley and Hobbie, 1975; Hobbie et al., 1977). Samples were preserved in sterile, particle-free, 30-ml screw-capped tubes containing formalin (final concentration: 2%, by vol). After staining, the water samples were filtered through 0.2-μm membrane filters (Nuclepore Corp., Pleasanton, California) pre-stained with Irgalan black. The total number of cells were counted using a Zeiss Standard 18 microscope equipped with an IV FL epifluorescence condensor, 100-W halogen lamp, BP450-490 band-pass filter, FT 510 beam splitter, and an LP 520 barrier filter (Carl Zeiss, Inc., New York, New York). For each sample, a minimum of 10 randomly selected fields, containing at least 50 cells per field, were counted to obtain the acridine orange direct count (AODC) of total bacteria.

To identify bacteria one MA plate from each station was randomly selected, and the colonies were purified and identified to genus. The number of colonies purified and identified depended on the total colony count. Culture plates with more than 25 colonies were marked into halves or quarters and all colonies on one section were picked, purified, and identified; for plates with less than 25 colonies, all colonies on the plate were picked for identification. In general, a minimum of 25 colonies per culture plate were processed for identification. Isolates were screened for appropriate biochemical and morphological characteristics (Buchanan and Gibbons, 1974) and identified in accordance with the schema of Bain and Shewan (1968), Gibson et al. (1977), Furniss et al. (1978), and LeChevallier et al. (1980).

Water samples collected during the June 1981 cruise were also analyzed for ammonia, nitrite, nitrate, orthophosphate, dissolved organic phosphate, and dissolved organic nitrogen using a Technicon Model II autoanalyzer (Technicon, Tarrytown, New York), and for nonfilterable residue by gravimetric analysis (American Public Health Association, 1976). The samples were also examined for waste-specific volatile organic compounds according to the methods of Schwab et al. (1981). Temperature and salinity were determined at each station using a (Plessey 6230N; Plessey Environmental Systems, San Diego, California) salinometer. Measurements were made using water samples collected with a 5-liter Niskin bottle fitted with a reversing thermometer.

10.3. RESULTS

10.3.1. Microcosm Studies

10.3.1a. Mixed Bacterial Communities

Culturable bacteria present in surface water samples collected from the lower portion of the Chesapeake Bay, to which sterile composite waste had been added, increased in number after incubation for 6 d (Fig. 10.2). Maximum numbers of culturable bacteria in the microcosms were detected within 48 h after addition of waste and were directly proportional to the concentration of waste added ($r = 0.912$). Following a maximum increase in population size, the viable count decreased in the composite waste-enriched microcosms, with stable community sizes established after 48 h additional incubation.

Since the viable (culturable) bacterial community of the Chesapeake Bay water microcosms increased in number with addition of composite waste, an additional series of microcosms was established to determine what effects on the culturable bacteria were apparent within 24 h after addition of the composite waste (Fig. 10.3). Samples collected from the microcosms 30 min after waste addition revealed no significant decline in culturable bacteria. During the balance of the 24-h incubation, a gradual increase in numbers of culturable bacteria in all microcosms was

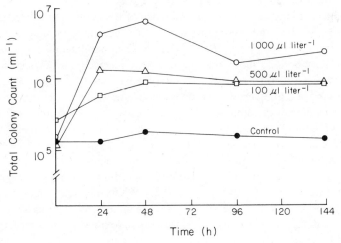

Figure 10.2. Effects of composite pharmaceutical waste on the culturable bacterial community in Chesapeake Bay water microcosms over a 144-h period.

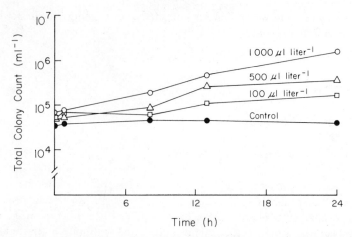

Figure 10.3. Effects of composite pharmaceutical waste on the culturable bacterial community in Chesapeake Bay water microcosms over a 24-h period.

noted, except in the controls, with final population sizes being proportional to the concentration of waste added ($r = 0.946$).

10.3.1b. Gnotobiotic Communities

Isolates from the dumpsites, distinguishable on the basis of colonial morphology and pigmentation (Table 10.1), were prepared as a mixed culture and exposed to composite waste. Quantitative changes in viable counts were monitored. Microcosms containing PR-110, the predominant *Vibrio* sp. isolated from water samples collected within the dumpsite, and PR-211, a *Pseudomonas* sp. also isolated from the dumpsite, demonstrated a typical influence of the composite waste; in control microcosms not receiving composite waste, the bacterial community was dominated by strain PR-211 (Table 10.2). After a 72-h stabilization (pre-composite-waste addition) period, those microcosms that received low concentrations of composite waste (≤ 500 μl liter^{-1}) were still dominated by strain PR-211, after incubation for 5 d. However, when a final composite waste concentration of ≥ 500 μl liter^{-1} was employed, dominance within the two-species community began to shift. Beginning with an inoculum of approximately 50% PR-110 and 50% PR-211 after a 72-h stabilization period, PR-211 comprised approximately 65% of the two-species community, as determined by plate count. Following an incubation period of 48 h after addition of 50 μl composite waste per liter, the culturable community was comprised of 58% PR-211 (Table 10.2). When the final concentration was increased to 1000 μl liter^{-1}, the microcosms contained communities dominated by PR-110, even though PR-211 was inoculated in approximately equal or larger numbers.

To improve the simulation of *in situ* pharmaceutical waste disposal, an additional series of microcosms was established. These were allowed to stabilize for 48

Table 10.2. Dominance in a Gnotobiotic Community Composed of *Vibrio* PR-110 and an Additional Bacterial Strain after 5- to 6-Day Exposure to Composite Pharmaceutical Waste[a]

Waste (μg liter^{-1})	Added Bacterial Strain (%)			
	PR-211	PR-106	AO-17	AO-66
0	70	41	21	11
100	78	34	29	4
500	58	17	29	1
1000	40	19	13	0

[a]Differences between populations for each waste treatment were significant ($p < 0.05$), as determined by t-test. The *Vibrio* PR-110 percentage is obtainable by subtracting the bacterial strain percentage from 100% at a given waste concentration.

h, after which they were inoculated with two successive additions of composite waste, the second addition occurring 48 h after the first. Two of the *Vibrio* strains isolated from seawater collection at the dumpsite, PR-110 and PR-106, were placed in flasks in approximately equal inoculation sizes. The control community (the flask without addition of waste) became dominated by PR-110, ranging from 65% to 59%, and decreasing with length of incubation. When communities of strains PR-110 and PR-106 were supplemented with 100 μl liter^{-1} composite waste (final concentration), the proportion of the community occupied by each strain was approximately the same as that found to occur in the control microcosms (Table 10.2). However, with an increased concentration of the first addition to 500 μl liter^{-1}, enrichment occurred. Although the absolute number of viable cells of each strain increased after each addition of composite waste, the final community composition ratio was similar to that detected after the first addition of composite waste. Concentrations ≤ 1000 μl liter^{-1} resulted in increased cell numbers, as well as an increase in the proportion of the community occupied by PR-110 (Table 10.2).

The response of a combination of strains PR-110 and *Pseudomonas* sp. AO-17 was similar to that of strains PR-110 and PR-106 (Table 10.2). The control microcosms showed a gradual increase in the proportion of the culturable community occupied by PR-110 throughout the test period. A composite waste addition of 100 μl liter^{-1} (final concentration) did not alter community composition, and PR-110 continued to dominate. However, the number of viable cells of strain AO-17 did not decrease, as occurred in control microcosms. When two composite waste additions of 500 μl liter^{-1} were made, only after the first addition did the viable counts of AO-17 decrease, with the final community still being dominated by PR-110. Community composition was altered when 1000 μl liter^{-1} of the composite waste was added. In these microcosms, the percentage of the culturable community occupied by PR-110 increased, compared to the control flasks. The growth responses exhibited by PR-110 and AO-17, illustrated in Fig. 10.4, are typical of those measured for all strains employed in the microcosm studies.

A community comprised of strains PR-110 and AO-66, the latter being a *Pseu-*

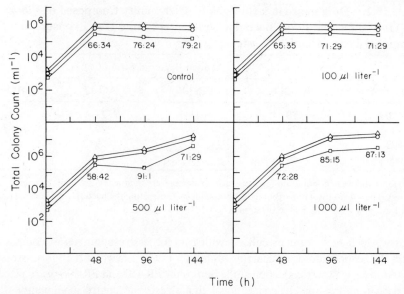

Figure 10.4. Effects of composite pharmaceutical waste on the composition of a two-species-membered community ($\triangle$) comprised of *Vibrio* PR-110 ($\bigcirc$) and Pseudomonas AO-17 ($\square$). Numbers represent the percentage of the community occupied by PR-110 and AO-17, respectively. Waste additions occurred immediately after the 48-h and 96-h samplings.

domonas sp., was also found to be dominated by strain PR-110 in the absence of composite waste (Table 10.2). In these microcosms, PR-110 was found dominate by 9:1, with dominance of PR-110 increasing with increasing concentration of the composite waste up to 500 μl liter^{-1}, after which AO-66 was no longer detectable on MA (Table 10.2).

10.3.2. Field Observations

10.3.2a. *Physical and Chemical Characteristics of the Sampling Regions*

Water temperature and salinity at the June 1981 stations (Fig. 10.1) ranged from 26.8 to 28.2°C (mean: 27.6°C) and 35.54 to 36.39‰ (mean: 36.01‰), respectively. Concentrations of ammonia in the seawater samples averaged 1.3 ± 0.5 μM; nitrate and nitrite concentrations averaged 1.22 ± 0.72 and 0.14 ± 0.02 μM, respectively. Orthophosphate concentrations, on average, were 0.20 ± 0.05 μM; dissolved organic phosphorus averaged 0.05 ± 0.08 μM, and dissolved organic nitrogen averaged 7.9 ± 2.5 μM. The mean concentration of nonfilterable residue (total suspended matter) was 20.2 ± 2.7 mg liter^{-1}, with significant ($p < 0.01$) increases noted at dumpsite stations G and H. Toluene was detected at stations A, C, I, K, L, and N; benzene was also detected at stations C and K. The selected physical and chemical parameters were not correlated with microbiological parameters, nor were significant trends noted, except that the nonfilterable residue increased at the dumpsite station.

10.3.2b. Enumeration of Bacteria in Seawater

Surface waters sampled near the land, the pharmaceutical waste, or the domestic sewage effluent contained the largest numbers of culturable, aerobic, heterotrophic bacteria when plated on MA and PCA (Table 10.3). Seawater collected at stations located near the Barceloneta wastewater treatment outfall contained the largest numbers of bacteria. The mean number, calculated from MA counts, was 164 ml^{-1}, and from PCA, 0.55 ml^{-1}, respectively, for samples collected during November 1980 (Table 10.3). At the station located within the outfall confluence, station 3C3, the counts were 20 ml^{-1} on MA and ~1 ml^{-1}, respectively, on PCA.

At stations located on a trackline from station 3C3 to 3C1, bacteria culturable on MA increased in number with increasing distance from the outfall. Moving away from shore, the number of bacteria culturable on PCA exhibited an approximate inverse relationship with distance from the outfall and shore (Fig. 10.5). Seawater collected at stations distant from shore, that is, the open ocean stations 2, 2A, 4, 5, and 6 (Table 10.2), yielded mean culturable bacterial counts of 6 (MA) and 0.08 (PCA) per ml.

Total bacterial numbers obtained for seawater samples collected in November 1980, determined by AODC, followed the same distribution pattern as that of the culturable bacteria, with largest numbers detected near the Barceloneta outfall (Table 10.3). The total numbers of bacteria at the outfall were three- to ninefold larger than those for open ocean seawater samples. Although the distribution pattern for AODC and MA counts tended to be parallel, the proportion of the total bacteria (measured by AODC) that grew on MA decreased, by a factor of 2, with increasing distance from shore (from station 4 to 6, Fig. 10.6a). At station 3C1, 16 km north of the Barceloneta outfall, the percentage of bacteria (measured by AODC) that were culturable on MA was maximum, 0.148%. The numbers of viable bacteria grown on PCA present in seawater collected at stations 4, 5, and 6 were relatively constant (Table 10.3), as was the ratio of AODC versus plate count at these three stations.

Culturable bacterial counts on MA, for the June 1981 seawater samples, are listed in Table 10.3. Open-ocean (stations E, F, I, J, K, L, M, and N) counts on MA averaged 5 per ml and PCA counts averaged 0.10 per ml. The MA counts decreased, by a factor of 8, on the trackline north, in the direction away from Puerto Rico (stations D, E, F, I, J, K, L, M, N), and omitting the dumpsite (stations G and H. Large numbers of culturable bacteria were detected in seawater samples collected at stations within the dumpsite area. However, the MA counts were largest at stations A, B, and C, located in the Caribbean Sea.

The MA and PCA counts were observed to be influenced by proximity to land or the dumpsite, but the total number (measured by AODC) did not change significantly for seawater samples collected during the June 1981 cruise (Table 10.3).

Table 10.3.   Sampling Locations and Bacterial Counts

Station	Location	Bacterial Count (per ml)		
		AODC[a] ($\times 10^4$)	MA[b] ($\times 10^0$)	PCA[c] ($\times 10^{-1}$)
November 1980				
1	24°00.7′N, 81°21.0′W	—	4.7	1.9
2	20°31.0′, 72°39.9′	7.3	4.9	1.7
2A	19°10.0′, 68°00.3′	4.4	4.8	0.9
3C1	18°39.6′, 66°30.3′	31.0	460.0	3.4
3C2	18°30.9′, 66°33.7′	37.0	12.0	4.3
3C3	18°29.8′, 66°32.8′	—	20.0	8.8
4	19°00.2′, 67°19.2′	12.0	11.0	0.5
5	19°42.0′, 67°18.7′	8.9	5.2	0.2
6	20°01.7′, 67°19.0′	11.0	4.7	0.7
June 1981				
A	15°33.2′, 63°54.7′	14.0	11.0	3.1
B	16°02.0′, 64°35.8′	34.0	24.0	0.4
C	16°38.0′, 65°29.0′	2.4	50.0	1.0
D	18°34.8′, 66°47.9′	26.0	7.7	3.4
E	18°39.8′, 66°47.9′	25.0	9.4	0.6
F	19°00.1′, 66°48.0′	15.0	5.8	0.9
G	19°12.0′, 66°48.0′	13.0	10.0	9.4
H	19°18.0′, 66°48.0′	30.0	7.4	4.0
I	19°29.8′, 66°48.0′	15.0	9.3	1.4
J	19°50.1′, 66°46.9′	23.0	5.9	3.8
K	20°00.0′, 66°48.0′	24.0	4.5	0.7
L	21°50.7′, 66°29.5′	19.0	2.7	0.7
M	25°30.0′, 65°51.4′	23.0	1.1	0.1
N	27°53.3′, 65°24.4′	14.0	2.2	0.1

[a]Acridine Orange direct count.
[b]Marine Agar.
[c]Plate Count Agar.

Nevertheless, while AODC numbers did not change significantly, bacteria culturable on MA and PCA varied considerably (Fig. 10.6b). The relationship of MA to AODC demonstrated that, with the exception of the dumpsite region, as distance from land increased, the proportion of total bacteria (measured by AODC) which grew on MA decreased (Fig. 10.6b). At station M, within the Sargasso Sea, the percentage of AODC bacteria culturable on MA was 0.0005%, compared to 0.003% obtained near the shore (station D) and 0.008% within the dumpsite. The PCA versus percentage showed a similar trend, decreasing, by a factor of 30, as distance from land increased (Fig. 10.6b).

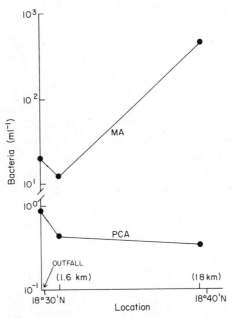

Figure 10.5. Bacteria from the Barceloneta wastewater outfall region culturable on Marine Agar (MA) and Plate Count Agar (PCA) for the November 1980 sampling.

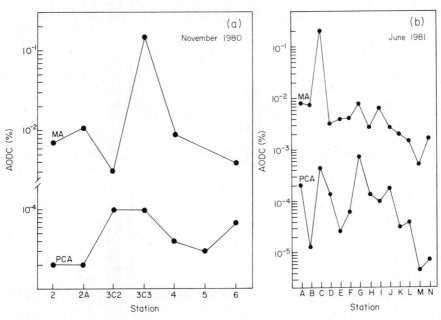

Figure 10.6. Percentage of Acridine Orange Direct Count (AODC) bacteria culturable on Marine Agar (MA) and Plate Count Agar (PCA) for (a) the November 1980 sampling and (b) the June 1981 sampling.

10.3.2c.   *Identification of Bacteria Isolated from Seawater*

The predominant genera of bacteria isolated from all surface water samples (1–5 m depths) were found to be representative of the genus *Vibrio*, comprising 70% (120 of 171) of the cultures isolated from the MA plates prepared during November 1980 (Fig. 10.7). In June 1981, 57% (143 of 251) of the cultures isolated from MA were members of the genus *Vibrio* (Fig. 10.8). Overall, *Vibrio* comprised 62% of the cultures, with the next most frequent being *Acinetobacter* (13% in 1980 and 29% in 1981), followed by *Pseudomonas* (3%), *Flavobacterium* (3%), and *Staphylococcus* (1%). The genera *Vibrio* and *Acinetobacter* comprised the majority of bacteria isolated at all of the 23 stations sampled, ranging from 64% at station L to 100% at stations C, E, and F, the mean percentage being 85% with a standard deviation of ± 10%.

In general, members of the genus *Vibrio* occurred more frequently at stations

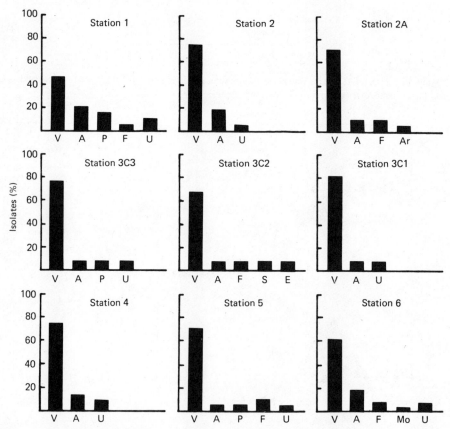

Figure 10.7. Taxonomic distribution of isolates for the November 1980 sampling: *V* = *Vibrio*, *A* = *Acinetobacter*, *P* = *Pseudomonas*, *F* = *Flavobacterium/Cytophaga* group, *Ar* = *Arthrobacter*, *S* = *Staphylococcus*, *Mo* = *Moraxella*, *E* = *Enterobacteriaceae*, and *U* = unidentified.

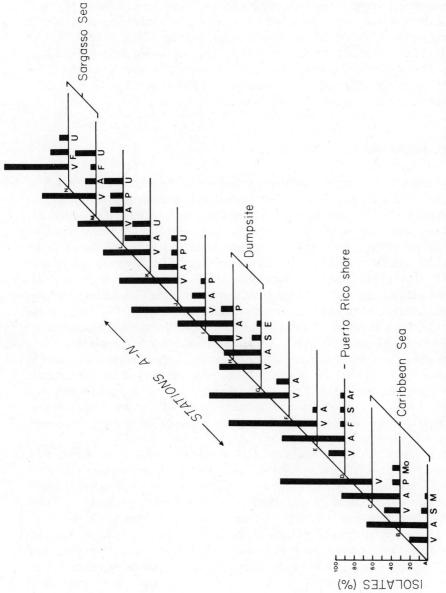

Figure 10.8. Taxonomic distribution of isolates for the June 1981 sampling: $V = Vibrio$, $A = Acinetobacter$, $P = Pseudomonas$, $F = Flavobacterium/Cytophaga$ group, $Ar = Arthrobacter$, $S = Staphylococcus$, $M = Micrococcus$, $E = $ Enterobacteriaceae, $Mo = Moraxella$, and $U = $ unidentified.

where increased proportions of the AODC bacteria could be recovered on MA (Fig. 10.6). In November 1980, this trend was evident at the station located closest to shore (station 4) and at the Barceloneta outfall (station 3C1, Fig. 10.1). In June 1981, the shore stations and the dumpsite revealed the lowest incidence of *Vibrio* (Fig. 10.8) and the lowest proportion of AODC bacteria recoverable on MA (Table 10.3, Fig. 10.6b). The decrease in incidence of *Vibrio* paralleled an increase in *Acinetobacter* at those stations (Fig. 10.8).

10.4. DISCUSSION

The Puerto Rico dumpsite was used for disposal of pharmaceutical wastes from January 1972 until August 1981. Bacteriological examinations of water samples collected within and surrounding the dumpsite demonstrated that the culturable bacterial community was dominated by *Vibrio* spp. (Peele et al., 1981). This finding was unexpected, because it had become almost axiomatic that the culturable bacterial community of the open ocean is dominated by *Pseudomonas* spp. (ZoBell and Upham, 1944; Pfister and Burkholder, 1965; Wood, 1967; Sieburth, 1971; Okami and Okazaki, 1972). Although the proportion of the seawater bacterial populations that can be cultured on laboratory media is usually <0.1% (Jannasch and Jones, 1959), plate counts of indicator microorganisms are nevertheless considered useful in estimating water quality (American Public Health Association, 1976). Furthermore, selected species of culturable bacteria such as coliforms are used to monitor effects of pollutants, as well as to document recovery of an aquatic system from those effects (Cherry et al., 1977). Hence, if the species composition of a bacterial community is employed as an indicator of environmental impact, the indigenous community composition, both in the presence and absence of environmental stress, must be understood and documented.

Previous studies of the microbial flora of surface waters at the Puerto Rico dumpsite included an array of methods employed to measure not only culturable bacterial populations, but also activity of the total bacterial community (Peele et al., 1981; Singleton et al., 1983). However, only by careful taxonomic analysis of the bacterial community was the direct and unequivocal evidence of an impact on that community confirmed. In light of the documented change in the bacterial community from dominance of *Pseudomonas* spp. to *Vibrio* spp., it is hypothesized that this change, arising from oceanic disposal of pharmaceutical wastes containing material that can be utilized by many marine bacteria as a growth substrate, could also occur in other surface waters where the nutrient concentration is high.

During our study chemicals present in the pharmaceutical wastes (toluene and benzene; Schwab et al., 1981) were detected in surface water collected several hundred kilometers from the dumpsite, indicating that the pharmaceutical wastes are not confined to the dumpsite (Peele et al., 1981). Without proper control sites (areas free of pharmaceutical wastes) a comparison of the bacterial flora between waste-affected waters and unaffected waters cannot be made. To circumvent the problem, water samples collected elsewhere than at or near the dumpsite and containing an indigenous bacteria flora were used to evaluate, in the laboratory, the effects of the addition of waste. Also, to ensure proper replication of experiments, as well as close approximation of the *in situ* environmental conditions, laboratory microcosms were employed. Thus, seawater samples collected at stations located in the lower portion of the Chesapeake Bay were used in the microcosm studies. Filter-sterilized composite pharmaceutical waste, to a maximum concentration of 1000 μl liter^{-1}, was added to the microcosm units. This concentration of waste was calculated to approximate the initial dumpsite dilution, 10^3 to 10^4, after dispersal in the surface waters of the open ocean (Csanady, 1981). The culturable bacterial flora responded to the perturbation by increasing in number, with the increase being proportional to the quantity of waste added (Fig. 10.3), demonstrating a bacterial community response in which components of the waste serve as a growth substrate for selected bacterial species present in natural waters. Further supporting this hypothesis was the response of the culturable bacterial community to waste addition, monitored during a 24-h period, following addition of waste to the microcosm (Fig. 10.3). Results of bacteriological analyses of samples taken 30 min after addition of waste did not indicate a toxic effect. Growth occurring after the addition of waste demonstrated that the response was linear and is interpreted to indicate utilization of the waste as a growth substrate. Not only did the number of culturable bacteria increase upon addition of waste, but also the number of bacteria throughout the test period remained signficantly larger than in the control microcosms. Hence, the microbial carrying capacity of this laboratory-simulated environment was greater when waste was added.

Although growth of selected species of bacteria present in the Chesapeake Bay water did occur after addition of waste, it was not evident whether all species of culturable bacteria therein increased equally or whether only certain species increased in activity and number. Similar response for surface water samples collected at the Puerto Rico dumpsite is inferred from the changes in species composition at the time of release of waste into the water, documented by Peele et al. (1981).

In the present study, microcosms that contained two bacterial species (the predominant *Vibrio* sp. in water samples from the dumpsite and either another *Vibrio* or a *Pseudomonas* sp.) and one or more waste additions demonstrated that, in general, the *Vibrio* sp. from the dumpsite dominated the community (Table 10.2, Fig. 10.4).

In microcosms without added waste, community composition remained at ~50% for each strain or became dominated by the *Pseudomonas* sp. Upon addition of sterilized waste, the *Vibrio* sp. consistently dominated, assuming a greater proportion of the community, relative to increasing waste concentration.

The relationship between increased nutrient concentration and altered community structure, with a selective advantage conferred on some bacterial species, has been demonstrated for other aquatic bacteria (Veldkamp, 1979). Results obtained from microcosm studies reported here, in combination with data from two recent cruises, as well as previous cruise data (Peele et al., 1981), provide support of the hypothesis that pharmaceutical wastes affect bacterial community structure.

The first cruise, completed in November 1980, was designed to gather quantitative and qualitative bacteriological data for seawater samples collected along a trackline from Key West, Florida, through the Barceloneta Regional Wastewater Treatment Plant and west of the dumpsite (Fig. 10.1). At the time of the cruise, the Barceloneta facility was treating only municipal wastewater; after August 1981, it is scheduled to receive and treat pharmaceutical wastes (Anderson and Dewling, 1981). The second cruise, in June 1981, permitted collection of samples from Barbados to Puerto Rico, through the dumpsite, and north through the Sargasso Sea to Bermuda (Fig. 10.1). The two cruises allowed for comparison of bacteriological data gathered south, west, and north of the dumpsite.

Total counts and viable counts in the open ocean (Table 10.3) were consistent with those obtained in previous studies (Sieburth, 1971; Orndorff and Colwell, 1980; Peele et al., 1981). Counts for seawater samples collected in the Barceloneta outfall area, at the dumpsite, and near the shore were also consistent with nutrient enrichment via terrestrial runoff and wastewater addition. The trends observed in the Barceloneta outfall (Fig. 10.5) may be a result of dilution and die-off of PCA-recoverable bacteria with increasing distance from the outfall.

Taxonomic analyses of bacterial isolates from seawater samples collected during November 1980 showed that members of the genus *Vibrio* were predominant (Fig. 10.7). Similarly, in June 1981, at stations south and north of the dumpsite, the culturable bacterial community was dominated by *Vibrio*. It should be noted that *Vibrio* spp. represented similar proportions of the culturable community in both the enriched microcosm and cruise samples. Surprisingly, *Acinetobacter* spp., and not *Pseudomonas* spp., were second most abundant. *Acinetobacter* has been reported as a common marine isolate in other studies (Austin et al., 1979; Kaneko et al., 1979; Simidu et al., 1980); since it has only been recently described (Buchanan and Gibbons, 1974), the taxonomy of this group of bacteria is not complete (Austin et al., 1979). Furthermore, the role of *Acinetobacter* in the marine environment needs to be examined further.

Because a single culture medium will provide proper growth conditions for only a fraction of the total bacteria in a sample, the efficiency of recovery of the marine agar employed in this study, and in others (ZoBell and Upham, 1944; Peele et al., 1981) should be considered. Austin et al. (1979) found marine agar to be selective neither for, nor against, *Vibrio* spp., although it did not provide for growth of the greatest variety of culturable species. Kaneko et al. (1979) used marine agar in a study of the Beaufort Sea and found the selective *Flavobacterium* spp. to predominate over *Vibrio*. Thus, based on these studies, it would seem that *Vibrio* dominance was not due to the medium used.

As a result of studies reported here, the validity of the concept that *Pseudomonas* spp. predominate in surface waters of the temperate and tropical ocean is open to question. In the past, incidence of more than 75% *Pseudomonas* spp. was typical. Sieburth (1971), for example, reported close to 100% *Pseudomonas* at stations that approximate the June 1981 trackline (stations F through N). Pfister and Burkholder (1965), in a numerical taxonomic study of seawater samples collected near Puerto Rico, reported ~66% of their isolates to be *Pseudomonas* spp. Methods for the identification and classification of bacteria have been improved during the past 10 y, so that vibrios and pseudomonads can be more clearly differentiated. Certain bacteria classified as *Pseudomonas* spp. in the earlier literature would today be identified as *Vibrio* and *Aeromonas*. For example, several of the glucose-fermenting *Pseudomonas* spp. of ZoBell and Upham (1944) and the high incidence of glucose-fermenting, indole-producing bacteria among isolates reported by Pfister and Burkholder (1965) as pseudomonads probably would now be classified as vibrios. However, changes in methodology and taxonomy alone can not account for the results reported here.

A shift in dominance from *Pseudomonas* to *Vibrio* appears to have occurred in other regions of the temperate and tropical oceans. Such dominance has been observed in the East China Sea by Simidu el al. (1980), in the Chesapeake Bay by Austin et al. (1979), and in the Gulf of Mexico (R. Sizemore, personal communication). A possible explanation for these shifts in dominance, and those observed in this study, is suggested by the studies of Sizemore and Colwell (1977) and Hada and Sizemore (1981). Marine vibrios possess a high degree of environmental adaptiveness, possibly due to the variety of cryptic plasmids carried by the majority of isolates. However, this hypothesis must be investigated further, especially since pseudomonads are also known to carry degradative and resistance plasmids.

A comparison of total bacterial counts (measured by AODC) and numbers of culturable bacteria shows that the latter comprise a small fraction of the total community, but also that this fraction is site-dependent. In regions where nutrient concentrations would be expected to be elevated and allochthonous bacteria more numerous (nearshore, within a dumpsite, or at the Barceloneta outfall), the fraction of the total bacteria recoverable on non-salt-containing PCA increased (Fig. 10.6), suggesting that a biological index can be established related to nutrient input above ambient. If such an index were applied to samples collected during November 1980 and June 1981, during which time the culturable bacteria (PCA) fraction of total bacteria (measured by AODC) was >0.00005%, those water samples could be considered to have nutrient concentrations above ambient. Similarly, when the fraction is <0.00005%, fewer nutrients would be available, as occurred at stations 2, 2A, 4, and 5 (Fig. 10.6a), and B, E, K, L, M, and N (Fig. 10.6b). Such an index would, of course, only allow for comparison of results obtained at a specified time and geographical location. However, within such confines, a trophic-index, indicating regions affected by nutrient input via anthropogenic material, could prove to be informative.

10.5. CONCLUSION

Results of laboratory and field studies suggest that a significant effect of surface-water enrichment at deep ocean dumpsites receiving pharmaceutical waste is an alteration, or restructuring, in species composition of the autochthonous bacterial community. Representatives of the genus *Vibrio* became dominant in both microcosms and surface-water samples exposed to pharmaceutical wastes. It is concluded that quantitative and qualitative bacteriological assessment can be useful in determining effects of wastes on marine bacterial communities. If, in fact, the microbial flora can be significantly affected to the extent of alteration of community composition by influx of anthropogenic materials such as pharmaceutical wastes, the ability of that water mass to assimilate additional burdens of materials must be considered before allowing continued waste disposal.

ACKNOWLEDGMENTS

The technical assistance of R. Attwell and N. Carlson is gratefully acknowledged. M. L. Guerinot provided data on the nonfilterable residues, C. Keefe the nutrient analyses, and J. M. Brooks the gas chromatographic analysis of samples. Special thanks are extended to the officers and crew of the *R/V Gyre* and the *R/V Endeavor*. Appreciation is expressed to R. Barber and O. Pilkey for their assistance in scheduling the November cruise, made possible through the auspices of the University of Maryland National Oceanographic Laboratory System. This study was supported by the U.S. National Oceanic and Atmospheric Administration (NA79AA-D00062) and by the U.S. National Science Foundation (DEB-77-14646).

REFERENCES

American Public Health Association. 1976. Standard Methods for the Examination of Water and Wastewater, 14th Edition. American Public Health Association, Washington, D.C., 1193 pp.

Anderson, P. W., and R. T. Dewling, 1981. Industrial ocean dumping in EPA Region II—regulatory aspects. *In:* Ocean Dumping of Industrial Wastes, B. H. Ketchum, D. R. Kester, and P. K. Park (Eds.). Plenum Press, New York, pp. 25–37.

Atlas, E., G. Martinez, and C. S. Giam. 1981. Chemical characterization of ocean-dumped waste materials. *In:* Ocean Dumping of Industrial Wastes, B. H. Ketchum, D. R. Kester, and P. K. Park (Eds.). Plenum Press, New York, pp. 275–293.

Austin, B., S. Garges, B. Conrad, E. E. Harding, R. R. Colwell, U. Simidu, and N. Taga. 1979. Comparative study of the aerobic, heterotrophic bacterial flora of Chesapeake Bay and Tokyo Bay. *Applied and Environmental Microbiology,* **37,** 704–714.

Bain, N., and J. M. Shewan. 1968. Identification of *Aeromonas, Vibrio* and related organisms. *In:* Identification of Methods for Microbiologists, Part B, B. M. Gibbs, and D. A. Shapton (Eds.) Academic Press, New York, pp. 79–84.

Buchanan, R. E., and N. E. Gibbons (Eds.). 1974. Bergey's Manual of Determinative Bacteriology, 8th Edition. The Williams and Wilkins Company, Baltimore, Maryland, 1268 pp.

Cherry, D. S., R. K. Guthrie, F. L. Singleton, and R. S. Harvey, 1977. Recovery of aquatic bacterial populations in a stream after cessation of chemical pollution. *Water, Air and Soil Pollution,* **7,** 95–101.

Csanady, G. T. 1981. An analysis of dumpsite diffusion experiments. *In:* Ocean Dumping of Industrial Wastes, B. H. Ketchum, D. R. Kester, and P. K. Park (Eds.). Plenum Press, New York, pp. 109–129.

Daley, R. J., and J. E. Hobbie. 1975. Direct counts of aquatic bacteria by a modified epifluorescence technique. *Limnology and Oceanography,* **20,** 875–882.

Francisco, D. E., R. A. Mah, and A. C. Rabin. 1973. Acridine orange-epifluorescence technique for counting bacteria in natural waters. *Transactions of the American Microscopical Society,* **92,** 416–421.

Furniss, A. L., J. V. Lee, and T. J. Donovan. 1978. The Vibrios. Public Health Laboratory Service, Monograph Series, Her Majesty's Stationery Office, London, 58 pp.

Gibson, D. W., M. S. Hendrie, N. C. Houston, and G. Hobbs. 1977. The identification of some Gram-negative heterotrophic aquatic bacteria. *In:* Aquatic Microbiology, F. A. Skinner and J. M. Shewan (Eds.). Academic Press, New York, pp. 135–159.

Hada, H. S., and R. K. Sizemore. 1981. Incidence of plasmids in marine *Vibrio* spp.isolated from an oil field in the northwestern Gulf of Mexico. *Applied and Environmental Microbiology,* **41,** 199–202.

Hobbie, J. E., R. J. Daley, and S. Jasper. 1977. Use of Nuclepore filters for counting bacteria by fluorescence microscopy. *Applied and Environmental Microbiology,* **33,** 1225–1228.

Ishikawa, T., and Y. Ikegaki. 1980. Control of mercury pollution in Japan and the Minamata Bay cleanup. *Journal Water Pollution Control Federation,* **52,** 1013–1018.

Jannasch, H. W., and G. E. Jones. 1959. Bacterial populations in sea water as determined by different methods of enumeration. *Limnology and Oceanography,* **4,** 128–139.

Kaneko, T., M. I. Krichevsky, and R. M. Atlas. 1979. Numerical taxonomy of bacteria from the Beaufort Sea. *Journal of General Microbiology,* **110,** 111–125.

LeChevallier, M. W., R. J. Seidler, and T. M. Evans. 1980. Enumeration and characterization of standard plate count bacteria in chlorinated and raw water supplies. *Applied and Environmental Microbiology,* **40,** 922–930.

Okami, Y., and T. Okazaki. 1972. Studies on marine microorganisms. I. Isolation from the Japan Sea. *The Journal of Antibiotics,* **25,** 456–460.

Orndorff, S. A., and R. R. Colwell. 1980. Distribution and identification of luminous bacteria from the Sargasso Sea. *Applied and Environmental Microbiology,* **39,** 983–987.

Park, P. K., and T. P. O'Connor. 1981. Ocean dumping research: historical and international development. *In:* Ocean Dumping of Industrial Wastes, B. H. Ketchum, D. R. Kester, and P. K. Park (Eds.). Plenum Press, New York, pp. 3–23.

Peele, E. R., F. L. Singleton, J. W. Deming, B. Cavari, and R. R. Colwell. 1981. Effects of pharmaceutical wastes on microbial populations in surface waters at the Puerto Rico dump site in the Atlantic Ocean. *Applied and Environmental Microbiology* **41,** 873–879.

Pfister, R. M., and P. R. Burkholder. 1965. Numerical taxonomy of some bacteria isolated from Antarctic and tropical seawaters. *Journal of Bacteriology,* **90,** 863–872.

Schwab, C. R., T. C. Sauer, Jr., G. F. Hubbard, H. Adbel-Reheim, and J. M. Brooks. 1981. Chemical and biological aspects of ocean dumping at the Puerto Rico dumpsite. *In:* Ocean Dumping of Industrial Wastes, B. H. Ketchum, D. R. Kester, and P. K. Park (Eds.). Plenum Press, New York, pp. 247–273.

Sieburth, J. McN. 1971. Distribution and activity of oceanic bacteria. *Deep-Sea Research*, **18**, 1111–1121.

Simidu, U., N. Taga, R. R. Colwell, and J. R. Schwarz. 1980. Heterotrophic bacterial flora of the seawater from the Nansei Shoto (Ryukyo Retto) area. *Bulletin of the Japanese Society of Scientific Fisheries*, **46**, 505–510.

Singleton, F. L., R. W. Attwell, M. S. Jangi, and R. R. Colwell. 1982. Influence of salinity and organic nutrient concentration on survival and growth of *Vibrio cholerae* in aquatic microcosms. *Applied and Environmental Microbiology*, **43**, 1080–1085.

Singleton, F. L., J. W. Deming, E. R. Peele, B. Cavari, B. Gunn, and R. R. Colwell. 1983. Microbial communities in surface waters at the Puerto Rico dumpsite. *In:* Wastes in the Ocean, Vol. 1: Industrial and Sewage Wastes in the Ocean, I. W. Duedall, B. H. Ketchum, P. K. Park, and D. R. Kester (Eds.). Wiley-Interscience, New York, pp. 201–218.

Sizemore, R. K., and R. R. Colwell. 1977. Plasmids carried by antibiotic-resistant marine bacteria. *Antimicrobial Agents and Chemotherapy*, **12**, 373–382.

Veldkamp, H. 1979. Ecological studies with the chemostat. *In:* Advances in Microbial Ecology, Vol. 1, M. Alexander (Ed.). Plenum Press, New York, pp. 59–94.

Wood, E. J. F. 1967. Microbiology of Oceans and Estuaries. Elsevier Scientific Publishing, Amsterdam, 319 pp.

ZoBell, C. E., and H. C. Upham. 1944. A list of marine bacteria including descriptions of sixty new species. *Bulletin of the Scripps Institute of Oceanography Technical Series* (University of California), **5**, 239–292.

11

ZOOPLANKTON POPULATION RESPONSES TO INDUSTRIAL WASTES DISCHARGED AT DEEPWATER DUMPSITE-106

Judith M. Capuzzo and Bruce A. Lancaster

Woods Hole Oceanographic Institution
Woods Hole, Massachusetts

Abstract   209

11.1. Introduction   210

11.2. Experimental Methods   211

    11.2.1. Laboratory Studies   211
    11.2.2. Field Studies   212

11.3. Results   213

11.4. Discussion and Conclusions   221

Acknowledgments   224

References   224

ABSTRACT

In laboratory studies with copepods, acute toxic effects of wastes discharged at Deepwater Dumpsite (DWD)-106 were detected at waste dilutions of 1.0–5.0 $\times$ 10^{-4} for Du Pont Grasselli waste and American Cyanamid waste and 1.0–5.0 $\times$

10^{-5} for Du Pont Edgemoor waste. Exposure of copepods to sublethal concentrations of each of the wastes resulted in a reduction in the rates of feeding, metabolism, and egg production as compared to control animals. Thus the energetics and reproductive potential of zooplankton entrained in waste plumes at DWD-106 may be seriously impaired. In field studies zooplankton collected from a waste plume that formed within several hours after an American Cyanamid waste dump showed a disruption in energetics similar to that of laboratory animals. The sublethal effects of the various wastes observed in laboratory and field animals were not reversed to control values when animals were removed from waste exposure and transferred to uncontaminated seawater. Progeny of exposed animals, however, did not retain stress symptoms. Entrainment of zooplankton in waste plumes at DWD-106 appears to be a single, short-term event involving only a small percentage of the zooplankton community within this water mass. Thus, even with toxic effects well documented, at the present rate of dumping, long-term consequences to zooplankton populations at DWD-106 appear to be minimal.

11.1. INTRODUCTION

Ocean dumping of industrial wastes provides an alternative to land-based disposal of toxic materials, but the impact of waste disposal on marine ecosystems is not well understood. Because of their fragile nature and ecological importance in marine food chains, the sensitivity of plankton populations to industrial wastes is of great concern. Exposure to industrial wastes may result in either reduced plankton biomass at several trophic levels or accumulation and transfer of toxic materials from one trophic level to another. Either response may lead to significant imbalances or alterations in food chain dynamics.

Deepwater Dumpsite (DWD)-106 is located on the continental slope, ~ 200 km southeast of New York City. Wastes from Du Pont Grasselli and Edgemoor plants and American Cyanamid operations have been dumped at this site for several years. The physical and chemical characteristics of each waste and their dispersal at sea have been investigated since dumping was initiated (Orr and Hess, 1978; Csanady, 1981; Kester et al., 1981, Orr and Baxter; 1983). Du Pont Edgemoor waste is derived from titanium dioxide production and is a highly acidic solution of ferric chloride containing several trace metals, including Cr, Cu, V, Cd, Zn, Ni, and Pb. Du Pont Grasselli waste is an alkaline solution of sodium sulfate containing trace amounts of methyl sulfate, methanol, phenol, and other organic compounds. American Cyanamid waste is derived from the production of organophosphorus pesticides and waste treatment chemicals, with additional wastes coming from the production of intermediates, surfactants, and chemicals used in the rubber mining and paper industries (Csanady et al., 1979). The wastes are diluted by a factor of 5×10^{-4} or greater within 2 h after dumping; in the absence of storms, subsequent dilution of wastes occurs slowly (O'Connor and Park, 1982). At the present rate of dumping, each waste plume is a separate occurrence, restricted to a small area of the ocean and to the mixed layer or pycnocline in depth. Thus, it would appear that exposure of planktonic organisms is limited to a single, short-term exposure of several days.

To adequately predict the assimilative capacity of DWD-106, the long-term effects and bioaccumulation of waste chemicals for each component of the pelagic ecosystem must be evaluated. The response of zooplankton populations to environmental stress may be manifested in disruption of normal energetic pathways and alterations in reproductive and developmental patterns, leading to unstable reproductive rates for this trophic level. The objectives of this study were to evaluate the responses of zooplankton populations to waste additions and to predict the long-term consequences on zooplankton production.

11.2. EXPERIMENTAL METHODS

11.2.1. Laboratory Studies

Collection of the copepods *Centropages typicus, Temora longicornis, Pseudocalanus sp.* and *Acartia tonsa* were made by plankton tows at a depth of 10 m off Gay Head in Vineyard Sound, Massachusetts, and off the Elizabeth Islands in Buzzards Bay, Massachusetts. Male and female specimens were isolated for laboratory culture. Copepods collected during the winter months, when seawater temperatures ranged from 0 to 10°C, were acclimated to 10°C and cultured at 10–12°C at constant illumination and fed a mixed algal diet consisting of *Isochrysis* and *Phaeodactylum* (1×10^5 cells ml^{-1}); *Artemia* nauplii provided an additional food source for *Centropages*. Copepods collected during the summer months, when seawater temperatures ranged from 15 to 20°C, were acclimated to 20°C and cultured at 20–22°C under the conditions described above. Estimates of feeding requirements and egg production rates of each copepod species were made before using adults for bioassays.

Each species of copepod was exposed to each of the wastes at concentrations ranging from 1 to 1000 μl liter^{-1} for 96 h at either 10° or 20°C, depending on acclimation temperature. The assay chambers were 100-ml crystallizing dishes, and 10 copepods were added to each assay chamber; all assays were conducted in triplicate. Survival of copepods exposed to two batches of Du Pont Grasselli waste (5-78 and 1-79), one batch of Du Pont Edgemoor waste (4-79) and one batch of American Cyanamid waste (7-80) were evaluated.

Percent mortality of test organisms was determined at the end of the experimental period. Enumeration of live and dead copepods was made by a modification of the neutral red technique developed by Crippen and Perrier (1974) as described by Capuzzo (1979). Experimental data on mortality were compared to data from control groups; estimates of LC$_{50}$ values were determined by log-probit analysis as described by Finney (1971).

Metabolic rates, feeding rates, and egg production rates of copepods were measured during the 96-h exposure period and up to 1 week following transfer to uncontaminated seawater. Respiration rates were determined using all glass differential microrespirometers (Grunbaum et al., 1955) as described by Capuzzo et al.

(1976). Feeding rates and fecal pellet production rates were determined according to the techniques described by Capuzzo and Lancaster (1981). Feeding rates were determined by measuring the reduction in cell concentration of *Isochrysis* over a 6-h interval, and cell counts were converted to micrograms of carbon after known cell concentrations were assayed for C and N on a Perkin-Elmer CHN analyzer (Perkin-Elmer Corporation, Norwalk, Connecticut). After determination of feeding rates, five copepods were transferred to a 15-ml centrifuge tube, and fecal pellets were collected after 24 h. Copepods were removed and the fecal pellets were collected on a glass fiber filter (1 μm) and assayed for C and N. For egg production rates, five pairs of copepods were placed in 100-ml crystallizing dishes and maintained on an algal diet of *Isochrysis* (1×10^5 cells ml^{-1}, 1 μgC ml^{-1}); egg production and hatching success were monitored daily. The various metabolic parameters were used to calculate energy budgets. Significant differences in energetics and egg production rate of control and exposed copepods were determined by analysis of variance (Sokal and Rohlf, 1969).

Production rates of zooplankton were estimated by (1) calculation of daily energy budgets and scope for growth indices, and (2) egg production (Elster, 1954; Edmonson, 1960; Petrovich et al., 1961). The components of an energy budget include Q_C, calories of food ingested; Q_R, calories lost in respiration; Q_U, calories lost in feces; and Q_G, calories available for growth and reproduction (Warren and Davis, 1967). Production rates based on scope for growth indices (Q_G) are on the basis of production per biomass (P/B) and can be calculated by the equation

$$P/B = Q_G(\text{weight of individual})^{-1} \, d^{-1} \qquad 1$$

Production rates based on egg production can be estimated by the equation

$$P = N_{ov}(D_{ov})^{-1} \qquad 2$$

where P is production, N_{ov} is egg production per female per day, and D_{ov} is duration of development.

This equation is used to estimate the population reproductive potential during a set time interval assuming no mortality of the population. A more realistic approximation of production would include an estimate of the loss in reproductive potential due to the mortality of individuals from waste exposure. This estimate is given by the equation

$$P' = N_t N_{ov}(D_{ov})^{-1} \qquad 3$$

where N_t is the percentage of the population surviving waste exposure and natural environmental stresses.

11.2.2.   Field Studies

The responses of zooplankton to an experimental dump of American Cyanamid waste were monitored during a cruise aboard the *R/V Mt. Mitchell* (RP-27-MI-80, 7–14 July 1980).

Egg production rates of zooplankton collected in the dumpsite area (38°48′N–39°00′N; 72°00′W–72°30′W) prior to and after the dump were compared to values obtained from zooplankton collected outside of the dumpsite area. The copepod *Temora stylifera* was the dominant species within both water masses and was used in all shipboard studies. Copepods were collected by bongo net tows (333-μm net), towed for 15 min at a depth of 10 m and a speed of 2–4 km h^{-1}. Specimens of *T. stylifera* were isolated from plankton samples and cultured aboard ship on a diet of *Isochrysis* and *Monochrysis* (1×10^5 cells ml^{-1}) at 20–22°C. Five pairs of copepods were placed in 100-ml crystallizing dishes, maintained on an algal diet, and estimates of egg production were made.

On 11 July 1980, at 1430 Greenwich Mean Time (GMT) barge dumping of American Cyanamid waste was initiated. The barge load of American Cyanamid waste was dyed to an initial rhodamine-WT® (Joseph Turner Company, Ridgefield, New Jersey) concentration of 32 μg g^{-1}. Waste dilution was monitored by sampling the concentrations of both volatile organic substances (such as toluene) by gas chromatography and rhodamine-WT by fluorescence spectroscopy using a Turner flow-through fluorometer (Wiesenburg and Brooks, 1983). Plankton samples were taken by bongo net tows within the waste plume 3 h after dumping was initiated (1730 GMT), at the same depth as chemical sampling. The net was rinsed for 2 min in seawater outside of the plume area before the plankton sample was removed to avoid surface contamination with the waste. Specimens of *Temora* were isolated from the plankton sample and incubated for estimates of egg production. Sampling in the vicinity of the waste plume was repeated on 12 July 1980 at 1430 GMT, 24 h after the initial dump. Estimates of egg production were made for at least 48 h. Significant differences in egg production rates between copepods collected inside and outside the dumpsite area were determined by analysis of variance (Sokal and Rohlf, 1969).

11.3. RESULTS

The LC$_{50}$ values, estimated by log-probit analysis, are presented in Table 11.1. Mortality rates of copepods exposed to Grasselli, Edgemoor, and American Cyanamid wastes are presented in Figs. 11.1–11.3. There was no significant difference ($P < 0.01$) in mortality of copepods exposed to the two batches of Grasselli waste, and no change in pH was observed at concentrations < 1 ml liter^{-1} (Table 11.2). *Centropages, Pseudocalanus,* and *Temora* were similar in their responses to Grasselli waste: significant mortality (>20%) was observed only at concentrations >100 μl liter^{-1}. The increased susceptibility of *Centropages* acclimated to 20°C suggests a synergistic effect of temperature on the toxicity of Grasselli waste.

The mortality rates of *Acartia, Centropages,* and *Pseudocalanus* exposed to Edgemoor waste were similar, and significant mortality (>20%) was observed at concentrations >5 μl liter^{-1} at both exposure temperatures. Alterations in pH at concentrations <100 μl liter^{-1} were not sufficient to cause significant mortality

Table 11.1.　Comparison of Toxic Levels of Du Pont Grasselli Waste for Marine Copepods

Species	Temperature (°C)	96 h LC_{50} (μl liter^{-1})[a]	
		5-78	1-79
Centropages typicus	10	273 ± 2	293 ± 2
	20	106 ± 2	—
Pseudocalanus sp.	10	200 ± 2	223 ± 2
Temora longicornis	10	225 ± 2	216 ± 2

[a]The ± indicates 95% confidence limits. Dash indicates no data available.

(Table 11.2). The LC_{50} values are presented in Table 11.3. Comparing the findings at the two exposure temperatures, it is apparent that there is a slight synergistic effect of temperature on the toxicity of Edgemoor waste and that this waste is slightly more toxic than Grasselli waste to these species of copepods.

Bioassays on the toxicity of American Cyanamid waste to the copepod *Acartia tonsa* have been completed, and an LC_{50} value of 233 ± 2 μl liter^{-1} has been

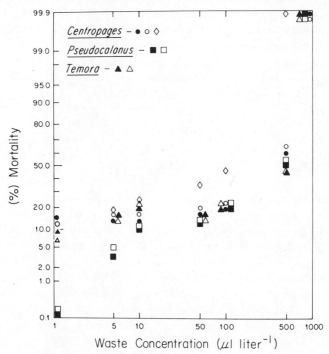

Figure 11.1.　Log-probit plot of the mortality of copepods exposed to Du Pont Grasselli waste for 96 h: ●, ▲, and ■ = 1-79 waste sample; ○, △, and □ = 5-78 waste, exposure at 10°C; and ◇ = 5-78 waste, exposure at 20°C. Each point represents the mean of 12 replicate assays.

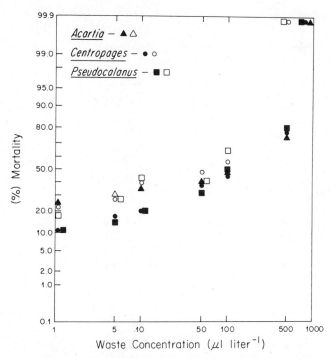

Figure 11.2. Log-probit plot of the mortality of copepods exposed to Du Pont Edgemoor waste for 96 h: closed symbols, exposure at 10°C; open symbols, exposure at 20°C. Each point represents the mean of 12 replicate assays.

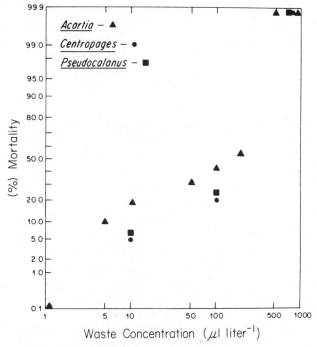

Figure 11.3. Log-probit plots of the mortality of copepods exposed to American Cyanamid waste for 96 h at 20°C. Each point represents the mean of 12 replicate assays.

Table 11.2.   The pH of Waste–Seawater Dilutions

Waste Concentration	Seawater pH		
(μl liter^{-1})	Grasselli	Edgemoor[a]	American Cyanamid
0	7.9	8.0	8.0
1	7.8	8.0	7.9
5	7.9	7.9	7.9
10	7.9	7.9	8.0
50	7.9	7.7	8.0
100	7.9	7.4[b]	8.0
500	8.0	6.1[c]	8.1
1000	8.1	4.1[c]	7.9
5000	8.5	2.3	8.0

[a]When diluted with seawater at each concentration, a particulate phase (hydrous ferric oxide) is formed; 99% of the particles were $\leq 15 \mu$m.
[b]Ferric oxide precipitate aggregated immediately.
[c]Ferric oxide precipitate aggregated after 24 h.

Table 11.3.   Comparison of Toxic Levels of Du Pont Edgemoor Waste for Different Marine Copepods

	96-hLC$_{50}$ (μl liter^{-1})[a]	
Acartia tonsa	171 $\pm$ 2.3	----
Centropages typicus	104 $\pm$ 2	97 $\pm$ 2
Pseudocalanus sp.	121 $\pm$ 2	91 $\pm$ 2

[a]The $\pm$ indicates 95% confidence limits. Dash indicates no data available.

calculated. Bioassays with other species of copepods, including *Centropages* and *Pseudocalanus,* have given similar results (Fig. 11.3), but there are not sufficient data to allow calculation of LC$_{50}$ values. No change in pH was observed at any of the waste concentrations tested.

Cannibalism of eggs by adult copepods did not appear to be a problem in estimating egg production by *Temora* and *Acartia* if eggs were removed daily. *Pseudocalanus* maintains eggs in a sac and thus can not cannibalize its eggs. Initial evaluations of egg production by *Centropages* revealed that adults could prey on newly released eggs and a false bottom of Nitex® (Tetko, Inc., Elmsford, New York) mesh was added to each crystallizing dish to separate adults from eggs.

Egg production rates of *Temora* and *Pseudocalanus* exposed to sublethal concentrations of Grasselli waste are presented in Table 11.4. Egg production rates were significantly reduced ($P < 0.01$) in both species with exposure to 1, 10, and 100 μl liter^{-1} and were not restored to the control levels even 1 week after expo-

Table 11.4.   Egg Production of *Temora* and *Pseudocalanus* Exposed to Various Concentrations of Du Pont Grasselli Waste for 96 h[a]

Waste Concentration (μl liter^{-1})	*Temora* (eggs per female per day)			*Pseudocalanus* (eggs per clutch per female)		
	1[b]	2[c]	3[d]	1[b]	2[c]	3[d]
0	1.7	1.8	1.6	8.2	8.0	7.6
	(0.1)	(0.1)	(0.2)	(0.2)	(0.2)	(0.4)
1	1.3	1.5	1.7	3.6	3.2	7.8
	(0.1)	(0.1)	(0.2)	(0.2)	(0.2)	(0.2)
10	1.3	1.3	1.8	3.6	2.8	7.6
	(0.1)	(0.1)	(0.1)	(0.2)	(0.2)	(0.2)
100	1.0	1.0	1.7	2.0	0.0	7.8
	(0.1)	(0.1)	(0.1)	(0.2)		(0.2)

[a]Mean values of 10 groups of five pairs of copepods per group with the standard error given in parentheses.
[b]Measured during 96-h exposure at 10°C.
[c]Measured 1 week after end of 96-h exposure.
[d]Measured from second generation copepods.

sure. Reductions were equivalent to 77% of control values for *Temora* exposed to 1 and 10 μl liter^{-1} and 59% for exposure at 100 μl liter^{-1}; reductions for *Pseudocalanus* were equivalent to 44% of control values with exposure to 1 and 10 μl liter^{-1}, and 24% with exposure to 100 μl liter^{-1}. During the post-exposure period reductions in egg production rates were similar for *Temora* but even greater reductions were observed for *Pseudocalanus*. The hatching time of eggs for both species was 3.0 d, and there was no significant difference in hatching time for exposed and control groups. The second generation of copepods of both species (offspring from exposed copepods) appeared to develop normally after hatching and attained reproductive state in ~20 d.

Significant reductions ($P < 0.01$) in egg production rates of *Centropages* and *Pseudocalanus* were also observed with exposure to 10 μl liter^{-1} Edgemoor waste (Table 11.5). Reductions were equivalent to 55% and 64% of control values for *Centropages* and *Pseudocalanus*, respectively. No egg production was observed with either species from the exposed groups during the week following exposure, and copepods from these groups experienced high mortality by the end of the post-exposure period. Control copepods continued to reproduce during the post-exposure period and no significant mortality was recorded. The hatching time of eggs was 2.5 d for *Centropages* and 3.0 d for *Pseudocalanus*, and there was no significant difference in hatching time for exposed and control groups. The second generation of copepods developed normally and attained sexual maturity in 20 d for *Pseudocalanus* and 26 d for *Centropages;* egg production rates of second generation copepods were the same as control organisms.

Egg production rates of *Acartia* exposed to American Cyanamid waste are pre-

Table 11.5.   Egg Production of *Centropages* and *Pseudocalanus* Exposed to Du Pont Edgemoor Waste for 96 h[a]

Waste Concentration (μl liter^{-1})	*Temora* (eggs per female per day)			*Pseudocalanus* (eggs per clutch per female)		
	1[b]	2[c]	3[d]	1[b]	2[c]	3[d]
0	14.6	18.5	20.5	11.3	9.8	11.2
	(1.0)	(1.0)	(1.2)	(1.0)	(0.9)	(0.9)
10	8.0	0.0	15.0	7.2	0.0	10.6
	(0.8)		(0.9)	(0.6)		(0.9)

[a]Mean values of 20 groups of five pairs of copepods per group with the standard error given in parentheses; *Centropages* at 20°C, *Pseudocalanus* at 10°C.
[b]Measured during 96-h exposure.
[c]Measured 1 week after end of 96-h exposure.
[d]Measured from second-generation copepods.

sented in Table 11.6. Exposure to concentrations of 1, 10, and 100 μl liter^{-1} resulted in significant reductions ($P < 0.01$) in egg production equivalent to 67%, 58%, and 46% of control values, respectively; egg production was also slightly delayed among copepods exposed to the higher concentrations. Hatching time was 2.5 d for both control and exposed copepods.

The energy budgets of *Centropages, Pseudocalanus,* and *Temora* exposed to 10 μl liter^{-1} and 100 μl liter^{-1} Grasselli waste are presented in Table 11.7. Compared to control animals, exposed copepods of all three species showed significant reductions ($P < 0.01$) in respiration rates and feeding rates. Reduced values for Q_G or scope for growth indices among exposed copepods were equivalent to 26.9% for *Centropages* at 100 μl liter^{-1}, 57% and 44% for *Pseudocalanus* at 10 and 100 μl liter^{-1}, respectively, and 77% and 59% for *Temora* at 10 and 100 μl liter^{-1}, respectively. This disruption in energetics could account for the reduced egg produc-

Table 11.6.   Fecal Pellet Production and Egg Production Rates of *Acartia* Exposed to American Cyanamid Waste[a]

Waste Concentration (μliter^{-1})	Fecal Pellet Production (pellets per copepod per day)	Egg Production (eggs per copepod per day)
0	8.0	4.8
	(0.4)	(0.3)
1	5.9	3.2
	(0.5)	(0.4)
10	4.0	2.8
	(0.8)	(0.2)
100	2.9	2.2
	(0.5)	(0.1)

[a]Mean values of eight replicate assays with standard error given in parentheses.

Table 11.7. Energy Budgets of *Centropages, Pseudocalanus,* and *Temora* Exposed to Du Pont Grasselli Waste for 96 h[a]

Species	Temperature (°C)	Waste Concentration (μl liter^{-1})	Calories (d^{-1})			
			Q_C	Q_R	Q_U	Q_G
Centropages	20.0	0	1.8×10^{-2}	3.0×10^{-3}	7.2×10^{-3}	7.8×10^{-3}
		10	—	—	—	—
		100	4.9×10^{-3}	8.1×10^{-4}	1.9×10^{-3}	2.1×10^{-3}
Pseudocalanus	10.0	0	1.3×10^{-2}	2.0×10^{-3}	6.0×10^{-3}	4.6×10^{-3}
		10	7.3×10^{-3}	1.1×10^{-3}	3.4×10^{-3}	2.6×10^{-3}
		100	5.7×10^{-3}	8.9×10^{-4}	2.6×10^{-3}	2.0×10^{-3}
Temora	10.0	0	8.4×10^{-3}	2.4×10^{-3}	3.4×10^{-3}	2.2×10^{-3}
		10	6.4×10^{-3}	1.8×10^{-3}	2.6×10^{-3}	1.7×10^{-3}
		100	5.0×10^{-3}	1.4×10^{-3}	2.0×10^{-3}	1.3×10^{-3}

[a]Caloric equivalents of Q_C and Q_U are based on the conversion of carbon to calories by the method of Salonen et al. (1976); caloric equivalents of Q_R were 4.8×10^{-3} cal μl^{-1} O_2 consumed (Brody, 1945); Q_G was calculated by difference. Dashes indicate no data available.

tion observed in *Temora* and *Pseudocalanus*. Similar results were observed among copepods exposed to 10 μl liter^{-1} Edgemoor waste (Table 11.8) with reductions in scope for growth indices equivalent to 55% and 54% for *Centropages* and *Pseudocalanus*, respectively. Complete energy budgets are not available for copepods exposed to American Cyanamid waste; however, feeding rates, as inferred from fecal pellet production, were significantly reduced (Table 11.6). Preliminary measurements of respiration rate of *Acartia* were equivalent to 9.6×10^{-3} cal d^{-1} for control copepods and 4.1×10^{-3} cal d^{-1} for those exposed to 10 μl liter^{-1}, a reduction of 43% of control values.

Production rates based on scope for growth indices and egg production rates of copepods exposed to Grasselli waste are presented in Table 11.9 and those exposed to Edgemoor waste in Table 11.10. The reductions in production rates attributable to waste exposure are comparable as estimated by the two methods. Production rates for copepods exposed to American Cyanamid waste were only calculated on

Table 11.8. Energy Budgets of *Centropages* and *Pseudocalanus* Exposed to Du Pont Edgemoor Waste for 96 h[a]

Species	Temperature (°C)	Waste Concentration (μl liter^{-1})	Calories (d^{-1})			
			Q_C	Q_R	Q_U	Q_G
Centropages	20.0	0	1.8×10^{-2}	3.0×10^{-3}	7.2×10^{-3}	7.8×10^{-3}
		10	9.9×10^{-3}	1.7×10^{-3}	4.0×10^{-3}	4.3×10^{-3}
Pseudocalanus	10.0	0	1.3×10^{-2}	2.0×10^{-3}	6.0×10^{-3}	4.6×10^{-3}
		10	7.2×10^{-3}	1.1×10^{-3}	3.4×10^{-3}	2.5×10^{-3}

[a]Definitions and units are given in Table 11.7.

Table 11.9.   Production Rates of *Centropages, Pseudocalanus,* and *Temora* Exposed to Grasselli Waste for 96 h.

	Waste Concentration (μl liter^{-1})	Production Rate		
		Energetics[a] (P/B d^{-1})	Egg Production	
Species			P	P'
Centropages	0	0.22	—	—
	10	—	—	—
	100	0.06	—	—
Pseudocalanus	0	0.23	0.41	0.39
	10	0.13	0.18	0.16
	100	0.10	0.10	0.08
Temora	0	0.09	0.09	0.09
	10	0.07	0.07	0.06
	100	0.05	0.05	0.04

[a]$P/B = Q_G$ wt^{-1}; average dry weights at 70°C for 24 h for each species: *Centropages* = 35 μg, *Pseudocalanus* = 20 μg, *Temora* = 25 μg. Dashes indicate no data available.

Table 11.10.   Production Rates of *Centropages,* and *Pseudocalanus* Exposed to Du Pont Edgemoor Waste for 96 h[a]

	Waste Concentration (μl liter^{-1})	Production Rate		
		Energetics[a] (P/B d^{-1})	Egg Production	
Species			P	P'
Centropages	0	0.22	0.56	0.53
	10	0.12	0.31	0.17
Pseudocalanus	0	0.23	0.57	0.54
	10	0.13	0.31	0.25

[a]Average dry weights as in Table 11.9.

the basis of egg production rates using a value of 18 d for development time of *Acartia* (Table 11.11).

In field studies, egg production rates of *Temora stylifera* were determined before and after dumping of American Cyanamid waste. There was no significant differ- ence ($P < 0.01$) in egg production rates at any of the control stations (Table 11.12).

Most of the dumped waste consisted of highly volatile organic compounds. Wie- senburg and Brooks (1983) found little mixing of the waste with depth and rapid loss of the volatile components through evaporation and surface mixing. Waste concentrations were equivalent to 2.1 mg liter^{-1} total volatile organic compounds (VOC) within 0.1 h after the dump, 860 μg liter^{-1} total VOC within 3 h, and 2 μg liter^{-1} total VOC after 9 h.

Copepods collected in the waste plume 3 h after dumping exhibited sluggish swimming behavior, and no egg production was observed after incubation in un-

**Table 11.11.   Production Rates of *Acartia*
Exposed to American Cyanamid Waste for 96 h**

Waste Concentration (μl liter^{-1})	Egg Production Rates	
	P	P'
0	0.27	0.25
1	0.18	0.17
10	0.16	0.12
100	0.12	0.07

**Table 11.12.   Egg Production Rates of *Temora stylifera* Collected during the
July 1980 Sampling aboard the *R/V Mt. Mitchell* in the Vicinity of DWD-106**

Station	Location	Egg Production Rates[a] (eggs per copepod per day)
17	38°59′53″N, 72°00′24″W	2.5 (0.6)
21	38°50′15″N, 72°10′04″W	2.2 (0.3)
22	38°50′00″N, 72°20′00″W	2.4 (0.5)
34	38°41′11″N, 72°10′10″W	2.5 (0.5)
A[b]	38°46′20″N, 72°07′15″W	0.0
B[c]	38°56′48″N, 71°41′54″W	0.0

[a]Mean value of four replicate assays with standard error given in parentheses.
[b]Copepods collected 3 h after dumping of American Cyanamid waste.
[c]Copepods collected 24 h after dumping of American Cyanamid waste.

contaminated seawater for 48 h. The lack of egg production among copepods collected from the waste plume might have been due to the inhibitory effects of higher exposure concentrations (730–78 μg ml^{-1}, 0–3 h) or a delayed response in egg production as observed in laboratory studies. Copepods collected 24 h later in the vicinity of the waste plume also appeared sluggish and failed to produce eggs. This sustained reduction in activity might have been the result of a lack of recovery of copepods exposed to acute chemical stress rather than the effects of continuous waste exposure, as no waste was detected in the waste plume at 24 h.

11.4. DISCUSSION AND CONCLUSIONS

Biological effects of waste disposal can be evaluated only in light of adequate information on the chemical composition of the wastes, their persistence in the dumpsite area, their bioavailability and bioaccumulation, and their toxicological effects. If the waste components are restricted to a plume and do not persist beyond a few days, exposure of plankton in the dumpsite area would be minimal, and permanent alterations in primary and secondary production would not be expected. If, on the other hand, waste components continue to persist in the dumpsite area and are not readily assimilated or dissipated, chronic, long-term exposure of plankton populations could result in localized reductions in productivity and changes in community structure. Thus, estimates of the assimilative capacity of a dumpsite area must be based on the ultimate fate of waste chemicals and the effects on populations of the dumpsite area, including both acute and chronic long-term effects. The high natural variability of water masses at DWD-106, however, prevent adequate *in situ* field estimates of population changes related to waste dumping.

Laboratory assessments of biological effects of wastes dumped at DWD-106 include reduced microbial heterotrophic activity (Vaccaro and Dennett, 1981), reduced growth rates of phytoplankton (Murphy and Belastock, 1980; Murphy et al., 1981) and high mortality of copepods (Capuzzo and Lancaster, 1981; this chapter). All of these responses, however, occurred at concentrations in excess of those normally encountered within a waste plume. Understanding the sublethal effects that may occur with exposure to concentrations normally detected within the waste plumes (10–50 μl liter^{-1}) is essential to predicting the impact on productivity of the dumpsite area.

The responses of zooplankton populations to environmental stress may be manifested in reduced egg production rates, lower rates of survival after hatching, delayed development, extended generation times, and an increase in the number of abnormal offspring, leading to unstable reproductive rates. Reeve et al. (1977) suggested that the most sensitive short-term index of sublethal stress to adult copepod populations was egg production, and reduced rates were measured among several species of copepods exposed to sublethal concentrations of copper and mercury. Berdugo et al. (1977) observed reduced egg production rates of *Eurytemora affinis* with short-term exposure to the water soluble fraction of a high aromatic heating oil. Chronic long-term exposure of *Eurytemora* resulted in reductions in life span, number of nauplii produced, mean brood size, and egg production rates (Ott et al., 1978); the toxic effects might not have been due to specific inhibition of reproductive processes, but related to reduced feeding rates of exposed copepods. Reductions in egg production rates of copepods exposed to each of the industrial wastes discharged at DWD-106 have been documented in the present study. Although fecundity was significantly reduced among exposed copepods, acute exposure to these wastes did not result in changes in hatching survival or development time.

Alterations in metabolic activity have been used by several investigators as an index of acute stress in copepod populations (Gaudy, 1977; Capuzzo, 1980). Reeve et al. (1977), however, found respiration rates not to be a sensitive indicator of stress for copepods exposed to sublethal concentrations of copper and mercury and suggested that other indices, such as egg production, should be used in predicting sublethal stress. Other zooplankton forms have shown reductions in metabolic rates with exposure to petroleum hydrocarbons and heavy metals (Corner, 1978; Davies, 1978) and it is generally assumed that any compound that interferes with normal energy utilization and storage mechanisms will result in an alteration of metabolic rate.

In the present study, reductions in respiration rates were observed in copepods exposed to industrial wastes discharged at DWD-106, suggesting that components of each of the wastes interfere with oxidative metabolism. Similar reductions in feeding activity of copepods exposed to the wastes led to a disruption in energy budgets. Reduction in feeding rates might be a result of either impairment of feeding mechanisms or inhibition of chemosensory receptors used in detecting food. This reduction in energetics could account for the reduced fecundity of exposed copepods, as less energy was available for growth and reproduction. Several investigators have reported the effects of declining food concentrations on copepod egg production. Dagg (1977) found that egg production of *Acartia tonsa* and *Centropages typicus* declined rapidly during brief periods of starvation; *Pseudocalanus minutus*, however, was more resistant to starvation, presumably due to a high accumulation of energy reserves, and egg production continued unimpaired for several days. Checkley (1980) found that egg production of *Paracalanus parvus* was severely limited at low food levels. These studies suggest that inhibition of feeding could indeed account for the reductions in egg production of *Acartia, Centropages,* and *Temora* exposed to the various wastes in the present study. The reduced fecundity of *Pseudocalanus* may also be related to an inhibition of utilization of stored reserves.

Using both LC_{50} data and sublethal response indices, the order of toxicity of the industrial wastes discharged at DWD-106 is as follows: American Cyanamid $\cong$ Du Pont Grasselli $<$ Du Pont Edgemoor. Sublethal responses are important in predicting disruptions in population stability and production associated with waste exposure. Estimates of production rates based on scope for growth indices and fecundity of zooplankton exposed to the various industrial wastes were comparable. Thus, both the immediate metabolic responses and the delayed reductions in fecundity of copepods exposed to industrial wastes may be used as sensitive indices of sublethal stress. Changes in energetics result from interference of toxicants with metabolic processes that could lead to inefficient utilization of food and subsequent reductions in growth and reproduction. Measurements of respiration rates and scope for growth indices can provide a first approximation of disruption in energetics and potential disruption in population stability, but should be coupled with fecundity measurements to be used in predictions of changes in actual production rates. All of the response parameters discussed in this chapter are amenable to both laboratory and shipboard studies. Future ocean dumping studies could compare the responses of zooplankton collected from actual field exposures with those exposed through a simulated shipboard dumping experiment.

The significance of reduced production rates of copepods exposed to industrial wastes at DWD-106 must be evaluated with consideration given to the volume of ocean affected by waste plumes. At the present rate of dumping only a small percentage of the area adjacent to DWD-106 appears to be affected by waste dumping. Dispersion and persistence of wastes varies with the prevailing hydrographic conditions, but the high rate of waste dilution and dissipation evident at DWD-106 results in only a small percentage of the zooplankton community being exposed to waste additions.

ACKNOWLEDGMENTS

This research was supported by the Office of Marine Pollution Assessment, U.S. National Oceanic and Atmospheric Administration, under grant No. NA79AA-D-00027. The authors gratefully acknowledge the assistance of J. P. Clarner and N. Corwin for carbon analyses. This chapter is Woods Hole Oceanographic Institution Contribution No. 5038.

REFERENCES

Berdugo, V., R. P. Harris, and S. C. O'Hara. 1977. The effect of petroleum hydrocarbons on reproduction of an estuarine planktonic copepod in laboratory cultures. *Marine Pollution Bulletin,* **8,** 138–143.

Brody, S. 1945. Bioenergetics and Growth. Reinhold Publishing, New York, 1023 pp.

Capuzzo, J. M. 1979. The effects of halogen toxicants on survival, feeding and egg production of the rotifer *Brachionus plicatilis. Estuarine and Coastal Marine Science,* **8,** 307–316.

Capuzzo, J. M. 1980. Impact of power-plant discharges on marine zooplankton: A review of thermal, mechanical and biocidal effects. *Helgoländer Meeresuntersuchungen,* **33,** 422–433.

Capuzzo, J. M., and B. A. Lancaster. 1981. The effects of pollutants on marine zooplankton at Deep Water Dumpsite 106: Preliminary findings. *In:* Ocean Dumping of Industrial Wastes, B. H. Ketchum, D. R. Kester, and P. K. Park (Eds.). Plenum Press, New York, pp. 411–419.

Capuzzo, J. M., S. A. Lawrence, and J. A. Davidson. 1976. Combined toxicity of free chlorine, chloramine and temperature to stage I larvae of the American Lobster *Homarus americanus. Water Research,* **10,** 1093–1099.

Checkley, D. M. Jr. 1980. Food limitation of egg production by a marine planktonic copepod in the sea off southern California. *Limnology and Oceanography,* **25,** 991–998.

Corner, E. D. S. 1978. Pollution studies with marine plankton. Part I. Petroleum hydrocarbons and related compounds. *In:* Advances in Marine Biology, Vol. 15, Sir F. S. Russell and Sir M. Yonge (Eds.). Academic Press, London, pp. 289–380.

Crippen, R. W, and J. L. Perrier. 1974. The use of neutral red and Evans blue for live–dead determinations of marine plankton (with comments on the use of rotenone for inhibition of grazing). *Stain Technology,* **49,** 97–104.

Csanady, G. T. 1981. An analysis of dumpsite diffusion experiments. *In:* Ocean Dumping of Industrial Wastes, B. H. Ketchum, D. R. Kester, and P. K. Park (Eds.). Plenum Press, New York, pp. 109–129.

Csanady, G., G. Flierl, D. Karl, D. Kester, T. O'Connor, P. Ortner, and W. Philpot. 1979. Deepwater Dumpsite 106. *In:* Proceedings of a Workshop on Assimilative Capacity of U.S. Coastal Waters for Pollutants, Crystal Mountain, Washington, E. Goldberg (Ed.). Special report, U.S. National Oceanic and Atmospheric Administration, Boulder, Colorado, pp. 123–147.

Dagg, M. 1977. Some effects of patchy food environments on copepods. *Limnology and Oceanography,* **22,** 99–107.

Davies, A. G. 1978. Pollution studies with marine plankton. Part II. Heavy metals. *In:* Advances in Marine Biology, Vol. 15, Sir F. S. Russell and Sir M. Yonge (Eds.). Academic Press, London, pp. 381–508.

Edmonson, W. T. 1960. Reproductive rates of rotifers in natural populations. *Memorie dell'Istituto Italiano di Idrobiologia Dott Marco de Marchi,* **12,** 21–77.

Elster, H. J. 1954. Uber die populationsdynamik von *Eudiaptomus glacilis* Sars and *Heterocope borealis* Fisher im Bodensee-Obersee. *Archiv für Hydrobiologie,* **20**(Supplement), 546–614.

Finney, D. J. 1971. Probit Analysis, 3rd Edition. Cambridge University Press, Cambridge, England, 333 pp.

Gaudy, R. 1977. Etude des modifications du métabolisme respiratorie de populations d'*Acartia clausi* (Crustacea: Copepoda) après passage dans le circuit de refroidissement d'une centrale thero-électrique. *Marine Biology,* **39,** 179–190.

Grunbaum, B. W., B. V. Siegel, A. R. Schulz, and P. Kirk. 1955. Determination of oxygen uptake by tissue grown in an all glass differential microrespirometer. *Mikrochimica Acta,* **6,** 1069–1075.

Kester, D. R., R. C. Hittinger, and P. Mukherji. 1981. Transition and heavy metals associated with acid-iron waste disposal at Deep Water Dumpsite 106. *In:* Ocean Dumping of Industrial Wastes, B. H., Ketchum, D. R. Kester, and P. K. Park (Eds.). Plenum Press, New York, pp. 215–232.

Murphy, L. S., and R. A. Belastock. 1980. The effect of environmental origin on the response of marine diatoms to chemical stress. *Limnology and Oceanography,* **25,** 160–165.

Murphy, L. S., P. R. Hoar, and R. A. Belastock. 1981. The effects of industrial wastes on marine phytoplankton. *In:* Ocean Dumping of Industrial Wastes, B. H. Ketchum, D. R. Kester, and P. K. Park (Eds.). Plenum Press, New York, pp. 399–410.

O'Connor, T. P., and P. K. Park. 1982. Consequences of industrial waste disposal at the 106-mile ocean waste disposal site. *In:* Ecological Stress and the New York Bight: Science and Management, G. F. Mayer (Ed.). Estuarine Research Federation, Columbia, South Carolina, pp. 675–697.

Orr. M. H., and L. H. Baxter III. 1983. Dispersion of particles after disposal of industrial and sewage wastes. *In:* Wastes in the Ocean, Vol. 1: Industrial and Sewage Wastes in the Ocean, I. W. Duedall, B. H. Ketchum, P. K. Park, and D. R. Kester (Eds.). Wiley-Interscience, New York, pp. 117–137.

Orr, M. H., and F. R. Hess. 1978. Acoustic monitoring of industrial chemical waste released at Deep Water Dumpsite 106. *Journal of Geophysical Research,* **83,** 6145–6154.

Ott, F. S., R. P. Harris, and S. C. M. O'Hara. 1978. Acute and sub-lethal toxicity of naphthalene and three methylated derivatives to an estuarine copepod, *Eurytemora affinis. Marine Environmental Research,* **1,** 49–59.

Petrovich, P. G., E. A. Shushkina, and G. A. Pechen. 1961. Calculation of zooplankton production (Russian). *Doklady Akademii Nauk SSSR,* **139,** 1235–1238.

Reeve, M. R., M. A. Walter, K. Darcy, and T. Ikeda. 1977. Evaluation of potential indicators of sub-lethal toxic stress on marine zooplankton (feeding, fecundity, respiration, and excretion): Controlled Ecosystem Pollution Experiment. *Bulletin of Marine Science,* **27,** 105–113.

Salonen, K., J. Sarvala, I. Hakala, and M. -L. Viljanen. 1976. The relation of energy and organic carbon in aquatic invertebrates. *Limnology and Oceanography,* **21,** 724–730.

Sokal, R. R., and F. J. Rohlf. 1969. Biometry: The Principles and Practice of Statistics in Biological Research. W. H. Freeman, San Franscisco, 859 pp.

Vaccaro, R. F., and M. R. Dennett. 1981. The environmental responses of marine bacteria to waste disposal activities at Deepwater Dumpsite 106. *In:* Assessment Report on the Effects of Waste Dumping in the 106-Mile Ocean Waste Disposal site. Dumping Evaluation Report 81-1, U.S. National Oceanic and Atmospheric Administration, Boulder, Colorado, pp. 295–308.

Warren, C. E., and G. E. Davis. 1967. Laboratory studies on the feeding, bioenergetics, and growth of fish. *In:* The Biological Basis of Freshwater Fish Production, S. D. Gerking (Ed.). Blackwell Publications, Oxford, pp. 175–214.

Wiesenburg, D. A., and J. M. Brooks. 1983. Eddy-enhanced dispersion of ocean-dumped organic waste at Deep Water Dumpsite-106. *Canadian Journal of Fisheries and Aquatic Sciences,* **40** (Supplement 2), 248–261.

12

PHARMACEUTICAL WASTES AT THE PUERTO RICO DUMPSITE: SUBLETHAL EFFECTS ON A MARINE PLANKTONIC COPEPOD, *TEMORA TURBINATA*

Wen Yuh Lee and Jerry L. Bird

Marine Sciences Institute
The University of Texas
Port Aransas, Texas

Abstract

12.1.	**Introduction**	**228**
12.2.	**Materials and Methods**	**229**
	12.2.1. Waste Material	229
	12.2.2. Feeding Experiment	229
	12.2.3. Growth and Fecundity Experiment	230
12.3.	**Results**	**231**
	12.3.1. Feeding Behavior of Copepods	231
	12.3.2. Survival, Growth, and Fecundity	232
12.4.	**Discussion**	**236**
12.5.	**Summary and Conclusions**	**238**

Acknowledgments   238

References   239

ABSTRACT

Copepods were affected when they were chronically exposed to pharmaceutical waste concentrations >0.1 μg g^{-1}. No consistent pattern of change in feeding rates that could be attributed to waste toxicity was discerned. Copepod ingestion rates in all treatments were essentially similar, and increased with cell density up to about 250 cells ml^{-1}. At higher phytoplankton density (>250 cells ml^{-1}) there was little variation in ingestion rates. Chronic exposure of copepods reared from eggs to adults in 1.0 and 10 μg g^{-1} waste concentrations significantly affected developmental rate, body length, and egg production, but did not influence survival rates. The overall survival percentages for the control, 0.1, 1.0, and 10 μg g^{-1} concentrations at day 15 were 68, 63, 72, and 66%, respectively. Copepod growth rates at 1.0 and 10 μg g^{-1} concentrations differed from that of the control, and were characterized by hormesis. In addition, at comparable ages, *Temora turbinata* grown at higher waste concentrations were smaller than the copepods raised at lower concentrations. At day 10, the average adult female length (tip of cephalothorax to the end of the anal segment) in the control, 0.1, 1.0 and 10 μg g^{-1} concentrations were 1077, 1070, 1017, and 1020 μm, respectively. Egg production by the 1.0 and 10 μg g^{-1} treated copepods was also much less than that of the control animals. Fecundity of copepods, expressed as the mean number per surviving female, was 15.4 for the control group, and declined to 5.5 for the 10 μg g^{-1} exposed copepods. Results of this experiment suggest that *T. turbinata* is affected only slightly by short-term exposure (≤ 24 h) to sublethal concentrations of pharmaceutical wastes, but longer exposures (>10 d) may lead to changes in copepod condition.

12.1. INTRODUCTION

Zooplankton play an important role in the functioning of marine ecosystems by preying on phytoplankton and transferring energy to the higher trophic levels. Zooplankton control marine phytoplankton species composition and size distribution through grazing (Steele and Frost, 1977; Ryther and Sanders, 1980). Their abundance and concentration also influence the success of larval fish recruitment (Steele, 1974; Smith and Lasker, 1978). Hence, a chronic pollutant stress on zooplankton may directly affect both the primary producer and carnivores, and eventually lead to alterations in the structure of the ecosystem.

Previous studies have shown that the pharmaceutical wastes disposed at the Puerto Rico dumpsite ($19°10'-19°20'$N and $66°35'-66°50'$W) were acutely toxic to many marine animals, including a sponge (*Microciona prolifera*), a hydrome-dusa (*Nemopsis bachei*), a sargassum anemone (*Anemonia sargassensis*), a poly-chaete worm (*Platynereis dumerilli*), amphipods (*Marinogammarus finmarchicus, Amphithoe valida,* and *Caprella penantis*), an isopod (*Sphaeroma quadridenta-tum*), a portunid crab (*Callinectes similis*), a grass shrimp (*Palaemonetes pugio*), mixed zooplankton, and redfish (*Sciaenops ocellatus*) eggs and larvae (Lee and Nicol, 1981; Lee, 1983). The 96-h LC_{50} (concentration lethal to 50% of the or-ganisms after 96 h) values were estimated to be 2.5–14 mg g^{-1} composite wastes. Concentrations lower than this range have not as yet been examined for chronic effects on marine zooplankton. We investigated sublethal effects of the wastes on feeding, growth, fecundity, and egg hatching success of the planktonic copepod *Temora turbinata* Dana. Experimental waste concentrations (0.1–10 μg g^{-1}) were comparable to levels detected in the sea following actual dumping (O'Connor, 1979; Schwab et al., 1981).

12.2. MATERIALS AND METHODS

12.2.1. Waste Material

The waste material tested was a mixture of wastes from seven industrial plants: Bristol, Merck, Pfizer, Squibb, Upjohn, Shering, and Puerto Rico Olefins. Chem-ical and physical properties of the composite waste have been characterized by Atlas et al. (1981), Presley et al. (1981), and Schwab et al. (1981). In general, the waste composite contained 1–3% organic carbon and 0.05–4% suspended solids (by wt). The waste samples had a density of 1.025 g cm^{-3} and were slightly acidic (pH 6.43–6.92) and enriched with a relatively persistent compound, *N,N*-dimethyl-aniline, and contained ~ 34 g $liter^{-1}$ dissolved solids. Heavy metals were generally present at very low concentrations, except for iron and manganese, which were present at 170 and 5.2 μg g^{-1}, respectively.

The stock samples used in the bioassays were not sterilized; they were sealed in 50-ml ampoules and stored in a refrigerator. Prior to each experiment, samples were equilibrated to room temperature (23°C). They were then mixed and diluted to desired concentrations with 0.2-μm-filtered seawater (30‰ salinity), which had been aerated for 30 min.

12.2.2. Feeding Experiment

Copepods (*T. turbinata*) were collected from the Aransas Pass Ship channel with a No. 10 net (mesh size 150 μm). This species has a wide distribution along the Atlantic coast, ranging from Puerto Rico to Cape Hatteras (González and Bowman, 1965). In Texas coastal waters, it is common during most of the year, except in January and July (Wormuth, 1978).

The copepods were acclimated to room temperature (23–24°C) for 2–3 d before the experiments and fed the dinoflagellate *Prorocentrum micans* (~35-μm diameter). *Temora turbinata* has been successfully maintained on a unialgal culture of *P. micans* (Bird, 1981). Grazing rates for copepods exposed to each waste concentration (0, 0.1, 1.0, 10, and 100 μg g^{-1}) were determined at four phytoplankton densities, and for each treatment eight 250-ml bottles (three control and five experimental) were utilized. Initial particle counts were made with a TA-II Coulter Counter (Coulter Electronics, Inc., Hialeah, Florida) for each bottle. After the initial counts five adult female *T. turbinata* were added to the experimental bottles, and all bottles were placed on a wheel rotating (~2 RPM) through a 24°C waterbath for 24 h in the dark. Final counts were made with the TA-II after passing the sample through a 303-μm mesh filter to remove the copepods and any large particulates. The size channels of the TA-II were also adjusted to prevent problems related to fecal pellet interference during counts.

Copepod feeding rates were estimated by the changes in phytoplankton density at time t_1 and t_2 in both the control (C_1 and C_2) and the experimental jars (C_1^* and C_2^*), and expressed as either filtration rates, that is, volume swept clear (ml h^{-1} per copepod), or as ingestion rates (cells h^{-1} per copepod). To determine the two parameters, the equations described by Frost (1972) were employed and summarized as follows:

$$F = V\left(\frac{g}{N}\right) \qquad\qquad 1$$

where F is filtration rate, V is the jar volume (250 ml), N is the number of copepods per jar (5), and g is the grazing coefficient; and

$$I = \bar{C} \times F \qquad\qquad 2$$

where I is ingestion rate and $\bar{C}$ is the average cell concentration in the jars. The variables g and C are derived from

$$C_2 = C_1\, e^{k(t_2 - t_1)}$$

$$C_2^* = C_1^*\, e^{(k-g)(t_2 - t_1)} \qquad\qquad 3$$

$$\bar{C} = \frac{C_1^*\, [e^{(k-g)(t_2 - t_1)} - 1]}{(t_2 - t_1)(k - g)}$$

where k is the algal growth constant and $(t_2 - t_1)$ is the experimental duration (24 h).

Dissolved oxygen content of the media and pH were also monitored.

12.2.3. Growth and Fecundity Experiment

Copepods were obtained and acclimated to room temperature in the same manner as that for feeding experiment. Eggs produced by these copepods were used in assessing the chronic effects of waste dilutions of 0, 0.1, 1.0, and 10 μg g^{-1}. For each waste concentration, 375 eggs were randomly divided into 15 1-liter jars (25 eggs per jar) and rotated on the plankton wheel. The growth bioassays were conducted under the condition of 12 h light and 12 h dark for 15 d. Four to five jars from each concentration were removed at 5-d intervals, and the copepods were fixed with 10% buffered formalin. At this time, one-half of the medium in the remaining jars was replaced with fresh medium. The preserved copepods were used for observations on egg hatching success, survival, developmental stages, body length, sex ratio, and egg and naupliar production. The last two indices were determined only on days 10 and 15, after the copepods had fully matured.

The phytoplankton food source added to the jars was a mixture of the two dinoflagellates, *P. micans* and *Cachonina niei,* in the ratio of 1:2 to 1:4. *Cachonina niei* were 12–15 μm in size and suitable for growth of nauplii and early copepodites. *Temora turbinata* has been successfully raised from egg to adult on unialgal cultures of both of these dinoflagellates (Bird, 1981). Algal density averaged 2420 cells ml^{-1} at the beginning of the experiment, 2523 cells ml^{-1} at day 5, 2298 cells ml^{-1} at day 10, and 1558 cells ml^{-1} at day 15, while the fresh media added to jars at days 5 and 10 contained 3702 and 5144 cells ml^{-1}, respectively.

12.3. RESULTS

12.3.1. Feeding Behavior of Copepods

There were two variables in the feeding experiments, phytoplankton cell density and pollutant concentration. The feeding behavior of the control copepods was very similar to that reported previously for *T. turbinata* (Bird, 1981) and for copepods such as *Calanus hyperboreus* (Mullin, 1963) and *Calanus pacificus* (Frost, 1972). Copepod ingestion rates increased with cell density up to a maximum level (250 cells ml^{-1}), then varied slightly with further increase in phytoplankton density (Fig. 12.1). This relationship is represented by the power equation $Y = 34.95\ X^{0.35}$ ($R^2 = 0.44$), where Y is the ingestion rate and X is the cell density. Filtration rates showed the reverse trend, with the maximum filtration rates at lower cell densities (Table 12.1).

Exposure to the waste concentrations of 0.1, 1.0, 10, and 100 μg g^{-1} did not change the copepod response to phytoplankton density relative to the control. No consistent relationship could be discerned between ingestion rates and waste toxicity. However, there was a tendency to increase ingestion rate with increasing pollutant concentration at the densities of 120 and 1850 cells ml^{-1}. The results of Duncan's multiple-range test suggested that at the lower cell density of 120 the differences of ingestion rates between the control and all the experimental groups were statistically significant ($p < 0.01$). At the cell density of 1850, the ingestion rate of the control was significantly different ($p < 0.05$) from that of the 1.0 and 10.0 μg g^{-1} groups only.

Changes in the pH and dissolved oxygen content of the test media were small during the 24-h experiment (Table 12.2). The pH values of all dilutions were close

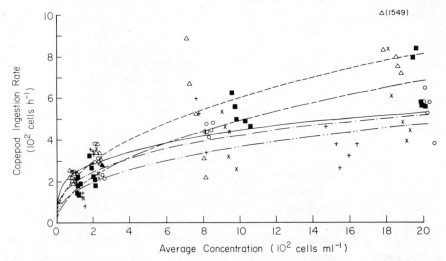

Figure 12.1. Ingestion rates of copepods exposed to pharmaceutical wastes: (+) control, (○) 0.1, (■) 1.0, (△) 10, and (×) 100 μg g^{-1}. Power curves ($Y = AX^B$) are used to describe the ingestion rates of copepods in each treatment. The control ($- \cdot \cdot -$) is represented by the equation $Y = 34.95 \ X^{0.35}$, $R^2 = 0.44$. The 0.1 (——), 1.0 (— —), 10 (----), and 100 ($- \cdot \cdot -$) μg g^{-1} curves are described by the equations $Y = 66.28 \ X^{0.28}$, $R^2 = 0.80$; $Y = 18.05 \ X^{0.48}$, $R^2 = 0.89$; $Y = 27.30 \ X^{0.45}$, $R^2 = 0.70$; and $Y = 43.75 \ X^{0.33}$, $R^2 = 0.65$, respectively.

to that of normal seawater, whereas dissolved oxygen content had declined slightly by the end of the experiment; in most cases, the reduction was < 1 mg liter^{-1}. The lowest oxygen content was recorded at the highest waste concentration (100 μg g^{-1}), and was about 17% lower than the value determined at the beginning of the experiment.

12.3.2. Survival, Growth, and Fecundity

Survival of copepods was high in all waste dilutions (Table 12.3). At day 5, average survival ranged from 65% in the 0.1 μg g^{-1} group to 86% for the controls. It should be noted that the 5-d mortalities included those eggs which failed to hatch and the nauplii which died due to waste toxicity. The reason for the higher mortality at 0.1 μg g^{-1} waste concentration was not apparent. In a separate test, 120 eggs, divided into six groups, were immersed in waste dilutions for 24 h, and hatching success (75–95%) was slightly higher than those rotated on the plankton wheel at day 5, suggesting that survival of the hatched nauplii during the initial exposure to waste dilutions was high. The overall survival at day 15 was 68% for the controls, 63% for 0.1 μg g^{-1} group, 72% for the 1.0 μg g^{-1} group, and 66% for the 10 μg g^{-1} group.

Chronic exposure of copepods to low levels of waste concentrations affected developmental rate, body length, and egg production. The copepods were raised from eggs to about 5 d past the final molt (adults). Therefore, we examined only

Table 12.1. Effects of Pharmaceutical Wastes and Phytoplankton Density on the Filtration Rate of *Temora turbinata*

Waste Concentration (μg g^{-1})	Average Cell Density, cells ml^{-1} (Filtration Rate, ml h^{-1})			
	Experiment 1	Experiment 2	Experiment 3	Experiment 4
Control	1556 ± 63 (0.23 ± 0.05)	798 ± 24 (0.59 ± 0.14)	207 ± 17 (1.52 ± 0.35)	138 ± 14 (1.03 ± 0.40)
0.1	2022 ± 22 (0.27 ± 0.05)	841 ± 15 (0.54 ± 0.04)	240 ± 21 (1.22 ± 0.39)	100 ± 5 (2.42 ± 0.18)
1.0	1975 ± 24 (0.34 ± 0.06)	995 ± 24 (0.53 ± 0.08)	208 ± 13 (1.21 ± 0.31)	128 ± 9 (1.52 ± 0.24)
10.0	1823 ± 64 (0.51 ± 0.22)	772 ± 45 (0.70 ± 0.40)	242 ± 13 (1.36 ± 0.25)	95 ± 9 (2.27 ± 0.45)
100.0	1866 ± 50 (0.30 ± 0.10)	940 ± 31 (0.43 ± 0.13)	232 ± 6 (1.21 ± 0.28)	119 ± 14 (1.75 ± 0.52)

Table 12.2.   Average pH Values and Dissolved Oxygen Contents of the Test Media at 24°C

Waste Concentration (μg g^{-1})	pH		Dissolved Oxygen (mg liter^{-1})	
	0 h	24 h	0 h	24 h
Control	7.99 ± 0.03	7.93 ± 0.02	7.13 ± 0.04	6.55 ± 0.07
0.1	7.94 ± 0.01	7.87 ± 0.01	7.08 ± 0.04	6.73 ± 0.04
1.0	7.95 ± 0.02	7.91 ± 0.03	7.10 ± 0.08	6.67 ± 0.12
10.0	7.96 ± 0.02	7.92 ± 0.04	7.36 ± 0.03	6.48 ± 0.59
100.0	7.94 ± 0.02	7.93 ± 0.04	7.15 ± 0.01	5.95 ± 0.53

Table 12.3.   Survival of *Temora turbinata* Exposed to Pharmaceutical Wastes[a]

Waste Concentration (μg g^{-1})	Number of Survivors		
	Day 5	Day 10	Day 15
Control	22 ± 4	19 ± 2	17 ± 2
0.1	16 ± 1	17 ± 3	16 ± 3
1.0	21 ± 4	16 ± 4	18 ± 1
10.0	21 ± 2	19 ± 2	17 ± 3

[a]Results are the means (± 1 standard deviation) of four to eight replicates; each replicate initially contained 25 eggs.

the total number of eggs released during the last 5 d instead of the egg production potential of a female during its life cycle.

Compared with the copepods at the control and 0.1 μg g^{-1} waste concentration, *T. turbinata*, in the 1.0 and 10.0 μg g^{-1} treatments developed faster during the initial 5 d of the experiment, and development was retarded thereafter (Table 12.4). At day 5, copepodite I stage constituted the majority (>70%) of the population in the control and 0.1 μg g^{-1} waste dilution, whereas at the higher waste concentration, >90% of the copepods had grown to copepodite II and III. The pattern was reversed at days 10 and 15, at which time a greater percentage of adults was observed at the control and the lower waste concentrations. The percentage of adults at the highest concentration (10 μg g^{-1}) was 84% at day 10 and reached to 98% at day 15, relative to 92% and 100% of the controls.

Changes in body length (from head to the end of the anal segment) had been noted in those copepods chronically exposed to diluted pharmaceutical wastes. At comparable stages, *T. turbinata* raised at higher waste concentrations were always shorter than the copepods at lower waste dilutions. For example, at day 10 control females averaged 1.077 mm, whereas females in 0.1, 1.0, and 10 μg g^{-1} waste concentrations averaged 1.070, 1.017, and 1.020 mm, respectively. Similar trends were also found for adult males at days 10 and 15. The growth patterns of copepods during the course of chronic exposure to pharmaceutical wastes are shown in Fig. 12.2.

Table 12.4. Percentage Composition of Developmental Stages of *Temora turbinata* during Chronic Exposure to Pharmaceutical Wastes

| | | *T. turbinata* Composition (%) | | | |
| | | Waste Concentration (μg g^{-1}) | | | |
Day	Stage[a]	Control	0.1	1.0	10.0
5	N4	0	2	0	0
	N5	27	4	0	0
	C1	73	71	10	8
	C2	0	23	76	56
	C3	0	0	14	36
10	C3	0	0	0	3
	C4	5	3	0	3
	C5	3	0	0	10
	C6 (male)	34	46	51	46
	C6 (female)	58	51	49	38
15	C5	0	0	0	2
	C6 (male)	45	51	45	42
	C6 (female)	55	49	55	56

[a]Nauplius stages (N) 4 and 5, and copepodite stages (C) 1–6.

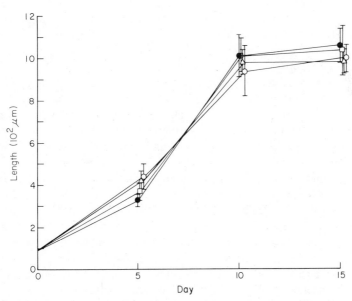

Figure 12.2. Average increase in copepod length from egg to adult. *Temora turbinata* were exposed to control (●), 0.1 (□), 1.0 (△), and 10 (○) μg g^{-1} waste concentrations. The vertical bars represent one standard deviation.

Table 12.5.   Mean Egg Production of *Temora turbinata* in Diluted Pharmaceutical Wastes

Waste Concentration ($\mu g\ g^{-1}$)	Mean Egg Number (number per jar)	Number of Observations	Fecundity (eggs per female)	Fecundity (eggs per pair)
Control	145 ± 30	8	15 ± 5	22 ± 8
0.1	217 ± 143	6	27 ± 11	39 ± 15
1.0	26 ± 12	8	3 ± 2	3 ± 2
10.0	40 ± 23	8	6 ± 4	7 ± 5

Egg production of exposed copepods was affected by the treatment concentrations. The difference between treated and untreated copepods was also significant (t-test, $p < 0.01$), with the exception of the 0.1 $\mu g\ g^{-1}$ exposed group versus the controls (Table 12.5). The total eggs produced by a surviving female during the last 5 d averaged 15 in the controls and declined to 6 in the waste dilution at 10 $\mu g\ g^{-1}$. Fecundity expressed as the mean number of eggs released by a male-female pair exhibited a similar pattern.

12.4.   DISCUSSION

Changes in the feeding behavior of marine animals are often used in the diagnosis of sublethal stress due to pollution. Short-term exposure to toxic material generally results in reduced feeding rates. For example, in a 96-h bioassay, filtration rates of copepods exposed to 10 and 100 $\mu g\ g^{-1}$ Du Pont Grasselli waste were significantly lower than those in the control (Capuzzo and Lancaster, 1981). Similar patterns have also been reported for copepods (*Calanus helgolandicus, Temora longicornis, Tigriopus brevicornis,* and *Pseudocalanus elongatus*) exposed to 10 $\mu g\ liter^{-1}$ Kuwait oil (Spooner and Corkett, 1979). Berman and Heinle (1980) reported that the planktonic copepod *Acartia tonsa* was able to change feeding mode, depending on the sublethal concentrations of water-accommodated fraction of a No. 2 fuel oil.

In the present study, *T. turbinata* feeding behavior did not vary significantly, even at high waste concentrations (100 $\mu g\ g^{-1}$). Three reasons could explain the discrepancy among the results of the different studies: (1) the inherent toxicity of the pharmaceutical wastes was possibly less than that of the No. 2 fuel oil or Du Pont Grasselli wastes; (2) the length of exposure was too brief for the pollutant to cause significant changes; and (3) *T. turbinata* was more resistant than animals of other studies. Berdugo et al. (1977) did not observe significant effects on the feeding of *Eurytemora affinis* chronically (10 d) treated with 10 and 50 $\mu g\ liter^{-1}$ naphthalene. Nevertheless, long-term studies should be conducted to determine whether changes in copepod fecundity and developmental patterns result from reduced feeding caused by the pharmaceutical wastes.

As suggested in previous studies (Reeve et al., 1977; Lee, 1978; Ott et al., 1978; Paffenhöfer and Knowles, 1978; Lee and Nicol, 1981), growth rate, body length, and egg production are sensitive indicators of sublethal stress. The present study showed that chronic exposure of copepods to low levels of pharmaceutical wastes resulted in smaller adult size and fewer eggs per female when compared with untreated *T. turbinata*. Copepods reared in the 1.0 and 10 μg g^{-1} waste dilutions also exhibited a very different growth pattern in which there was an enhanced initial growth rate followed by a reduced growth rate. This phenomenon (hormesis) has been described for the mud crab (*Rhithropanopeus harrisii*) during a short-term exposure to low aqueous hydrocarbon concentrations (Laughlin et al., 1981). It is suggested that the initial stress of low doses of pollutants will stimulate organisms to grow faster, but extended exposures or higher concentrations reverse the effects. Similar sequential reactions in zooplankton respiration and excretion have also been reported for animals exposed to low concentrations of oils (Gyllenberg and Lundqvist, 1976; Lee et al., 1978; Vargo, 1981).

In the present study, production of offspring at the end of a 15-d exposure to four concentrations of pollutants was compared. Egg production per female exposed to the higher concentrations (1.0 and 10 μg g^{-1}) of pollutants was significantly less than that of females in the lower waste concentrations (control and 0.1 μg g^{-1}). Eggs were observed in the rearing experiments as early as day 10 in some samples, but offspring were not quantified until day 15. This may have led to an underestimation of egg production because unfertilized eggs of *T. turbinata* degrade in <24 h and individual adult females may have begun reproducing on different days.

Results of *T. turbinata* egg production, however, were comparable to results observed for *Eurytemora affinis* (Ott et al., 1978) and *Pseudodiaptomus coronatus* (Paffenhöfer and Knowles, 1978). In these two studies copepods exposed to either 10 μg liter^{-1} naphthalene or 5 μg liter^{-1} cadmium had daily production rates of about 50% of untreated copepods. In the present study, production rates of *T. turbinata* reared in 10 μg g^{-1} waste concentration averaged 36% of that of the control population.

The importance of the results of these experiments depends on how well the laboratory study simulates the environment. Waste plumes at the Puerto Rico dumpsite have been characterized by Presley et al. (1981) and Schwab et al. (1981), and the deep ocean dumping studies have been summarized by O'Connor (1979) and Simpson et al. (1981). They suggest that the plume behavior observed at Deepwater Dumpsite (DWD)-106, off New York, was similar to plume behavior at the Puerto Rico dumpsite. The initial dilution was caused mainly by turbulence due to the barge, followed by oceanic processes. The maximum concentrations 24 h after a dump of 2.5 × 10^6 liters of pharmaceutical waste was estimated to be 10 μl liter^{-1} and covered an area of 35 km^2 above 15 m depth (O'Connor, 1979). The concentration declined to 0.5 μl liter^{-1} within 7 d. Schwab et al. (1981) did not observe a significant difference in phytoplankton populations between the samples taken from comparable depths inside and outside the dumpsite. Results of the present study suggest that migratory zooplankton were probably not seriously affected unless consecutive dumps occurred very near each other in time and space and consequently resulted in an increased exposure of these animals to the pollutants.

In such a case, copepod adult size and egg production may change as a result of chronic exposure to the pharmaceutical wastes, and eventually lead to alterations in the ecosystem. The magnitude of these variations is difficult to predict due to the complexity of many factors involved at the dumpsite and the different responses of marine organisms to waste toxicity (Murphy et al., 1981). Extrapolation of the laboratory results to the field should therefore be made and viewed cautiously.

The pharmaceutical wastes are now no longer barge-dumped off the coast of Puerto Rico, but are treated at a sewage treatment plant and discharged nearshore. The biological consequences of waste discharge at the two locations are probably different. Because of shallower water depths and potential longer residence times of the wastes, the nearshore environment is likely subject to greater damage than the offshore environment. The actual effects, however, will depend on the dynamics of waste plumes in the environment and the sensitivity of biological communities to the pollutants.

12.5. SUMMARY AND CONCLUSIONS

Copepod feeding behavior was not affected in a 24-h exposure to 0.1, 1.0, 10, and 100 μg g^{-1} pharmaceutical wastes. Ingestion rates of copepods exposed to these waste concentrations were comparable to that of the controls at the four phytoplankton cell densities (1850, 870, 225, and 115 cell ml^{-1}). Exposure for longer than 24 h may have been required to induce significant changes in the feeding rates of *T. turbinata.*

Results of the chronic exposure experiments indicate that body size, egg production, and growth rate are good indicators of sublethal stress from pharmaceutical wastes. Compared with untreated *T. turbinata,* copepods raised at waste concentrations ≥ 1.0 μg g^{-1} were characterized by smaller adult size (35–60 μm shorter), reduced egg production (about 36% of the control), and an abnormal growth pattern (hormesis), and these changes have also been often observed in animals chronically exposed to low levels of environmental pollutants. The present study shows that chronic exposure to sublethal concentrations of the pharmaceutical wastes reduces copepod fitness as expressed in adult length and fecundity; however, the environmental impact of the disposed materials on the planktonic community probably depends to a large extent on both the frequency of dumping and the behavior of waste plume at the dumpsite.

ACKNOWLEDGMENTS

This work was supported by the Ocean Dumping and Monitoring Program of the U.S. National Oceanic and Atmospheric Administration, Grant No. NA80AA-D-0061. We wish to thank P. L. Parker for providing us with special assistance during the final phase of this study. This chapter is University of Texas Marine Science Institute Contribution No. 603.

REFERENCES

Atlas, E., G. Martinez, and C. S. Giam. 1981. Chemical characterization of ocean-dumped waste materials. *In:* Ocean Dumping of Industrial Wastes, B. H. Ketchum, D. R. Kester, and P. K. Park (Eds.). Plenum Press, New York, pp. 275–293.

Berdugo, V., R. P. Harris, and S. C. O'Hara. 1977. The effect of petroleum hydrocarbons on reproduction of an estuarine planktonic copepod in laboratory cultures. *Marine Pollution Bulletin,* **8,** 138–143.

Berman, M. S., and D. R. Heinle. 1980. Modification of the feeding behavior of marine copepods by sub-lethal concentrations of water-accommodated fuel oil. *Marine Biology,* **56,** 59–64.

Bird, J. L. 1981. Relationships between Vertical Distributions of Zooplankton and Phytoplankton on the Texas Continental Shelf and in Laboratory Water Columns. Ph.D. Dissertation, Marine Science Institute, University of Texas at Austin, 149 pp.

Capuzzo, J. M., and B. A. Lancaster. 1981. The effects of pollutants on marine zooplankton at Deep Water Dumpsite 106: preliminary findings. *In:* Ocean Dumping of Industrial Wastes, B. H. Ketchum, D. R. Kester, and P. K. Park (Eds.). Plenum Press, New York, pp. 411–419.

Frost, B. W. 1972. Effects of size and concentration of food particles on the feeding behavior of the marine planktonic copepod *Calanus pacificus. Limnology and Oceanography,* **17,** 805–815.

González, J. G., and T. E. Bowman. 1965. Planktonic copepods from Bahía Fosforescente, Puerto Rico, and adjacent waters. *Proceedings of the United States National Museum,* **117,** 241–303.

Gyllenberg, G., and G. Lundqvist. 1976. Some effects of emulsifiers and oil on two copepod species. *Acta Zoologica Fennica,* **148,** 1–24.

Laughlin, R. B., Jr., J. Ng, and H. E. Guard. 1981. Hormesis: a response to low environmental concentrations of petroleum hydrocarbons. *Science,* **211,** 705–707.

Lee, W. Y. 1978. Chronic sublethal effects of the water soluble fractions of No. 2 fuel oils on the marine isopod, *Sphaeroma quadridentatum. Marine Environmental Research,* **1,** 5–17.

Lee, W. Y. 1983. Copepods and ichthyoplankton: Laboratory studies of pharmaceutical waste toxicity. *In:* Wastes in the Ocean, Vol. 1: Industrial and Sewage Wastes in the Ocean, I. W. Duedall, B. H. Ketchum, P. K. Park, and D. R. Kester (Eds.). Wiley-Interscience, New York, pp. 235–250.

Lee, W. Y., and J. A. C. Nicol. 1981. Toxicity of biosludge and pharmaceutical wastes to marine invertebrates. *In:* Ocean Dumping of Industrial Wastes, B. H. Ketchum, D. R. Kester, and P. K. Park (Eds.). Plenum Press, New York, pp. 439–454.

Lee, W. Y., K. Winters, and J. A. C. Nicol. 1978. The biological effects of the water-soluble fractions of a No. 2 fuel oil on the planktonic shrimp, *Lucifer faxoni. Environmental Pollution,* **15,** 167–183.

Mullin, M. M. 1963. Some factors affecting the feeding of marine copepods of the genus *Calanus. Limnology and Oceanography,* **8,** 239–250.

Murphy, L. S., P. R. Hoar, and R. A. Belastock. 1981. The effects of industrial wastes on marine phytoplankton. *In:* Ocean Dumping of Industrial Wastes, B. H. Ketchum, D. R. Kester, and P. K. Park (Eds.). Plenum Press, New York, pp. 399–410.

O'Connor, T. P. 1979. Ocean Dumping Research and Monitoring at the Puerto Rico Dumpsite. Unpublished manuscript, Ocean Dumping and Monitoring Program, U.S. National Oceanic and Atmospheric Administration, Rockville, Maryland, 35 pp.

Ott, F. S., R. P. Harris, and S. C. M. O'Hara. 1978. Acute and sublethal toxicity of naphthalene and three methylated derivatives to the estuarine copepod, *Eurytemora affinis*. *Marine Environmental Research*, **1**, 49–58.

Paffenhöfer, G.-A., and S. C. Knowles. 1978. Laboratory experiments on feeding, growth, and fecundity of and effects of cadmium on *Pseudodiaptomus*. *Bulletin of Marine Science*, **28**, 574–580.

Presley, B. J., J. S. Schofield, and J. Trefry. 1981. Waste material behavior and inorganic geochemistry at the Puerto Rico waste dumpsite. *In:* Ocean Dumping of Industrial Wastes, B. H. Ketchum, D. R. Kester, and P. K. Park (Eds.). Plenum Press, New York, pp. 233–246.

Reeve, M. R., M. A. Walter, K. Darcy, and T. Ikeda. 1977. Evaluation of potential indicators of sub-lethal toxic stress on marine zooplankton (feeding, fecundity, respiration, and excretion): Controlled Ecosystem Pollution Experiment. *Bulletin of Marine Science*, **27**, 105–113.

Ryther, J. H., and J. G. Sanders. 1980. Experimental evidence of zooplankton control of the species composition and size distribution of marine phytoplankton. *Marine Ecology–Progress Series*, **3**, 279–283.

Schwab, C. R., T. C. Sauer, Jr., G. F. Hubbard, H. Abdel-Reheim, and J. M. Brooks. 1981. Chemical and biological aspects of ocean dumping at the Puerto Rico dumpsite. *In:* Ocean Dumping of Industrial Wastes, B. H. Ketchum, D. R. Kester, and P. K. Park (Eds.). Plenum Press, New York, pp. 247–273.

Simpson, D. C., T. P. O'Connor, and P. K. Park. 1981. Deep-ocean dumping of industrial wastes. *In:* Marine Environmental Pollution, Vol. 2: Dumping and Mining, R. A. Geyer (Ed.). Elsevier Scientific Publishing, New York, pp. 379–400.

Smith, P. E. and R. Lasker. 1978. Position of larval fish in an ecosystem. *Rapports et Pròces-Verbaux des Réunions*, **173**, 77–84.

Spooner, M. F., and C. J. Corkett. 1979. Effects of Kuwait oils on feeding rates of copepods. *Marine Pollution Bulletin*, **10**, 197–202.

Steele, J. H. 1974. The Structure of Marine Ecosystems. Harvard University Press, Cambridge, Massachusetts, 128 pp.

Steele, J. H., and B. W. Frost. 1977. The structure of plankton communities. *Philosophical Transactions of the Royal Society of London*, **280**(B), 485–534.

Vargo, S. L. 1981. The effects of chronic low concentrations of No. 2 fuel oil on the physiology of a temperate estuarine zooplankton community in the MERL microcosms. *In:* Biological Monitoring of Marine Pollutants, J. Vernberg, A. Calabrese, F. P. Thurberg, and W. B. Vernberg (Eds.). Academic Press, New York, pp. 295–322.

Wormuth, J. H. 1978. Determination of average dry weights of important neuston species collected in 1976. *In:* Environmental Studies, South Texas Outer Continental Shelf, Biology and Chemistry. Unpublished report, submitted to the Bureau of Land Management, Washington D.C. Marine Science Institute, University of Texas, Port Aransas, pp. 3-1–3-37.

PART IV: DEEP-SEA MINING WASTES

13

MODELLING THE COAGULATION OF A SOLID WASTE DISCHARGE FROM A MANGANESE NODULE PROCESSING PLANT

Charles L. Morgan and F. Thomas Lovorn

Lockheed Ocean Science Laboratory
San Diego, California

Abstract		**244**
13.1.	**Introduction**	**244**
13.2.	**Methods**	**245**
	13.2.1. Dispersion Model	245
	13.2.2. Coagulation Model	246
	13.2.3. Laboratory Tests	248
13.3.	**Results**	**250**
	13.3.1. Laboratory Tests	250
	13.3.2. Modelling	252
13.4.	**Discussion**	**253**
	13.4.1. Laboratory Tests	253
	13.4.2. Modelling	255
13.5.	**Conclusions**	**257**

Acknowledgments   257

References   257

ABSTRACT

Simple sedimentation tests using mixtures of seawater or freshwater and simulated wastes from a research-scale hydrometallurgical processing scheme for a manganese nodule processing plant show that the net vertical flux of the solids is greatly affected by the total solids concentration. The results of the tests, throughout much of the concentration range tested, are consistent with a model in which the flux rate is completely determined by simple second-order coagulation of fine-grained solids. Examination of results from a plume dispersion model incorporating coagulation shows that the scale of the discharge is an important factor. Settling rates estimated from relatively small-scale field test observations may dramatically underestimate the settling rates for a full-scale operation.

13.1. INTRODUCTION

In the research and development work directed toward the establishment of a deep-seabed mining industry, the effects of potential waste discharges from the metallurgical processing operations are of great concern. Potential environmental impacts must be accurately assessed as early as possible to avoid commitments of resources to practices that may prove environmentally unsound. Lacking specifications for actual discharge compositions or sites, preliminary assessment efforts must concentrate on the identification of the major processes involved in any potential discharge. At this stage, predictive exercises with mathematical models can serve to establish general relationships and to provide a crude estimation of overall impacts. One operation in particular is considered here: the discharge of process tailings (wastes) from a land-based or at-sea metallurgical processing plant into the surface waters at or near the mine site.

The basic premise in this consideration is that metallurgical processing of manganese nodules is likely to result in substantial quantities of fine particulate wastes that may be discharged into the ocean. The environmental consequences of such a discharge will depend on the settling rate of the particulate matter through the water column.

A key problem for this predictive exercise is to quantify the mechanisms that transform very fine-grained discharge solids into particles having significant settling velocities. One such mechanism is coagulation, the increase of particle size due to the collision and subsequent coalescence of small particles into large ones.

The importance of coagulation in removing colloidal and fine-grained particles from the ocean is widely recognized, but no general analytical solution of the phenomenon has been devised. However, numerical methods such as the one used in this work (Yue and Deepak, 1979) provide a means of simulating the theoretical sensitivity of coagulation rates to variables such as particle concentration, size distribution, and time.

The application of laboratory tests to this predictive exercise is similarly indirect. Stumm and Morgan (1970) note that simple experiments with sedimentation columns occasionally produce sedimentation rates that exhibit second-order kinetics with respect to overall particle concentration. Heicklen (1976), using the principles of chemical kinetics, discusses the assumptions that must be made for this situation to occur. In this chapter, second-order rate coefficients are derived from sedimentation tests conducted with waste slurries produced from proprietary bench-scale process development tests. In computer simulations of discharge plume dispersion, these rate constants are assumed to be directly proportional to the collision efficiency (fraction of collisions that result in coalescence) for various collision mechanisms. Results of this simulation suggest that coagulation is generally a nonlinear function of particle concentration and can be of prime importance in controlling the removal of discharged solids from the water column.

13.2. METHODS

To examine the theoretical effect of coagulation on discharge solids, we use a combination of three computer models: one for a negatively buoyant turbulent jet discharged in a current (Koh and Chang, 1973; Brandsma and Divoky, 1976), one for passive dispersion with advection and turbulent diffusion (Csanady, 1973), and one that includes four mechanisms of coagulation (Hunt, 1980).

13.2.1. Dispersion Model

The jet model has been used by the U.S. Army Corps of Engineers for prediction of the short-term fate of dredged material. The equations governing the motion of the jet are those for conservation of mass, momentum, buoyancy, and particle size distribution. The rates of change of these quantities are determined with respect to distance from the discharge point, and Runge-Kutta methods are used for numerical integration of the equations along the jet axis. A round jet is assumed to discharge at some angle downward into a horizontal current. The jet entrains ambient fluid and momentum, thereby diluting the discharge and growing in size while bending in the direction of the current. As the jet descends, it behaves more like a plume, spreading horizontally and collapsing vertically. Subsequent dilution is calculated using a simple puff model, which advects discrete parcels of discharge-receiving water mixtures in a constant current of 10 cm s^{-1} while dispersing each parcel horizontally with a constant dispersion coefficient of 10^4 cm^2 s^{-1}. The density structure of the receiving waters is taken from Ozturgut et al. (1978) as representative of surface waters in the northeastern tropical Pacific, and is presented in

Table 13.1. Vertical Density Profile of Receiving Waters[a]

Depth (m)	Density $(g\,cm^{-3})$
0–40	1.0230
40–50	1.0250
50–60	1.0250
60–100	1.0255
100–200	1.0270
>200	1.0273

[a]Adapted from Ozturgut et al. (1978).

Table 13.1. Particle settling may occur throughout the descent, advection, and dispersion phases.

13.2.2. Coagulation Model

For a continuous size distribution, the time evolution of the number concentration (number cm^{-3}) of particles, $N(r, t)$, having radius r in the range of r to $r + dr$ at time t, can be expressed as (Fuchs, 1964):

$$\frac{\partial N(r, t)}{\partial t} = -N(r, t) \int_0^\infty K(r, r_i)\, N(r_i, t)\, dr_i$$

$$+ \frac{1}{2} \int_0^\infty \int_0^\infty K(r_i, r_j)\, N(r_i, t)\, N(r_j, t)\, dr_i\, dr_j \qquad\qquad 1$$

The first term on the right-hand side of equation 1 describes the reduction in number of particles with radius r by coagulation between particles with radius r and other particles. The second term describes the production of new particles with radius r by the coagulation of particles with radius r_i and r_j such that

$$r_i^3 + r_j^3 = r^3 \qquad\qquad 2$$

The frequency of collisions between particles r_i and r_j depends on the collision mechanism. We have considered four mechanisms, each with its own coagulation constant K. These are:

Brownian motion:

$$K_b(r_i, r_j) = \frac{2}{3} \frac{kT}{\mu} \frac{(r_i + r_j)^2}{r_i r_j} \qquad\qquad 3$$

fluid shear:

$$K_{sh}(r_i, r_j) = \frac{4}{3} \left(\frac{\epsilon}{\nu}\right)^{1/2} (r_i + r_j)^3 \qquad\qquad 4$$

inertial:

$$K_I(r_i, r_j) = 1.2 \frac{\rho_p}{\rho_f} \left(\frac{\epsilon^3}{\nu^5}\right)^{1/4} (r_i + r_j)^2 \left|r_i^2 - r_j^2\right| \qquad 5$$

differential sedimentation:

$$K_{ds}(r_i, r_j) = \frac{2}{9} \frac{\pi g}{\nu} \frac{(\rho_p - \rho_f)}{\rho_f} (r_i + r_j)^2 \left|r_i^2 - r_j^2\right| \qquad 6$$

where r_i = radius of particle i; k = Boltzmann constant, T = temperature (°K), μ = fluid viscosity, ν = kinematic viscosity, ϵ = turbulent energy dissipation per unit mass, ρ_p and ρ_f = density of particle and fluid respectively, and g = the acceleration of gravity. While the Brownian motion depends upon fluid properties at rest (such as temperature and viscosity), the other three mechanisms depend also on relative particle motion induced by turbulent fluid motion and gravity. The net coagulation constant is:

$$K_{TOT} = K_b + (K_{sh}^2 + K_I^2 + K_{ds}^2)^{1/2} \qquad 7$$

The geometric addition of K_{sh}, K_I, and K_{ds} is necessary because of the geometric addition of velocities (Heubsch, 1967). The condition that frequencies are restricted to particles smaller than the appropriate turbulent microscale is satisfied for our size range of interest, 0.02–100 μm.

For the range of particle sizes we will consider, the radius covers a range of four orders of magnitude, but the volume (the parameter actually conserved in a coagulating system) covers 12 orders of magnitude. If the volume range is divided into 100 equal size classes, the first 10 orders of magnitude will be in the first size class. To circumvent this problem, the range is divided into equal size classes on a logarithmic scale, so that each order of magnitude is described in the same detail.

Transforming from radius space into logarithmic space is accomplished by the following (Yue and Deepak, 1979):

$$r_i = r_1 a^{b(i-1)} \qquad 8$$

where r_1 is the radius of the smallest particle under consideration, and a and b are constants. In our model, we chose $a = 10$ and $b = \frac{1}{3}$. Hence, the volume of each bin is 10 times the volume of the previous bin. This enables us to cover the full range of particle sizes with 12 bins. However, by using particle sizes that are equally spaced on the basis of the logarithm of their volumes, the arithmetic sum of any two standard volumes does not produce another standard volume. That is, when standard sizes V_i and $V_j (V_i \geq V_j)$ coalesce, $V_i + V_j$ is between standard sizes V_i and V_{i+1}. Therefore, the mass of the new particle is factored between bins i and $i + 1$ in the manner:

$$V_i + V_j = F_{ij}V_i + (1 - F_{ij})V_{i+1} \qquad 9$$

where F_{ij} is the fraction assigned to bin i and $(1 - F_{ij})$ the fraction assigned to bin $(i + 1)$. This factoring conserves mass before and after coagulation. Equation 1 is evaluated by the trapezoidal rule and, when the logarithmic transformation and volume factoring are included, can be rewritten in the form:

$$
\begin{aligned}
\frac{\Delta N_i}{\Delta t} = &- \sum_{j \neq i} K_{ij} N_i N_j - \frac{1}{2} K_{ij} N_i^2 \\
&+ \sum_{j < i} F_{ij} K_{ij} N_i N_j + \frac{1}{2} F_{ii} K_{ii} N_i^2 \\
&+ \sum_{j < i-1} (1 - F_{i-1,j}) K_{i-1,j} N_{i-1} N_j \\
&+ \frac{1}{2} (1 - F_{i-1,i-1}) K_{i-1,i-1} N_{i-1}^2
\end{aligned}
\qquad 10
$$

Kritz (1975) and Yue and Deepak (1979) used such a formulation to study the time evolution of aerosol size distributions.

The transport and coagulation processes in the jet are treated separately. For each time step, the jet configuration, particle concentration, and settling are calculated using the Runge-Kutta method for integrating the conservation equations. Then, equation 10 is applied for the same time step to obtain a new set of values for each size class.

This method is applicable to an arbitrary initial size distribution. Because we do not presently know the likely size distribution for manganese nodule metallurgical process wastes, we chose a normal distribution with a maximum volume concentration at 4 μm and a standard deviation of 3 μm. To test the sensitivity of the model to this distribution, we also consider a similar distribution with a maximum concentration at 23 μm.

We also do not know the value or variation of the rate of viscous dissipation of turbulent energy per unit mass, denoted as ϵ in equations 4 and 5, for the flow conditions being modelled. However, based on equations for pipe flow and measurements in and above the thermocline by Grant et al. (1968), ϵ was estimated to range from 22 cm^2 s^{-3} at the discharge to 0.001 cm^2 s^{-3} for ambient conditions. Therefore, the values of ϵ for the jet and passive dispersion phases selected for this study are 1 and 0.1, respectively, to reflect intermediate but increased levels of turbulence in each phase relative to ambient.

13.2.3. Laboratory Tests

Ideally, laboratory simulations of solid waste discharges should be designed to measure the suspended particle size distribution and sedimentation flux independently during the course of an experiment. Also, to test the hypothesized coagulation mechanisms that depend on the turbulent flow field (shear and inertial coagulation), typical shear gradients present at the discharge site must be known and in some way reproduced in the laboratory. The experiments described here are standard sedimentation tests that measure only the particle flux rate in a nonturbulent column. With these limitations, we can directly examine only the Brownian and differential-sedimentation mechanism and can only test the results for consistency with the postulated coagulation-driven sedimentation.

Heicklen (1976), using the principles of chemical kinetics and assuming a suspension of particles in a nonturbulent chamber, defines coagulation as follows:

$$\frac{dC_n}{dt} = D_n \nabla C_n + R'_n - K_n C_n \qquad 11$$

The first term on the right represents simple Fickian diffusion along the concentration gradients within the sample ("wall loss"); R'_n is the production of particles by coagulation of small particles and disintegration of larger particles; and $K_n C_n$ represents loss of particles by disintegration (assumed to be a first-order reaction); C_n is the concentration of the nth particle size.

If losses to the sample wall are insignificant and if coagulation is irreversible (no disintegration of particles), then equation 11 is reduced to the following:

$$\frac{dC_n}{dt} = R_n = \sum_{j=1}^{n-1} K_{j,n-j} C_j C_{n-j} \qquad 12$$

If we further assume that the total flux of particles out of the column can be approximated by the sedimentation of one critical size class (C_{cr}) which is a constant fraction (f) of the total particle concentration ($C_{cr} = f C_{TOT}$) and which is produced by the coagulation of another, nonsettling size class ($C_1 = C_{TOT} - C_{cr}$), then equation 12 describes a process of simple second-order kinetics:

$$\frac{dC_{cr}}{dt} = -\beta (C_{TOT})^2 \qquad 13$$

where $-\beta$ is directly proportional to $f(1 - f)$.

Sedimentation tests for this study were carried out with experimental process rejects (sample label OMCO PRM2) suspended either in seawater or distilled water (Table 13.2). Initial subsampling of this 57-liter batch for sedimentation tests was done by pumping the material through Tygon® tubing into 1-liter aliquots; the tube was affixed to a large, perforated plunger, which was moved vigorously through the sample to keep the solids in suspension while pumping. Seven 1-liter aliquots taken in this manner contained an average of 0.021 g cm^{-3} nonfilterable (through a 0.4-μm membrane filter) solids with a range of between 0.0203 and 0.0214 g cm^{-3} and a standard deviation of ± 0.0004 g cm^{-3}. Final subsampling for each test was done by pipetting from a vessel that was mixed vigorously in a wrist-action shaker and then allowed to settle for 1 min. Repetitive 5-ml pipetting of the same aliquot by this method gave a reproducibility of ± 0.0003 g cm^{-3}. Samples pipetted from aliquots in which no time for settling was allowed contained 0.0311 $\pm$ 0.0003 g cm^{-3}. Since we were concerned primarily with the sedimentation characteristics of slowly settling particles, and since the 1 min delay before pipetting greatly enhanced the pipetting reproducibility, all sedimentation tests were carried out with the delay.

The tests used an electrobalance with a sedimentation accessory housed in an

Table 13.2.   Average Initial Suspended Particle Concentrations (mg cm^{-3})^a

Tailing Sample Number	Medium	
	Seawater	Distilled Water
1	0.01(9)	0.01(3)
2	0.07(4)	0.06(3)
3	0.12(5)	0.14(2)
4	0.25(2)	0.26(1)
5	0.61(2)	0.69(3)
6	1.26(6)	1.35(1)

^{a}Number of replicates in parentheses.

isothermal water bath. The maximum fall height in the tube was 25.3 cm. The water bath temperature was held at 25.1 $\pm$ 0.1°C, about 2–3°C above the normal room temperature. The sedimentation fluid volume was 930 ml for all runs. Before each run, the recorder output from the electrobalance was calibrated with M-class weights that covered the range of interest. The sample was pipetted into the settling tube and thoroughly mixed throughout the water column. The electrobalance was then engaged, and the data recorded. Chart records generated in the test were subsequently digitized on an automatic digitizer using a 2.5-min increment.

Values of the second-order rate coefficient β were calculated from equation 13 for each time increment. The average particle concentration in the column, C_{TOT}, was estimated for each increment from the volume of the sedimentation column and the difference between the maximum weight of sedimented particles and the weight accumulated at the midpoint of the increment. In the particle concentration range where the observed values of β were approximately independent of particle concentration, we assumed that irreversible coagulation occurred (collision efficiency = 1). At concentrations greater than this range, we estimated the collision efficiency to be the ratio of the calculated β to the value of β in the region with assumed irreversible coagulation. A more satisfactory treatment for this high concentration range would involve the specific surface chemistry of the particle suspension being used.

13.3.   RESULTS

13.3.1.   Laboratory Tests

Figure 13.1 summarizes the relationship between concentration and the second-order rate coefficient, β, as described by the average of all test results. These data come almost entirely from measurements made during the first 3 h. For the modelling analysis, the coagulation collision efficiency was set at 1 for concentrations

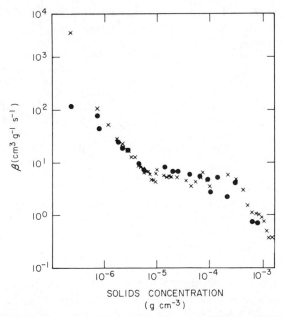

Figure 13.1. The relationship between the second-order rate coefficient and solids concentration in seawater ($\times$) and in distilled water ($\bullet$).

$< 3.2 \times 10^{-4}$ g cm^{-3}. For higher concentrations, the efficiency was set at the ratio of the measured value to $\beta = 8.1$ cm^3 g^{-1} s^{-1}.

Analysis of variance performed on all the data indicated that the experiments made with the lowest and highest initial particle concentrations were significantly different from the midrange runs for the β values measured at the lowest (< 0.005 g cm^{-3}) concentration interval (Table 13.3). Runs with one initial concentration

Table 13.3. Analysis of Variance between Tests with Different Initial Particle Concentrations

Initial Concentration (mg cm^{-3})	F Values ($F_{0.95} = 3.84$)					
	0.011	0.071	0.112	0.323	0.566	1.16
0.011	—					
0.071	1052[a]	—				
0.112	2093	9.35	—			
0.323	752	0.044	8.72	—		
0.566	1095	1.85	1.73	2.20	—	
1.16	765	12.1	55.5	7.58	21.2	—

[a]Runs for <0.005 g cm^{-3} concentration interval.

Table 13.4.   Analysis of Variance among Sedimentation Tests with the Same Initial Particle Concentrations

Average Initial Concentration (mg cm^{-3})	F^a	$F_{0.95}{}^b$
0.011	11.2	1.94
0.071	2.13	2.60
0.112	0.786	2.37
0.323	3.21	3.84
0.566	0.522	3.84
1.16	1.90	2.21

[a] Runs compared for β values obtained from the lowest concentration interval only, that is, when the column particle concentration is <0.005 g cm^{-3}.
[b] The F values $>F_{0.95}$ indicate significant between-test variance.

were reproducible except for those at the lowest initial concentration (Table 13.4.) Freshwater results were statistically distinct from seawater runs at the lowest concentration interval (Table 13.5). The overall coefficient of variation of β values calculated for all runs (Fig. 13.2) was greatest in the lowest concentration intervals.

13.3.2. Modelling

Figures 13.3–13.6 show the key results of the various coagulation mechanisms (equations 3–7) incorporated into the dispersion models. The results are displayed in terms of the evolution with time or dilution of the relative distributions of particle volume concentrations expressed as cm^3 solids per cm^3 slurry during the dispersion of the plume. An ordinate value of 1.0 in Figs. 13.4–13.6 indicates that the volume concentration for that size fraction is the same for the two cases compared. A value less than or greater than one indicates that the volume concentration for that size

Table 13.5.   Analysis of Variance between Distilled Water and Seawater Tests[a]

Initial Concentration (mg cm^{-3})	F^b
0.01	3.28
0.06–0.07	4.84
0.11–0.13	20.8
0.6	6.50

[a] $F_{0.95} = 3.84$.
[b] Run groups for <0.005 g cm^{-3} concentration interval.

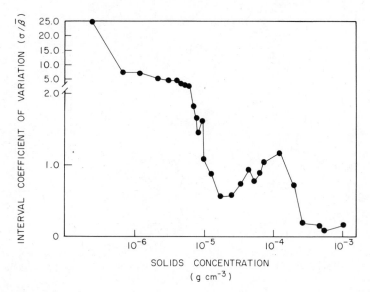

Figure 13.2. The relationship between the coefficient of variation of the second-order rate coefficient for each solids concentration.

class is decreased or increased, respectively, for one case over another. The full-scale mass flux of the process plume is set at 10^4 t d^{-1}.

13.4. DISCUSSION

13.4.1. Laboratory Tests

Over a particle concentration range that varies by a factor of 60 (between 10^{-5} and $10^{-3.5}$ g cm^{-3}), the values of β vary by a factor of < 1.2, and thus are consistent with the assumption that the collision frequency is unity within this range (Fig. 13.1). At higher concentrations, the assumed efficiencies drop off rapidly and contribute very little to the net calculated coagulation. Intuitively, we could attribute the abrupt change observed in Fig. 13.1 at $C = 10^{-3.5}$ g cm^{-3} to some fundamental change in particle surface chemistry that occurs at this dilution, and would expect this particular value of C to vary significantly with changes in the waste composition. If this is true, then a primary goal for any discharge should be to increase the concentration at which this transition point occurs.

At particle concentrations less than about $10^{-3.5}$ g cm^{-3}, the apparent value for β increases rapidly, as does the standard deviation of the individual estimates (Fig. 13.2). The large variation is possibly due to the fact that the changes in sedimented mass used to derive these estimates are on the same order as the random variations of the instrument itself. The systematic change in β may be due to either instrument drift or a relatively slow precipitation reaction (such as diffusion-limited oxidation).

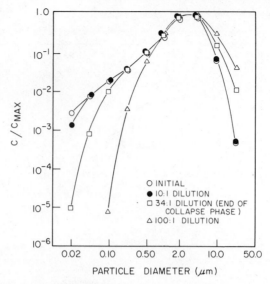

Figure 13.3. Change in the relative distribution of the particle volume concentration during plume dispersion; C_{Max} is the maximum concentration at each dilution.

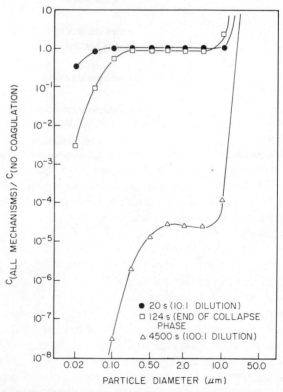

Figure 13.4. The effects of coagulation: 4 μm mode.

The distinct difference between the seawater and the distilled water experiments (Table 13.5) is consistent with the latter explanation.

13.4.2. Modelling

The action of coagulation in transferring mass from the fine to the coarser size fractions is clearly evident in Fig. 13.3. The results illustrate how the size distribution of a coagulating system varies throughout a 75-min simulation relative to the size fraction with maximum volume concentration. The initial size distribution does not include any particles in the 20-μm size class, but the results show that this class is rapidly populated by coagulation of smaller particles. The total particle volume concentration in surface waters during this period decreases more than four orders of magnitude, due to dilution and sedimentation.

The volume concentrations of each size class with and without coagulation are compared in Fig. 13.4, which shows the history of the process plume, beginning with rapid depopulation of the very fine-grained size classes in the jet phase and resulting in the essentially complete transition to the large size classes after <2 h. With the specified current of 10 cm s^{-1}, this would mean that the solids would be

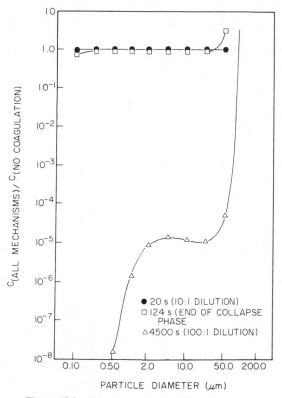

Figure 13.5. The effects of coagulation: 23 μm mode.

completely converted to the large size classes <0.5 km downstream from the discharge point. This case clearly demonstrates the importance of considering coagulation as well as settling as potential mechanisms for particle removal.

A comparison of Fig. 13.5 with Fig. 13.4 shows the net effect of moving the mode of the initial particle size distribution up two size classes (from 4 μm to 23 μm). At 100:1 dilution, the two cases have similar size distributions relative to the mode. In both cases, there is a rapid coagulation and depopulation of the fine size classes to the larger size classes. There is a slightly greater depopulation of the size classes near the 23-μm mode, presumably due to the increased effectiveness of the shear, inertial, and differential-sedimentation mechanisms in the larger size classes.

The significant difference in the predicted coagulation between tenth-scale and full-scale discharges at similar dilutions is shown in Fig. 13.6. At a dilution of 10:1, the full-scale discharge has essentially completed the process of coagulation to the largest size class. Measurement of the size distribution of a tenth scale plume after an equivalent dilution had occurred will result in a serious underestimation of the full-scale particle size distribution if the nonlinear effects of coagulation are not included in the extrapolation.

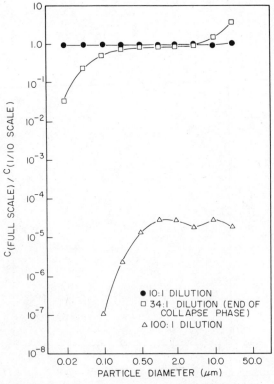

Figure 13.6. The effects of discharge scale on coagulation.

13.5. CONCLUSIONS

1. Coagulation is an important mechanism for particle removal.
2. Coagulation increases as a nonlinear function of discharge scale.
3. This discharge model is sensitive to the original particle size distribution, but predicts that most solids will be converted to large, rapidly settling particles over a fairly wide range of sizes.
4. Laboratory sedimentation experiments with a bench-scale manganese nodule processing waste are consistent with a system in which sedimentation is dominated by irreversible coagulation of fine particles to rapidly settling particles over almost two orders of magnitude of particle concentration.

ACKNOWLEDGMENTS

The authors wish to thank J. Boaz for assistance in running the laboratory tests and D. Hamm for computer programming support. This work was supported by Ocean Minerals Company and Lockheed Missles and Space Company.

REFERENCES

Brandsma, M. G., and D. J. Divoky. 1976. Development of Models for Prediction of Short-Term Fate of Dredged Material in the Estuarine Environment. Grant No. DACW39-74-C-0075, U.S. Army Corps of Engineers Waterways Experimental Stations, Vicksburg, Mississippi, 133 pp.

Csanady, G. T. 1973. Turbulent Diffusion in the Environment. D. Reidel Publishing, Boston, Massachusetts, 173 pp.

Fuchs, N. A. 1964. The Mechanics of Aerosols. Pergamon Press, New York, 408 pp.

Grant, H. L., A. Moilliet, and W. M. Vogel. 1968. Some observations of the occurrence of turbulence in and above the thermocline. *Journal of Fluid Mechanics*, **34**, 443–448.

Heicklen, J. 1976. Colloid Formation and Growth: A Chemical Kinetics Approach. Academic Press, New York, 178 pp.

Huebsch, I. O. 1967. Relative Motion and Coagulation of Particles in a Turbulent Gas. USNRDL-TR-67-49, U.S. Naval Radiological Defense Laboratory, San Francisco, California, 94 pp.

Hunt, J. R. 1980. Prediction of oceanic particle size distributions from coagulation and sedimentation mechanisms. *In:* Particulates in Water: Characteristics, Fates, Effects and Removal, C. Kavanaugh and J. O Leckie (Eds.). Advances in Chemistry Series No. 189, American Chemical Society, Washington, D.C., pp. 246–268.

Koh, R. C. Y., and Y. C. Chang. 1973. Mathematical Model for Barged Ocean Disposal of Waste. Environmental Protection Agency Technology Series EPA 600/2-73-029, U.S. Environmental Protection Agency, Washington, D.C., 583 pp.

Kritz, M. A. 1975. Formation Mechanism of the Stratospheric Aerosol. Ph.D. Dissertation, Graduate School of Yale University, New Haven, Connecticut, 428 pp.

Ozturgut, E., G. C. Anderson, R. E. Burns, J. W. Lavelle, and S. A. Swift. 1978. Deep Ocean Mining of Manganese Nodules in the North Pacific: Pre-mining Environmental Conditions and Anticipated Mining Effects. Technical Memorandum ERL MESA-33, U.S. National Oceanic and Atmospheric Administration, Boulder, Colorado, 133 pp.

Stumm, W., and J. J. Morgan. 1970. Aquatic Chemistry: An Introduction Emphasizing Chemical Equilibria in Natural Waters. Wiley-Interscience, New York, 583 pp.

Yue, G. K., and A. Deepak. 1979. Modeling of coagulation-sedimentation effects on transmission of visible/IR laser beams in aerosol media. *Applied Optics,* **18,** 3918–3925.

14

DISTRIBUTION OF Cr, As, Se, Ag, Cd, Ba, Hg AND Pb IN PACIFIC OCEAN FERROMANGANESE NODULES

Jane Z. Frazer

Science Applications International Corp.
La Jolla, California

Benjamin W. Haynes

Bureau of Mines
United States Department of the Interior
Avondale, Maryland

Robert R. Sims, Jr.

Science Applications International Corp.
La Jolla, California

Abstract		**260**
14.1.	**Introduction**	**260**
14.2.	**Methods**	**261**
	14.2.1. Sample Preparation	261
	14.2.2. Sample Analysis	264
	14.2.3. Accuracy and Precision	264
14.3.	**Results and Discussion**	**265**
	14.3.1. Chromium	265
	14.3.2. Arsenic	266

14.3.3. Selenium   267
14.3.4. Silver   267
14.3.5. Cadmium   267
14.3.6. Barium   267
14.3.7. Mercury   268
14.3.8. Lead   268

14.4. Implications for Disposal of Nodule Rejects   **268**

References   **269**

Ms. Frazer's present address: Chevron Research Company, 576 Standard Avenue, Richmond, California 94802.

ABSTRACT

Fifty-five bulk ferromanganese nodule samples from the Pacific Ocean were analyzed for total content of Cr, As, Se, Ag, Cd, Ba, and Hg. Concentrations of Pb and other metals had been determined previously for the same samples. Cadmium and Ba are correlated positively with Mn, Ni, Cu, and Zn, and negatively with Fe, Co, As, and Pb. Cadmium seems to occur primarily in the 10 Å manganate phase of the nodules, whereas Ba occurs at least partly in the form of barite. Chromium probably occurs in the sediments incorporated within the nodules, and is correlated positively with As and Si, and negatively with Mn. Arsenic and Hg are correlated with Fe, and As is also correlated positively with Co and Pb, and negatively with Mn, Ni, Cu, and Zn. Arsenic and Hg are associated presumably with the iron oxide phases. Like Co, they are especially concentrated in regions characterized by seamounts and may be of volcanic origin. Silver and Se showed no clear trends. Concentrations of the toxic elements in nodules from the region between the Clarion and Clipperton Fracture Zones, where deep ocean mining is most likely to occur, can be compared with the maximum levels allowed by the U.S. Environmental Protection Agency (EPA) if a solid is not to be considered a toxic waste. Concentrations of Cr, Ag, and Hg are so low that they are of no environmental concern. Levels of As, Cd, and Ba are borderline; they could present a toxicity problem if they occurred in the rejects entirely in soluble form. Lead and Se are observed in nodules in concentrations considerably higher than allowed by EPA for nonhazardous wastes. Since Se and Pb are the most likely elements to make the rejects toxic, further studies should pay particular attention to these elements.

14.1. INTRODUCTION

One of the most striking characteristics of deep ocean ferromanganese nodules is their ability to concentrate trace elements from seawater. The most notable of these elements are Ni, Cu, and Co, which account for the interest in nodules as a mineral resource. However, some elements concentrated by nodules can be toxic. It is conceivable that some of the toxic elements may be concentrated in the solid wastes from nodule processing, or rejects, in amounts and chemical forms that might create hazards from disposal of the processing rejects.

In order to determine potential environmental effects of toxic elements in nodules, it is necessary to know the concentrations of such elements in the bulk nodules, the mineral structures in which they occur, and their chemical forms after processing. This chapter addresses the first two questions.

14.2. METHODS

Fifty-five bulk ferromanganese nodule samples from the Pacific Ocean have been analyzed for total content of Cr, As, Se, Ag, Cd, Ba, and Hg by atomic absorption spectrophotometry (AAS). The samples were chosen to represent the different environments in which nodules occur with typically different compositions. The environments include three separate areas between the Clarion and Clipperton Fracture Zones (CC Zone) in the northeastern equatorial Pacific, where nodule deposits are most promising for mining. Other environments are an area just north of the CC Zone, a seamount region, the North Pacific red clay province, the East Pacific Ridge, and a portion of the South Pacific. Table 14.1 shows locations from which the samples were collected and sample types and portions analyzed. The samples had previously been analyzed by x-ray energy spectrometry for Ca, Mn, Fe, Co, Ni, Cu, Zn, and Pb content (Frazer et al., 1978; Fisk et al., 1979; Frazer and Fisk, 1980). These results are also shown in Table 14.1.

14.2.1. Sample Preparation

Most of the samples had previously been dried and ground for x-ray energy dispersion analysis. This undoubtedly removed some fraction of the volatile elements such as Hg. In addition, some of the samples had been stored for years in unprotected environments, for example, in burlap bags. Thus, we cannot rule out sample contamination. Contamination levels, however, would surely be insignificant in comparison with concentration levels that would create a disposal hazard from nodule rejects.

After a portion of each sample was set aside for the Hg analysis, samples were freeze-dried to constant weight and ground to homogeneous powders. Samples were digested in Teflon® bombs with HCl, HNO_3, and HF in a 90° water bath. This procedure produced total dissolution of the samples.

For the Hg analyses, the undried portion of each sample was digested in HNO_3 and Hg-free H_2SO_4 and then oxidized with Hg-free $KMnO_4$. These samples were later reduced with a 10% solution of $NH_2OH \cdot HCl$ in 10% NaCl to destroy the excess $KMnO_4$. Finally they were reduced to Hg(O) with a 20% solution of $SnCl_2$ in $3N$ HCl.

Table 14.1. Sampling Sites and Ferromanganese Nodule Composition[a] ($\mu g\ g^{-1}$)

Sequence Number	Station Name[b]	Location	Water Depth (m)	Sample Type and Section Analyzed	Dimension (mm)	Nucleus
Area A:	**Near DOMES site A**					
3400160	MN7401-04G12	8.663°N,152.630°W	5100	Half nodule	40x35x22	Present;U[c]
3400165	MN7401-05G15	2.938°N.151.010°W	5025	Half nodule	33x27x18	Nodule fragment
3400247	80C75-46-7	9.327°N,150.845°W	5116	Whole nodule	35(diameter)	
3400257	80C75-47-12	9.058°N,151.185°W	5005	Whole nodule	32(diameter)	
3400262	80C75-48-21	8.293°N,151.220°W	5097	Whole nodule		Nodule fragment
3400265	MULLER-40111	7.970°N,152.287°W	5189	Whole nodule	19x19x18	None apparent
Area B:	**DOMES site B**					
3380114	MN7402-15G26	9.000°N,139.850°W	5031	Cross section	56x50x33	None apparent
3750092	MN7401-08G32	11.000°N,140.000°W	4850	Cross section	96x65x62	None apparent
3750094	MN7401-08D01	11.117°N,140.000°W	4810	Half nodule	17x14x10	Nodule fragment
3750096	MN7402-16G28	10.950°N,140.000°W	4835	Half nodule	57x31x17	Nodule fragment
3750103	MN7402-16G37	11.100°N,140.017°W	4800	Crust fragments		
3750446	K79-05-99BC	11.012°N,140.067°W	4900	Whole nodule	13x11x10	Rock
3750453	K79-05-010BC	11.012°N,140.080°W	4290	Quarter nodule	60x45x28	Nodule fragment
3750486	K79-05-54BC	11.012°N,140.088°W	4910	Half nodule	24x18x15	Present;U
Area C:	**DOMES site C**					
3730070	MN7402-13G04	16.017°N,124.983°W	4430	Nodule fragments		
3730073A	MN7402-13G07	14.983°N,125.000°W	4505	Half nodule	46x36x26	Nodule fragment
3730073B				Cross section	71x42x28	
3730075	MN7402-13G09	14.993°N,125.067°W	4590	Nodule fragments	35x28x13	
3730076	MN7402-13G10	14.967°N,125.067°W	4515	Nodule fragments		
3730077	MN7402-13G11	15.000°N,125.067°W	4510	Whole nodule	33x21x19	None apparent
3730080	MN7402-13D02	15.033°N,125.083°W	4500	Quarter nodule	45x35x17	Nodule fragment
3730148	SEASCOPE72-8CC	15.100°N,125.167°W	4390	Nodule fragment	27x20x17	None apparent
Area D:	**Around 21°N,114°W**					
4080342	MR-8	21.100°N,114.150°W	3560	Quarter nodule	70x60x45	Nodule fragment
4080385	MR-70	20.883°N,114.333°W	3750	Cross section	80x55x40	Nodule fragment
4080473	SEASCOPE72-23DB	20.943°N,113.932°W	3567	Quarter nodule	60x48x32	Nodule fragment
4080476	SEASCOPE72-33DB	20.950°N,113.960°W	3685	Quarter nodule	54x34x33	Nodule fragment
4080477	SEASCOPE72-20DB	20.930°N,113.953°W	3567	Half nodule	47x41x30	Nodule fragment
4080483	SEASCOPE72-30DB	20.913°N,113.970°W	3621	Quarter nodule	59x45x32	Nodule fragment
4080485	SEASCOPE72-25DB	20.952°N,113.988°W	3658	Quarter nodule	65x40x35	Nodule fragment
Area E:	**Seamounts**					
3770153	7TOW-143D	19.512°N,168.875°W	1805	Whole Nodule	30x24x15	None apparent
3790020	ARIES-10D	19.313°N,176.735°E	1753	Crust fragments	69x41x40	
4130165	7TOW-144D	21.535°N,167.930°W	1690	Quarter nodule	80x42x30	
4150104	ARIES-12D	20.752°N,173.440°E	1623	Crust fragments	67x50x35	
4160105	ARIES-19D	21.145°N,163.397°E	1575	Mn-coated sed.		
4160136	ARIES-20D	21.160°N,163.147°E	1437	Crust fragments		
4180403	SB930001	27.818°N,145.700°E	1116	Cross section	65x63x60	Present;U
Area F:	**North Pacific Red Clay Province**					
4100004	STYX-3FF	20.067°N,130.067°W	4959	Half nodule		None apparent
4120469	SEASCOPE72-149DB	27.572°N,150.572°W	5123	Half nodule	34x30x14	None apparent
4460093	SEASCOPE72-155DB	36.023°N,132.907°W	5048	Quarter nodule	34x30x17	Present;U
4490033	SEASCOPE72-132DB	30.660°N,164.348°W	3045	Half nodule	42x35x25	None apparent
4490038	SEASCOPE72-127DB	30.687°N,164.440°W	5560	Quarter nodule	46x35x18	Shark tooth
4510011	ARIES-45PG	36.577°N,174.950°E	5195	Quarter nodule	42x28x28	Present;U
Area G:	**East Pacific Ridge**					
3350069	DPSOND-4	9.130°N,105.010°W	2957	Half nodule	40x30x18	Rock
3350072	DPSOND-3	9.142°N,105.182°W	3240	Quarter nodule	55x40x18	Rock
3350090	SIQ-D4	8.157°N,104.457°W	3325	Outer layer		Basalt
3350124	RISE-III-D3	8.825°N,103.917°W	2095	Quarter nodule	78x50x26	None apparent
3710159	RISE-III-D6	11.500°N,103.292°W	2703	Half nodule	45x35x25	None apparent
Area H:	**South Pacific**					
1580009	ET24-RS8	43.000°S,139.933°W	5139	Quarter nodule	56x43x42	None apparent
1900007	ET21-RS11	39.850°S, 96.867°W	3639	Cross section	76x70x43	Sediment
2320028A	SOTW-40D	27.943°S,159.785°W	4558	Quarter nodule	62x59x58	Present;U
2320028B				Cross section	45x42x34	Rock
2680041	SCAN-72-G	18.997°S,155.005°W	4605	Half nodule	28x28x27	Sediment
3040105	CNEXO-B5	4.982°S,154.983°W	4990	½ Mn-coated rock	21(diameter)	
3050039	SOTW-68D	9.805°S,164.743°W	4199	Crust	50x30x20	
3050057	STYX-81FF42	3.800°S,166.100°W		Half nodule	25x20x20	Present;U

[a] x denotes mean concentration; ± denotes standard deviation.

[b] DOMES is an acronym for Deep Ocean Mining Studies.

[c] Undetermined.

[d] Not determined.

	Ca	Mn	Fe	Co	Ni	Cu	Zn	Pb	Cr	As	Se	Ag	Cd	Ba	Hg
	16000	244000	59000	1600	15400	14600	1400	400	11	162	52	<0.1	20	2100	0.13
	22000	298000	102000	1500	12300	11500	1400	400	6	148	43	<0.1	19	2600	0.27
	15000	189000	63000	4600	12600	8400	1100	500	12	231	50	0.3	11	1900	0.40
	17000	280000	47000	3500	15900	15100	1500	300	12	146	54	<0.1	20	2000	0.19
	20000	284000	60000	1600	14600	14500	1500	400	8	149	53	0.7	30	2300	0.08
	18000	284000	40000	1300	16100	16100	1900	300	11	118	58	0.2	24	1800	0.03
x̄:	18000	263000	62000	2400	14500	13400	1500	400	10	159	52		21	2100	0.19
±:	3000	41000	22000	1400	1700	2900	300	100	2	38	5		6	300	0.14
	18000	302000	50000	1600	14900	11900	1600	300	10	140	63	<0.1	23	2900	0.03
	17000	303000	50000	1700	15200	10600	1500	300	10	139	48	<0.1	21	2800	0.09
	20000	278000	39000	1400	15100	14800	1700	300	11	116	34	0.3	21	2800	0.67
	18000	296000	42000	1500	16000	13400	1800	300	11	123	49	<0.1	23	2600	0.04
	13000	180000	86000	3200	11100	7700	1000	500	17	208	41	0.1	8	3900	0.20
	17000	197000	54000	2800	12900	11500	1300	400	20	176	47	0.1	12	2000	0.45
	20000	294000	45000	1900	14100	12900	1700	400	10	141	52	<0.1	24	3900	0.06
	21000	271000	21000	2100	14600	14300	1800	300	13	145	50	<0.1	20	2300	0.06
x̄:	18000	265000	51000	2000	14200	12100	1600	400	13	148	48		19	2900	0.20
±:	3000	49000	15000	600	1600	2300	300	100	4	30	8		6	700	0.23
	17000	254000	80000	2300	13900	9500	1600	500	19	194	45	<0.1	20	2500	0.09
	16000	295000	60000	2000	13100	11800	1800	400	12	165	33	<0.1	24	2800	0.03
	15000	276000	54000	1700	11600	11000	1700	300	12	145	38	0.3	31	3000	0.02
	17000	270000	77000	4300	14200	9000	1200	500	10	106	31	<0.1	18	3200	0.05
	17000	278000	69000	2300	13800	10100	1400	500	9	172	48	0.4	20	3700	0.44
	16000	286000	67000	2400	13700	11300	1600	500	13	176	38	<0.1	26	3100	0.06
	16000	278000	64000	2100	14900	13100	1500	400	13	169	31	<0.1	19	3200	0.05
	23000	327000	44000	1600	14300	12600	2400	300	10	141	32	0.2	26	2100	0.08
x̄:	17000	283000	64000	2300	13700	11100	1700	400	12	169	37		23	2800	0.10
±:	2000	21000	12000	800	1000	1500	400	100	3	20	7		5	400	0.14
	14000	259000	109000	5900	10200	6700	1600	500	11	169	56	0.2	12	1900	0.29
	ND	267000	9600	ND	11700	6700	ND	ND	8	141	55	0.2	32	2300	0.09
	17000	272000	9000	600	11500	7400	2000	400	10	88	68	<0.1	28	4400	0.07
	17000	270000	9800	800	12500	7900	1600	400	12	154	61	<0.1	24	3000	0.36
	18000	272000	102000	1100	11100	7000	1800	500	14	212	61	<0.1	24	2000	0.41
	17000	260000	103000	1300	10800	7200	1600	400	12	214	57	<0.1	22	2200	0.11
	18000	272000	106000	900	10100	6400	1800	500	8	87	77	<0.1	22	2900	0.06
x̄:	17000	267000	101000	1800	11100	7000	1700	500	11	152	62		23	2700	0.20
±:	1000	6000	6000	2000	9000	500	200	100	2	52	8		6	900	0.15
	57000	215000	131000	6900	5100	1100	700	1700	9	266	54	<0.1	5	1600	0.67
	25000	190000	162000	6800	4400	1300	600	1500	13	203	61	<0.1	24	2100	0.08
	27000	169000	171000	7300	3900	100	700	1400	14	204	63	0.2	22	2400	0.42
	36000	221000	163000	9200	4600	500	600	1700	10	352	46	<0.1	5	1900	0.11
	36000	145000	143000	5400	3200	400	500	1400	34	314	44	<0.1	3	1600	0.08
	75000	239000	95000	5900	7100	1200	1000	1400	14	273	47	0.4	5	1800	0.14
	21000	286000	103000	5200	12900	700	1100	1200	16	274	52	0.1	22	1300	0.07
x̄:	39000	209000	138000	6700	5900	800	700	1500	16	269	52		12	1800	0.23
±:	20000	47000	30000	1400	3300	500	200	200	8	54	7		10	400	0.23
	16000	273000	83000	3500	12500	8500	1200	700	21	229	54	<0.1	6	1200	0.09
	9000	154000	80000	1800	10000	6200	800	600	13	307	69	<0.1	8	1400	0.23
	15000	167000	136000	900	6300	4200	700	1100	17	301	54	<0.1	6	1600	0.09
	14000	225000	117000	2700	10300	5900	900	900	14	241	47	<0.1	7	1300	0.14
	15000	207000	120000	2800	9700	6100	700	1000	15	234	49	<0.1	7	1800	0.07
	13000	154000	99000	0	5500	4100	1200	700	19	237	54	<0.1	10	1500	0.03
x̄:	14000	197000	106000	2000	9100	5800	900	800	17	269	55		7	1500	0.11
±:	3000	47000	22000	1300	2600	1600	200	200	3	36	8		2	200	0.07
	ND	78000	190000	ND	1000	1000	ND	ND	11	113	52	<0.1	24	1900	0.06
	ND	196000	158000	ND	6600	3500	ND	ND	12	189	58	<0.1	22	2200	0.10
	ND	141000	227000	ND	4800	1500	ND	ND	11	168	56	0.1	26	2100	0.20
	128000	383000	ND	ND	400	0	100	0	12	195	55	<0.1	24	1900	0.03
	21000	138000	236000	1000	1500	1300	600	500	17	297	42	0.3	4	1600	0.28
x̄:	75000	187000	203000	500	2900	1500	400	300	13	192	53		20	2000	0.13
±:	76000	117000	36000	700	2700	1300	400	400	3	67	6		9	200	0.10
	17000	203000	129000	3100	7100	4000	600	1100	6	305	50	0.3	8	1500	0.10
	18000	213000	118000	700	11300	4300	1200	400	57	243	53	0.4	16	1700	0.24
	17000	146000	164000	5900	2500	1500	500	1100	9	344	47	0.2	5	1200	0.02
	16000	151000	166000	5000	3400	2100	500	1000	10	349	58	_0.1	6	1500	0.02
	23000	160000	191000	5400	2700	1800	600	1200	19	339	55	<0.1	4	1900	0.05
	10000	141000	89000	1900	8900	5800	1000	300	25	235	57	11.3	12	1000	0.09
	ND	195000	319000	ND	2800	1000	ND	ND	13	327	50	<0.1	4	1800	2.81
	21000	199000	177000	4100	4100	3000	600	900	38	349	49	0.1	3	2000	0.01
x̄:	17000	176000	169000	3700	5400	2900	700	900	22	311	52		7	1600	0.42
±:	4000	29000	69000	1900	3300	1600	300	400	18	47	4		5	300	0.97

14.2.2. Sample Analysis

Samples were analyzed for Cr, As, Se, Ag, Cd, and Ba by AAS using a Perkin-Elmer No. 603 (Perkin-Elmer Corporation, Norwalk, Connecticut) equipped with air/C_2H_2-N_2O/C_2H_2 burners, HGA-2200 graphite furnace, AS-1 autosampler, deuterium (D_2) lamp background corrector and No. 056 recorder. The D_2 background corrector was used for the Cr, Ag, and Cd analyses. The wavelengths of Ba, As, and Se prevent the use of the D_2 corrector for these elements.

The AAS working standards, except for Ag, were prepared from a mixed 10 mg liter^{-1} stock in 1% HNO_3 using Fisher 1000 mg liter^{-1} standards (Fisher Scientific Company, Pittsburgh, Pennsylvania). Silver standards were prepared separately in a similar matrix.

Standard additions were routinely performed along with standard calibration curves. Where the two methods produced significantly different results, the calculations were based on the standard addition calibration alone. Where they were approximately the same, a curve fitted to both sets of points was used.

Samples were analyzed for Hg by cold vapor AAS using a Laboratory Data Control No. 1235 mercury monitor (Laboratory Data Control, Riviera Beach, Florida) equipped with a Perkin-Elmer No. 023 recorder. Working standards were prepared from a 10 mg liter^{-1} stock solution in 1% HNO_3 using Fisher 1000 mg liter^{-1} standards.

14.2.3. Accuracy and Precision

As a check of accuracy, five control samples, including U.S. Geological Survey reference materials A-1 and P-1 (Flanagan and Gottfried, 1980) were analyzed by AAS at the Bureau of Mines Avondale Research Center. At Science Applications International Corp., La Jolla, California, where the reported analyses were performed, five replicates of these control samples were analyzed to determine precision. Results are shown in Table 14.2.

Except for As, results from the two laboratories agree in most cases within the limits of precision. Science Applications International Corp., results for As are consistently higher than those of the Bureau of Mines by as much as a factor of four for samples at the low end of the As range. To resolve this discrepancy the As content of samples A-1 and P-1 was measured by neutron activation. Absolute amounts could not be determined by this method because the necessary standards were not available; however, repeated measurements showed relative amounts of As for A-1 : P-1 to be 2.74 : 1.00 (T. Mellin, personal communication). We conclude that the correct values for As lie between those reported by the two laboratories.

Where our results could be compared with published values for nodules from similar environments, they were generally within the same range. Again the exception was As. There was good agreement for nodules from high-As environments, but our results were much higher for samples from low-As environments.

Table 14.2.   Toxic Elements in Control Samples (μg g^{-1})

Element	Laboratory[b]	Control Samples[a]				
		USGS (A-1)	USGS (P-1)	3730073 (B)	4180403	2320028 (A)
Ag	1	<0.1	<0.1	<0.1	<0.1	<0.1
	2	0.03 ± 0.04	0.12 ± 0.10	0.05 ± 0.08	0.06 ± 0.12	0.20 ± 0.12
As	1	305	45	75	235	188
	2	349 ± 7	180 ± 6	154 ± 27	274 ± 9	344 ± 7
Ba	1	1830	3100	ND	ND	ND
	2	1700 ± 100	2600 ± 200	2600 ± 400	1200 ± 200	1200 ± 100
Cd	1	8	22	27	8	4
	2	9.0 ± 0.04	23.9 ± 1.3	23 ± 3	21.8 ± 0.9	5.3 ± 0.6
Cr	1	22	15	ND	ND	ND
	2	20.3 ± 0.5	13.9 ± 0.2			
Hg	1	0.21	<0.10	<0.10	0.46	<0.10
	2	0.29 ± 0.04	0.07 ± 0.02	0.03 ± 0.05	0.07 ± 0.01	0.021 ± 0.007
Se	1	ND	ND	ND	ND	ND
	2	36 ± 2	61 ± 3	31 ± 4	52 ± 8	47 ± 1

[a]The term ND denotes not determined.
[b]Laboratory 1 is Bureau of Mines; laboratory 2 is Science Applications International Corp.

Neither control analyses by the Bureau of Mines nor published analyses are available for Se, so we cannot verify the accuracy of the results for this element.

14.3.   RESULTS AND DISCUSSION

Results of the AAS analyses are shown in Table 14.1. Nodules are highly enriched in some of the toxic elements (As, Se, Cd, and Pb) relative to deep-sea clays or oceanic basalts. The other elements (Cr, Ag, Ba, and Hg) occur in concentrations similar to or less than commonly reported for other seafloor sediments.

By examining correlations between each of these elements and the major nodule constituents (Table 14.3) one can obtain some clues about the mineral structures in which the toxic elements occur. Arrhenius et al. (1979) provide a discussion of the partitioning of elements among mineral phases in nodules. These results could lead to conjecture about the form in which these elements would occur in the processing rejects. Each of the toxic elements is discussed separately.

14.3.1.   Chromium

Chromium concentrations average 14 μg g^{-1} and are the lowest in and near the CC Zone, with a mean of 11 μg g^{-1} (Areas A–D), and the highest in the South Pacific Ocean. There is a definite but small overall negative correlation between Mn and Cr. This is especially marked in nodules from the CC Zone ($r = -0.65$) but disappears when one considers only nodules from the other areas.

Table 14.3.   Interelement Correlation Coefficients[a]

	Pb	Cr	Se	As	Cd	Ba	Hg
Mn	−0.55	−0.30*	NS	−0.54	0.56	0.45	NS
Fe	0.69	NS	NS	0.58	−0.45	−0.37	0.46
Co	0.80	NS	NS	0.52	−0.45	NS	NS
Ni	−0.63	NS	NS	−0.62	0.50	0.44	NS
Cu	−0.73	NS	−0.28*	−0.66	0.49	0.46	NS
Zn	−0.65	NS	NS	−0.80	0.70	0.52	NS
Pb	1.00	NS	NS	0.69	−0.58	−0.40	NS
Cr	NS	1.00	NS	0.37	−0.34*	−0.28*	NS
As	0.69	0.37	NS	1.00	−0.84	−0.63	NS
Cd	−0.58	−0.34	NS	−0.84	1.00	0.54	NS
Ba	−0.41	−0.28	NS	−0.63	0.54	1.00	NS

[a] All correlation coefficients shown are significant at better than the 99% confidence level except those marked with asterisks, which are >95%. The term NS indicates correlation coefficients insignificant at <90%.

Chromium content in deep-sea clays is 90 μg g^{-1} (Turekian and Wedepohl, 1961). Since Cr content in nodules is lower by a factor of six, it is quite likely that Cr is associated with the sediment incorporated in the nodules. That this may be the case is indicated further by the fact that an analysis of data from the sediment data bank of Scripps Institution of Oceanography indicates that Cr and Si are positively correlated.

14.3.2.   Arsenic

Arsenic would be expected to be present from the fact that As is strongly concentrated in terrestrial iron deposits. This element is markedly correlated with Fe. Arsenic is also correlated positively with Co, Cr, and Pb, and negatively with Mn, Ni, Cu, Zn, and Ba. This element is probably associated with the Fe oxide phases.

Arsenic concentrations are generally lowest in the CC Zone areas, with a mean of 159 μg g^{-1} for our analyses. However, as discussed in Section 14.2.3., there is an apparent systematic error in these results. Arsenic values reported by others for nodules from the CC Zone are in fact considerably lower. Calvert et al. (1978) analyzed 19 nodule samples by x-ray fluorescence and found As values ranging from 50 to 105 μg g^{-1}, with a mean of 73. These nodules were from a location at the western edge of our Area A, and their mean composition was similar, except for 16% less Cu and 25% less Ni. A value of 75 μg g^{-1} is probably a better estimate for the mean As concentration in the areas of the CC Zone likely to be mined.

High concentrations of As are characteristic of nodules from seamount provinces. Arsenic is high not only in nodules from the seamounts themselves (Area E) but also in abyssal nodules from areas near seamounts (South Pacific Area H). Arsenic values reported by other investigators (Willis, 1970) range from 113 to 272

μg g^{-1}, with a mean of 152. Willis (1970) and Summerhayes and Willis (1973) reported nodules containing more than 350 μg g^{-1} As, but these were from the Agulhas (off South Africa) and Blake (off the southwestern United States) Plateaus.

14.3.3. Selenium

With an average concentration of 51 μg g^{-1} in Pacific Ocean nodules, as compared to 0.17 μg g^{-1} in deep-sea clays and carbonate sediments, Se appears to be one of the elements most highly concentrated by nodules. On land Se is associated with iron hydrates, so one might expect Se to be correlated with Fe in nodules. This is not the case, however; there are no clear associations between Se and any of the other metals. Selenium concentrations are generally lower in the CC Zone than elsewhere, although they vary more within each area than between areas.

14.3.4. Silver

Silver content in the nodules is quite low, generally <0.1 μg g^{-1}. This is the mean Ag content of deep-sea clays. There is some indication that Ag content in nodules from the CC Zone is higher than in nodules from other areas, in spite of one anomalously high value for the South Pacific.

14.3.5. Cadmium

Cadmium is correlated with Mn, Cu, Ni, and especially Zn. This is not surprising, since Cd and Zn are similar in atomic radii and exhibit similar chemical behavior. The Cd:Mn correlation is especially strong ($r = 0.79$) in the CC Zone. It appears that Cd is primarily concentrated in the 10 Å manganate phase, which is the predominant constituent of nodules from the CC Zone. This element is probably incorporated in the same sites of the 10 Å structure as are Ni, Cu, and Zn.

14.3.6. Barium

Barium content is higher in nodules from the CC Zone than in those from elsewhere in the Pacific, with a mean value of 2.6 mg g^{-1} for this region. This element is known to occur in nodules in the form of barite ($BaSO_4$) (Arrhenius, 1963; Mero, 1965; Hering, 1971) and can also substitute into the lattice of the 10 Å manganates. In the samples analyzed, Ba is correlated with Mn, Ni, Cu, and Zn; however, most of these correlations become insignificant when one considers separately the groups of nodules from the CC Zone and those from other areas. The meaning of this is not yet clear. Perhaps Ba content is actually independent of Mn and its associated elements and is only coincidentally high in the region where nodules are most enriched in those elements.

14.3.7. Mercury

Mercury content in Pacific nodules averages 0.2 μg g^{-1}, in the same range as in deep-sea clays. It is significantly correlated only with Fe. Harriss (1968) has presented data suggesting that Hg in deep-sea manganese nodules is from submarine volcanic and hydrothermal emanations. Our data cannot confirm this, since we find variations in Hg content within each area at least as great as variations between different geographical areas. As mentioned previously, the samples available for this study had not been stored to prevent loss or contamination by Hg; in addition, most of these samples had previously been dried at 110°C. Thus we cannot draw any firm conclusions about Hg from our data.

14.3.8. Lead

Lead content in these nodules is positively correlated with Fe, Co, and As to a marked degree, and negatively correlated with Mn, Ni, Cu, and Zn. Lead is generally believed to be associated with the Fe oxide phases and absent from the 10 Å manganates. The lowest lead content is in samples from the East Pacific Ridge and the highest is in seamount samples. Concentrations in the CC Zone average 0.04%, five times the concentration in deep-sea clays.

14.4. IMPLICATIONS FOR DISPOSAL OF NODULE REJECTS

According to U.S. Environmental Protection Agency (EPA) regulations, a solid waste must be listed as a hazardous waste if it exhibits toxicity as a result of the extraction procedure. Briefly, the toxicity test consists of leaching one part of the solid in 16 parts distilled water and four parts 0.5N acetic acid. The resulting extract is not to exceed 100 times the National Drinking Water Standard (reference) for the concentrations of eight metals: As, Ba, Cd, Cr, Pb, Hg, Se and Ag. Table 14.4 lists the maximum allowed concentrations.

If one makes the extreme assumption that these elements are 100% extracted from nodule processing rejects by the prescribed test, then the maximum concentrations allowed in the solids would be 20 times the amount allowed in the extract. In Table 14.4 these allowable maxima are compared with the concentration levels in bulk nodules from the region where ocean mining is likely to occur, the CC Zone.

Chromium, Ag, and Hg occur at such low levels in all the nodules studied that we can safely conclude these elements present no toxicity problems. Arsenic levels in nodules from the CC Zone appear to be less than the allowable maximum. Although much higher As concentrations do occur in some Pacific Ocean nodules, these nodules are too low in Ni and Cu to be mined in the foreseeable future. Nodule rejects should present no hazard with respect to As. Cadmium also occurs in CC-Zone nodules at about the same level as its allowable maximum. This ele-

Table 14.4.   Toxic Element Concentrations in Ferromanganese Nodules Compared with U.S. Environmental Protection Agency Standards for Nonhazardous Solid Wastes (μg g^{-1})

Element	Maximum Concentration in Leach[a]	Concentration in Solid if Element is 100% Leached	Average Concentration in Nodules from CC Zone
Cr	5	100	12
As	5	100	159 (73)[b]
Se	1	20	45
Ag	5	100	<0.5
Cd	1	20	21
Ba	100	2000	2650
Hg	0.2	4	0.16
Pb	5	100	360

[a]The maximum concentration in leach is given by the EPA in units of mg liter^{-1}; we have assumed the density of leach to be 1 g cm^{-3} to convert to μg g^{-1}.
[b]The average for analyses is too high; 73 μg g^{-1} is a more likely value (see Section 14.3.2.).

ment is almost certainly associated with the 10 Å manganate phase in the same manner as Ni, Cu, and Zn. Thus it should be possible to remove some of the Cd from the bulk material along with these elements of economic interest and either utilize it or dispose of it separately. Nodules from the CC Zone contain more Ba than those from other Pacific regions, and more than enough to make the rejects toxic if the total Ba content existed in extractable form. We know, however, that this is not the case. At least some of the Ba, and perhaps most of it, occurs in nodules in the form of barite, an extremely stable mineral. A study of the partitioning of Ba between barite and the 10 Å manganates in natural nodules might show that Ba in the rejects will present no hazard. Selenium and Pb are the toxic elements in nodules with the highest levels as compared to EPA maximum allowances, exceeding those allowances by factors of two and four, respectively. Most of the Pb is probably associated with the Fe phases in the nodules, but Se in nodules has not been studied to date.

REFERENCES

Arrhenius, G. 1963. Pelagic sediments. *In:* The Sea—Ideas and Observations on Progress in the Study of the Seas, Vol. 3: The Earth Beneath the Sea History, M. N. Hill (Ed.). Wiley-Interscience, New York, pp. 655–727.

Arrhenius, G., K. Cheung, S. Crane, M. Fisk, J. Frazer, J. Korkisch, T. Mellin, S. Nakao, A. Tsai, and G. Wolf. 1979. Counterions in marine manganates. *Colloques Internationaux du Centre National de la Recherche Scientifique,* **289,** 333–356.

Calvert, S. E., N. B. Price, G. R. Heath, and T. C. Moore, Jr. 1978. Relationship between ferromanganese nodule compositions and sedimentation in a small survey area of the equatorial Pacific. *Journal of Marine Research,* **36,** 161–183.

Fisk, M. B., J. Z. Frazer, J. S. Elliott, and L. L. Wilson. 1979. Availability of Copper, Nickel, Cobalt and Manganese from Ocean Ferromanganese Nodules (II). Reference 79-17, Unpublished report, Scripps Institution of Oceanography, La Jolla, California, 68 pp.

Flanagan, F. J., and D. Gottfried. 1980. USGS Rock Standards, III: Manganese-Nodule Reference Samples USGS-Nod-A-1 and USGS-Nod-P-1. Geological Survey Professional Paper 1155, U.S. Government Printing Office, Washington, D.C., 39 pp.

Frazer, J. Z., and M. B. Fisk. 1980. Availability of Copper, Nickel, Cobalt and Manganese from Ocean Ferromanganese Nodules (III). Reference 80-16, Unpublished report, Scripps Institution of Oceanography, La Jolla, California, 117 pp.

Frazer, J. Z., M. B. Fisk, J. Elliott, M. White, and L. Wilson. 1978. Availability of Copper, Nickel, Cobalt and Manganese from Ocean Ferromanganese Nodules (I). Reference 78-25, Unpublished report, Scripps Institution of Oceanography, La Jolla, California, 138 pp.

Hering, V. N. 1971. Metalle aus Tiefsee-Erzen. *Stahl Eisen,* **91,** 452–459.

Harriss, R. C. 1968. Mercury content of deep-sea manganese nodules. *Nature,* **219,** 54–55.

Mero, J. L. 1965. The Mineral Resources of the Sea. Elsevier Scientific, Publishing, Amsterdam, 312 pp.

Summerhayes, C. P., and J. P. Willis. 1973. Manganese encrustations from the Agulhas Bank. *In:* Joint Geological Survey—University of Cape Town Marine Geology Program Technical Report 5, pp. 121–126.

Turekian, K. K., and K. H. Wedepohl. 1961. Distribution of the elements in some major units of the earth's crust. *Bulletin of the Geological Society of America,* **72,** 175–192.

Willis, J. P. 1970. Investigation on the Composition of Manganese Nodules with Particular Reference to Certain Trace Elements. Master's Thesis, University of Cape Town, South Africa, 111 pp.

15

DISPOSAL OF REJECTS FROM FERROMANGANESE NODULE PROCESSING

Francis C. Brown and Nelson L. Nemser

Department of Chemical Engineering
Northeastern University
Boston, Massachusetts

Abstract		**272**
15.1.	**Introduction**	**272**
	15.1.1. The Nature of the Resource	272
	15.1.2. Elements of a Nodules Processing Venture	273
	15.1.3. Current State of Development	273
15.2.	**Extractive Metallurgy**	**274**
	15.2.1. Analogies to Terrestrial Ores	274
	15.2.2. First-Generation Nodule Processing	275
15.3.	**Characterization of Processing Wastes**	**277**
	15.3.1. Types and Amounts of Waste	277
	15.3.2. Classes of Wastes	278
	15.3.3. Key Properties of Wastes	279
15.4.	**Disposal of Processing Wastes**	**280**
	15.4.1. Classification of Nodule Rejects for Disposal	280
	15.4.2. Waste Treatment Options	281
	15.4.3. Needs for Additional Information	282

Acknowledgments   283

References   284

ABSTRACT

Although many types of wastes will be produced in a nodule processing plant, disposal of rejects, the residues of the raw nodule material that remain after the metals of interest have been recovered, presents the main problem. The rejects from nodule processing may be grouped in three main classes: (1) tailings from three-metal hydrometallurgical processes, (2) tailings from four-metal hydrometallurgical processes, and (3) smelting slags. The tailings from both three- and four-metal hydrometallurgical processes will be extremely fine grained and may be difficult to stabilize. Smelting slags will be coarse, stable, and free draining. A toxicity test developed by the U.S. Environmental Protection Agency involves contacting waste materials with a dilute acetic acid solution. Based on analogies to rejects from terrestrial mining and milling operations, it is possible that rejects from hydrometallurgical processes may show characteristics of toxicity. Smelting slags, however, will be inert under these conditions. The tailings may not exhibit toxicity when subjected to the American Society for Testing and Materials D3987-81 extraction test or the U.S. Army Corps of Engineers–U.S. Environmental Protection Agency elutriate analysis. Therefore, it will be necessary to define an appropriate test protocol to determine the toxicity of nodule rejects prior to their disposal. Because reject material produced on bench-scale or small, pilot-scale systems may not be representative of that produced in a commercial-scale plant, it will be necessary to operate a fully integrated 1:10 to 1:20 scale demonstration plant to obtain representative material for testing.

15.1. INTRODUCTION

15.1.1. The Nature of the Resource

Manganese nodules are composed mainly of oxides of manganese and other metals dispersed in a fine-grained, layered structure. They are found on the seabeds of low-sedimentation-rate, deep-ocean basins throughout the world. In prospective mining sites, their abundance exceeds 10 kg m^{-2} (dry wt). The bulk chemical composition and the occurrence of trace elements in nodules varies greatly among samples from various regions (Sorem, 1979). Extensive prospecting and exploration over the past 20 y has shown that deposits of commercial interest lie at depths of 4000–6000 m in a region of the Pacific from south of Hawaii to south of Baja California, Mexico. Not only are the nodules abundant in this region, but they contain high concentrations of copper, nickel, cobalt, and manganese, which are generally considered the most valuable constituents of the ore. Molybdenum, zinc, and other metals can also be recovered as secondary products if justified economically. The valuable metals are disseminated throughout the nodules in extremely fine-grained mineral phases. They cannot be concentrated to produce smaller amounts of more enriched materials for subsequent processing as is the case for many terrestrial ores. Therefore, the entire nodule must be processed for metal recovery. This not only limits the range of possible choices in the extractive metallurgy, but dictates, by overall material balance, the amount of reject material that will be produced.

15.1.2. Elements of a Nodule Processing Venture

Development of the technology for mining and processing of manganese nodules will require an increasing commitment of funds over an extended period of time as technical problems are addressed on successively larger scales. Most attention has been paid to problems involved in defining the resource and developing the technology for mining and prospecting. It is assumed that the resolution of problems in other areas of the venture is already achievable.

One possible scenario for the development of the necessary technology involves simultaneous prospecting and exploration at sea to define the mine site, and research and development activities on land to develop techniques to retrieve and process the nodules. A variety of process concepts could be explored in bench-scale experiments on a few kilograms of material, and proof of concept tests could be carried out with a pilot plant designed to treat on the order of 1 t of nodules per day. Data to support the design of a commerical scale plant could be obtained from the operation of a 1:10 to 1:20 scale demonstration plant.

A nodule mining and processing venture may consist of six essential elements: mining and at-sea storage, transportation to port, unloading and storage at the port, transportation of raw nodules to and rejects from the processing plant, nodule processing for metals recovery, and rejects disposal. Although the mine site may be fixed, the developer will select the location of the port, processing plant, and waste disposal area, and the method of disposal in order to optimize the total venture, not any one element of it. For example, higher transportation costs might be incurred if the processing plant is located where abundant and relatively inexpensive energy is available. If adverse local climate or land-use restrictions prevent waste disposal in the immediate vicinity of the processing plant, wastes might be transported a significant distance—over 100 km, if necessary—to a more favorable area. Disposal of wastes at sea would be considered only if it could be shown that such an approach would be environmentally and economically acceptable.

15.1.3. Current State of Development

Several industrial consortia have been active in the development of technology for the mining and processing of ferromanganese nodules. Reports of their activities have been widely published (Arthur D. Little, Inc., 1979; Black et al., 1981). Experimental mining systems have been tested at retrieval rates of hundreds of tonnes of nodules per day. This compares to the commercial operations on the order of thousands of tonnes per day. Furthermore, these small-scale tests have been run for only short periods of time, due to mechanical problems. Reliable operation of the mining system is crucial to the success of a nodule venture. It also represents a major technical advance in the state of the art and a significant capital and operating cost. Therefore, additional extensive testing of the mining system at the prototype scale will need to be undertaken.

It is possible to draw analogies to the well-developed technologies used in the processing of terrestrial ores to guide the development of nodule processing schemes. Potential processes have been tested extensively on the bench and in small-scale pilot plants, at rates of up to 1 t d^{-1}. While additional testing in larger scale pilot or demonstration plants is likely, the remaining technical and economic problems are easier to address than is the mining system.

Operation of demonstration-scale plants will produce significant quantities of metals for market acceptance testing and generate design data for construction of a commercial plant. The plants will also produce large quantities of rejects, perhaps 10^4–10^5 t over the course of a 1- or 2-y test period. The properties of these wastes will be representative of those to be produced in the commercial plant.

Development of suitable techniques for the treatment and disposal of rejects from nodule processing is only one of the problems to be overcome in the development of an economically viable, environmentally acceptable nodule processing venture. Although waste disposal has been identified as a key environmental problem (Dames and Moore and EIC Corporation, 1977), sufficient experience exists with the disposal of wastes from the terrestrial ores to suggest that this should not present insurmountable problems.

15.2. EXTRACTIVE METALLURGY

15.2.1. Analogies to Terrestrial Ores

Manganese nodules could be regarded as high-grade copper-nickel-cobalt oxide ore with manganese and iron oxides and various claylike materials constituting the balance. As such, processing routes that have been developed for the recovery of nickel and cobalt from terrestrial lateritic ores might be applicable. The presence of copper and other metals complicates the metal separation and purification sequence. Alternatively, the nodules might be considered a low-grade manganese ore that would require upgrading to eliminate impurities such as copper, nickel, and cobalt. The techniques used on terrestrial manganese ores would be difficult, if not impossible, to apply directly. If upgrading could not be accomplished, conventional reductive smelting techniques to produce ferro- or silicomanganese could be modified to permit removal of impurities. These would be more energy intensive because of the lower grades involved.

A review of the scientific and patent literature published up to the mid-1970s (Dames and Moore and EIC Corporation, 1977), as well as more recent reviews

Table 15.1. Classification of Extractive Metallurgical Process Systems

System	Process
Sulfate	High-temperature sulfuric acid leach
	Smelting–sulfuric acid leach
	Sulfuric acid reduction leach
	Sulfurous acid reduction leach
	Reduction roast–sulfuric acid leach
	Sulfation roast
Ammonia	Reduction–ammonia leach
	CUPRION[a]–ammonia leach
	High-temperature ammonia leach
Chloride	Hydrochloric acid reduction leach
	Hydrogen chloride reduction roast–acid leach
	Segregation roast
	Molten salt chloridation

[a]CUPRION is a Kennecott Corporation trade name for two processes involving cupric ion catalyzed hydrometallurgical reduction with carbon monoxide.

(Hubred, 1980), shows that nodule processing schemes could be classified according to the chemical solvent used to dissolve the metals of interest (Table 15.1). Since energy costs and capital charges are expected to be high for nodule processing plants, it will be necessary to control carefully other operating costs such as solvent consumption and loss. This limits the possibility of developing viable options from the systems listed in Table 15.1, unless they can be optimized for process reagents and waste disposal. For example, the sulfur dioxide requirement for a sulfuric acid reduction leach process plant treating 1×10^6 (dry) t of nodules per year is ~ 1000 t d^{-1}. This would require burning 500 t of sulfur per day or 1000 t of pyrites per day, or using the sulfur dioxide removed from the stack gases of a 1500-MW power plant burning 3% sulfur coal. Since the burning of expensive raw materials to produce a reagent is not economically attractive, and synergistic association with a utility power plant would probably be difficult to achieve, adoption of this alternative may be difficult even though the chemistry is well developed. Other routes such as a high-temperature ammoniacal leach may be technically feasible, but they do not appear to offer significant advantages over the use of more familiar technology such as the Caron process, which involves a reduction and low-temperature ammoniacal leaching sequence.

15.2.2. First-Generation Nodule Processing

It is evident from a review of the literature that only a few of the options summarized in Table 15.1 have received serious consideration as candidates for develop-

Table 15.2.   First-Generation Nodule Processing Techniques

Process	Extractive Metallurgy	Products
Reduction–ammonia leach	Reduction of dried nodules with CO-rich reducing gas followed by metal extraction into ammoniacal–ammonium carbonate solution	Cu, Ni, Co
CUPRION–ammonia leach	Reduction and extraction of metals from nodules at low temperature in ammoniacal–ammonium carbonate solution using CO gas	Cu, Ni, Co
High-temperature sulfuric acid leach	Extraction of metals from nodules without dissolution of significant amounts of Mn or Fe by leaching at high temperature with concentrated sulfuric acid	Cu, Ni, Co
Smelting–sulfuric acid leach	Reductive smelting of nodules with separation of Cu, Ni, and Co as an alloy phase for subsequent subsidizing and acid leaching, and further reduction of Mn-rich slag to ferromanganese and silicomanganese	Cu, Ni, Co, Mn
Reduction–hydrochloric acid leach	Reduction of dried nodules with HCl, with subsequent reduction and recycling of Cl_2, followed by metal extraction into HCl solution	Cu, Ni, Co, Mn

ment of viable, integrated processes. They are summarized in Table 15.2, along with the extractive metallurgy used and the primary products.

The key question in selecting a possible processing route for further development is whether manganese is to be recovered along with copper, nickel, cobalt, and perhaps molybdenum and other secondary products. The fundamental chemistry of the reduction and CUPRION (cupric ion catalyzed hydrometallurgical reduction with carbon monoxide) ammonia leach and high-temperature acid leach processes dictates that manganese will not be dissolved in the solvent. If manganese is desired, it could be obtained only through a sequence of physical or chemical steps subsequently carried out on the rejects from which copper, nickel, and cobalt had been removed. These processes are basically adaptations of technology developed for the recovery of nickel from laterites, although the low-temperature reduction step in the CUPRION process is uniquely applicable to nodules. The metal separation steps are more complex than is the case for laterites processing.

The smelting–sulfuric acid processes also are adaptations of technology used on terrestrial ores, both lateritic and sulfide. The smelting step, carried out at 1400°C, is quite energy intensive, and although recovery of manganese from smelting slags is not necessary, it is highly likely that it would be practiced to improve process economics. A variety of options exists for the recovery and purification of manganese in the reduction–hydrochloric acid leach process. Development of a viable route to the production of electrolyte manganese, or other commercially acceptable manganese products, from impure chloride solutions is a prerequisite for the success of this approach. Unlike the other processes in Table 15.2, this process has no direct terrestrial analog, and its commercial success may depend on the existence of a special buy-back arrangement with an adjacent chlorinated hydrocarbon production facility; for example, trading the chlorine evolved in the reduction steps for the hydrogen chloride reagent required.

Process flow diagrams and material and energy balances have been developed for each of these processes (Dames and Moore and EIC Corporation, 1977). These show the amounts, types, and compositions of wastes produced. Such detailed information is not available for the recovery of manganese from the three-metal process rejects, although the essential features of this operation have been described (Lai, 1980).

15.3. CHARACTERIZATION OF PROCESSING WASTES

15.3.1. Types and Amounts of Wastes

It is useful to distinguish between those wastes that are unique to the processing of nodules and those that are generated in other manufacturing operations. Examples of general manufacturing wastes include sludges produced from water treatment plants, flue gas desulfurization sludges from steam boilers, and miscellaneous scraps and trash generated from normal plant operations. This type of material is generated routinely in many locations and in amounts comparable to those expected in a nodule plant. Treatment and containment requirements are well known, and disposal at sea will not be required.

The residue after the extraction of the valuable metals from the raw nodules would be unique to nodule processing. Examples of this type of waste, generically called rejects, include leached tails, slags, and fused salts from a reduction–hydrochloric acid leach process. Since only 2–3% of the mass of the raw nodules is recovered as product in three-metal plants, and 25–30% is recovered in four-metal plants, the mass of these rejects will approach that of the raw nodules processed.

Nodule processing plants also will produce a third type of waste which, although generally known from processing analogous terrestrial ores or other manufacturing operations, may have chemical or physical properties strongly influenced by its association with nodule processing. Examples of this type of waste include tank-house slime, dust from smelting operations, substances removed from liquid ion-exchange reagents, and sludge produced from lime boiling procedures. Disposal of this type of waste will be carried out using conventional practices unless it is found to contain significant amounts of toxic elements, derived from nodules, which would be released if normal methods were used. With the exception of lime boil solids produced in the sulfuric acid process, the amount of these materials will be very small compared to the amount of rejects produced.

15.3.2. Classes of Wastes

The physical and chemical properties of rejects from nodule processing are uniquely determined by the composition of the raw nodules and the processing sequence to which they have been subjected. However, it is not necessary to examine every possible process or process modification to carry out a preliminary evaluation of the impacts of the terrestrial or at-sea disposal of rejects. A classification scheme can be developed based on the amount of rejects produced and their key chemical and physical properties.

It is well known from the processing of terrestrial ores that smelting slags have properties that are quite different from leached tails. The latter are generally fine grained, not free draining, and may or may not settle to form stable sludges that are easily reclaimed. Slags are generally coarse, free draining, stable, and chemically inert by virtue of their vitreous structure. Laterite tailings are relatively stable, and some waste disposal areas have been reclaimed by direct revegetation (Reed, 1979). Rejects from leaching processes that are extremely fine grained, such as phosphate slimes, may be very difficult to stabilize. Although no good direct analogs are available, it is likely that rejects from a reduction–hydrochloric acid leach process or other four-metal hydrometallurgical process that dissolves nearly the entire raw nodule matrix will be hydrous and finer grained than those from three-metal processes.

Estimates of the likely mining and processing rates for the first-generation nodule processing ventures have generally ranged from 1×10^6 to 3×10^6 (dry) t y^{-1}. Data available in 1977 led to the conclusion that capital and market penetration limitations would result in four-metal plants with lower capacities than three-metal plants. More recent estimates suggest that four-metal plants would also process nodules at the higher rate, at least if the products are ferromanganese and silicomanganese. Since production of this much electrolytic manganese would exceed current world consumption, the following intermediate situations might arise:

1. Three-metal plants would be designed to process 3×10^6 t of nodules per year.
2. Four-metal plants based on a process that recovers ferromanganese from smelting slags would be designed to process 3×10^6 t of nodules per year. Recovery of manganese to the maximum possible extent could be optional.
3. Four-metal plants based on the recovery of manganese from the rejects from a three-metal plant with subsequent upgrading to ferro- or silicomanganese would be designed to process 3×10^6 t of nodules per year. Recovery of manganese at lower yields than obtainable from a smelting process is likely.
4. Four-metal plants based on a process that recovers electrolytic manganese would be designed to process 1×10^6 t of nodules per year.

Table 15.3.   Amounts and Types of Wastes from Nodule Processing

Major Class of Wastes	Amount of Reject[a] $[10^3$ (dry) t d^{-1}]
Leached tails from three-metal hydrometallurgical processes and lime boil solids, if produced	12.0^b, 2.5^c
Residues from these processes from which some manganese has been removed by physical separation techniques	9.0
Slags from smelting processes, from ferro- or silicomanganese production, or from electrolytic manganese production, if appropriate	6.5^d
Leached tails from four-metal hydrometallurgical processes and non-slag residues from electrolytic manganese production	1.0^b, 0.8^e

[a]Material balance derived from Dames and Moore and EIC Corporation. (1977).
[b]From leached tails.
[c]From lime boil solids.
[d]From smelting slags.
[e]From fused salts.

The amounts of rejects produced from each process are summarized in Table 15.3. The lime boil solids would be produced only from a sulfuric acid leach process, and fused salts are produced only if electrolytic manganese is recovered. A significant amount of dust, up to 700 t d^{-1}, could be produced in a smelting process. Although most would be recycled, some will probably have to be purged to prevent the build-up of volatile impurities, and this dust may present a waste disposal problem.

15.3.3. Key Properties of Wastes

The types of information on the chemical and physical properties of wastes that are required for the design of land-based containment areas are chemical composition and index and geotechnical properties. Although not all of this information, particularly geotechnical data, would be required for disposal at sea, it will be necessary to determine both the chemical composition and the grain-size distribution and density of the solids. Since no commercial nodule processing plants have been operated, and only limited amounts of wastes have been produced in small scale pilot plants, it is necessary to rely on analogies to the properties of wastes from terrestrial ores to estimate these properties.

Bulk chemical compositions, including the distribution of potentially toxic trace elements of nodule rejects, have been estimated based on a consideration of the basic extractive metallurgy involved (Dames and Moore and EIC Corporation, 1977). However, it is also necessary to determine the mineralogy of the rejects to find whether or not trace metals are present as benign or toxic compounds and whether they are chemically bound in a stable matrix or are subject to migration in contact with rain or seawater. Unfortunately, none of this information is available.

The leaching solutions used throughout the plants contain varying amounts of reagents, dissolved metals, dissolved sea salts, and trace elements. Over 98% of the dissolved metals and reagents are removed as product or recycled in washing and recovery steps. Since the composition, temperature, and pH of the solutions change throughout the process, some of the dissolved trace elements may be either incorporated with process wastes, co-reduced and sold with the metals, or may exit with the rejects stream. All rejects will, at a minimum, be treated to adjust their pH, probably into the range 6–9, and this will result in the precipitation of most of the heavy metals and some trace metals as hydrated oxides. With the exception of the smelting process, liquids accompanying the leached tailings will contain dissolved sea salts, and other soluble salts formed in processing, at concentrations up to a few percent. In the smelting process, these salts will have been either incorporated into the slag or vaporized with other volatile reduced elements, and collected in the smelter dusts. Attempts to remove these dissolved salts from the liquids accompanying the rejects would be very complex and costly.

Very little information is available on the index or geotechnical properties of nodule rejects. It is possible to estimate the specific gravity of the solid phase based on the density of the constituents assumed to be present, and the void volume could be estimated if the grain size distribution were known. It has been reported that rejects from a hydrometallurgical process will be fine-grained (generally below 0.007–0.1 mm) (Keith and Jenkins, 1981), and they should therefore resemble laterite tailings. It has also been reported that rejects from a hydrometallurgical process settle rapidly to relatively high densities, which is also characteristic of laterite tailings (Reed, 1979). Other characteristics will have to be estimated by analogy until such time as test data become available.

15.4. DISPOSAL OF PROCESSING WASTES

15.4.1. Classification of Nodule Rejects for Disposal

A key question for each of the rejects listed in Table 15.3 is: Should the material be considered hazardous? The waste characteristics defined in the U.S. Resource Conservation and Recovery Act that are relevant to the classification of the rejects from processing manganese nodules are toxicity (acetic acid extraction), corrosivity, radioactivity, and presence of cyanide. The last two are not of concern: the nodules contain small negligible amounts of radioactive substances (6×10^3 to 2×10^5 Bq kg^{-1}; D. R. Anderson, personal communication, cited in Park et al., 1983) and cyanide is not used in their extractive metallurgy. Corrosivity, defined as a characteristic of streams having pH <2.0 or >12.5, is of little concern. The nodule rejects will be treated to maintain a nearly neutral pH. The rejects will be considered hazardous by virtue of their toxicity, however, if any of the toxic contaminants are leachable to concentrations that exceed limits established by the EPA.

In preliminary surveys, certain samples of mining and milling wastes were hazardous by this criterion (PEDCO Environmental, Inc., 1981). Although none of the wastes tested are mineralogically similar to nodule rejects, and none of the samples tested showed toxicity when extracted with water, all contained the potentially toxic elements expected to be present in nodule rejects.

In the absence of data to the contrary, it is reasonable to assume that the rejects from three-metal hydrometallurgical processes also may be considered toxic by this criterion. This conclusion would apply also to rejects from four-metal hydrometallurgical processes, and fused salts, which are highly soluble, in particular. On land where leachate could migrate into a freshwater system, it is likely that these wastes would have to be disposed of in impervious containment areas, if only to prevent the seepage of sea salts into groundwater. However, if they are found to be particularly susceptible to leaching under more realistic conditions such as prolonged contact with acid rain, an elaborate monitoring system may be required for the disposal area.

Based on experience with the inert behavior of smelting slags in a wide variety of environments, it may be presumed that slags from nodule smelting processes will not be considered hazardous. The toxic elements will be stabilized within the vitreous matrix and are not likely to be mobilized by extraction in acetic acid. It would only be necessary to locate the land-based disposal site for this material in a manner that is consistent with local land use requirements and according to normal practice in the disposal of slags.

It is difficult to see the relevance of the acetic acid extraction procedure to the toxicity of elements in the rejects when placed in a seawater medium. The American Society for Testing and Materials (ASTM) has recently adopted a standard, D3987-81, for determining the toxicity of wastes based on an extraction in freshwater (ASTM, 1981). This may be a more relevant test for at-sea as well as land-based material. An alternate approach might involve testing according to the protocol of the Elutriate Analysis defined by the U.S. Army Corps of Engineers (ACOE) and the EPA for wastes to be disposed of at sea (for a discussion of this procedure, see Kester et al., 1983). Although these tests could determine the extent to which toxic elements could be dissolved from the nodule rejects under more realistic conditions, issues such as toxicity would have to be addressed by other means.

15.4.2 Waste Treatment Options

The chemical and physical properties of nodule rejects that are critical in determining toxicity depend on the conditions in the processing steps used to recover the desired metals. Since the economics of the venture as a whole should be optimized, the extent to which process conditions can be manipulated to improve waste properties is limited. For example, if raw nodules were not ground finely in an attempt to produce rejects of larger grain size, metal recovery efficiencies would probably be reduced. The unrecovered metals might then be subject to leaching after prolonged contact with seawater. Consequently, it is not likely that modifications will be made in the processing schemes to control properties of rejects.

Further treatment of rejects after processing, such as chemical fixation, might be considered. Pozzolanic reagents are siliceous materials that react with calcinaceous components of wastes to form cementlike aggregates. Addition of the proper types and amounts of pozzolanic reagents would improve the index properties and increase chemical stability by providing a more stable matrix to prevent extraction of potentially toxic elements. However, such an approach would be very costly because of the large amounts of rejects to be treated. It is not likely to be used unless it can be shown to mitigate an otherwise difficult disposal problem from three-metal or four-metal hydrometallurgical processes, and it would not be required for slags under any circumstances.

15.4.3. Needs for Additional Information

Since only a few tens of tonnes of nodules have been subjected to testing under conditions that would result in the production of real wastes, and this material has not been made generally available, the characterization of waste properties is somewhat speculative. Furthermore, additional process research and development work may well result in the design of demonstration or commercial-scale plants that produce wastes which differ considerably from those currently available. Nevertheless, important data could be obtained on the salient properties of each class of nodule rejects by subjecting raw nodules to a series of tests, under either batch or semicontinuous conditions with pilot plant equipment, in order to simulate the sequence of operations expected in commercial plants. The amount of testing carried out on the rejects would be constrained, however, by the few tonnes of material that would be generated at this scale. It is also important that a realistic, acceptable test protocol be developed to characterize the properties of these rejects.

In addition, as part of the internal process evaluation work, rejects characterization should be given the same scrutiny as the development of leaching or smelting conditions. Physical and chemical properties should be evaluated considering the possible ultimate destinations of the waste. Specific examples are suggested in Tables 15.4 and 15.5.

It is clear that development work on the wastes and their disposal must occur simultaneously with technical efforts in the mining and processing of this new and yet untapped resource. Industries will have to provide information and sufficient samples of rejects so that others can evaluate proposed disposal options. The government must develop the tests and criteria to characterize the wastes appropriately and decide on acceptable and unacceptable methods of treatment and disposal. Many alternatives will be site-specific, such as land versus sea and arid versus wet. Industries will have to work closely with local, state, and federal agencies initially to screen and determine the safest, most economical, most environmentally sound solution to waste disposal.

Reject handling is one part of what will ultimately be a billion-dollar venture. It is an area where material goes across process boundaries and requires approval

Table 15.4.   Considerations Required for Containment Area Design

Chemical Composition	Index Property	Geotechnical Property
Solids		
Bulk chemical composition	Specific gravity of solids	Consolidation
Mineralogical analysis	Bulk in-place density	Permeability
Ion exchange capacity	Grain size distribution	Shear strength
Chemical stability	Atterberg limits	Compaction
Liquids		
Bulk chemical composition		
Solution pH and buffering capacity		

Table 15.5.   Considerations Required for Waste Evaluation

Physical Property	Chemical Property	Miscellaneous
Stability	Chemical analysis	Revegetation potential
Particle size distribution	Mineral analysis	Effect on wildlife, toxicity
Dewatering ability	Leachability in the environment	
Angle of repose	(chemical stability)	
Dusting	Impurity build-up in the	
Bulk density	liquid portion of wastes	
Porosity and permeability	pH and buffering capacity	
Specific gravity	of solutions	
Moisture content	Corrosivity	
Compression strength	Ion exchange capacity	
Shear strength	Solution composition	

and decisions from outside any consortium of companies. It would be beneficial to both the regulatory agencies and industry to collaborate so that the methodology of waste evaluation develops along with the mining and processing technology. Effective collaboration will promote the development of the industry and assist in meeting the need for the critical metals contained in nodules.

ACKNOWLEDGMENTS

The work on the characterization of wastes from nodule processing was carried out at EIC Laboratories, Inc., Norwood, Massachusetts, under subcontract to Rogers, Golden & Halpern, Philadelphia, Pennsylvania, during the preparation of a report for the U.S. Bureau of Mines on a state-of-the-art environmental assessment of onshore disposal of manganese nodule rejects. This is part of an ongoing effort sponsored by the U.S. National Oceanic and Atmospheric Administration to address environmental issues related to the mining and processing of nodules. The authors wish to thank these parties for permission to publish this work.

REFERENCES

American Society for Testing and Materials (ASTM). 1981. Shake Extraction of Solid Wastes with Water. Standard D3987-81, 5 pp.

Arthur D. Little, Inc. 1979. Technological and Economic Assessment of Manganese Nodule Mining and Processing. Contract No. 14-01-0001-79-C-44, Office of Minerals Policy and Research Analysis, U.S. Department of the Interior, 75 pp.

Black, J. R. H., T. B. King, and J. P. Clark. 1981. An analysis of four processing schemes for recovering metal values from deep-sea nodules. *Materials and Society,* **5,** 191–209.

Dames and Moore and EIC Corporation. 1977. Description of Manganese Nodules Processing Activities for Environmental Studies, Vol. 3, Processing Systems Technical Analysis. Contract No. 6-35331, Office of Marine Minerals, U.S. National Oceanic and Atmospheric Administration, 540 pp.

Hubred, G. L. 1980. Manganese nodule extractive metallurgy review, 1973–1978. *Marine Mining,* **2,** 191–212.

Keith, K. M., and R. W. Jenkins. 1981. The State of Hawaii Manganese Nodule Program: Infrastructure and Other Studies. *Thirteenth Annual Offshore Technology Conference,* OCT4090, 195 pp.

Kester, D. R., B. H. Ketchum, I. W. Duedall, and P. K. Park. 1983. The problem of dredged-material disposal. *In:* Wastes in the Ocean, Vol. 2: Dredged-Material Disposal in the Ocean, D. R. Kester, B. H. Ketchum, I. W. Duedall, and P. K. Park (Eds.). Wiley-Interscience, New York, pp. 3–27.

Lai, R. 1980. Flotations of Fine Manganese Carbonate from CUPRION Process Tailings. *In:* Proceedings, International Symposium on Fine Particulate Processes, New York, AIME, pp. 654–666.

Park, P. K., D. R. Kester, I. W. Duedall, and B. H. Ketchum. 1983. Radioactive wastes and the ocean: an overview. *In:* Wastes in the Ocean, Vol. 3: Radioactive Wastes and the Ocean, P. K. Park, D. R. Kester, I. W. Duedall, and B. H. Ketchum (Eds.). Wiley-Interscience, New York, pp. 3–46.

PEDCO Environmental, Inc. 1981. Evaluations of Best Management Practices for Mining Solid Waste Storage, Disposal and Treatment. Presurvey Study, Preliminary Draft, Resource Extraction and Handling Division, U.S. Environmental Protection Agency, 33 pp.

Reed, J. G. 1979. Operation of the Greenvale Nickel Project Mine and Refinery. *In:* Proceedings, International Laterites Symposium, New York, pp. 145–154.

Sorem, R. K. 1979. Manganese Nodules. Plenum Publishing, New York, 150 pp.

PART V: ECONOMIC ASPECTS OF DEEP-SEA DISPOSAL

16

ECONOMIC AND OPERATIONAL CONSIDERATIONS OF OFFSHORE DISPOSAL OF SEWAGE SLUDGE

Thomas M. Leschine

Institute for Marine Studies
University of Washington
Seattle, Washington

James M. Broadus

Marine Policy and Ocean Management Program
Woods Hole Oceanographic Institution
Woods Hole, Massachusetts

Abstract   **288**

16.1. Introduction   **288**

16.2. Economic Site Selection in Ocean Sludge Dumping   **291**

**16.3. Relative Internal Costs of Nearshore and Deepwater Ocean
Dumping**   **294**

    16.3.1. New York City: Comparative Costs at Three Ocean
                Dumpsites   295
                16.3.1a. Hauling Capacity   *296*
                16.3.1b. Time and Personnel   *297*
                16.3.1c. Comparative Short-Run Transportation Costs *298*
                16.3.1d. Capital Modifications for Distant Water
                         Ocean Dumping   *298*
    16.3.2. Comparative Costs for All Dumpers   305
    16.3.3. Comparative Long-Run Transportation Costs   308

16.4. Future Trends and Costs   310

16.5. Summary and Conclusions   312

Acknowledgments   314

References   314

ABSTRACT

A simplified economic analysis relates the comparative internal costs of nearshore and distant sewage dumpsite options in the New York Bight to the reduction in external costs required to move to a more distant site. Indicative approximations of the relative internal costs associated with the alternative sites are generated using three different approaches. First, an assumption that deepwater dumping is just a projection of current nearshore practice and capability to the distant sites leads to a ratio of Deepwater Dumpsite-106 to 12-mile site of about 4.6 for New York City's short-run variable transportation costs. Second, annual cost estimates reported by all dumpers in the region show ratios ranging from 2.7 to 5.5, with a weighted average ratio of 4.0. These estimates also suggest that there may be a minimum efficient scale for ocean sludge dumping in the $(0.5–1.0) \times 10^6$ m^3 y^{-1} range, and that there may be unexploited economies of scale in current practice. Third, using a sludge disposal transportation cost algorithm developed for the U.S. Environmental Protection Agency, we find ratios for long-run total transportation costs ranging from 3.6 to 4.7 for those examples closest to current practice. Long-run cost estimates are quite sensitive to vessel size and sludge thickness. We do not measure dynamic cost behavior but argue that there is reason to expect long-run total costs to be lower than simple projections of current short-run costs. A reasonable, rough method for planning purposes might be that the ratio of total internal cost for dumping at the deepwater site to that for the nearshore site is about 4, although the use of sludge dewatering or other technologies not now in use in the region could alter this estimate.

16.1. INTRODUCTION

Despite nearly a decade of increasingly stringent federal policies aimed at discouraging and ultimately eliminating the practice of ocean dumping of sludges from municipal sewage treatment plants, the quantity of sludge dumped annually into U.S. coastal waters has increased. Swanson and Devine (1982) report that the 1981 volume of sewage sludge dumped off the U.S. East Coast [3.2×10^5 t (dry wt), or 6.3×10^6 t (wet wt)] represents a 50% increase over the 1977 sludge disposal. The significance of this comparison lies partly in the fact that the U.S. Environmental Protection Agency (EPA) first implemented policies in 1974 to eliminate all sludge dumping by 31 December 1981. Although it is difficult to project the future U.S. policy on ocean dumping, it appears that the volume of sludge dumped nationwide could increase substantially in the 1980s (Swanson and Devine, 1982).

All of the U.S. sewage sludge that has been ocean-dumped since 1980 has come from publicly owned sewage treatment plants in the New York–New Jersey metropolitan region and has been dumped at the 12-mile site in the New York Bight. Modern sewage treatment technology has developed along lines that emphasize the removal of debris, oxygen-demanding material, and pathogens from wastewater derived from households and other sources. A primary treatment plant typically achieves 30–45% biochemical oxygen demand (BOD) removal by mechanically separating solids from liquid effluent. Sequential processing by screening, settling, and maceration is employed to produce a homogeneous sludge of about 3–5% solids. Secondary treatment processes achieve 85–90% BOD removal by incorporating additional biological or chemical processing into the treatment sequence (U.S. EPA, 1979). Secondary treatment significantly increases the amount of sludge produced per unit of wastewater treated, regardless of the particular secondary process employed. Most sludge dumped in the New York Bight at present results from secondary treatment.

Sludge production in the New York Bight region has continued to increase. New treatment plants have become operational in the region, some older plants have been converted to secondary treatment, and sewage collection systems in New Jersey and on Long Island (New York) have been extended outward into suburbs, where most of the growth of the past decade has occurred. The sludge volumes dumped by municipalities into the New York Bight in 1981 are summarized in Table 16.1. As the figures show, New York City generated about 52% of the total sludge produced for ocean disposal in 1981.

Although several major studies of sludge management alternative and their costs for the New York Bight Region have been completed over the past decade (Interstate Sanitation Commission, 1976; Camp, Dresser & McKee, 1978), no comprehensive technical feasibility studies comparing deep versus shallow water ocean dumping alternatives have been undertaken until recently. The earlier studies were aimed primarily at finding land-based alternatives to ocean dumping, under the assumption that the ocean dumping of sludge would cease by law at the end of 1981. Since the 1980 decision against EPA in *City of New York versus U.S. Environmental Protection Agency* (Farrington et al., 1982), however, studies of the relative technical requirements and costs of ocean dumping at the 12-mile, intermediate (65 mile), and deep ocean [Deepwater Dumpsite (DWD)-106] sites have been completed as well (Ecological Analysts, Inc., and SEAM Ocean, Inc., 1983a, 1983b, 1983c).

The 1976 Interstate Sanitation Commission report recommended a coordinated regional system for the processing and disposal of sludge from wastewater treatment plants in the New York–New Jersey metropolitan area. Although the report found that ceasing ocean dumping would greatly increase the costs of sludge dis-

Table 16.1.   Volume of Sewage Sludge Ocean
Dumped at the New York Bight 12-Mile Site in 1981

Sewerage Authority	Sludge Volume[a] (10^6 m^3)
New York City Department of Environmental Protection	3.3
Middlesex County, New Jersey	0.82
Passaic Valley, New Jersey[b]	0.52
Nassau County, New York[b]	0.48
Essex-Union Joint Meeting, New Jersey[b]	0.44
Rahway-Linden Roselle, New Jersey	0.26
Bergen County, New Jersey	0.26
Westchester County, New York	0.21
Monmouth County, New Jersey	0.057
Glen Cove, New York	0.023
Middletown, New Jersey	0.020
Total	6.4

[a]Estimates from U.S. EPA Region II and municipal sewerage authorities.
[b]Where direct sludge volume was unavailable, volume was calculated from reported wet weight using the conversion $1 \text{ m}^3 = 0.96 \text{ t}$ (wet wt) sludge.

posal, the commission proposals were based solely on land-based alternatives, in keeping with the EPA's policy at the time to end ocean dumping by 1981.

The 1978 Camp, Dresser & McKee study was designed to identify a feasible alternative to ocean dumping for New York City which could be implemented before the deadline of 31 December 1981. It selected an option involving sludge dewatering and composting. Although the costs of individual components of the recommended sludge treatment and disposal systems were estimated in considerable detail, the study did not provide a detailed justification of the estimated total cost of the recommended plan. The plan was estimated to involve a capital investment of 250 million (1978) dollars and annual operating expenses to the city of about 30 million (1978) dollars. The earlier study had estimated that its plan would require a capital investment of 200 million (1975) dollars and yearly operating and maintenance costs of 16 million (1975) dollars (Interstate Sanitation Commission, 1976). By contrast, New York City's 1978 expenses for operating its ocean disposal system to the 12-mile site were about 2 million dollars (Camp, Dresser & McKee, 1978).

Philadelphia is the largest municipality to have actually implemented a phase-out of ocean dumping in favor of a land disposal alternative. Its costs (1981 dollars) based on operational experience with its land reclamation program, was estimated to be 220 dollars t^{-1} (dry wt). Guarino et al. (1975) reported on the ocean disposal costs of both dewatered (10% solids) and unthickened (3.5% solids) Philadelphia sludge at nearshore (21.3 km) and more distant (93 km) locations. Costs of installing and operating dewatering equipment, as well as the potential savings from reducing sludge volume for transport by dewatering, were included. They found the total cost in 1975 (annualized capital costs plus annual operation and maintenance costs) for the ocean alternatives they considered to range from 43 to 50 dollars t^{-1} (dry wt), with costs of land-based alternatives ranging from 67 to 117 dollars.

Despite the exclusive use of the 12-mile site for sewage sludge dumping in the New York Bight at present, both the chemical waste dumpsite (DWD-106) and the intermediate or 65-mile site are also candidates for future sludge dumping in the area. The City of Camden, New Jersey, used DWD-106 for sludge dumping during 1977–1978 while a composting facility was being constructed (P. Anderson, personal communication). About 18,200 t (wet wt) of the cleanout wastes from sludge digester tanks was also conveyed to the site in 1981. The 65-mile site has not been used for any ocean disposal to date. It was identified as an alternative candidate to the 12-mile site in the EPA's 1978 Environmental Impact Statement (EIS) on the 12-mile dumpsite, and approved for use on a contingency basis should use of the 12-mile site affect Long Island beaches (U.S. EPA, 1978). The three sites are discussed and compared with respect to their environmental characteristics in Swanson et al. (1985).

Costs of ocean dumping at the three sites are discussed in the EIS for the nearshore sewage-sludge dumpsite (U.S. EPA, 1978). These estimates focus on projected increased vessel transport costs and consider the adequacy of present fleet capacity at the distant sites. Although the factors that contributed to estimated total costs are not described in detail, the EIS identifies some additional costs, such as monitoring and surveillance costs. It also lists potential adverse impacts on recreation, navigation, fisheries, and offshore mining that could result from dumping activities. These potential environmental costs can contribute to the total social costs.

The 1983 studies conducted by Ecological Analysts, Inc., for New York City project the city's present costs at the 12-mile site as well as at the intermediate and deepwater dumpsites; the method used is similar to the first of the projections made in this chapter (Section 16.3.1). A 1982 Temple, Barker and Sloane study describes cost estimates that were prepared for the EPA by all the sewerage authorities in the region that used the 12-mile site in 1981 (Temple, Barker and Sloane, Inc., 1982). We use this same information in Section 16.3.2. Because all of these studies, including ours, provide estimates of only the internal cost portion of the total cost, we describe in Section 16.2. how the ratio of internal costs at two candidate dumpsites can be used to estimate the size of external costs necessary to justify a switch from the low internal cost to the high internal cost options.

16.2. ECONOMIC SITE SELECTION IN OCEAN SLUDGE DUMPING

Some level of environmental pollution is essentially unavoidable (or avoidable only at unrealistic expense) in the ocean dumping of municipal sewage sludge. It may be the case that for some wastes the greater dispersion achieved at more distant dumping sites is less environmentally desirable than the relative degree of containment achieved at closer sites. We assume, however, that in general the most troublesome pollution can be reduced by the use of more distant sites when the quantity of sludge to be disposed of is unvarying. In this way, distance, d, and pollution, p, are treated as substitute inputs in the accomplishment of a fixed level of sludge disposal, D^*. Modelling environmental pollution as a productive input is a consistent and analytically useful device implicit in much of the economic literature on the relationship between productivity and environmental regulation (Christainsen and Haveman, 1981). The economic problem then is to find the optimal mix of pollution level and distance offshore at which to dump.

For any activity, net benefit is the difference between gross or total benefit and total cost. From society's point of view, the optimum is obtained where there is the greatest margin of total social benefit over total social cost. In the case of ocean sludge dumping, however, there appear to be substantial external costs or spillover effects, where some pollution-related costs of dumping activities are imposed on parties beyond the consideration of economic planning by ocean dumping authorities. Thus there is likely to be a difference between the decision reached by ocean dumpers and the social optimum. At sites where pollution and associated external costs are greatest, this divergence will lead to private net benefit calculations in excess of social net benefits. As a result, such polluted sites are likely to be, from a social point of view, excessively favored in dumpers' decision making. Situations such as this, where an agent's decisions result in excessive levels of some activity and impose external costs on other groups, often lead to a demand for public regulation. This is one way to explain the economic rationale for federal regulation of site designation for ocean sludge disposal.

To identify the site distance with the greatest net social benefit in this context, it is necessary to know total social costs, including the dumpers' internal costs and the external costs (those real costs borne by the public). This greatly complicates identification of the site with greatest net social benefit, because we know very little about the pollution imposed at various distances and the social cost of that pollution (Swanson et al., 1985). Because the present regulatory situation considers only three prospective dumpsites, however, we do know the relevant distances involved. It is therefore possible to estimate the dumpers' costs associated with those alternative distances. Achieving those comparative estimates of internal costs, in fact, permits us to reach some conclusions about the size of external costs required to change the social decision from one site to another.

We start with the proposition that the economically preferred dumping site, S, is that with the greatest net social benefit (B_{net}); though other, noneconomic, criteria may be applied in the actual decision. The choice criterion is:

$$B_{(net)S} > B_{(net)L} \tag{1}$$

where the subscript L signifies the losing site. Assume that New York and other municipal dumpers pay only the direct cost of their dumping. All pollution costs can then be treated as external to the dumpers' decisions. We also assume that, whatever distance, d, offshore is chosen for the dumping, D, a level of pollution, p, results (which may in general decrease, and at a diminishing rate, with greater d). Whatever combination of d and p is employed, it is assumed to lie on a production isoquant representing a fixed level of sludge disposal, D^*. The total benefits of all site options are therefore just those associated with D^* of sludge disposal and, thus, are treated as equal:

$$TB_{(total)A} = TB_{(total)B} = \overline{TB}_{(total)} \tag{2}$$

where $TB_{(total)A}$ is total benefit of the nearshore site, $TB_{(total)B}$ is total benefit for the distant site, and $\overline{TB}_{(total)}$ is the total benefit derived from accomplishing the disposal of an amount D^* of municipal sewage sludge. This reduces the choice of the site with greatest net social benefit to a search for the site with least total cost. Designating external costs, X, where

$$X = X(D, d, p)$$

$$\frac{\delta X}{\delta d} < 0; \quad \text{but } D = D^* \text{ and } p = p(d),$$

gives

$$X = X(d) \tag{3}$$

Any site's net benefit, $B_{(net)}$, then just equals the difference between its total benefit and the total cost of using the site:

$$B_{(net)i} = \overline{TB}_{(total)} - TC_{(total)i} \tag{4}$$

where subscript i designates the particular site. The total cost, $TC_{(total)i}$, of each option is just the sum of internal cost of dumping, C_i, and the external cost associated with the site, X_i:

$$TC_{(total)A} = C_A + X_A$$
$$TC_{(total)B} = C_B + X_B \tag{5}$$

So that

$$B_{(net)A} = \overline{TB}_{(total)} - C_A - X_A$$
$$B_{(net)B} = \overline{TB}_{(total)} - C_B - X_B \tag{6}$$

Thus

$$B_{(net)B} > B_{(net)A} \tag{7}$$

if and only if $C_B + X_B < C_A + X_A$.

Rearranging terms to move all internal costs to one side, we can express the choice condition in a way that allows us to specify the necessary relationship between the options' external costs if we can estimate their respective internal costs:

$$(C_B - C_A) < (X_A - X_B) \tag{8}$$

That is, site B will be the economic choice only if the internal costs of site B exceed those of site A by less than the difference between site A's external cost and site B's. If we can estimate C_B with respect to C_A, then we can specify the relative magnitudes of X_B and X_A necessary to justify selection of site B by criterion (1). For example, if we find that $C_B = rC_A$, for $r > 1$, then this condition requires that:

$$(rC_A + X_B) < (C_A + X_A) \tag{9}$$

This is equivalent to:

$$(X_A - X_B) > [(r - 1) \, C_A] \tag{10}$$

This simply restates the proposition that if the total social cost of dumping at site B is to be less than that of dumping at site A, and if we know that the internal cost of site B is r times the cost of site A, that is, exceeds the internal cost of site A by the amount $(r - 1)(C_A)$, then the difference between external costs at site A and the smaller ones at site B must be greater than $(r - l)$ times C_A. In this way, if we can estimate the relative sizes of internal costs for sites A and B, we can provide a target value for the reduction in external costs required to change the dumpsite from site A to site B.

16.3.   RELATIVE INTERNAL COSTS OF NEARSHORE AND DEEPWATER OCEAN DUMPING

When ocean dumping is the ultimate disposal method, the associated costs can be thought of as segmented in correspondence with the major components of the sludge treatment and disposal process. This process consists of a number of well-identified steps: (1) production; (2) thickening; (3) stabilization; (4) disinfection; (5) conditioning and dewatering; (6) storage; (7) loading; (8) hauling; (9) ultimate disposal; and (10) monitoring and control (U.S. EPA, 1979). In practice, some steps may be omitted from the processing train and others may be added.

For purposes of comparing costs, we enter this process only at the step where divergence in cost is expected to occur for different site distances. The conditioning and dewatering step appears to be that point of divergence. Thus, the total internal cost of each site option can be thought of as the sum of the costs of conditioning and dewatering, storage, loading, hauling, dumping, and monitoring and control employed to dump at that site. Transportation costs are seen here as the sum of internal costs for each step in the process after conditioning and dewatering. The relative shares of total cost assigned to each of these steps are likely to differ for each distance. This is because as distance changes it often becomes more economical to devote relatively more resources to one step than another, shifting the proportionate share of each step in order to achieve the lowest possible total cost for each site.

To evaluate the relative internal cost of dumping at each site and the major factors influencing the size and composition of those costs, we employ three alternative approaches. First, using data provided by the New York City Department of Environmental Protection and other sources, we estimate New York's short-run variable transportation costs for disposal at each site. These estimates are based on the simplifying assumption that deepwater dumping is merely a projection of nearshore practice and capacity to more distant sites, with minimal alteration in existing technology.

As a second approach to the question, we report and examine cost data and estimates provided for the EPA by all municipal dumpers in the New York Bight region. These data seem more nearly to reflect total short-run transportation costs, rather than just variable transportation costs, and they afford complete coverage for the Bight on a more or less consistent and comparable basis. The underlying parameters and assumptions for these estimates are not always clearly stated, however, and there is likely to be considerable variation in methodology across municipalities. Therefore, taken by themselves, these estimates must be used very cautiously in comparing nearshore versus deep-ocean dumping costs.

As a third approach to estimating comparative dumping costs, a transportation cost algorithm developed by Ettlich (1977) was employed, using appropriate parameters for the New York Bight case. This approach more nearly estimates long-run total transportation costs, but it too omits additional costs or cost savings that might occur at earlier stages in the sludge treatment and disposal process. By generating approximations of cost differences with different vessel sizes, different sludge thicknesses, and dumpsite distances, however, the potential savings in transportation costs resulting from investment in vessels and in dewatering can be better determined and weighed against the expected cost of such investment.

No one of these three approaches is entirely satisfactory or complete in itself. By examining them all together, however, we hope the reader will obtain an improved appreciation of the comparative costs associated with the alternative sites and of the major factors determining the differences in those costs. Before we proceed, an important note of caution is in order. These approaches measure different things in different ways. Quantitative comparison of results between methods, therefore, is not appropriate and could be misleading.

16.3.1. New York City: Comparative Costs at Three Ocean Dumpsites

A transition to deep-ocean or distant water sewage sludge dumping in the New York Bight would likely occur in two stages. In the short term, present capacities and capabilities would be employed to the extent feasible to move sludge farther offshore. In the longer term, capital investment in technologies or equipment not presently in wide use in the region would be employed to develop a system more efficient on a cost-per-unit-volume basis for the increased distance. The short-term adjustment would demand more transport time and higher utilization of present equipment than does the current operation at the 12-mile site. The risk of weather-related delays or accidents would also be greater.

In the case of New York City, the present fleet of hauling vessels has insufficient

Table 16.2.   Annual Hauling Capacity of New York City Sewage Transport Vessels

Number of Vessels	Trips per Day	Trips per Year[a]	Surplus or Deficit[b] (%)
3	2	1872	+34.4
3	1	926	−33.5
4	1	1248	−10.4

[a]To conform with present city practice, 25% inoperative time should be assumed, effectively leaving only three vessels available on any given day. At present, the three operating vessels typically make a total of five trips per day to the nearshore dumpsite (G. Lutzic, New York City Department of Environmental Protection, personal communication). Trips per year are calculated using 312 available days per year.

[b]A total of 1393 trips per year are required to haul 3.3×10^6 m^3 at 2400 m^3 per trip.

capacity to go the longer distance on a regular basis, and would have to be augmented. Weather-related delays could run to 5 d or more at a time, so some capital investment might have to be made immediately in land-based sludge storage. The need to contract for private hauling services because of the anticipated capacity shortfall accounts for a major portion of increased short-run costs, providing the incentive to invest capital in more cost effective methods of moving sludge farther out to sea over the longer term.

New York City operates a fleet of four sludge transport ships to haul sludge from its 12 operating sewage treatment plants to the 12-mile site. The city is unique among the region's ocean dumpers in that it is able to run its own disposal operations, essentially independent of the private contractors who lease tug or barge services to the other permittees. Both the city's and the private contractors' vessel fleets are described in U.S. EPA (1978).

16.3.1a.   Hauling Capacity

In its present operations to the 12-mile site, New York City has the advantage of considerable excess fleet capacity. Though its four vessels are among the smallest in the region's sludge dumping vessel fleet, with an average capacity of about 2400 m^3, each is capable of making two trips per day to the 12-mile site. As Table 16.2 shows, however, this surplus of hauling capacity becomes a capacity deficit if travel distance is such that each vessel is limited to one trip per day.

Even with all four vessels in operation, a 10% shortfall in hauling capacity could exist with full-day trips. For practical purposes, however, no more than three vessels are considered to be available at any one time in the calculations which follow. Back-up capacity is essential for any sludge hauling operation, as well as for all other phases of the sewage treatment and disposal process. In addition, New York City's weekly sludge production currently shows a 30% variation between winter and summer. Although short-term increases are not significant (Camp, Dresser &

Table 16.3. Hauling Capacity of Sludge Vessels in the New York-New Jersey Metropolitan Area[a]

	Vessel Operator	
	New York City	Private Contractors
Total number of vessels	4	9
Average number of vessels available	3	8
Average vessel capacity (m³)	2400	4300
Average number of trips per day per vessel	1	1
Available days per year	312	312
Total annual volume (10^6m)	2.3[b]	10.7[b]

[a]The vessels available are described in U.S. EPA (1978). The vessel *Liquid Waste No. 1*, which formerly operated in Puerto Rico, is now available for use in the New York Bight. General Marine Transport Corporation also owns a barge, the *Leo Frank*, not included in the EPA report but included in the above table. The barge *Westco I* is not included above.

[b]The amount of sludge dumped at the 12-mile site in 1981 was 6.4×10^6 m³ (P. Anderson, personal communication). Therefore the projected hauling capacity with respect to the 1981 amount is 36% for New York City and 170% for the private contractors.

McKee, 1978), it appears reasonable to allow at least 15% above the nominal capacity for maximum production. We follow conventional practice in treating one extra unit for each phase of the processing and disposal operation as a reasonable backup capability for weather-related delays, or equipment breakdown (Camp, Dresser & McKee, 1978).

It should be noted, however, that the present hauling capacity is in considerable excess of present uses in the region, especially when the capacity of the commercial haulers is taken into account. This is true even under the assumption that all vessels in the fleet are limited to a single trip per day to whichever dumpsite is chosen. Table 16.3 compares the hauling capacity of the commercial fleet to that of New York City. The present fleet can deal with a near doubling of sludge volume, even when allowances are made for backup capacity and circumstances that restrict all vessels to one trip per day.

16.3.1b. Time and Personnel

As time estimates for the operations in Table 16.4 show, both the intermediate and deepwater sites are sufficiently far offshore to impose a limit of one trip per day per vessel. As the time per day each vessel must spend at sea increases, personnel requirements also increase.

The eight crew members per 12-h watch crewing arrangement is certified by the U.S. Coast Guard for city sludge hauling vessels. As time at sea increases, other arrangements would have to be made to meet vessel certification standards. Vessels such as New York City's sludge ships would probably require two five-person watches for a 16-h trip. A 24-h trip would most likely require three five-person watches.

Sludge hauling operations, regardless of the dumpsite chosen, can be grouped into a number of distinct activities: vessel loading, travel within waterways and New York Harbor to and from sea lanes, navigation in sea lanes to and from the dumpsite, and discharge of sludge at sea. In New York City's present operations, a vessel typically leaves one of the city's treatment plants at the beginning of the day's work shift, after having been loaded the previous night. The vessel returns at midday, usually to a different plant, is loaded again, and makes another trip, possibly returning to a third plant. The operating day is about 12 h, with an eight-person crew working alternate days for a 36-h week. Two crews are thus sufficient to keep one vessel in use 6 d per week.

16.3.1c. Comparative Short-Run Transportation Costs

The annual variable transportation costs associated with each of the three disposal options can now be computed. To simulate the short-run approach described above, we simply project the present three-vessel fleet operations to the more distant sites, using private contractors to haul the surplus. This method is similar to one used in 1981 by New York City to calculate an estimate of its costs for using DWD-106 (G. Lutzic, personal communication). Cost categories include personnel, repair, maintenance and supply, fuel, and private contractor service as needed to haul sludge which exceeds the capacity of the fleet (Table 16.5).

16.3.1d. Capital Modifications for Distant Water Ocean Dumping.

In the longer term, or if a sufficiently long delay is permitted in the transition period to distant water ocean dumping, capital will be invested by ocean dumping permittees in the expectation that appropriate investments in new technologies will lower future unit costs of dumping; the same rationale would apply to the private dumping contractors, and it might also work to attract new firms to the industry. Such new entrants might bring with them innovative technologies and operating methods that could eventually reduce relative unit costs even further.

If distant water sites are to be used for ocean dumping, then the possible changes in treatment and disposal practices are (1) increase in onshore sludge storage capacity in anticipation of more frequent and longer weather-related disruptions in sludge transport schedules; (2) change in sludge treatment and handling techniques, most likely associated with the introduction of dewatering equipment to

Table 16.4. Estimated Time and Crew Requirements for Vessels Carrying New York City Sludge to Three Dumpsites

Site	Number of Trips per Day	Crew Required	Loading While Crew Aboard	Travel in Harbor and Waterways	Sea Lane Travel	Discharge[c]
				Handling and Travel Time (h)[a,b]		
12-mile	2	8 persons, 1 watch	2	2+	2	1
65-mile	1	10 persons, 2 watches	0	2+	9	3–5
DWD-106	1	15 persons, 3 watches	0	2+	16	3–5

[a]Vessel speed is assumed to be 12 knots in open seas and 5 knots during discharge.
[b]This information differs somewhat from the estimates of Camp, Dresser & McKee (1978) and U.S. EPA (1978).
[c]The EPA will likely impose stricter discharge rules on the more distant sites than are currently in effect for the 12-mile site (P. Anderson, personal communication).

Table 16.5. Estimated Variable Costs of Dumping New York City Sewage Sludge at Three Dumpsites [million (1982) dollars]

Cost Factor	12-Mile Site	65-Mile Site	DWD-106
Personnel[a]	1.6	2.3	3.2
Estimated number of people	(55)	(75)	(90)
Repairs, maintenance, and supplies[b]	1.0	1.3	2.0
Fuel[c]	1.5	2.2	3.2
Private contractor services[d]	—	7.0	10.5[e]
Total annual cost	4.1	12.8	18.9
Cost per m^3	($1.24)	($3.87)	($5.70)
Cost per 10^3 (dry) kg	($37.00)	($117.00)	($172.00)
Current annual sludge production (10^6 m^3, at 3% solids)	(3.3)	(3.3)	(3.3)

[a]Vessel crew size in each case is sufficient for three vessels at sea per day (Table 16.4). Fifteen additional shore support and backup crew members are assumed in each case. Average salary and overtime estimates are from G. Lutzic (personal communication).

[b]The 12-mile site estimate is current as of August 1982 (G. Lutzic, personal communication). Other estimates are proportional to expected increased daily vessel use.

[c]The 12-mile site estimate is based on 1393 vessel trips needed to move 3.3 × 10^6 m^3 of sludge (Table 16.2). Others calculated are for a 926-trip limit (Table 16.2), which moves 2.3 × 10^6 m^3. Per-trip mileage is computed as $(30 + d) \times 2$, where d is one-way sea lane distance to the dumpsite. Fuel consumption is estimated to be 24 liter km^{-1}, and fuel cost 0.33 dollars per liter (G. Lutzic, personal communication).

[d]For intermediate and deep-ocean sites, private contractors are assumed to haul 1.1 × 10^6 m^3 excess. Cost is figured on a cost-per-unit-volume basis, assuming 9.54 dollars per m^3 for DWD-106 and 6.36 dollars per m^3 for the 65-mile site (P. Anderson, personal communication).

[e]In its 1981 estimate for EPA Region II, New York City reported its hauling capacity to DWD-106 as 2.07 × 10^6 m^3 y^{-1}; 2.25 × 10^6 m^3 y^{-1} is assumed here. Private contractor service costs increase if the former is assumed.

reduce sludge volume for subsequent transport to distant sites; and (3) change in configuration of the hauling fleet to improve the efficiency and safety of long-distance sludge transport, most likely by employing larger and more seaworthy vessels.

Sludge storage requirements associated with the use of distant dumpsites would likely increase over present requirements. Vessels that spend more time at sea would make fewer trips to service individual treatment plants, thus requiring that sludge slated for disposal be held longer. Should larger vessels be used, then it might also prove economical to accumulate more sludge at the smaller treatment plants before ordering a sludge pickup. Weather delays, which would affect the whole system simultaneously, require that all plants have some degree of backup storage capacity, and such delays would likely be longer and more frequent than at present. Long delays (3–5 d) could require considerable additional time to reduce the backlog resulting from continued sludge production by treatment plants. If dewatering facilities are constructed, these could be at one or two central locations, necessitating the construction of storage capability at these facilities as well (Camp, Dresser & McKee, 1978).

While the need for increased storage capacity is impossible to estimate without more precise knowledge of the sludge management system to be employed, some elements that contribute to the cost of increasing storage capacity can be described. Estimates of storage capacities at operating New York City treatment plants were used to calculate the system-wide storage time at various sludge production rates (Camp, Dresser & McKee, 1978). System-wide storage time is about 10 d when daily sludge production is 12,600 m^3, a level that will be reached by 1985, assuming no dewatering occurs to decrease sludge volume (Camp, Dresser & McKee, 1978).

If storage time is estimated by this approach, then adding 1 d additional storage capacity is equivalent to a sludge volume of 9000 m^3 at the system's present operating level. An additional five days' storage time would thus require a capacity increase of 45,000 m^3, or 36% increase in the total storage capacity.

Table 16.6 provides estimates for the costs of a sludge storage system. According to private contractors, towed barge transport to the 12-mile site is affected by weather 10% of the time, whereas self-propelled vessels of the type New York City uses are affected about 2% of the time. A 5-d increase in storage capacity, in addition to the 10-d capacity already available, seems sufficient to cover the additional requirements of DWD-106.

It is quite likely that at least some of the sludges that might be dumped at distant dumpsites would be dewatered prior to hauling for disposal. Under New York City's current practice, the sludge treatment process ends with sludge stabilization, without dewatering. Digested sludge is piped to storage tanks, from which it is ultimately loaded into vessels for disposal at sea. Practices of the other treatment

Table 16.6. Associated Storage Costs for a 299 Metric Ton per Day Sludge Production System (1982 values)[a]

Expenditures	System Costs	Expansion Costs[b]
Capital (10^6 dollars)		
Structures	5.0–10.1	
Equipment	0.6–1.1	
Total	5.6–11.	2.0–4.0
Operation and Maintenance (10^3 dollars)		
Operation and attendance	85–231	
Maintenance	8–17	
Total	93–248	34–89

[a]Computed from cost information in Camp, Dresser & McKee (1978).
[b]Expansion costs are based on a 36% expansion of the system, which provides an additional 5-d storage capacity.

plants in the region are similar, though some produce thicker digested sludges than New York City's 3% sludge.

The need for sludge dewatering, which dramatically reduces sludge volume, is a major reason why land-based disposal alternatives tend to be more costly than ocean disposal. Composting, incineration, and other thermal destruction methods all require that sludge be dewatered to a relatively high solids content. A sludge residue of at least 18–20% solids is desirable for composting, and some combustion processes might not prove economical unless the sludge is more than 35% solids. Where hauling capacity is limiting, dewatering can be used to reduce sludge volume to the existing fleet capacity. Because annual fuel costs are directly proportional to the total distance traveled, dewatering can lower fuel costs by reducing the total annual vessel trips required. If fleet replacement is necessary, then capital costs of replacement will be lowered by sludge dewatering because less hauling capacity will be required. Thus clear tradeoffs exist between the additional costs of installing and operating dewatering equipment and the potential savings in other phases of the storage and disposal systems.

How much dewatering capability is required to achieve significant savings in other aspects of operations to deliver sludge to distant water dumpsites? For an initial sludge quantity Q_0 and solids concentration, τ_0 percent, an increment in solids content $\Delta\tau$ produces a corresponding reduction in sludge quantity, ΔQ:

$$\Delta Q = \left(\frac{\Delta\tau}{\tau_0 + \Delta\tau}\right)Q_0 \qquad (11)$$

Increasing the percent solids content of a given quantity of New York City's sludge from 3% to 4% produces a 25% reduction in total sludge volume. Table 16.7 shows the approximate volume reduction achievable by dewatering New York City sludge to various percent solids >3%. The possible effects of adding chemicals to condition sludge prior to dewatering are not considered. An increase in sludge solids content to 4.8% would reduce its volume to 2.07×10^6 m³, the volume New York City vessels could haul to DWD-106 according to the 1981 capacity and cost estimates supplied to the EPA. The cost-effective level of dewatering appears to be far below the 18–20% solids content envisioned for many land-based alternatives.

Table 16.7.   Reduction in Volume of New York City Sludge as a Function of Percent Solids[a]

Volume (10^6 m³)	Solids (%)	Reduction (%)
3.31	3	
2.49	4	25
1.98	5	40
1.25	8	63
0.85	12	75

[a]Calculated using equation 11.

Camp, Dresser & McKee (1978) give cost estimates for the construction and operation of solid bowl-type centrifuges which could be operated in combination with polymer sludge conditioning to process liquid sludge at a rate of 1100 liters min^{-1}. Each unit can produce a sludge with 8% solids content from a digested sludge stream of 3% solids. It appears that six such units could process New York City's current daily sludge production. Because the purpose of introducing dewatering capability is to reduce subsequent transportation costs, and because placing dewatering equipment at one or two locations would require some costly plant-to-plant transfers of sludge, it seems reasonable to assume that one such unit is placed at each of New York City's operating treatment plants. Capital and operating and maintenance costs given in Table 16.8 are estimated for a seven-unit installation (one extra unit for backup) and for 12 units using cost information provided by Camp, Dresser & McKee (1978). Twelve units in separate locations might require different support structures from those assumed for the purpose of cost estimates here.

The introduction of a dewatering process into a sludge processing and disposal system that has ocean dumping as its ultimate disposal method affects other operational aspects of the system. First, dewatered sludge is difficult (and thus costly) to pump, compared to sludge with higher water content. Though opinions vary, treatment plant engineers believe that 6% solids is an upper limit to the sludge thickness for routine operations. In particular, a vessel-based disposal system requiring pumping of sludge for transfers could have its overall efficiency impaired considerably by the introduction of dewatered sludge. Sludge dewatering might also affect the dispersion of sludge dumped at sea (Swanson and Devine, 1982), although dewatering to 18–20% solids content is unlikely. An additional consid-

Table 16.8.   Estimated Costs of 7-Unit and 12-Unit Centrifuge-Type Dewatering Installations [million (1982) dollars][a]

Expenditures	12 Unit	7 Unit
Capital		
Equipment	4.8	2.8
Structures	11.7	8.3
Parts and supplies	6.0	3.5
Total	22.6	14.6
Annual Operation and Maintenance		
Chemicals	3.4	3.4
Electric usage	0.4	0.2
Staffing	0.9	0.6
Total	4.7	4.2

[a]Computed from cost information in Camp, Dresser & McKee (1978).

eration is that dewatering only decreases the unit capital costs of vessel transport if it succeeds in reducing vessel capacity requirements in units of whole ships which can be removed from the fleet. Also, a vessel 50% full has approximately the same crew and fuel requirements as a full vessel.

Industry representatives, city officials, and wastewater engineers in the region expressed a consensus that New York City's present vessels cannot make the trip to DWD-106 on a regular basis. This consideration would also eliminate some of the vessels from the private contractors' fleet, which are self-propelled vessels purchased from New York City.

To approximate the cost of a new barge fleet to haul New York City's sludge to the deepwater dumpsite, we estimate barge fleet capital and operation and maintenance costs from the vessel transport cost information developed by Ettlich (1977). The calculations shown in Table 16.9 are for barge fleets sufficient to haul the volumes that result with and without dewatering, with one extra unit assumed for backup. We assume that 7.6×10^6 liter barges will be used, the largest for which Ettlich provides cost information. This is the approximate size of the larger barges in the present commercial haulers' fleet. Towed barges appear to be preferred to self-propelled transport ships for long-distance hauling, in part because of the cost advantages afforded by their larger capacity.

Table 16.9.   Estimated Cost of Transport Barges for New York City Sludge [thousand (1982) dollars][a]

Item	3% Solids[b]	10% Solids[b]
Barges[c]		
Number of barges	(4)	(2)
Total capital cost	19,235	9,617
Maintenance cost	229	114
Facilities		
Total capital cost	1,566	1,125
Operation and maintenance		
Supplies	35	22
Holding and pumping		
maintenance labor	38	27
Dock maintenance	17	10
Electricity	26	8
Administration and overhead	29	16
Total operation and maintenance	145	83

[a]Calculations are based on Ettlich (1977). Sludge holding and pumping operation labor cost and towing costs are omitted because they depend on distance traveled.
[b]Sludge volume is assumed to be 3.3×10^6 m^3 at 3% solids, and 1.0×10^6 m^3 at 10% solids.
[c]Barge capacity is 7.6×10^6 liters.

16.3.2.   Comparative Costs for All Dumpers

To better determine relative total costs for the alternative dumpsites, and also to broaden our scope to all sludge dumpers in the New York Bight, we examine cost information supplied to the EPA in early 1981 by the ocean dumping permittees who now use the 12-mile site (Table 16.10). This information is of only limited usefulness as a prediction of long-run comparative costs, in part because the full set of operating assumptions and underlying parameters used by the dumpers in forming their estimates are not provided in detail and probably vary from case to case.

In each case, the cost of using the 12-mile site is the actual reported cost for calendar year 1980. Minor costs for surveillance and monitoring are included, but not costs for conditioning and dewatering. The corresponding sludge volume, used to derive unit costs, is either the volume supplied by the permittee as the basis for the calculation or derived from annual permittee sludge tonnage as reported by EPA (U.S. House of Representatives, 1981). In all but two cases, costs for the 12-mile site are based on service fees charged by commercial haulers under short-term (1- to 3-y) contracts. These contracts are usually negotiated on a fixed charge per-unit-volume or per-unit-weight basis, and some contain escalator clauses to cover increased fuel and labor costs. New York City and Westchester County are the exceptions in use of private haulers. New York limits its use of contractors to emergency or special purposes, and Westchester County relies only in part on private contractor services.

For cost estimates to DWD-106, all dumpers except New York City assumed that private contractors would haul all of their sludge. New York City assumed that private contractors would be needed to carry about one-third of its annual sludge production, as in the calculation of Table 16.5. No major alterations in sludge processing or hauling techniques were assumed by any of the permittees in estimating their costs for using DWD-106. Therefore, the estimates in Table 16.10 are probably best interpreted as short-run total transportation costs.

The differences between New York City's short-run total transportation cost for dumping at the 12-mile site (Table 16.10) and its short-run variable transportation cost (Table 16.5) are explained in part by the fact that costs in Table 16.10 are for 1980, whereas those in Table 16.5 are for a greater 1981 volume at more inflated prices. In any case, the interpretive taxonomic cost labels have been assigned by us to conform to conventional usage. The estimates themselves were not constructed to conform to our labels. For New York City, fixed costs in the form of current capital costs represent a relatively insignificant portion of the City's total ocean dumping cost because of the vintage of its existing plant and equipment. The fees charged for hauling services by the region's three private contractors, on the other hand, presumably do reflect both their fixed and variable costs. These charges may form a major portion of costs reported by all other permittees (Table 16.10).

It is probable, however, that in the fleet as a whole, fixed costs of ocean disposal operations are comparatively small, since equipment is old and, in expectation that

Table 16.10. Costs of Ocean Dumping in the New York Bight in 1980[a]

Permittee	Sludge Volume (10^6 m^3)	Total Cost, 12-Mile Site (10^6 dollars)	Unit Cost, 12-Mile Site (dollars m^{-3})	Total Cost, DWD-106 (10^6 dollars)	Unit Cost, DWD-106 (dollars m^{-3})	Ratio of DWD-106 to 12-Mile Costs
New York City Department of Environmental Protection	3.12	4.0	1.30	18.6	5.96	4.6
Passaic Valley Sewerage Commission	1.61	2.4	1.50	13.2	8.20	5.5
Middlesex County Utility Authority	1.16	3.3	2.84	11.5	9.91	3.5
Nassau County	0.44	0.7	1.63	2.5	5.69	3.5
Westchester County	0.40	1.3	3.26	3.5	8.72	2.7
Joint Meeting	0.39	0.8	1.93	2.1	5.21	2.7
Bergen County Utility Authority	0.23	0.9	3.93	2.6	11.48	2.9
Rahway	0.28	0.8	2.80	2.3	8.37	3.0
Linden-Roselle	0.05	0.2	2.96	1.9	15.65[b]	NA
Total or Average	7.68	14.4	2.46	58.2	8.80	4.0[c]

[a]Information supplied by P. Anderson, EPA (personal communication). Amounts are adjusted to 1982 dollar values. Actual 1980 volumes may differ from those reported by dumpers as the basis for their cost calculations, which are shown here.
[b]Based on Linden-Roselle's projected sludge volume of 0.12×10^6 m^3 rather than the actual 1980 volume used for the 12-mile site calculations.
[c]Weighted average ratio for entire New York Bight, excluding Linden-Roselle.

dumping would cease in 1981, little capital has been invested in recent years. Regulatory uncertainty and the belief that ocean dumping might be discontinued altogether has generally led to reduced investment in new plants and equipment for ocean dumping. As existing capital depreciates, total costs attributable to capital expenditures diminish and are replaced by escalating maintenance and operation costs. To the extent that this has occurred in the New York Bight, most of the costs calculated for the 12-mile site (Table 16.10) are probably composed chiefly of short-run variable costs. Because no major alterations in sludge hauling techniques were factored into the cost projections for DWD-106, these projections are likely to be heavily skewed toward short-run variable cost, with a consequent under-representation of the role of new capital expenditures in reducing long-run unit and total costs.

Both the unit costs and the ratios of 1980 12-mile site costs to estimated DWD-106 costs show considerable variation (Table 16.8). Bergen County reports the highest unit cost at the 12-mile site, spending over 3 dollars m^{-3}. This is due to navigational difficulties, which permit only small vessels to service the county's facilities. For the distant site, however, Bergen County expects to spend nearly three times as much. All dumpers expect at least a 2.7 ratio of deepwater to nearshore dumping cost, but none expects more than a 5.5 ratio. The weighted-average projected ratio for the cost of all dumping in the New York Bight is 4.0.

There is at least suggestive evidence in these estimates about economies of scale in ocean sludge dumping. In Fig. 16.1, unit costs from Table 16.10 are plotted against volume for each ocean dumper. The resulting pattern for the nearshore site indicates an economy of scale in which unit costs drop with increasing volumes $\leq 0.5 \times 10^6$ m^3, and then decline much more gradually for greater volumes. This suggests that there is a minimum efficient scale for ocean sludge dumping, a volume beyond which most scale economies have been realized. The minimum efficient scale would occur to the right of that volume at which the shaded trend area in Fig. 16.1 bends or breaks; for dumping at the 12-mile site this is about 10^6 m^3, or at least 0.5×10^6 m^3. Middlesex County is an exceptional case in the extent to which it, like Bergen County, is hampered by difficult access to its treatment plant. This difficulty imposes water draft restrictions on hauling vessels, forcing a severe underutilization of vessel capacity.

A similar plot for the deepwater site estimates is also shown in Fig. 16.1. In this case, no pattern is evident. This does not mean that economies of scale would be absent in deepwater dumping, but rather reflects and reinforces the fact that the cost projections for DWD-106 are rough estimates using a variety of different assumptions.

Scale economies are one reason why sewage sludge disposal tends to be treated as a public responsibility, rather than being left to the marketplace. Further consolidation of this responsibility among the region's sewage authorities might permit more efficient disposal practices, whether or not dumping continues at the 12-mile site or is moved to a more distant site.

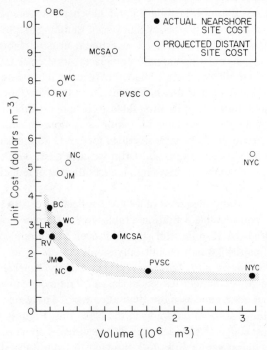

Figure 16.1.   Distribution of unit cost by volume for New York Bight ocean dumping in 1980. Values plotted are unadjusted costs from Table 16.10 for: BC, Bergen County; JM, Joint Meeting; LR, Linden-Roselle; MCSA, Middlesex County Sewerage Authority; NC, Nassau County; NYC, New York City; PVSC, Passaic Valley Sewerage Commission; RV, Rahway Valley; WC, Westchester County. The shaded area indicates an apparent systematic relationship between unit costs and annual sludge volume.

16.3.3.   Comparative Long-Run Transportation Costs

In this section we apply Ettlich's (1977) general algorithm, by which the costs of sludge transport can be estimated as functions of the transport mode, sludge thickness, and transport distance. This method is based on a generalized description of cost conditions obtained for several different transport modes, but it permits detailed cost calculations using actual operating parameters for sludge hauling by barge. Appropriate price indices are employed as noted to account for the effects of inflation. The resulting cost estimates include such components as operation and maintenance costs (including fuel and electricity), capital costs for barges and handling facilities, labor costs, and towing charges. They do not include the costs of dewatering and other activities occurring before the transportation stage of the sludge treatment and disposal process. Therefore, these estimates are best interpreted as approximations of long-run total transportation costs. As such, they are "applicable to preliminary estimates for general planning, studies of alternatives, or to long-range financial or facilities planning." (Ettlich, 1977). Ettlich cautions that apparent cost differences of less than 15% may not be real. To approximate the New York Bight situation and to estimate the effects on cost of using different barge sizes and sludge thicknesses (to reduce total volume), we apportion the current New York Bight region sludge production between New York City and the other sludge dumpers (Table 16.11). We treat the New York Bight sludge hauling problems as if all sludge originated from two sources, New York City and one source representing the rest of the area.

We consider both the current sludge volume as 3% sludge, and the reduced volumes which would result at 4% and 10% thicknesses. Hauling costs for both 3.2×10^6 and 7.6×10^6 liter barges (the largest Ettlich considers) are computed. The 7.6×10^6 liter barges are roughly the same size as the largest barges in the present fleet (7300 t). Ettlich's assumptions were modified slightly. Towing cost was assumed to be 300 (1982) dollars per hour. Round-trip towing time was assumed to be 8 h to the 12-mile site, 24 h to the 65-mile site, and 48 h to DWD-106. Labor charges are based on an annual average salary of 26,000 dollars per year, plus 20% for fringe benefits. Fifty-two weeks per year, 6 days per week operation was assumed, with 12-h work days assumed for the 12-mile site and 24-h days for the others. No excess fleet capacity is assumed, except as necessary to use whole barge units for the operation. Ten-, 60-, and 120-mile estimates were

Table 16.11. Estimated 1981 Barging Costs in the New York Bight as Functions of Distance, Barge Size, and Percent Solids [million (1982) dollars][a]

	12-Mile Site		65-Mile Site		DWD-106	
Solids (%)	Small Barge	Large Barge	Small Barge	Large Barge	Small Barge	Large Barge
New York City Sources[b]						
3[c]	4.09	2.02	9.59	4.96	18.32	8.60
4	3.05	1.73	7.25	3.38	13.73	6.39
10	1.35	1.08	2.92	1.74	5.56	2.74
Other Sources						
3[c]	3.50	1.92	8.20	4.45	16.52	7.98
4	2.85	1.64	6.70	3.14	12.62	5.91
10	1.28	1.05	2.68	1.65	5.12	2.54
Total New York Bight Sources						
3	7.59	3.94	17.79	9.21	34.84	16.58
4	5.90	3.37	13.96	6.51	26.34	12.30
10	2.63	2.13	5.60	3.39	10.68	5.28

[a]Calculated from Ettlich (1977). The barge capacities are 3.2×10^6 and 7.6×10^6 liters for small and large barges, respectively.
[b]New York City volume is assumed to be 3.3×10^6 m^3 at 3% solids; other sources are assumed to be 3×10^6 m^3 at 3%. Volumes at other thicknesses are calculated as in Table 16.7.
[c]This line is calculated by applying Ettlich's information for 4% sludge to the volume at 3% thickness.

used for site calculations, and all values were adjusted to New York City's actual 1982 costs (Table 16.5).

The table illustrates the dramatic effect increasing barge size or decreasing sludge volume, or both, can have on subsequent transportation costs. According to these estimates, New York City could haul 10% sludge to the deepwater site in large barges for less transportation cost than the current total operating costs it reports for the 12-mile site (Table 16.5), provided investment is made in both new barges and dewatering equipment.

The highest costs are incurred for hauling 3% sludge to the 12-mile site in small barges. The lowest costs are incurred in hauling 10% sludge to the 12-mile site in large barges. Similarly, the smallest percentage increase in hauling costs as a function of distance is represented in the change incurred in going from hauling 10% sludge in large barges to the 12-mile site to hauling it to the 65-mile site. The largest such change occurs in making a transition from hauling 3% sludge in small barges at the 12-mile site to the same system projected to DWD-106. The ratio of DWD-106 to 12-mile site costs, with 3% and 4% thickness and constant barge size, ranges over values similar to those shown in Table 16.10; in this case the range is from 3.6 to 4.7. With 10% sludge thickness, the ratio falls as low as 2.4.

16.4. FUTURE TRENDS AND COSTS

All of the cost comparisons described are based on single point estimates of costs for fixed sludge volumes disposed at given sites. By simplifying the problem with parametric assumptions (such as fixed volumes, fixed distances, equal total benefits, best-practice technology, and indefinite or infinitesimal time horizon) certain basic properties of the comparative costs become more obvious (Tihansky, 1974). Yet this simplification ignores some important dimensions of the problem.

Up to this point, we have largely ignored the difficult question of how costs are likely to change with time and with increasing quantities of sludge. It is important, though, to determine, at least qualitatively, how short-run costs, where the dumping fleet and other plant and equipment cannot be augmented or modified, differ from long-run costs, where all available efficiency-enhancing modifications have been incorporated into the operating technology.

Generally speaking, except near the long-run equilibrium, short-run average cost will be greater than long-run average cost. This is almost certainly the case for nearshore sludge dumping in the New York Bight, because capital modifications for sludge dumping have been in abeyance while sludge quantities have grown. Short-run cost observed in current practice, with deteriorating and obsolescing capital, overstates long-run cost. Using this short-run cost as a basis for costs at distant sites would then tend to amplify this possible overstatement in the estimates of long-run costs for deepwater dumping.

In the short-run, if an immediate transition is made to a distant site, then the initial response of ocean dumping permittees might well be to apply present capabilities and methods to longer distance travel as best they can. The costs given in Tables 16.5 and 16.10 might then represent reasonable estimations of the range of immediate cost increases to be expected. Otherwise, all of our point estimates, based on projection of current practice to the distant sites (that is, all but those derived from the Ettlich method) probably tend to overstate somewhat the real (inflation-adjusted) costs that would be approached over the longer term. The resulting misimpression might be corrected by reference to estimates generated by the Ettlich method, which attempts to simulate long-run cost. However, the correction is imperfect because it is confined to transportation cost and omits the cost of dewatering and other possible changes in processing and handling.

A more profound dynamic consideration concerns the time profile of costs at the various sites. The simple comparison of net benefits among alternatives becomes, in a dynamic setting, the more complicated comparison of the discounted sums of flows of net benefits (or costs) over a relevant time period. This problem underlies the choice of optimal distance for ocean dumping, and its resolution depends on knowledge of the likely behavior of both internal and external costs over time with (presumably) increasing sludge volumes. Little is known about such dynamic cost behavior in ocean dumping.

Even if we knew that the total (internal and external) cost of dumping at site A were two times the cost at site B, we could not select site B with confidence if there were reason to suspect that cost at site B would increase rapidly over time or with increasing load, while cost at site A would remain relatively constant. The dilemma would be particularly acute if the site selection choice were very costly or could be made only infrequently. Of course, the present value of future cost is sensitive to the rate at which future values are discounted (Baumol, 1968; Krutilla and Fisher, 1975). The correct choice of social discount rate in various contexts is a largely unresolved issue (Fisher and Krutilla, 1975).

Two other qualitative adjustments to our results are suggested by the dynamics of the distance choice. The first involves learning. In moving to a new operating environment, such as a deepwater dumpsite, there is some reason to expect that, with increasing experience, cost-saving will take place (Zimmerman, 1982). Where such a prospect exists, there is some presumption that a higher level of activity might be chosen than would be selected solely on the basis of apparent initial cost (Spence, 1981). The second adjustment concerns irreversibility. When there is a reasonable expectation that irreversible damage might be imposed, a lower level of activity than would otherwise be chosen might be preferred (Arrow and Fisher, 1974; Russell, 1982).

There are, in addition to dynamic considerations, several other important aspects of the problem that we have not attempted to address. We have proceeded on the assumption that the municipalities' entire sludge load will be disposed of through the same mode (ocean dumping) and at a single site. Because of the possible scale economies involved, this is probably so. Conceivably, though, lower-cost disposal could be achieved through a multimedia, multisite approach, in which various proportions of the total sludge load are dispatched through different disposal modes at different times, depending on prevailing conditions. The sludge disposal question has increasingly turned to one of comparing land disposal to ocean disposal, rather than a strict comparison of ocean disposal alternatives as we have done here. The question of environmental cost external to the disposal authority remains largely unresolved. As far as the ocean options are concerned, we know very little about the magnitude of those costs and how they change with distance, thickness, and sludge volume. This is a crucial part of the total cost equation and one about which great increases in knowledge should be possible. We have attempted to set some limits on these external costs by relating them to the comparative internal cost of ocean dumping. Nevertheless, the external costs remain highly uncertain.

The equity effects of different dumpsite choices is another important area that we have not attempted to explore here. If one of the motivations for regulatory choice of one site over another is to reduce the inequities of external costs, rather than simply to find the lowest total social cost, then this issue should be considered in greater depth. For example, it may be possible that external costs fall more heavily on a low-income group at one site and more heavily on a high-income group at another.

16.5. SUMMARY AND CONCLUSIONS

In comparing alternative sites for ocean dumping of municipal sewage sludges, the relevant costs from a social point of view are the total social costs of each option. These consist of total internal costs, those costs borne directly by the sludge dumpers, and total external costs, those costs imposed on others by effects such as environmental pollution. Presently, we are unable to measure the external costs of ocean dumping. It is possible, however, to estimate internal costs for alternative sites; these estimates provide limited information on the relative magnitudes of external costs necessary to change the social decision from one site to another. Specifically, if internal costs at site B are r times those at site A, $r > 1$, then the difference between external costs at site A and smaller ones at site B must be greater than $(r - 1)$ times the internal costs at site A.

In comparing the internal costs of ocean dumping at different distances, the relevant costs are those occurring after the point in the sludge processing and disposal system where costs diverge for different distances. Total internal cost, then, is the sum of those costs incurred in conditioning, dewatering, storage, loading, hauling, ultimate disposal, and monitoring and control. By total transportation cost, we refer only to those steps occurring after the conditioning and dewatering steps.

The cost estimates we report here, though largely confined to transportation costs, should capture the bulk of those costs that would be included in measures of relative total internal costs. These estimates provide three different approaches to measuring the relationship between the internal costs of nearshore and more distant ocean dumping. We have constructed an estimate of comparative cost for

New York City based on the assumption that deepwater dumping is just a projection of current nearshore practice and capability to more distant sites. This estimate is best interpreted as short-run variable transportation cost, which we found to be about 4.1×10^6 (1982) dollars for current operations at the 12-mile site, 12.8×10^6 dollars for the 65-mile site, and 18.8×10^6 dollars for DWD-106. The ratio of DWD-106 to 12-mile site costs, then, is about 4.8, whereas that of 65-mile to 12-mile site costs is about 3.2.

Estimates supplied to the EPA by all dumping permittees in the region in 1981 provide somewhat ill-defined, though useful, comparative costs (perhaps best considered to be short-run total transportation costs) for the New York Bight. These range from about 14.4×10^6 (1982) dollars at the 12-mile site to 58×10^6 dollars at DWD-106. This results in a weighted average ratio of DWD-106 to 12-mile site costs of about 4.1 for all Bight dumpers. The estimated ratios for individual dumpers range from 2.7 to 5.5. Estimates generated by the Ettlich (1977) method suggest long-run total transportation cost ratios that range from 2.5 to 4.6.

We caution against the mechanical application of these results. The three approaches we employed measure different things, and their results should not be compared directly. None of these approaches is complete or entirely satisfactory by itself, but combined they are useful in possibly bounding the likely comparative costs of distant and nearshore ocean dumping. On that basis, and assuming that total internal costs behave with site distance in a fashion similar to these proxies, we propose that, as a practical method, using DWD-106 for municipal sewage sludge ocean dumping will cost about four times the cost of dumping at the 12-mile site. In other words, we estimate that $r \cong 4$.

Obviously, much information is required before we can reach confident conclusions about the comparative total cost of dumping at each site. As a beginning, it would be useful for some appropriate agency, such as the EPA, to define carefully a consistent set of cost components about which information is needed, and collect them from sludge dumpers. Total costs of current dumping activities at the 12-mile site should be requested, as well as total costs for dumping at the other sites, estimated in the same manner. This should be relatively easy to accomplish without imposing too great a burden on the municipalities.

Even though our considerations have emphasized transportation costs, there can be major tradeoffs related to other aspects of the disposal problem. For example, there are preliminary indications that substantial unexploited economies of scale may exist for ocean dumping in the region. Reduction in total transportation costs might be available by consolidation of sludge disposal practices, such as by making use of a large tanker stationed in the harbor and serviced by the present fleet of smaller vessels. Reduction in transportation costs might also be achieved through additional emphasis on storage or dewatering capabilities. Therefore, simple projection of nearshore operating experience to deepwater sites is useful mainly to provide upper bound estimates for the total internal cost of deepwater dumping. Generally speaking, long-run total costs may be smaller than observed or projected short-run costs.

ACKNOWLEDGMENTS

We wish to gratefully acknowledge the assistance of K. Wellman and A. Goodwin in the preparation of this manuscript. R. Ladner deserves special thanks for her tireless and enthusiastic data analysis. In addition, numerous officials and executives in the New York City Department of Environmental Protection, the Nassau County Department of Public Works, U.S. EPA Region II Headquarters, the U.S. Coast Guard, and in private industry provided valuable information and assistance. Finally, we thank our reviewers for many helpful comments. This chapter is W.H.O.I. Contribution No. 5320, prepared with funds from the Office of Marine Pollution Assessment, U.S. National Oceanic and Atmospheric Administration, under Grant No. NA 81RA-D-00013, and from the Pew Memorial Trust under the auspices of the Marine Policy and Ocean Management Program at the Woods Hole Oceanographic Institution.

REFERENCES

Arrow K. J., and A. C. Fisher. 1974. Environmental preservation, uncertainty, and irreversibility. *Quarterly Journal of Economics,* **88,** 312.

Baumol, W. J. 1968. On the social rate of discount. *The American Economic Review,* **58,** 788–802.

Camp, Dresser & McKee. 1978. New York City Sludge Management Plan: Stage 1. Unpublished Draft Technical Report, 2 Vols. Submitted to the New York City Department of Environmental Protection, 109 pp.

Christainsen, G. B., and R. H. Haveman. 1981. The contribution of environmental regulations to the slowdown in productivity growth. *Journal of Environmental Economics and Management,* **8,** 381–390.

Ecological Analysts, Inc., and SEAMOcean, Inc. 1983a. Technical Information to Support the Redesignation of the 12-Mile Site for the Ocean Diposal of Municipal Sewage Sludge. Submitted to the U.S. Environmental Protection Agency Region II by the New York City Department of Environmental Protection, 20 chapters (paginated separately), 247 pp. plus appendices.

Ecological Analysts, Inc., and SEAMOcean, Inc. 1983b. Technical Information to Support the Redesignation of the 60-Mile Site for the Ocean Disposal of Municipal Sewage Sludge. Submitted to the U.S. Environmental Protection Agency Region II by the New York City Department of Environmental Protection, 20 chapters (paginated separately), 208 pp. plus appendices.

Ecological Analysts, Inc., and SEAMOcean, Inc. 1983c. Technical Information to Support the Redesignation of the 106-Mile Site for the Ocean Disposal of Municipal Sewage Sludge. Submitted to the U.S. Environmental Protection Agency Region II by the New York City Department of Environmental Protection, 20 chapters (paginated separately), 144 pp. plus appendices.

Ettlich W. F. 1977. Transport of Sewage Sludge. EPA-600/2-77-216. U.S. Environmental Protection Agency, Cincinnati, Ohio, 98 pp.

Farrington, J. W., J. M. Capuzzo, T. M. Leschine, and M. A. Champ. 1982. Ocean dumping. *Oceanus,* **25**(4), 39–50.

Fisher, A. C., and J. V. Krutilla. 1975. Resource conservation, environmental preservation, and the rate of discount. *The Quarterly Journal of Economics,* **89,** 358–370.

Guarino, C. F., M. D. Nelson, S. A. Townsend, T. E. Wilson, and E. F. Ballotti. 1975. Land and sea solids management alternatives in Philadelphia. *Journal of the Water Pollution Control Federation,* **47,** 2551–2564.

Interstate Sanitation Commission. 1976. Phase 2 Report of Technical Investigation of Alternatives for New York–New Jersey Metropolitan Area Sewage Sludge Disposal Management Program. Unpublished Report prepared by Camp, Dresser & McKee and Alexander Potter Associates, 259 pp. plus appendices.

Krutilla, J. V., and A. C. Fisher. 1975. The Economics of Natural Environments. Prepared for Resources for the Future, Washington, D.C. Johns Hopkins University Press, Baltimore, Maryland, 292 pp.

Russell, C. L. 1982. Economics and marine pollution. *In:* Impact of Marine Pollution on Society, V. K. Tippie, and D. R. Kester (Eds.). Praeger Publishers, New York, pp. 284–289.

Spence, A. M. 1981. The learning curve and competition. *The Bell Journal of Economics,* **12,** 49–70.

Swanson, R. L., and M. Devine. 1982. The pendulum swings again: ocean dumping policy. *Environment,* **24,** 14–20.

Swanson, R. L., M. A. Champ, T. O'Connor, P. K. Park, J. O'Connor, G. Mayer, H. Stanford, E. Erdheim, and J. L. Verber. 1985. Sewage sludge dumping in the New York Bight Apex: a comparison with other proposed ocean dumpsites. *In:* Wastes in the Ocean, Vol. 6: Nearshore Waste Disposal, B. H. Ketchum, J. M. Capuzzo, W. V. Burt, I. W. Duedall, P. K. Park, and D. R. Kester (Eds.). Wiley-Interscience, New York, pp. 461–488.

Temple, Barker and Sloane, Inc. 1982. Costs of Ocean Disposal of Municipal Sewage Sludge and Industrial Wastes. Prepared for U.S. Environmental Protection Agency under Contract No. 68-01-6341, 30 pp. plus appendices.

Tihansky, D. P. 1974. Historical development of water pollution control cost functions. *Journal of the Water Pollution Control Federation,* **46,** 813–833.

U.S. Environmental Protection Agency (EPA). 1978. Final Environmental Impact Statement on the Ocean Dumping of Sewage Sludge in the New York Bight. U.S. EPA Region II, New York, 226 pp. plus appendices.

U.S. EPA. 1979. Process Design Manual for Sludge Treatment and Disposal. EPA 625/1-79-011, U.S. Environmental Protection Agency, Cincinnati, Ohio, 1013 pp.

U.S. House of Representatives. 1981. Committee on Merchant Marine and Fisheries. Subcommittee on Oceanography and Subcommittee on Fisheries, Wildlife Conservation, and the Environment. *Waste Dumping Hearings.* 97th Congress, 1st session, p. 544.

Zimmerman, M. B. 1982. Learning effects and the commercialization of new energy technologies: The case of nuclear power. *The Bell Journal of Economics,* **13,** 297–310.

PART VI: CONCLUDING REMARKS

17

DISPOSAL OF WASTES IN THE DEEP SEA: OCEANOGRAPHIC CONSIDERATIONS

Dana R. Kester

Graduate School of Oceanography
University of Rhode Island
Kingston, Rhode Island

Wayne V. Burt

College of Oceanography
Oregon State University
Corvallis, Oregon

Judith M. Capuzzo

Department of Biology
Woods Hole Oceanographic Institution
Woods Hole, Massachusetts

P. Kilho Park

Office of Oceanic and Atmospheric Research
National Oceanic and Atmospheric Administration
Rockville, Maryland

Iver W. Duedall

Department of Oceanography and Ocean Engineering
Florida Institute of Technology
Melbourne, Florida

Abstract

17.1. Introduction   **320**

17.2. Comparison of Deep-Sea and Nearshore Regions for Waste Disposal   **321**

319

17.3.   Tracers: Application to Waste Disposal   322

    17.3.1.   Oceanic Properties   322
    17.3.2.   Lagrangian Tracers   324

17.4.   Oceanic Chemical Cycles   327

17.5.   Types of Wastes Suitable for Deep Ocean Disposal   331

17.6.   Summary and Conclusions   332

Acknowledgments   332

References   333

ABSTRACT

Oceanic processes that govern the dynamics of wastes in the ocean, from input to removal, are (1) the transport and mixing processes at all the depths, (2) a variety of chemical processes, (3) the interaction with organisms and solid phases, and (4) the accumulation in sediments. Recent investigations of oceanic properties, such as ^3H distribution in the North Atlantic Ocean, and of Lagrangian trajectories reveal very complex and unpredictable transport at various depths. However, we do know that the ocean's diffusive nature serves to dilute contaminants. A fairly good scientific database exists from which to predict the inorganic speciation of metals in wastes added to seawater. However, there is great uncertainty about the role and behavior of organic substances that affect metal chemistry and marine organisms. Incineration of combustible wastes at sea appears promising when we consider it as a dispersive strategy. Oceanographically, it is illogical to define a limited disposal site for incineration; incineration lanes across the ocean may harm the environment less. Attention should be given to the particulate material that results from incineration, because the particles emitted can be transported for large distances in the atmosphere before settling.

17.1.   INTRODUCTION

In this final chapter we examine several issues concerning the use of the deep ocean environment as a place for disposing of wastes. In nearly all instances the disposal of wastes in the deep ocean is likely to be more costly than land or nearshore disposal, if the principal costs are considered to be transportation and facilities. Consequently, the incentives for deep-sea disposal of wastes are based mainly on relative values of environmental protection and avoidance of costly treatment processes.

If choices must be made as to which portions of the human environment are most essential to protect, air and ground water quality are certain to rank high. The preservation of the quality of nearshore regions is likely to receive attention because of their use by and proximity to society. Protection of the ocean can be based on arguments for aesthetic and ethical values. These arguments may not carry much weight when we are faced with the need to preserve human habitats or when economics substantially favors oceanic, rather than alternate, disposal areas.

The challenge for marine scientists is twofold. What are the limits of waste input into the deep ocean, without causing unacceptable degradation? Are there demonstrable impacts on society that are caused by degrading the oceanic environment? In considering these problems in this volume, we have focused on the deep ocean as opposed to the nearshore environment, which is examined in Volume 6 of this series. There are a number of oceanic characteristics, in addition to depth of the water column, that distinguish nearshore environments from the deep ocean. The estuaries and continental shelves have a more pronounced coupling between benthic and euphotic portions of biological and geochemical cycles than does the deep ocean. In the oceanic regime, this coupling occurs at rates ranging from tens to hundreds of years, as determined by rates of circulation, whereas in nearshore environments the rates can be those ranging from tidal to seasonal cycles. Another distinction is that nearshore regions are generally more productive biologically than the deep ocean. By focusing on the deep ocean in this consideration of waste disposal, we do not imply that wastes will be discharged at great depths, though they could be, especially for contained wastes. It is likely that most wastes disposed of in the deep ocean will be discharged in the surface layer. Our concern is how their subsequent fate and possible effect on the ocean will be influenced by the fact that the open ocean is deeper and less productive than nearshore regions.

17.2. COMPARISON OF DEEP-SEA AND NEARSHORE REGIONS FOR WASTE DISPOSAL

One of the consequences of disposing of wastes in nearshore waters is the accumulation of contaminants in localized regions of the benthic environment. This effect has been evident in numerous studies in estuaries and inland seas (Topping, 1976) and continental shelves (Stanford et al., 1981). Although there have been far fewer investigations of wastes discharged in the deep ocean (Chapter 1), we would expect much less localized accumulation of contaminants in deep-sea sediments from wastes dispersed at the ocean surface.

A major concern of waste disposal in nearshore regions is the conflict that may arise with the utilization of marine resources, especially fisheries. Many of the most productive fishing grounds are in coastal regions, and the nearshore habitats are essential in the life cycles of many other organisms. Near many of the coastal urban areas of the United States of America, shellfish harvesting has been prohibited because of contamination caused by wastes. These conflicts between waste disposal and marine resource use appear to be less severe in the open ocean.

In both the nearshore and deep ocean environments we can strive to utilize natural biological and geochemical cycles to assimilate wastes. This objective requires that we understand the characteristics of these cycles and how they differ between coastal and oceanic regions. These considerations must be waste-specific. Some wastes are inherently more compatible with natural cycles, whereas others can disrupt the natural mechanisms of degradation and remineralization, and others may be toxic to marine life.

17.3.   TRACERS: APPLICATION TO WASTE DISPOSAL

17.3.1.   Oceanic Properties

During the past decade there have been major advances in the understanding of marine processes and in the development of instrumentation. Much of this work has been motivated by a desire for fundamental knowledge of the ocean, but it is quite useful to apply this information to the problem of waste disposal in the ocean. As a consequence we are in a far better position now to anticipate the effects of ocean disposal than was the case 10 years ago.

The main features of oceanic circulation have been evident for nearly half a century (Sverdrup et al., 1942). This knowledge has been based on the distributions of physical and chemical properties such as temperature, salinity, dissolved oxygen, and nutrients. Over the years these patterns have been further defined and their details have become better resolved. The Geochemical Ocean Sections Study (GEOSECS) program of the U.S. National Science Foundation contributed substantially to this work in the past decade by obtaining a systematic set of oceanographic data (Bainbridge, 1981; Craig et al., 1981; Spencer et at., 1982), including selected radioactive tracers (Craig and Turekian, 1976; Broecker and Peng, 1982). Distributions of oceanic properties reveal the large-scale, integrated effects of various processes such as advection, mixing, and biological productivity (Riley, 1951; Veronis, 1977), but the actual mechanisms are generally more complex than the representations of oceanic models.

Recent studies have shown clearly the dynamic nature of deep ocean transport processes. In 1972 the GEOSECS program obtained tritium (^3H) data in the North Atlantic Ocean that demonstrated the relatively rapid transfer of waters from the high-latitude surface region to mid-latitude ocean depths. Tritium provided a fortuitous tracer of rapid deepwater transport because of its 12.44-y radioactive decay half-life, and because of its sudden input into the environment in the early 1960s. The large-scale testing of nuclear weapons in the atmosphere by the United States and the Union of Soviet Socialist Republics from 1961 to 1962 increased the global inventory of ^3H from the pre-nuclear era of between 0.5 and 5.0 kg to 600 kg

(Östlund and Brescher, 1982). This ^3H became associated with water molecules in the atmosphere and thus entered the hydrological cycle. In the early 1960s the surface waters of the ocean, particularly in the northern hemisphere where the weapon tests occurred, became labeled with tritiated water. It has now been possible to follow the downward mixing and transport of these waters into the intermediate and great depths of the ocean.

By 1972 the ^3H had reached the deep waters at 40°N. The transport of waters from the region near Iceland to the latitude of Georges Banks, in the North Atlantic Ocean, in about 10 y was considerably more rapid than would have been expected based on traditional concepts of the rates of deep ocean transport processes. A second investigation of ^3H in the deep waters of the North Atlantic was conducted by the Transient Tracers in the Ocean (TTO) program of the U.S. National Science Foundation in 1981. Along with a more extensive sampling plan than the GEOSECS study, the TTO investigators resampled the North Atlantic GEOSECS transect and determined the extent of deep ocean ^3H transport after two decades. The results of the GEOSECS and TTO ^3H investigations are compared in Fig. 17.1. The ^3H data in Fig. 17.1 have been corrected for radioactive decay to a common date of 1 January 1981, so that radioactive decay is not a factor in comparing the two sets of data. The 1981 data continue to show the southward transport of deep waters, with significant ^3H concentrations as far south as 30°N. In much of the North Atlantic near-bottom waters, there has been a 50% increase in ^3H between 1972 and 1981. Between 1972 and 1981 there continued to be an infusion of surface waters, along with their ^3H tracer, into the depths of the North Atlantic, and these waters continued their southward extension. The shapes of the curves in Fig. 17.1 are remarkably similar for the two data sets. The slight decrease in ^3H between 64°N

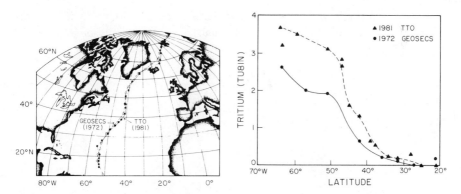

Figure 17.1. Tritium concentrations in near-bottom waters of the North Atlantic Ocean along a transect south of Iceland. The dots are GEOSECS data obtained in 1972; the triangles are TTO data obtained in 1981. Both sets of values are reported in tritium units (TU), defined as the atom ratio of ^3H to ^1H multiplied by 10^{18}; one *TU* unit is 7.088 disintegrations per minute per kilogram of water (H_2O). The scale for these tritium units is designated (TU81N), meaning that the values have been decay-corrected to 1 January 1981 using the new half-life of 12.44 y for ^3H. These data are from Östlund and Brescher (1982) and from Östlund (1983a).

and 48°N, followed by the large gradient from 48°N to 38°N, suggests significant differences in the transport rates of near-bottom waters with latitude along the transect of the stations.

A three-dimensional analysis along with considering the effects of mixing will be required for a detailed interpretation of the ^{3}H data in terms of deep ocean transport processes. Such information is available for the 1981 TTO expedition (Östlund, 1983a, 1983b). However, if the data along this one transect is representative of other North Atlantic Oceans sections, it could substantiate the views of Worthington (1976), who argued that there are several large-scale, linked gyres that transport and exchange waters at mid- and great depths in the ocean. The region between 48°N and 64°N could be one gyre system with rapid mixing processes within, and the region from 20°N to 35°N could be a second gyre system. The boundary between these two gyres at 35°N to 45°N could be a region of slower transfer of waters with latitude. These concepts of deep ocean transport, even though presently hypothetical and unproven, are of importance to considerations of deep ocean waste disposal. Only by improved understanding of oceanic processes can we expect to make reliable predictions about the fate of wastes placed in the deep ocean.

17.3.2. Lagrangian Tracers

Lagrangian tracer experiments have revealed the complexity of oceanic transport processes. Rossby and co-workers (Riser and Rossby, 1983; Rossby et al., 1983) have studied the trajectories of acoustically tracked floats at mid-depths in the western North Atlantic Ocean. The results of their work reveal several aspects of mid-ocean transport processes that are relevant to considerations of waste disposal and dumpsite site selection.

A large number of isobaric floats have been tracked for more than one year. Diagrams of the composite trajectories reveal the great diversity of water parcel displacements in the ocean (Fig. 17.2). Trajectories originating from a relatively

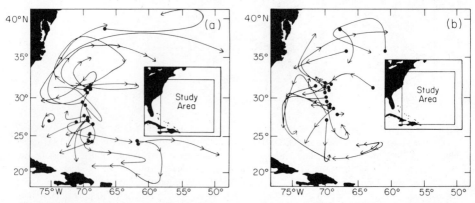

Figure 17.2. Trajectories of isobaric floats tracked over periods of months at depths of (a) 700 m and (b) 1500–2500 m. Adapted from Rossby et al. (1983).

small region of the ocean expand within months to cover substantial areas of the western Atlantic basin. There is considerable variation in the pattern of trajectories at 700 m and at depths of 1500–2500 m (Rossby et al., 1983). Riser and Rossby (1983) used these data to calculate the total kinetic energy within $2° \times 2°$ squares (Fig. 17.3). The influence of the Gulf Stream is evident in the northwestern portion of the area studied, but a larger scale gradient in kinetic energy is also evident, as well as the contrast between 700- and 2000-m depths. One of the very striking observations from these studies is the prevalence of eastward trajectories between 20°N and 28°N, which extends from the western boundary of the ocean basin to the Mid-Atlantic Ridge (Fig. 17.4). This eastward transport in the main thermocline is opposed to the main gyre circulation in the surface waters of the North Atlantic, and it is contrary to inferences based on a simple consideration of salt transport from the Mediterranean Sea outflow and of low-oxygen water from the productive regions off Africa (Rossby, 1981). A second revelation from these Lagrangian trajectories is the prevalence of eddy features in the mid-depth regions of the ocean (Fig. 17.5). These eddies tend to migrate westward, even in the region where the non-eddy trajectories are eastward. These observations support the notion that eddies can be self-propelled, rather than merely entrained in the large-scale flow field. Eddies may provide a mechanism for transporting both high-salinity water from the Mediterranean Sea and low-oxygen water from the eastern subtropical North Atlantic.

It is evident from these recent studies of oceanic circulation that waste plumes in oceanic regions may have very complex and unpredictable trajectories. The steady-state concepts of oceanic transport processes are of little value in anticipating how a specific parcel of water will be displaced in a specific region. The uncertainty of specific trajectories becomes even greater if one considers the shear

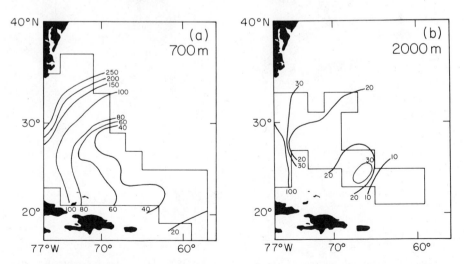

Figure 17.3. Kinetic energy contours (units of ergs g^{-1}) based on isobaric trajectories at (a) 700 m and (b) 2000 m. Based on the analysis of Riser and Rossby (1983).

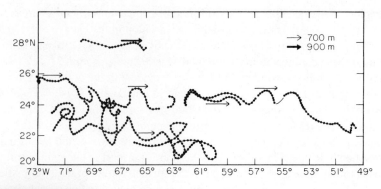

Figure 17.4. Trajectories of isobaric floats at depths of 700 m and 900 m, showing eastward displacements over periods of more that one month.

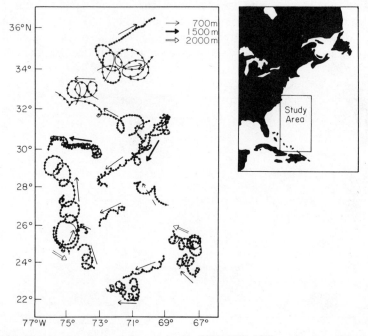

Figure 17.5. Trajectories of isobaric floats at depths of 700, 1500, 2000 m, showing eddy-type motion for periods of more than one month.

that exists vertically from the surface to the deep waters. The diversity of oceanic trajectories makes it difficult to define a region of impact from a particular disposal site, short of the entire ocean basin. On the other hand, this diversity implies the diffusive nature of oceanic displacements, which may serve to dilute contaminants.

17.4. OCEANIC CHEMICAL CYCLES

The basic premise in considering the open ocean as a potential site for waste disposal is that natural chemical cycles might be utilized to assimilate wastes without harm to humans or to the environment. These cycles reflect the combined effects of specific chemical processes, biological activity, and the long-term geochemical cycles that ultimately regulate the composition of the ocean. Several lines of research have converged in recent years to provide new insight into the principal aspects of these cycles. This information can be used in assessment of waste disposal in the deep ocean.

Recent advances in the reliability of sampling and analysis of seawater for trace elements have significantly expanded the number of chemical elements for which oceanic cycles can be delineated. Until recently it had not been possible to measure many trace elements in seawater without contaminating the samples. But reliable data now exist for Cu, Cd, Mn, Pb, Hg, Ni, Zn, Al, Ge, Se, V, and Fe (Bruland, 1983; Huizenga and Kester, 1983; Symes and Kester, 1985). These results show several distinctive types of chemical behavior for trace elements in the ocean. One characteristic is the nutrient-type distribution, similar to phosphate, nitrate, and silicate, in which the element is depleted in surface waters and is regenerated at depth (Chapter 1, Fig. 1.5). Biological processes in the ocean play a major role in the cycling of these trace elements, which include Cd, As, Ba, Zn, Ge, Ni, Se, and Fe. The inverse behavior in which there is surface enrichment and depletion at depth has been observed for Pb, and it is associated with input from the atmosphere and rapid removal from the water column (Bruland, 1983; Duce et al., 1972). Some elements such as Cu and Al show mid-depth minima in concentration, whereas others such as Mn have mid-depth maxima. For some elements, such as Fe, Mn, Cr, and As, it is evident that oxidation-reduction processes are very important in their oceanic chemical cycling. We can expect that when these elements enter the ocean from waste disposal operations, they will enter the prevailing chemical cycles, and as long as the incremental fluxes through the cycles caused by the wastes are small these elements should be assimilated or be blended into the background concentration.

Inasmuch as biological processes are a major cycling mechanism for many elements in the ocean, and since alterations in the natural ecosystem due to waste disposal should be avoided, it is important to define the influence of waste components on the biota. Considerable progress has been made on this problem relative to metals in marine systems. It has been demonstrated that Zn, Mn, and Fe can affect the reproductive rates of marine phytoplankton at very low ionic activities of

10^{-12}–10^{-10} (Brand et al., 1983). Studies have also shown that competitive interactions occur among metals such that the toxicity of copper to phytoplankton varies with the ionic activity of manganese (Sunda and Huntsman, 1983). Evidence has also been obtained that interactions among metals such as Fe, Mn, and Cu have different effects on related coastal and oceanic species of diatoms (Murphy et al., 1984).

It has been increasingly clear that the interactions between phytoplankton and trace metals depends greatly on the marine chemistry of the metals. Anderson and Morel (1982) have shown that the uptake of iron is influenced by solution phase complexation, redox, and photochemical reactions. Chemical data for quantitatively assessing these types of reactions in seawater are being continually improved (Kester et al., 1975; Turner et al., 1981; Millero and Schreiber, 1982; Zuehlke and Kester, 1983). A fairly good basis exists for predicting the inorganic speciation of metal constituents in wastes added to seawater, but there is great uncertainty concerning the role and behavior of organic substances that affect metal chemistry and marine organisms.

Some of the relationships among chemical processes, biological activity, and oceanic cycles are illustrated in Fig. 17.6. The factors that must be considered in going from chemical input to removal from the ocean include (1) a variety of chemical processes, (2) the interactions with organisms and solid phases, and (3) accu-

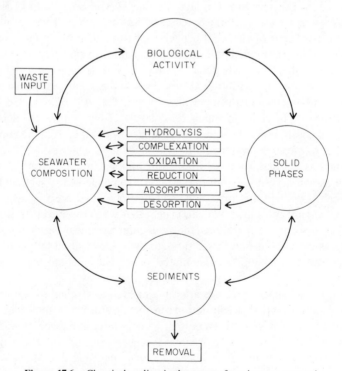

Figure 17.6. Chemical cycling in the ocean, from input to removal.

mulation in sediments. The ocean should be used for waste disposal only to the extent that the cycling and ultimate removal of harmful constituents are known.

One area of research that may be particularly helpful in the assessment of chemical cycles is the attempt to identify general relationships that exist between chemical properties of the elements and their marine geochemistry. The periodic behavior of the chemical elements with atomic number is well known. It is not surprising that this periodicity is also reflected in marine processes. Figure 17.7 shows the variation in seawater concentration with atomic number. Turner and Whitfield (1983) have shown that a few chemical properties of the elements, such as their electrostatic interactions, valence orbital energies, and covalent interactions can be related directly to biological activity and residence time in the ocean. As these relationships become defined more quantitatively, they will be helpful in predicting the consequences of waste input to the ocean.

The residence time, τ, of an element in the ocean provides another example of the role of chemical periodicity in marine chemistry. Residence time is the amount of an element in the ocean divided by the rate of its input to or removal from the ocean:

$$\tau = \frac{A}{r_i} = \frac{A}{r_o} \tag{1}$$

where A is the total amount of the element dissolved or in suspension in the ocean, r_i is the input rate, and r_o is the output rate. The concept of residence time assumes

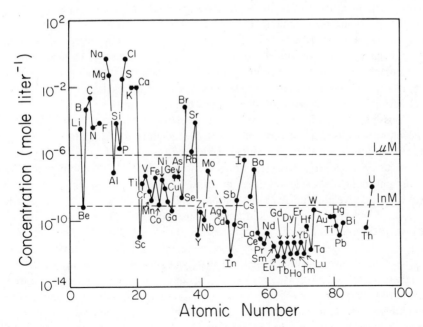

Figure 17.7. The concentration of elements in seawater as a periodic function of atomic number (after Turner and Whitfield, 1983).

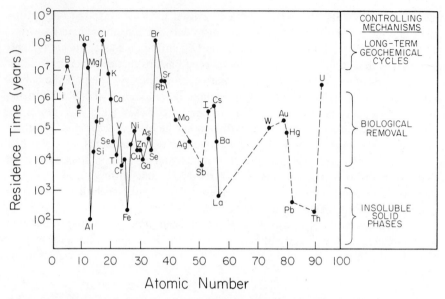

Figure 17.8.   Residence time (years) of elements in the ocean as a periodic function of atomic number. Solid lines connect adjacent elements (excluding the noble gases), and dashed lines span intervals where residence times are not available. Residence times are from Brewer (1975).

that the chemical cycles are in steady state, so that the rate of input and rate of output are equal for an element. Figure 17.8 shows the variation of residence time with atomic number. Figures 17.7 and 17.8 are not completely independent of each other, because residence times are based in part on the oceanic concentrations of the elements in seawater. However, residence times show a distinct periodicity with the alkali, alkaline earth, and halide ions having long residence times and with mid-period elements having short residence times.

A possible law of marine chemistry can be extracted from Fig. 17.8. Three basic controlling mechanisms determine the residence time of elements in the ocean: long-term geochemical cycles control residence times in the range of 10^7–10^8 y; biological cycles control residence times in the range of 10^4–10^6 y; efficient particle scavenging controls residence times of up to 1000 y. The long-term geochemical cycles include weathering reactions on land and in the ocean, and the subduction of oceanic sediments beneath continental plates (Chapter 1). These processes are of primary importance for B, Na, Mg, Cl, K, Br, Rb, Sr, and U. The role of biological cycling has long been known for elements such as Si, P, and Ca; recent studies have shown the importance of biological processes for many of the trace metals (Cu, Ni, Zn, Fe, Mn, V, Ba, Hg, I, and As). A few elements are distinguished by very short residence times (Al, Fe, La, Pb, and Th). The common denominator in the marine chemistry of these elements is their affinity for particulate phases, beyond mere biological removal. These elements form insoluble hydroxide phases at the seawater pH of ~8.

These general considerations of marine chemical cycles can be applied useful to the problem of waste disposal in the open ocean. From a classification of ele- ments in terms of their removal mechanisms and residence times it becomes pos- sible to project the time scales and perturbations to chemical cycles that can result from waste input to the ocean.

17.5 TYPES OF WASTES SUITABLE FOR DEEP OCEAN DISPOSAL

When evaluating a decision to dispose of wastes in the ocean, it is important to consider the specific nature of the waste, the method of disposal, and the charac- teristics of the marine environment in which the waste will be placed. It may be useful to examine what generalizations might be drawn about those wastes that are most likely to be assimilated by the marine environment without significant impacts.

Incineration of combustible wastes at sea appears to be a viable method of dis- posal. Large quantities of toxic organic chemicals can be incinerated to carbon dioxide, water, acidic gases (mainly HCl), and a small amount of residual material. The dispersive nature of the marine atmosphere and the upper layers of the ocean greatly reduce the likelihood that the products of incineration will be concentrated sufficiently in the ecosystem to produce an impact. The high buffering capacity of seawater (~ 2.4 meq liter^{-1}) reduces the chance that there will be a significant change in pH.

If incineration at sea is selected as the means of destroying certain wastes, it should be recognized that this is an inherently dispersive strategy, and dispersion should be maximized. For example, from an environmental point of view, it is illogical to define a limited geographical disposal site for incineration. If inciner- ation sites were lanes across the ocean, rather than a fixed 10 km $\times$ 10 km region, there would be less likelihood of the incineration activity harming the environment. Obviously, incineration sites should not be in close proximity to inhabited areas or fishing grounds. The identifiable plumes from an incineration ship should not im- pinge on maritime transportation. It may be justifiable to exclude incineration on coastal seas such as the Baltic Sea, the North Sea, the Mediterranean Sea, and the Gulf of Mexico.

It may seem ironic to consider incineration at sea as a method of waste disposal when there is increasing concern and data showing the detrimental effects of acid rain on land, but there are several important distinctions between these two issues. The effects of acid rain illustrate the long-term and cumulative consequences on land and on freshwater environments at long distances from the source of the acidic gases.

Three of the factors that distinguish acid rain from at-sea incineration plumes are that the land-based sources of acidic gases and particles are at fixed locations for decades, the fresh waters of lakes have on the average one-third lower buffering capacity than seawater (Stumm and Morgan, 1981), and vegetation can be directly

ances. Most investigations of incineration at sea have em-
nts of acidic gases (such as HCl), and indicators of com-
CO and CO_2), and residual waste components. Atten-
particulate material that results from the combustion process,
nsiderable evidence for long-range atmospheric transport of par-
al., 1980).

.o. SUMMARY AND CONCLUSIONS

The results obtained from marine research to date do not preclude the use of the open ocean for disposal of some types of wastes. It seems likely that some wastes can be dispersed and diluted in the ocean, and can be assimilated by natural biogeochemical cycles, without detriment to marine resources and biota. In fact, the ocean has been serving this role on a limited basis for centuries. Nevertheless, we should proceed with caution as we contemplate the ability of the ocean to accommodate additional types or quantities of wastes.

The capacity of the ocean to assimilate some wastes is finite. It is not sufficient to merely regard the ocean as a suitable disposal site because of its great volume, its massive background of natural substances, or its remoteness from human activity. Within the past two decades we have begun to recognize that human actions can produce global changes in the atmosphere, ocean, and biosphere. We have seen the effects of ocean contamination by persistent synthetic organic compounds. We are now seeing global increases in atmospheric CO_2.

One of the difficulties in using the open ocean for waste disposal is devising a method of verifying that wastes are not producing subtle, but significant, changes in the marine ecosystem. Estuaries and coastal waters generally have a smaller capacity to assimilate wastes than the open ocean, but they have the advantage that detrimental effects are more likely to be detected and addressed by society. We must develop effective means to assure that the quality of the deep ocean ecosystem will not be degraded by waste disposal practices.

Although a great deal is known about the ocean, we must remind ourselves that discoveries about the ocean are being made at a rapid rate. It is highly likely that future marine research will reveal presently unsuspected aspects of the ocean and of the processes occurring within the sea. One of the best safeguards for ensuring maximum utilization of the ocean's resources, including its use for waste disposal, without detrimental effects, is to continue the vigorous pursuit of marine research. Some of this research should be directed toward the specific issues related to marine pollution. But it is also essential that we recognize the importance of fundamental studies of oceanic processes.

ACKNOWLEDGMENTS

We thank T. P. O'Connor for discussions about this chapter. We also thank T. D. Bewig and E. E. Main for their editorial assistance in the preparation of this chapter. This work was supported by National Ocean Service, U.S. National Ocean and Atmospheric Administration. Opinions expressed are the authors' and do not necessarily reflect those of the U.S. Government.

REFERENCES

Anderson, M. A., and F. M. M. Morel. 1982. The influence of aqueous iron chemistry on the uptake of iron by the coastal diatom *Thalassiosira weisflogii*. *Limnology and Oceanography*, **27**, 789–813.

Bainbridge, A. E. 1981. GEOSECS Atlantic Expedition, Vol. 2, Sections and Profiles. U.S. National Science Foundation, Washington, D.C., 198 pp.

Brand, L. E., W. G. Sunda, and R. R. L. Guillard. 1983. Limitation of marine phytoplankton reproductive rates by zinc, manganese, and iron. *Limnology and Oceanography*, **28**, 1182–1198.

Brewer, P. G. 1975. Minor elements in sea water. *In:* Chemical Oceanography, 2nd Edition, Vol. 1, J. P. Riley and G. Skirrow, (Eds.). Academic Press, London, pp. 415–496.

Broecker, W. S., and T-H. Peng. 1982. Tracers in the Sea. Eldigio Press, Columbia University, Palisades, New York, 690 pp.

Bruland, K. W. 1983. Trace elements in sea water. *In:* Chemical Oceanography, 2nd Edition, Vol. 8, J. P. Riley and R. Chester, (Eds.). Academic Press, London, pp. 157–220.

Craig, H., and K. K. Turekian. 1976. The GEOSECS program: 1973–1976. *Earth and Planetary Science Letters*, **32**, 217–219.

Craig, H., W. S. Broecker, and D. Spencer. 1981. GEOSECS Pacific Expedition, Vol. 4, Sections and Profiles. U.S. National Science Foundation, Washington, D.C., 251 pp.

Duce, R. A., J. G. Quinn, C. E. Olney, S. R. Piotrowicz, B. J. Ray, and T. L. Wade. 1972. Enrichment of heavy metals and organic compounds in the surface microlayer of Narragansett Bay, Rhode Island. *Science*, **176**, 161–163.

Huizenga, D. L., and D. R. Kester. 1983. The distribution of total and electrochemically available copper in the northwestern Atlantic Ocean. *Marine Chemistry*, **13**, 281–291.

Kester, D. R., R. H. Byrne, and Y-J. Liang. 1975. Redox reactions and solution complexes of iron in marine systems. *In:* Marine Chemistry in the Coastal Environment, T. M. Church (Ed.). ACS Symposium Series No. 18, American Chemical Society, Washington, D.C., pp. 56–79.

Millero, F. J., and D. R. Schreiber. 1982. Use of the ion pairing model to estimate activity coefficients of the ionic components of natural waters. *American Journal of Science*, **282**, 1508–1540.

Murphy, L. S., R. R. L. Guillard, and J. F. Brown. 1984. The effects of iron and manganese on copper sensitivity in diatoms: Differences in the responses of closely related neritic and oceanic species. *Biological Oceanography*, **3**, 187–201.

Östlund, H. G. 1983a. Tritium and Radiocarbon, TTO Western North Atlantic Section, GEOSECS Re-Occupation. Tritium Laboratory Data Release 83-07, Rosenstiel School of Marine and Atmospheric Science, University of Miami, Florida, 66 pp.

Östlund, H. G. 1983b. TTO North Atlantic Study, Tritium and Radiocarbon. Tritium Laboratory Data Release 83-35, Rosenstiel School of Marine and Atmospheric Science, University of Miami, Florida, 100 pp.

3rescher. 1982. GEOSECS Tritium. Tritium Laboratory Data Re-
ᵉl School of Marine and Atmospheric Science, University of

...er, A. Semb, and T. J. Conway. 1980. High winter concentrations
...orwegian Arctic and transport from Eurasia. *Nature,* **287,** 824–826.

..ɔl. Oxygen, phosphate, and nitrate in the Atlantic Ocean. *Bulletin of the
..m Oceanographic Collection,* **13,** 1–126.

.ɔ. C., and H. T. Rossby. 1983. Quasi-Lagrangian structure and variability of the
subtropical western North Atlantic circulation. *Journal of Marine Research,* **41,** 127–
162.

Rossby, H. T., S. C. Riser, and A. J. Mariano. 1983. The western North Atlantic—A Lagrangian viewpoint. *In:* Eddies in Marine Science, A. R. Robinson (Ed.). Springer-
Verlag, Berlin, pp. 66–91.

Rossby, T. 1981. Eddies and the general circulation. *In:* Woods Hole Oceanographic Institution 50th Anniversary Volume, M. Sears (Ed.). Springer-Verlag, Berlin, pp. 137–161.

Spencer, D. W., W. S. Broecker, H. Craig, and R. F. Weiss. 1982. GEOSECS Indian Ocean
Expedition, Vol. 6, Sections and Profiles. U.S. National Science Foundation, Washington, D.C., 142 pp.

Stanford, H. M., J. S. O'Connor, and R. L. Swanson. 1981. The effects of ocean dumping
on the New York Bight ecosystem. *In:* Ocean Dumping of Industrial Wastes, B. H.
Ketchum, D. R. Kester, and P. K. Park (Eds.). Plenum Press, New York, pp. 53–86.

Stumm, W., and J. J. Morgan. 1981. Aquatic Chemistry: An Introduction Emphasizing
Chemical Equilibria in Natural Waters. Wiley-Interscience, New York, 780 pp.

Sunda, W. G., and S. A. Huntsman. 1983. Effect of competitive interactions between manganese and copper on cellular manganese and growth in estuarine and oceanic species
of the diatom *Thalassiosira. Limnology and Oceanography,* **28,** 924–934.

Sverdrup, H. U., M. W. Johnson, and R. H. Fleming. 1942. The Oceans. Prentice-Hall,
Englewood Cliffs, New Jersey, 1060 pp.

Symes, J., and D. R. Kester. 1985. The distribution of iron in the northwest Atlantic. *Marine
Chemistry,* in press.

Topping, G. 1976. Sewage and the sea. *In:* Marine Pollution, R. Johnston (Ed.). Academic
Press, London, pp. 303–351.

Turner, D. R., and M. Whitfield. 1983. Inorganic controls on the biogeochemical cycle of
the elements in the ocean. *In:* Environmental Biochemistry, R. Hallberg, (Ed.). Ecological Bulletin No. 35, Stockholm, pp. 9–37.

Turner, D. R., M. Whitfield, and A. G. Dickson. 1981. The equilibrium speciation of dissolved components in freshwater and seawater at 25°C and 1 atm pressure. *Geochimica
et Cosmochimica Acta,* **45,** 855–881.

Veronis, G. 1977. Use of tracers in circulation studies. *In:* The Sea: Ideas and Observations
on Progress in the Study of the Sea, Vol. 6, E. D. Goldberg, I. N. McCave, J. J.
O'Brien, and J. H. Steele (Eds.). Wiley-Interscience, New York, pp. 169–188.

Worthington, L. V. 1976. On the North Atlantic Circulation. The Johns Hopkins University
Press, Baltimore, Maryland, 110 pp.

Zuehlke, R. W., and D. R. Kester. 1983. Ultraviolet spectroscopic determination of the
stability constants for copper carbonate and bicarbonate complexes up to the ionic
strength of seawater. *Marine Chemistry,* **13,** 203–226.

AUTHOR INDEX

Italicized numbers indicate pages on which full references appear.

Abdel-Reheim, H., *207, 240*
Ackerman, D. G., 60, 63, 64, 65, 66, 67, *69, 71, 76, 88*
Adams, J. W., *69*
American Conference of Governmental and Industrial Hygienists, 68, *70*
American Public Health Association, 192, 202, *206*
American Society for Testing and Materials (ASTM), 281, *284*
Anastasi, J. L., *71*
Anderson, D. R., *26, 27*
Anderson, G. C., *258*
Anderson, M. A., 328, *333*
Anderson, P. W., 189, 204, *206*
Anderson, R. F., *25*
Andis, J. D., 68, *70*
Anonymous, 48, *50*
Arnold, R. G., *24*
Arrhenius, G., 265, 267, *269*
Arrow, K. J., 311, *314*
Arthur D. Little, Inc., 273, *284*
Atkinson, C. A., *70*
Atlas, E., 83, *88*, 189, *206*, 229, *239*
Atlas, R. M., *207*
Attwell, R. W., *208*
Austin, B., 204, 205, *206*

Baboolal, L. B., *51, 71, 113*
Bächmann, K., *114*
Backus, R. H., 137, *143*
Badley, J. H., 58, *70*, 77, 78, *88*
Bain, N., 192, *206*
Bainbridge, A. E., 322, *334*
Barber, R. T., 18, *24*
Barcelona Convention, 49, *50*
Barniske, L., 34, 35, *50*, 117, *122*
Bascom, W., 12, *24*
Baumol, W. J., 311, *314*
Bayer, A. G., 121, *122*
Beard, J. H., III, 64, *70*
Belastock, R. A., *240*

Bendiner, W. P., 13, *26*
Bensten, L. C., *29*
Berdugo, V., 236, *239*
Berman, M. S., 236, *239*
Bernstein, R. L., *29*
Bidleman, T. F., 83, *88*
Biggons, N. E., 192, *206*
Bird, J. L., 230, 231, *239*
Bisagni, J. J., 13, *24*, 79, *88*, 127, 131, *143, 144*
Bishop, W. P., 23, *24*
Black, J. R. H., 273, *284*
Bodennec, G., *24*
Bowman, T. E., 229, *239*
Boyle, E. A., 16, *24*
Brand, L. E., 328, *333*
Brandsma, M. G., 245, *257*
Breeding, R. J., 95, *113*
Brescher, R., 323, *334*
Brewer, P. G., 15, *24*, 173, *184*, 330, *333*
Broecker, W. S., 322, *333, 334*
Brooks, J. M., 12, *24*, 207, *240*
Brooks, N. H., 5, 14, *24*
Brown, D. P., *71*
Brown, J. F., 28, *333*
Brown, M. F., 172, 176, *184*
Bruland, K. W., 16, 17, *25, 27*, 327, *333*
Brush, L. H., *27*
Buat-Menard, P., *113*
Buchanan, R. E., 192, 204, *206*
Bundesgesetzblatt II, 116, *122*
Burkholder, P. R., 202, 204, *207*
Burns, R. E., *258*
Byrne, R. H., *333*

Calvert, S. E., 266, *269*
Camp, Dresser & McKee, 289, 290, 296, 297, *314*
Capuzzo, J. M., 15, *25*, 236, *239, 315*
Carey, A. G., Jr., *29*
Carmichael, G. R., 107, *113*
Carnes, M., *144*
Carnes, R. A., 81, *88*

'5

, 145, 245, 257
.ɔ9
.ₓ5
, ₂02, 206
. D., 15, 25
.ₑt, R., 107, 113
.ₑster, R., 17, 29
Cheung, K., 269
Christainsen, G. B., 292, 314
Clark, J. P., 284
Clausen, J. F., 59, 61, 69, 70, 75, 88, 93, 95, 113
Cole, F. A., 29
Colwell, R. R., 19, 25, 204, 205, 206, 207, 208
Compaan, H., 39, 50
Congdon, S. W., 88
Conrad, B., 206
Conway, I. J., 334
Corey, R. J., 68, 70
Corkett, C. J., 236, 240
Cotter, J. E., 71
Craig, H., 322, 333, 334
Crane, S., 269
Crawford, C. L., 71
Csanady, G. T., 12, 13, 25, 127, 128, 133, 135, 136, 144, 172, 184, 203, 207, 245, 257
Cunningham, N. J., 69
Curl, H., Jr., 29
Curtis, C. E., 7, 25

Daley, R. J., 192, 207
Dames and Moore and EIC Corporation, 274, 277, 279, 284
Darcy, K., 240
Dayal, R., 22, 25
Dean, D., 71
DeBeu, W. A., 29
Deepak, A., 245, 247, 248, 258
Defense Logistics Agency, 80, 88
deLappe, B. W., 17, 25
Deming, J. W., 19, 25, 207, 208
dePass, V. E., 29
Des Rosiers, P. E., 72, 90
Deuser, W. G., 15, 25
Devine, M., 288, 289, 315
Dewling, R. T., 189, 204, 206
Dickson, A. G., 334

Dietz, A. S., 30
Divoky, D. J., 245, 257
Dohnert, E. H., 69
Donaghay, P. L., 174, 184
Donovan, T. J., 207
Drehsen, M. E., 70
Duce, R. A., 327, 333
Duedall, I. W., 5, 7, 10, 11, 25, 27, 29, 281, 284
Dunst, M., 107, 113

Eagle, R. A., 20, 25
Ecological Analysts, Inc., and SEAM Ocean, Inc., 289, 314
Eimhjellen, K., 27
Elder, D. L., 15, 17, 26
Elder, J. W., 136, 144
Elliott, J. S., 270
Engleman, G. G., 70
Englert, T. R., 113
Eppel, D., 107, 110, 113
Erdheim, E., 315
Erickson, K. L., 27
Estes, E. D., 71
Ettlich, W. F., 295, 304, 308, 309, 314
Evans, T. M., 207
Ewart, T. E., 13, 26

Fabian, H., 118, 122
Fabian, H. W., 93, 113
Faisst, W. K., 14, 24, 26
Farmanfarmaian, A., 27
Farre, J. A., 20, 29
Farrington, J. W., 289, 315
Fay, R. R., 89
Ferguson, R. L., 19, 30
Fischer, H. B., 133, 136, 141, 144
Fisher, A. C., 311, 314
Fisher, H. J., 51, 68, 70, 71, 88, 113
Fisk, M. B., 261, 269, 270
Fitzgerald, W. F., 17, 26
Fitzsimmons, C. K., 72, 90
Flanagan, F. J., 264, 270
Fleer, A. P., 24
Fleming, R. H., 334
Flierl, G. R., 143, 150, 169
Flynn, F. E., 70
Flynn, N. W., 70
Forstner, V., 17, 29
Fowler, S. W., 15, 17, 25, 26, 30
Francisco, D. E., 192, 207
Franks, R. P., 16, 25
Frazer, J. Z., 261, 269, 270

Fredericks, A. D., *89*
Fredericks, E. M., *70, 88*
Frost, B. W., 228, 230, 231, *239, 240*
Frye, D., 127, *144*
Fuhrmann, M., *25*
Furniss, A. L., 192, *207*

Gardner, W. D., 15, 19, *29*
Garges, S., *206*
GESAMP, 42, *50*
Giam, C. S., 82, 83, *88, 206, 239*
Gibbons, N. E., 204, *206*
Gibson, D. W., 192, *207*
Gill, G. A., *26*
Goldberg, E. E., 83, *88*
Gomez, L. S., 18, *27, 28*
Gonzalez, J. G., 229, *239*
Gordon, R. B., 128, *144*
Gorman, P., 66, *71*
Gottfried, D., 264, *270*
Grant, A., *69*
Grant, H. L., 248, *257*
Grassle, J. F., 18, 19, *26*
Gregory, G. L., 103, *113*
Gross, M. G., 20, *29*
Guard, H. E., *239*
Guarino, C. F., 290, *315*
Guillard, R. R. L., 18, *30, 333*
Gunn, B., *208*
Guse, W., *122*
Guthrie, R. K., *206*
Gutknecht, W. F., *71*
Guttman, M. A., 65, 68, *70*
Gyllenberg, G., 237, *239*

Hada, H. S., 205, *207*
Haedrich, R. L., *29*
Hagen, A. A., 8, *26*
Hardiman, P. A., *25*
Harding, E. E., *206*
Harms, J., 100, *113*
Harrington, J., *71*
Harris, J. C., *69*
Harris, R. P., *239, 240*
Harriss, R. C., 268, *270*
Harvey, G. R., 17, *26*
Harvey, R. S., *206*
Haugen, E. M., *28*
Häuser, J., *113*
Hausknecht, K. A., *88*
Haveman, R. H., 292, *314*
Heath, G. R., 23, *26, 269*
Heaton, M. G., *25*

Heicklen, J., 245, 249, *257*
Heinle, D. R., 236, *239*
Helsinki Convention, 49, *50*
Hendrie, M. S., *207*
Hering, V. N., 267, *270*
Herrmann, W., 98, *114*
Hess, F. R., 127, *145*
Heubsch, I. O., 247, *257*
Higgo, J. J. W., *25*
Hites, R. A., 17, *27*
Hittinger, R. C., *27, 184*
Hoar, P. R., *240*
Hobbie, J. E., 192, *207*
Hobbs, G., *207*
Hoffman, K.-D., *122*
Holland, W. R., *29*
Hollister, C. D., 23, *24, 26*
Hood, D. W., 11, *26*
Houston, N. C., *207*
Hubbard, G. F., *89, 207, 240*
Hubred, G. L., 275, *284*
Huested, S. S., *24*
Huizenga, D. L., 19, *26,* 327, *333*
Hunt, J. R., 15, *26,* 245, *257*
Huntsman, S. A., 19, *26,* 328, *334*

Ichiye, T., 135, *144*
Ikeda, T., *240*
Ikegaki, Y., 189, *207*
Inoue, M., *144*
Inter-Governmental Maritime Consultative
   Organization (IMCO), 5, 11, *26,* 37, 41, 42,
   44, *50,* 75, *88*
Interstate Sanitation Commission, 289, 290,
   314, 315
Ishikawa, T., 189, *207*

Jackson, B., *71*
Jackson, G. A., 5, *24, 27*
James, B. M., *89*
Jangi, M. S., *208*
Jannasch, H. W., 19, *27,* 202, *207*
Jasper, S., *207*
Jenkins, R. W., 280, *284*
Johnson, B. H., 126, *144*
Johnson, M. W., *334*
Johnson, R. J., 68, *69, 70, 71, 88, 113*
Jones, G. E., 202, *207*
Jones, S. P., *24*
Joranger, E., *334*
Jungclaus, G., 66, *71*

Kamlet, K. S., 10, *27,* 37, *50*

Kaneko, T., 204, *207*
Keith, K. M., 280, *284*
Kennedy, E. A., *89*
Kester, D. R., 7, 12, 17, 19, *25, 26, 27, 28, 29, 143,* 172, 173, 184, 185, 281, *284,* 327, 328, *333, 334*
Ketchum, B. H., 5, *25, 27, 29,* 281, *284*
Kiefer, D. A., *70*
Kim, J. P., *26*
King, T. B., *284*
Klonis, H. B., *113*
Klos, E. G., 174, *184*
Knauer, G. A., 15, 19, *27*
Knowles, S. C., 237, *240*
Koh, R. C. Y., 14, *24, 27,* 126, *145,* 245, 257
Kohn, D., 127, *145*
Korkisch, J., *269*
Krichevsky, M. I., *207*
Kritz, M. A., 107, *113*, 248, *258*
Krutilla, J. V., 311, *315*
Kupferman, S. L., 14, *27*

Laflamme, R. E., 17, *27*
Lahmann, W., *113*
Lai, R., 277, *284*
Lancaster, B. A., 15, *25,* 236, *239*
Landing, W. M., 17, *27*
Lasker, R., 228, *240*
Laughlin, R. B., Jr., 237, *239*
Laul, J. C., *27*
Lavelle, J. W., *258*
LeChevallier, M. W., 192, *207*
Lee, J. V., *207*
Lee, W. Y., 229, 236, 237, *239*
Leinen, M., *26*
Lenhard, U., 97, *113*
Lentzen, D. E., 60, *71*
Lerman, A., 14, *27*
Leschine, T. M., *315*
Letterman, E. F., *25*
Levins, P. L., *69*
Liang, Y-J., *333*
Lin, C., *113*
Lisitzin, A. P., 22, *27*
Lodge, J. P., Jr., *113*
Lohse, H., *113*
Luft, T. A., 35, *51*
Lundqvist, G., 237, *239*
Lutzke, K., 120, *122*

MacLean, S. A., 12, *27*
McRoy, C. P., 11, *26*

McVey, D. R., 22, *27*
Maddalone, R. F., *88*
Mah, R. A., *207*
Mariano, A. J., 324, 325, *334*
Martin, J. H., 15, 19, *27*
Martinez, G., *206, 239*
Mattern, R. V., 79, *89*
Matthews, B. J., *88*
Mayer, G., *315*
Mellin, T., *269*
Mero, J. L., 267, *270*
Miller, J. N., 10, *25*
Millero, F. J., 328, *333*
Milliman, J. D., 22, *28*
Mitchell, N. T., 9, *28*
Mizenko, D., 132, 137, *145*
Moilliet, A., 248, *257*
Moon, E. L., *70, 88, 113*
Moore, T. C., Jr., *269*
Morel, F. M. M., 15, 19, *28,* 328, *333*
Morel-Laurens, N. M. L., 19, *28*
Morelli, J., *113*
Morgan, J. J., 245, *258,* 331, *334*
Moyer, R. H., 103, *113*
Mukherji, P., 12, 17, *27, 28,* 172, *184,* 185
Müller, A., *113*
Mullin, M. M., 18, *28,* 231, *239*
Murphy, L. S., 12, *28,* 238, *240,* 328, *333*

Nakao, S., *269*
Neff, G. S., *88*
Ng, J., Jr., *239*
Nicol, J. A. C., 229, 236, *239*
Niiler, P. P., *29*
Norton, M. G., *25*
Nozaki, Y., *24*
Nuclear Energy Agency-Organisation for Economic Co-Operation and Development, 7, *28*
Nunny, R. S., *25*

Oberacher, D. A., 81, *88*
O'Connor, J. S., *30, 315*
O'Connor, T. P., 8, *28,* 36, 40, *51, 145,* 188, *207,* 229, 237, *239, 315*
Offutt, C. K., *72, 90*
O'Hara, S. C., *239, 240*
Okami, Y., 202, *207*
Okazaki, T., 202, *207*
Okubo, A., 13, *28,* 135, *145*
Olney, C. E., *88, 333*
Olsen, D. B., 137, *143, 145*
Orndorff, S. A., 204, *207*

Orr, M. H., 127, *145*
Oslo Commission, 7, *29*
Oslo Convention, 49, *51*
Osterberg, C., 15, *29*
Östlund, H. G., *30,* 323, 324, *333, 334*
Ott, F. S., 236, 237, *240*
Ozturgut, E., 245, 246, *258*

Paffenhöfer, G.-A., 236, 237, *240*
Paige, S. F., 34, *51,* 68, *71,* 93, *113*
Palmer, H. D., 20, *29*
Park, P. K., 5, 11, *25, 27, 29,* 36, 40, 51,
    145, 188, *207, 240,* 280, 281, *284,*
    315
Pate, J. B., *113*
Patterson, C. C., 17, *29*
Pavish, D., 129, 130, *145*
Payne, J. R., *25*
PEDCO Environmental Inc., 281, *284*
Peele, E. R., 189, 191, 202, 203, 204, *207,*
    208
Peng, T-H., 322, *333*
Pequegnat, W. E., 75, 86, *89*
Pfister, R. M., 202, 204, *207*
Piotrowicz, S. R., *333*
Pokrowsky, P., 98, 103, *114*
Polloni, P. T., *29*
Presley, B. J., 22, *30,* 229, 237, *240*
Price, N. B., *269*
Pritchard, R. W., 13, *28*
Pulaski, E. P., *71*

Quay, P. D., *30*
Quinn, J. G., *333*

Rabin, A. C., *207*
Rahn, K. A., 332, *334*
Rancher, J., 107, *113*
Ray, B. J., *333*
Reed, J. G., 278, 280, *284*
Reeve, M. R., 236, *240*
Rex, M. A., 18, *29*
Rice, C. P., *88*
Richardson, P. L., *143*
Riley, G. A., 322, *334*
Riley, J. P., 17, *29*
Risebrough, R. W., *25*
Riser, S. C., 324, 325, *334*
Robertson, R., 141, *145*
Robias, R. F., *88*
Rolfe, M. S., *25*
Rose, C. D., 14, *29*
Ross, E. H., *25*

Rossby, H. T., 324, 325, *334*
Rowe, G. T., 15, 18, 19, *29,* 127, *145*
Russell, C. L., 311, *315*
Ryan, W. B. F., 20, *29*
Ryther, J. H., 5, 18, *24, 29,* 228, *240*

Salomons, W., 7, 17, *29*
Sanders, H. L., 18, *29*
Sanders, J. G., 228, *240*
Sarro, T. L., *70*
Sauer, T. C., Jr., *24, 207,* 229, *240*
Savelsberg, M., *114*
Schaule, B. K., 17, *29*
Schaum, J., 64, *70*
Scheyer, K. H., *51, 71,* 88, *113*
Schiff, S. L., 15, *28*
Schindler, R. N., 97, *113*
Schmidt, T. T., *25*
Schmitz, W. J., Jr., 13, *29*
Schofield, J. S., *240*
Schreiber, D. R., 328, *333*
Schwab, C. R., 189, 202, *207,* 229, 237,
    240
Schwarz, J. R., *208*
Sears, D. R., *113*
Segfried, W. E., Jr., *27*
Seidler, R. J., *207*
Semb, A., *334*
Shain, S. A., 79, *89*
Shaugh, A. M., *51, 71,* 113
Sheesley, T. R., *113*
Sheffield, S. J., *70*
Shepard, F. P., 20, *29*
Shepard, L. E., *27*
Shewan, J. M., 192, *206*
Shih, C. C., 56, *68, 69, 70, 71,* 88, *113*
Shokes, R. F., *70*
Sholkovitz, E. R., 15, *30*
Shropshire, J. C., *25*
Sieburth, J. McN., 202, 204, *208*
Sillig, M., 97, *114*
Simidu, U., 204, 205, *206, 208*
Simpson, D. C., 127, 133, *145,* 237, *240*
Singleton, F. L., 189, 191, 202, *206, 207, 208*
Sizemore, R. K., 205, *207, 208*
Sklarew, R. C., 128, 129, *145*
Small, L. F., 15, *30*
Smith, P. W., 228, *240*
Sorem, R. K., 272, *284*
Spaulding, M., 128, 129, 141, *145*
Spence, A. M., 311, *315*
Spencer, D. W., *24,* 322, *333, 334*
Spooner, M. F., 236, *240*

Springer, A. M., *25*
Stafford, T., *71*
Staff of SCCWRP, *24*
Stanford, H. M., 12, *30, 315,* 321, *334*
Stauffer, J. L., *69*
Steele, J. H., 228, *240*
Stegeman, J. J., 20, *30*
Steinhauer, W. G., 17, *26*
Stookey, L. L., 176, *185*
Stumm, W., 245, *258,* 331, *334*
Stuvier, M., 23, *30*
Summerhayes, C. P., 267, *270*
Sunda, W. G., 18, 19, *26, 30,* 328, *333,*
334
Sverdrup, H. O., 322, *334*
Swanson, R. L., *30,* 288, 289, 291, 292,
315
Swartz, R. C., 20, *29*
Swift, S. A., *258*
Symes, J., 327, *334*

Taga, N., *206, 208*
Tan, R. L., *51, 70, 71, 113*
Tanzer, F., *113*
Telfer, A., *70, 88*
Temple, Barker and Sloane, Inc., 291, *315*
TerEco Corporation, 65, 68, 69, *71,* 79, 80,
86, *89*
Thomas, T. J., 61, 64, *71*
Thorne, C. F., *51, 71, 113*
Thrun, K. E., *69*
Tihansky, D. P., 310, *315*
Tobias, R. F., *69, 70, 88, 113*
Toft, L., *71*
Topping, G., 321, *334*
Trefry, J. H., 22, *30, 240*
Tsai, A., *269*
Turekian, K. K., 266, *270,* 322, *333*
Turner, D. R., 328, 329, *334*

Unger, S. L., *70*
U.S. Air Force, 61, 63, *71*
U.S. Army Corps of Engineers, 10, *30*
U.S. Congress, 55, *71,* 74, *89*
U.S. Department of Commerce, 68, *71*
U.S. Department of State and U.S. Environ-
mental Protection Agency, 55, *71,* 76, *89*
U.S. EPA, 10, *30,* 56, 59, 61, 62, 67, 68, *71,*
72, 79, 80, 81, *90,* 289, 291, 294, 296, 297,
315
U.S. House of Representatives, 305, *315*
U.S. National Academy of Sciences, 17, *30*
Unlu, M. Y., *30*

Upham, H. C., 202, 204, 205, *208*

Van Boxtel, R., *30*
Van Dyke, G. R., *70*
Vargo, S. L., 237, *240*
Vastano, A. C., *143*
Veldkamp, H., 203, *208*
Venezia, R. A., 59, 69, *72*
Verber, J. L., *315*
Veronis, G., 322, *334*
Vier Korn-Rudolph, B., 97, 99, *114*
Vigon, B., *71*
Vogel, W. M., 248, *257*

Wade, T. L., *333*
Wagoner, D. E., *71*
Walter, M. A., *240*
Ward, T. J., *29*
Wastler, T. A., 58, 59, 68, 69, *72,* 75, 77, 80, *89, 90*
Webster, F., 13, *30*
Wedepohl, K. H., 266, *269*
Weikard, J., 93, *114*
Weisenburg, D. A., *24*
Weiss, R. F., *334*
Weitkamp, C., 99, *113, 114*
Weller, P. J., *70*
White, M., *270*
Whitfield, M., 329, *334*
Wiebe, P. H., *143*
Williams, G., 127, *144*
Williams, W. G., 13, *30*
Willis, J. P., 266, 267, *270*
Wilson, L. L., *270*
Wilson, T. R. S., 173, *185*
Winters, K., *239*
Wirsen, C. O., 19, *27*
Wolf, G., *269*
Wolf, S. D., *70*
Wood, E. J. E., 202, *208*
Woodland, L. R., *69*
Wormuth, J. H., *143,* 229, *240*
Worthington, L. V., 324, *334*
Wulf, H., 93, *114*

Yang, D. K., *113*
Yayanos, A. A., 19, *30*
Yudelson, J., 135, *145*
Yue, G. K., 245, 247, 248, *258*

Zee, C. A., *69, 70, 71, 88, 113*
Zimmerman, M. B., 311, *315*
ZoBell, C. E., 202, 204, 205, *208*
Zuehlke, R. W., 328, *334*

SUBJECT INDEX

Abyssal seafloor, as disposal site, 23
Acartia tonsa, 211, 213–223
Acid iron waste:
  composition of, 173
  dispersion of, 172, 183–184
  dispersion at DWD-106, 132–143
  effect of pycnocline, 176–184
  effect on copepods, 215–216, 218–220,
    223
  oceanic *vs.* MERL comparison, 183–184
  removal kinetics, 117–179, 182–184
  removal from surface waters, 176–179,
    180–184
  vertical profiles in MERL tank, 177
Acinetobacter, 200–202, 204
Acridine orange stain, 192, 197–199, 202,
  205
Aeromonas, 205
American Cynamid waste:
  characteristics of, 210
  effect on oceanic copepods, 212–213, 215,
    217–221, 223
Arsenic:
  in incineration wastes, 42
  in manganese nodules, 263, 266–267,
    268–269
  in organochlorine wastes, 78
Arthrobacter, 200–201
Atlantic circulation, 323–327
Atlantic Ocean, chemical profiles, 16
Atmospheric input of metals, 7, 17
At-Sea Incineration, Inc., 55

Bacteria, total counts from Puerto Rico,
  197–199, 202, 204–205
Baltic Sea, 7, 49
Barcelona Convention, 46, 49
Barceloneta outfall, bacterial study of,
  191–192, 197, 198–199, 202, 204–
  205
Barging costs for sewage sludge in New
  York Bight, 309

Barium, in manganese nodules, 263, 265–
  268
Basins of ocean, 21
Benthic biomass, 18
Benthic colonization in deep sea, 19–20
Bergen County, 306–308
Bioassays:
  of pharmaceutical wastes, 229–238
  in situ using BOM, 86
  use of copepods, 211–216
Biological characteristics of deep ocean,
  18–20
Biological effects:
  of incineration, 65–66, 69, 80, 84–87
  of wastes, 221–224
Biotal Ocean Monitors, 86

Cadmium, 7
  in incineration wastes, 42
  in manganese nodules, 263, 265–268
  in organochlorine wastes, 78
  vertical profiles of, 16
California pipeline discharges, 5
Capacity of incineration, ships, 47
Capital expenditures, effect on sludge
  dumping costs, 298, 300–304, 308–
  313
Carbon dioxide:
  from incineration, 59, 62, 65, 67
  measurements during incineration, 38,
    43–45
Carbon monoxide, 59–60, 62, 65, 67, 95–
  96
  measurements during incineration, 38,
    43–45
Caribbean Sea, microbial study, 191, 197–
  199
Centrifuge dewatering of sewage sludge,
  303
Centropages typicus, 211, 213–220, 223
Chemical characteristics of deep ocean, 16–
  18

Chemical cycles in ocean, 327–331
Chesapeake Bay bacteria, 193–194, 203, 205
Chevron, U.S.A., incineration platform, 68
China, importance of riverine sediment, 22
Chlorinated hydrocarbons:
  incinerated at sea, 58–60, 66–68
  incinerated in North Sea, 118
  see also Organochlorine
Chromium:
  from acid iron waste, 179–180
  in incineration wastes, 42
  in manganese nodules, 263, 265–266, 268–269
  measurements, 176, 180
  in organochlorine wastes, 78
Coagulation of waste solids, 245–257
Coal ash, 10
Coal wastes dumped by United Kingdom, 20
Colonization of benthos, 19–20
Combustion efficiency, 56, 61, 63, 65, 67, 77, 120
Conditions for incineration at sea, 37–38, 43–48
Copepods:
  culture of, 211–212
  effects of wastes on, 211–224
  egg production by, 211–213, 216–223
  energy budgets of, 212, 218–220, 223
  feeding rates, 211–212
Copper:
  effect on organisms, 18–19
  in incineration wastes, 42
  natural sources of, 7
  in organochlorine wastes, 78
  vertical profiles of, 16

DDT, 40, 42, 45, 80–85
Deep ocean disposal, definition of, 5
Deep sea–nearshore comparison, 12–23, 321–322
Deepwater dumpsite 106:
  economic factors, 299–300, 306–310, 313
  general characteristics, 172
  location, 7–9, 131
  physical characteristics, 13, 131–132, 148–149
  sewage sludge disposal, 291, 298–311
  wastes at, 210–211
Denmark, 7
Destruction efficiency, 56, 60–61, 63, 65, 67, 76, 81–84

Dewatering of sewage sludge, economic aspects of, 301–304, 309–310
Diffusivity, *see* Eddy diffusivity
Dispersion, effect of circular flow, 158–161
Dispersion of wastes, 12, 126–143
Drainage basins of major rivers, 22
Dredged material:
  dumped by United States, 20, 22
  ocean-dumped, 10
Du Pont Edgemoor waste, *see* Acid iron waste
Du Pont Grasselli waste, 210–211
  effect on copepods, 214, 217, 219–220, 223
Dust as source of metals, 7

Economics of ocean dumping, 291–313
Eddies:
  in channel, 161–167
  effect on dispersion, 148–157, 167–169
  effect on fluxes, 157–169
  in ocean, 325–326
Eddy diffusivity, 149, 152, 157, 160, 167
Egg production of *Temora turbinata*, 236–238
Energy budget for copepods, 212, 218–220, 223
Enterobacteriaceae, 200–201
Entrainment, into eddies, 156
Escape, from eddies, 156
Eulerian steps, in dispersion model, 129–130
European ocean dumpsites, 7–9
External costs of disposal, 292–294, 311–312
Extraction of metals from manganese nodules, 274–277

Fecal pellet production by copepods, 212, 218
Fecal pellets, role in vertical transport, 15
Fecundity, of zooplankton, 230–232, 236–238
Feeding rates:
  of copepods, 211–212
  of zooplankton, 229–232, 236, 238
Fisheries affected by ocean disposal, 321–322
Flavobacterium, 200–201, 204
Flocculation:
  of acid iron waste, 178–179
  of waste particles, 15
Forest fires, as source of metals, 7

GEOSECS, 322–323
Germany (FRG), 7, 116, 120
  waste disposal by incineration, 35–39, 47–48
Gnotobiotic bacteria, 194–196
Growth rates of zooplankton, 230–232, 235, 238
Gulf of Mexico:
  incineration site, 58–60, 64–66, 67
  incineration of wastes in, 75, 77–87
Gulf of Mexico dumpsite, location of, 7–8
Gulf Stream, 325
Gulf Stream rings, see Eddies

Halogenated hydrocarbons, incinerated at sea, 10
Hawaii, dredged disposal in deep sea, 10
HCl:
  determination of, 58, 97–107
  in incineration plume, 68
  from incineration of wastes, 10, 34–35, 68–69, 79, 81, 85, 93
  limits in stack emissions, 35
  measurements in plumes, 103–107
Helsinki Convention, 49
Herbicide orange:
  composition of, 63
  incineration of, 60–64, 75–77
Hexachlorobenzene, 40
Horizontal diffusion, effect on waste dispersion, 135–143
Hydrocarbons, incinerated at sea, 10

Impact indicators of waste disposal, 86–87
Incineration:
  effectiveness, 49, 69
  impact on organisms, 69
  products of, 34–35
  regulations for, 45
  at sea:
    European practices, 116–121
    special considerations, 48
  site selection, 41–43
  of solid wastes, 43
  system controls, 38, 40, 43–46
  of wastes, 34–39, 311
    conditions for, 34
    in North Sea, 10
Incineration equipment, 119
Incineration facility, land-based, 36
Incineration platform, in Gulf of Mexico, 68

Incineration ships:
  characteristics of, 39, 46–48
  safety requirements, 46–48
Incineration sites:
  lanes across ocean, 49
  in North Sea, 94
  of United States, 58–60, 64–68
Incineration waste, composition of, 41–42, 61, 63, 65, 67
India, importance of riverine sediment, 22
Industrial sources:
  of metals, 7
  of wastes for incineration, 42
Industrial waste deep ocean dumpsites, 8
Industrial waste disposal, economics aspects, 291–313
Industrial wastes:
  effects on pH of seawater, 216
  incinerated at sea, 117
Inputs of wastes to ocean, 5–7
Internal costs of disposal, 294–295, 297–313
International Maritime Organization, 37–47
Iron:
  in incineration wastes, 42
  measurements, 176–180
  penetration through pycnocline, 179–184
  removal from water column, 176–184
  see also Acid iron

Johnston Atoll:
  incineration of Agent Orange, 76
  incineration site, 60–64
Joint Meeting, 306–308

Kinetics of acid iron, removal from surface waters, 177–179, 182–184

Lagrangian steps, in dispersion model, 130–131
Lagrangian tracers, 324–327
Land-based incinerator, 36
Laser, use in HCl determination, 97–99
LC-50 for copepods, 213–216
Lead, 7
  in incineration wastes, 42
  in manganese nodules, 263, 266, 268–269
  in organochlorine wastes, 78
  vertical profiles of, 16
LIDAR, use in HCl determination, 99–102, 104–107

Linden-Roselle, 306, 308
London Dumping Convention, 55
  at-sea incineration provisions, 36–38, 40,
    43–48

Manganese, vertical profiles of, 16
Manganese nodule processing, 273–277
Manganese nodules:
  description of, 262–263
  methods of analysis, 261, 264–265
  properties of, 272–273
  trace element composition of, 262–269
Manganese nodule wastes, 244–257, 277–
    283
  toxicity of, 268–269, 280–281
  treatment of, 281–282
Marine agar, 191, 192, 197–199, 202
Matthias I, 6, 35–38, 47–48, 93
Matthias II, 36–39, 47–49, 106, 116
Matthias III, 37–38, 46–48
Mediterranean Sea, incineration of wastes
    in, 37, 46, 49
Mercury:
  in manganese nodules, 263, 265–266,
    268–269
  in North Atlantic, 16–17
  in organochlorine wastes, 78
MERL (Marine Ecosystems Research
    Laboratory), 173–175, 183–184
Mesocosm experiments, 173–184
Metals:
  effect on primary production, 18–19
  natural and industrial sources of, 7
Microbial aspects of pharmaceutical waste
    disposal, 189, 190, 192–206
Middlesex County, 306–308
Mid-ocean ridges, 20–21
Minimum efficient scale for disposal,
    307
Mississippi River, DDT in, 83
Model for coagulation, 246–248
Modelling, physical effects of eddies on
    wastes, 148–169
Model of waste dispersion, 128–131, 137–
    138, 245
MODIS (model for plume dispersion), 107–
    111
Moraxella, 200–201
Munitions disposed at sea, 11

Nassau County, 306, 308
Natural and industrial sources of metals,
    7

Nearshore vs. deepwater disposal costs, 305–
    309
New York Bight:
  barging costs for sewage sludge, 309
  wastes dumped in, 10
New York Bight Dumpsite, 290
New York City:
  barge capacity for sewage sludge, 296–
    297
  barge fleet for deepwater disposal, 304
New York sewage sludge, 289–291
Nickel, 7
  in incineration wastes, 42
  in organochlorine wastes, 78
  vertical profiles of, 16
North Atlantic chemical profiles, 16
North Atlantic circulation, 323–327
North Pacific chemical profiles, 16
North Sea, 7, 118
  incineration site, 93–94
  incineration of wastes in, 11, 35–36, 46,
    48–49, 64, 66–67
  termination of incineration 49
Nuclear Energy Agency, 7
Nutrient limitation in oceanic surface waters,
    18

Obsolete ship disposal, 11
Oceanic chemical cycles, 327–331
Oceanographic factors of waste disposal,
    322–331
Organic carbon in ocean, 19
Organic matter degradation in deep sea,
    19
Organic wastes:
  production of, in United States, 76
  for incineration, composition of, 41–42
Organochlorine:
  products, annual production of, 34
  residues from incineration, 68
  wastes, 92–93
    composition of, 78, 80–82
    disposal of, 34–35
    incinerated at sea, 120
    incineration of, 34–39, 75, 77–84
Oslo Commission, 7
Oslo Convention, relationship to
    incineration, 36–38, 46, 48
Oxidation-reduction cycling of elements,
    327–328
Oxygen consumption by organic matter, 19
Oxygen minimum zone, importance in ocean
    disposal, 23–24

Pacific Ocean chemical profiles, 16
PAHs:
  and marine organisms, 20
  in ocean and sediments, 17
Passaic Valley, 306, 308
PCBs:
  incineration at sea, 40, 42, 45, 49, 64–
    66, 68–69
  in deep ocean, 17
Personnel costs for sewage sludge dumping,
    297–300
Pesticides, incineration of, 80–85
pH:
  in bioassay experiments, 234
  effects of wastes, 79
  of seawater effected by industrial wastes,
    216
Pharmaceutical wastes:
  chemical properties of, 229
  effect on Chesapeake Bay bacteria, 193–
    194, 203
  LC-50 for marine organisms, 229
  microbial aspects, 189, 190, 192–206
  properties of, 189
Philadelphia sewage sludge, 290–291
Physical processes related to ocean
    disposal, 12–15
Phytoplankton:
  effect by incineration, 80
  effects of metals on, 327–328
  ingestion by zooplankton, 231, 233
Pipeline discharges, 5
Plate Count agar, 192, 197–199, 205
Primary production in ocean, 18
Production of organic waste in United
    States, 76
Products of incineration, 56
Pseudocalanus, 211, 213–220, 223
Pseudomonas bacteria, 190, 194–196,
    200–205
Puerto Rico dumpsite:
  contamination from, 202, 204–206
  location of, 7–8, 191
  microbial study of, 190–193, 196–
    206
  oceanographic characteristics of, 196,
    202, 205
  physical characteristics of, 13
  see also Pharmaceutical wastes
Pycnocline:
  effect on acid iron waste, 174–184
  importance in deep ocean, 23
  mixing across, in MERL tank, 180–181

Radioactive waste disposal in North Atlantic
    by Europe, 9
Rahway, 306, 308
Rate constants, for iron removal from water
    column, 177–179, 182
Regulations by United States for incineration
    at sea, 56
Residence time:
  and biological removal, 330
  of deep oceanic waters, 23
  of elements, 329–330
  and insoluble phases, 330
  and long-term geochemical cycles, 330
Resources affected by ocean disposal,
    321–322
Respiration rates of copepods, 211, 218–
    219, 223
Rings, see Eddies
Rivers, importance in sediment transport,
    22–23
Rossby floats, 324–327
Rossby wave, 149–151

Sargasso Sea, microbial study, 191, 197–
    199, 204–205
Scrubbers for incineration emissions, 35–
    36
Seafloor as disposal site, 23
Seasalt aerosols, as source of metals, 7
Sediment, composition of, 17
Sedimentation rates, 22
Selenium, in manganese nodules, 263, 265–
    269
Settling of particulate wastes, 14
Sewage sludge, 10
  barge capacity for New York, 296–297
  barging costs in New York Bight, 309
  dumped in ocean, 288–291
  economics of dewatering, 301–304, 309–
    310
  volume reduction by dewatering, 302
Sewage sludge dumping, personnel costs,
    298–300
Shell Chemical Company, 75, 77–78, 80
  incineration of waste at sea, 58–60
  waste composition, 61
Silver, in manganese nodules, 263, 265–
    269
Site selection:
  based on costs, 291–294
  for incineration, 84–85
Slope Water, role of eddies, 148, 149, 157ff
Staphylococcus, 200–201

Stoke's drift, 150
Storage costs for sewage sludge, 300–301
Stream function, 150, 152–157, 161–167
Sublethal effects on zooplankton, 217–224,
    236–238
Submarine canyons, 20
Surface mixed layer, importance in deep
    ocean disposal, 23
Surface ocean input of wastes, 12
Surface waters, removal of wastes from,
    176–184

TCDD, incineration of, 40, 45, 49, 60–63,
    65, 76
Temora longicornis, 211, 213–214, 216–220
Temora stylifera, 220–221
Temora turbinata, 229–238
Topography of deep sea, 20–22
Toxicity of managanese nodule wastes,
    268–269, 280–281
Trace elements:
    reliable analyses, 327
    role of biological cycling, 327–330
Tracers of ocean circulation, 322–327
Trajectories:
    in eddies, 150–152, 155–156
    of surface drogues, 13
    of waters in ocean, 324–327
Tritium applied to ocean circulation, 322–
    324
TTO, 323–324
Twelve-mile site for sewage sludge disposal,
    299–301, 306–307, 309

United Kingdom, 7
United States:
    deepwater dumpsites, 7–8, 10
    incineration regulations, 36
    organochlorine production, 34
    production of organic wastes, 76

Variable costs for sludge dumping,
    300
Vertical diffusion, effect on waste
    dispersion, 135
Vesta, 38–39, 47, 49, 93, 116–121

Vibrio bacterial strains, 190, 194–196, 200–
    206
Volcanic activity as source of metals, 7
Vulcanus, 36–38, 47, 49, 93, 116
Vulcanus I, 57–58
    incineration near Johnston Atoll, 76
    use in Gulf of Mexico, 75, 77–81
Vulcanus II, 57, 66–67

Warm core rings, 132, 137–141. See also
    Eddies
Waste dispersion:
    from incineration, 95, 103–111
    in ocean, 126–143
Waste displacement by eddies, 150–152,
    156, 158, 165
Waste disposal, oceanographic factors, 321–
    331
Waste Management, Inc., 54–55
Wastes:
    at deep ocean dumpsites by United States,
        10
    dumped in deep sea, 12
    incinerated at sea, 117
    for incineration, 56
    from manganese nodule processing, 277–
        283
    relative toxicity of, 236
Westchester County, 306, 308

Xenobiotic compounds, 17, 20

Zinc, 7
    effect on organisms, 19
    in incineration wastes, 42
    in organochlorine wastes, 78
    vertical profiles of, 16
Zooplankton:
    effect of incineration, 80
    effect of pharmaceutical wastes on, 210–
        238
    fecundity, 230–232, 236–238
    feeding rates, 229–232, 236, 238
    growth rates, 230–231, 234–235, 237–238
    survival during waste exposure, 234–235,
        237–238